Jody Stuchiner

Studies in Eighteenth-Century Culture

Volume 51

Studies in Eighteenth-Century Culture

Volume 51

Published by Johns Hopkins University Press for the
American Society for Eighteenth-Century Studies

Johns Hopkins University Press
Baltimore and London
2022

Johns Hopkins University Press
2715 North Charles Street
Baltimore, Maryland 21218-4363
www.press.jhu.edu

ISBN 978-1-4214-4342-3
ISSN 0360-2370

Articles appearing in this annual series are abstracted and
indexed in *America: History and Life, Current Abstracts, Historical
Abstracts, MLA International Bibliography, Poetry and Short Story
Reference Center, and RILM Abstracts of Music Literature*

Contents

The Art of Intercultural Engagement: A Cluster on Daniel O'Quinn's
Engaging the Ottoman Empire: Vexed Mediations, 1690–1815

ASECS Affiliate and Regional Societies

American Antiquarian Society
Aphra Behn Society
Bibliographical Society of America
British Society for Eighteenth-Century Studies
Burney Society of North America
Canadian Society for Eighteenth-Century Studies
Daniel Defoe Society
Early Caribbean Society
East-Central ASECS
Eighteenth-Century Scottish Studies Society
German Society for Eighteenth-Century Studies
Goethe Society of North America
Historians of Eighteenth-Century Art and Architecture
Ibero-American Society for Eighteenth-Century Studies
International Adam Smith Society
International Herder Society
Johnson Society of the Central Region
Lessing Society
Midwestern ASECS
Mozart Society of America
North American British Music Studies Association
Northeast ASECS
North American Kant Society
Rousseau Association
Samuel Johnson Society of the West
Samuel Richardson Society
Society of Early Americanists
Society for Eighteenth-Century French Studies
Society for Eighteenth-Century Music
Society for the History of Authorship, Reading and Publishing
South Central Society for Eighteenth-Century Studies
Southeast Asian Society for Eighteenth-Century Studies
Southeastern ASECS
Western Society for Eighteenth-Century Studies

A Note from the Editors

Volume 51 of *Studies in Eighteenth-Century Culture* is, in some ways, the American Society for Eighteenth-Century Studies's very own journal of the plague year. As COVID-19 hit North America in the early spring of 2020, the academic conferences and public lectures that serve as the seedbed for our contributions were all abruptly canceled or postponed. As the pandemic spread, almost everyone in the field found themselves scrambling to work in conditions unlike anything most of us were used to, all while experiencing levels of anxiety, uncertainty, and unsought responsibility that made stringing two sentences together often seem a daunting task. Nonetheless, some scholarly work found a way to bloom and we are fortunate that it did. With vaccinations and time, COVID-19 may recede into historical memory, much like the late seventeenth- and eighteenth-century outbreaks of plague that many of us have studied. But the new archives, shrewd questions, provocative insights, and methodological innovations offered up in this volume of *SECC* will long remain a resource for us. While none of us yet knows what the "after times" will be like and most of us are more than eager to put our own plague year behind us, we should be grateful that, amidst such tragedy and loss and dread, the contributors to this volume help us think in such exciting and generative new ways about the long eighteenth century. They, at least, found a way to bring some lasting good out of a year of such relentless bad.

David A. Brewer
The Ohio State University

Crystal B. Lake
Wright State University

Liberal Theory and Eighteenth-Century Criticism

DAVID ROSEN AND AARON SANTESSO

B y almost universal consent, professional literary criticism is an invention of the long eighteenth century, while literary *theory*, the systematic, metacritical practice that undergirds a great deal of academic work on literature, has its roots in nineteenth-century hermeneutics. Perhaps this is part of the reason that "high" theory, as it has been called, has often found a cold reception in the bastions of eighteenth-century studies. Although this situation has changed considerably in the last decade or so, even a cursory glance at conference proceedings or the indices of period journals confirms the strong and continuing presence of historicist and archive-focused scholarship. To the extent that theory *has* made inroads, moreover, it has often taken the shape of what Eve Kosofsky Sedgwick, following Silvan Tomkins, has termed "weak theory" (cognitive criticism, "thing theory," affective criticism, "distant reading," and the like)—modes, that is, that favor the descriptive and quantitative, in contrast to the aggressively interpretive energies of "strong theory."[1] In the present-day debate over the merits of "critique" versus "postcritique" (terms that overlap considerably with "strong" and "weak" theory, respectively) eighteenth-century studies has largely, if not exclusively, turned its head towards the latter.[2] Although, as Immanuel Kant put it, "our age is the genuine age of criticism, to which everything must submit," "critique," the methodology that Rita Felski and others have identified as central to most high-theoretical analysis, has long sat uncomfortably with eighteenth-century literary texts.[3] In particular, the subversive, destructive mode of critique that Paul Ricoeur termed the "hermeneutics of suspicion," a tradition that began with the likes of Friedrich Schleiermacher and Friedrich Schlegel and greatly accelerated with Ricoeur's three great masters of suspicion—Karl Marx, Friedrich Nietzsche, and Sigmund Freud—has always understood and presented itself as an undoing of Enlightenment rationalism and its (supposed) ideological simplicity.

To put it a slightly different way: it might be said that the eighteenth century provided the conditions that made the "hermeneutics of suspicion" necessary. In this view, many of the century's most notable achievements— the vast spread of empire and of market capitalism, the elaboration of the modern liberal subject, Enlightenment rationalism itself—were only so many masks of power waiting to be peeled off and identified as the epiphenomena of something sinister and brutish, or at the very least unreflectingly naive. It would come as no surprise, then, that the great elaborators of nineteenth-century hermeneutics would be particularly out of sympathy with eighteenth-century texts, both literary and otherwise. Under the best of circumstances, as Sedgwick and Felski (among others) have pointed out, the methodologies of critique have been destructive in their intention and often paranoid (Sedgwick's term) in their affect, placing

> an extraordinary stress on the efficacy of ... knowledge in the form of exposure, [acting] as though its work would be accomplished if only it could finally, this time, somehow get its story fully known. That a fully initiated listener could still remain indifferent or inimical, or might have no help to offer, is hardly treated as a possibility. [This] trust in exposure seemingly depends, in addition, on an infinite reservoir of naivete in those who make up the audience for these unveilings.[4]

To acknowledge, however, that many eighteenth-century authors were complicit, or worse, with the spread of systemic oppressions does not quiet a nagging sense that there may be more interesting, or in any case different, ways to approach period texts—ways that move beyond both suspicious reading and historicist contextualization to treat those texts' readers (both then and now) as something other than "infinitely" credulous and that bring some nuance to the complex intentionality of those authors.

We might, for example, acknowledge a certain pragmatic side to a great deal of eighteenth-century literature and to a main strand of period reading habits. We might recognize this tradition, too, as being intensely engaged with liberal thought—to the extent, anyway, that it recognizes all authors, and all readers, as autonomous agents with vastly different ideas about taste, morality, politics, etc., and as therefore requiring certain accommodations and conventions in order to communicate properly. In the discussion that follows, we will attempt to move past what seems to us a false choice for readers of eighteenth-century texts—indeed, though it far exceeds the scope of this essay, we would suggest that this false dichotomy plagues the entire field of literary studies. It is a choice between shooting fish in a barrel (which is what engaging in paranoid reading or "critique," or embracing those "strong" theories that make use of critique, can often feel like) and submitting to some species of weak theory or postcritique, which can feel like a failure of ambition or form of professional suicide.[5] In doing so, we will suggest that there exists a species of "theory" native to the eighteenth century, or at least implicit in its critical writings, that attains the complexity and consequence of "high" theory, without falling into the usual dichotomies of "strong" and "weak." In tracing the genealogy of this species of theory, we will further suggest that it indeed originates in early thinking about liberalism—that is, in the work of both John Locke's followers and his bitter opponents. A conviction that people are not naturally subject to hierarchical authority, but rather are free and equal; a high valuation of individual dignity and autonomy; a contractarian vision of society that revolves around toleration and mutual agreements: if one is to discover a "literary theory" endemic to the eighteenth century, one might expect it to be in conversation with the most intense modal energies of the day.

The Problem of a Liberal Criticism

Though earlier thinkers (e.g., Sir Philip Sidney) exercised an influence, liberalism during the eighteenth century was largely associated with and derived from Locke—and so the obvious place to look for the origins of a literary theory colored by liberalism would seem to be in the work of critics who actively espoused Lockean principles. In practice, however, this is less straightforward than it sounds—and it turns out that very few politically liberal critics produced anything of the kind. As numerous observers have noted, the line from Locke's political views, as articulated in the *Second Treatise on Government,* and his aesthetic views (such as they were), as they might be derived from the *Essay Concerning Human Understanding,* was never direct or obvious—and Locke's aesthetically inclined followers often struggled to square his Whiggishness with his indifference, or even hostility, towards creative literature.[6] Joseph Addison and Sir Richard Steele, for example, accepted the major aspects of both Locke's epistemology and his political philosophy and used their writings to promote these positions, from the celebration of republican resistance to tyranny in Addison's *Cato* and the late statement in *The Free-Holder* on "Civil Liberties, as the natural Rights of Mankind," to the various expositions on empiricism and Lockean language theory in *The Spectator*.[7] It is clear, moreover, that Addison endeavored to understand criticism itself in Lockean terms:

> Mr. Lock[e]'s *Essay on Human Understanding* would be thought a very odd book for a man to make himself master of, who would get a reputation by critical writings; though at the same time it is very certain, that an author who has not learned the art of distinguishing between words and things, and of ranging his thoughts, and setting them in proper lights, whatever notions he may have, will lose himself in confusion and obscurity.[8]

Unfortunately, the very terms with which Addison conveys his Lockeanism vividly indicate the limited utility of Locke for a serious literary criticism. Invoking the "art of distinguishing between words and things" and stressing the importance of avoiding "confusion and obscurity," Addison recalls Locke's own dim view of literature as such: figurative speech, metaphor, fictive associations, and so on, all belong to the realm of fancy, not the world of real experience, which it is the *philosopher*'s task to perceive clearly. In contrast to philosophical language (the topic of *An Essay Concerning Human Understanding*, Book III), which aims at precision and at drawing fine distinctions, the discourse of poetry and fiction commits rampant "abuses" of language—fine, perhaps, for the purposes of entertainment, but hardly fit to "inform and instruct."[9] To the meager extent that he is interested in them at all, literary taste and aesthetic judgment occupy for Locke a sphere separate from either political theory or epistemology.

This leaves Addison, far more interested in aesthetic questions, in something of a bind. Deriving his political principles from a figure actively hostile towards art (or at best dismissive of it), he is left with, essentially, two recourses. First, Addison helps to establish what becomes a longstanding tradition of politically minded critics (liberal or otherwise) valuing or devaluing literary works in light of the ways in which they pass or fail various ideological litmus tests: political virtue (having the right opinions) matches up remarkably well with literary value. Thus Addison defends John Milton against John Dryden's charge that the kingly, tyrannical "Devil was in reality Milton's Hero"; instead, he argues, "Milton never intended" any hero at all, and this move away from a central focus on a superior, controlling character is part of the poem's "Greatness of Plan."[10] What Addison pointedly does not offer is a vital link between politics and aesthetics: a considered account of the ways in which an author's political ideology might be relevant to aesthetic judgment and assessments of literary quality. Rather, in helping to pioneer the persona of the critic-grandee, rendering verdicts against those who deviate from acceptable doctrine, Addison stands as a kind of forefather to a whole host of liberal critics—from Leslie Stephen to Lionel Trilling and beyond—who scorn the illiberal without ever, themselves, reading or writing in a liberal manner.

Quite the opposite. The civic values that are Addison's meat and drink in his more political essays—the toleration of different beliefs, the promotion of the rights of the general public, the celebration of individual liberty and equality—fade away in his literary criticism, in which the canons of taste are ultimately aristocratic. When Addison defines taste as a "faculty of the Soul" that is "in some degree born with us," or when he expresses hostility and contempt toward "Mob Readers," he is explicitly contradicting both Locke's politics and his empiricism.[11] In contrast to Locke's scorn for those who rely on "the alms-basket" and "live lazily on scraps of begged opinions," *The Spectator* offers the neoclassical view that criticism must be founded upon received universal standards ("I shall always make Reason, Truth, and Nature the Measures of Praise and Dispraise"), rather than upon the "generality of Opinion."[12] "A little Wit," Addison comments, "is equally capable of exposing a Beauty, and of aggravating a Fault, and though such a Treatment of an Author naturally produces Indignation in the Mind of an understanding Reader, it has however its effect among the generality of those whose Hands it falls into, the Rabble of Mankind being very apt to think that every thing which is laughed at with any mixture of Wit, is ridiculous in itself."[13] Wearing the hat of a Whig apologist, Addison perceives all people to share a common "nature"; speaking as a critic, he perceives the opposite: some are born with the critical faculty, or acquire it through rigorous training, while the great majority never attain it.

For the early professional critics of the Enlightenment, the utility of liberalism was impeded, it seems likely, by the very novelty of their position. Undoubtedly aware of the need to establish and legitimize their authority as critics in a newly open and competitive marketplace, these critics tended, perhaps inevitably, to defend their insights as supported by timeless and inarguable standards; when it comes to questions of taste and value, there's little, ultimately, to distinguish Addison and Steele—or Nicholas Rowe, or William Congreve, for that matter—from many of their Tory counterparts.[14] The idea, therefore, that a liberal politics might actually become the basis for a literary criticism, or cause one to read in certain ways, is never seriously entertained by these writers. For that, ironically, one has to turn to authors of a more conservative stripe.

Authorial Contracts

When Dryden couched Achitophel's justifications for regicide in the language of contractarianism ("All Empire is no more than Pow'r in Trust"), he was at once attempting to discredit a political philosophy that he found dangerous and quietly acknowledging the extent to which such language had entered the public sphere by the early 1680s.[15] Although it is improbable that Dryden was conversant with Locke's *Second Treatise* when he wrote *Absalom and Achitophel*, he proved surprisingly fluent at articulating the foundations of (what would ultimately become) a liberal politics:

> What shall we think! can people give away
> Both for themselves and Sons, their Native sway?
> Then they are left Defensless, to the Sword
> Of each unbounded Arbitrary Lord:
> And Laws are vain, by which we Right enjoy,
> If Kings unquestiond can those laws destroy.
> Yet, if the Crowd be Judge of fit and Just,
> And Kings are only Officers in trust,
> Then this resuming Cov'nant was declar'd
> When Kings were made, or is for ever bar'd:
> If those who gave the Scepter, could not tye
> By their own deed their own Posterity,
> How then could *Adam* bind his future Race? ...
> Then Kings are slaves to those whom they Command,
> And Tenants to their Peoples pleasure stand.
> Add, that the Pow'r for Property allowd,
> Is mischeivously seated in the Crowd:
> For who can be secure of private Right,
> If Sovereign sway may be dissolv'd by might?[16]

For Dryden, the Hobbesian notion that the sovereign might only be an "Officer in trust," holding power at the "People[']s Pleasure," is self-evidently absurd, both an affront to religion (i.e., the absolute power of the Stuarts derived from God) and, paradoxically, itself the violation of a "Cov'nant." Following the logic of Sir Robert Filmer's *Patriarcha*, Dryden conceives of the Adamic "contract" as binding kings to their subjects for all of "Posterity."

One would look in vain, then, to Dryden's poetry and criticism for the political liberalism that Addison derived from Locke. Nevertheless, it is equally clear that the language of covenants and contracts had become common coin by the final decades of the seventeenth century. In Locke's earliest, and least sentimental, framing of his contractarianism, the 1667 *Essay on Toleration,* Locke himself showed little interest in the liberties and rights that he would later outline in the *Second Treatise,* and which were subsequently associated by Addison and others with political liberalism.[17] Compulsion and prejudice, Locke observed in the *Essay,* would only create more determined enemies, and therefore the "magistrate ought ... to meddle with nothing but barely in order to securing the civil peace and [property] of his subjects."[18] Contracts, in this early articulation, were little more than a form of deferred aggression: we tolerate and thus form covenants with people of whom we do not necessarily approve, but cannot justify attacking or ignoring—people with whom we need to find a *modus vivendi*. At the risk of compressing a great deal of intellectual history into a few sentences, we would contend that the instrumental agreement between real or potential rivals was the characteristic mode—political and economic, but also in some cases aesthetic—of the period that emerged in the wake of divine-right monarchy, and that even the Stuarts' staunchest defenders were on some level aware of this development. In the emerging market for literary goods, Dryden seems to recognize, the author would need to strike bargains, tender promises, and reach informal or tacit deals with his or her audience; thus in his *Discourse Concerning the Original and Progress of Satire,* Dryden praises Juvenal for the way "he fully satisfies my Expectation" and carefully presents his own satirical work as endeavoring to "give the Publick all the Satisfaction [I am] able in this kind."[19]

The relation between politics and literary theory, at the turn of the eighteenth century, might be described as chiastic. If Addison, both a producer and admirer of literary works expressing liberal sentiments, could not articulate (or was not interested in articulating) a vital link between his partisan beliefs and his critical practices, but instead held true to traditional and neoclassical aesthetic values, so writers of a more conservative, often monarchist, political bent, moved in the opposite direction, and spent the period slowly feeling their way into an aesthetic theory grounded in contractualism.[20] This seeming contradiction requires disentangling stances that in later ages would have been more closely bound up with each other— for instance, the notion that writing literature for a broad public, or writing literature of a populist bent, necessarily indicated a favorable view of democracy as such. Or, again, the notion—subsequently the cause of much mischief—that political liberalism and a commitment to the free market, both guided by the logic of the contract, necessarily went hand in hand.[21] Given their political leanings, it is unsurprising that these more conservative writers tended to couch these contracts not in civil but in economic terms— with their prefaces and introductions, in particular, often serving as bills-of-fare.[22] The best known example of such a gesture is arguably the work of a Whig—Fielding's Introduction to *Tom Jones*, in which he explicitly compares the novelist to an innkeeper:

> An Author ought to consider himself, not as a Gentleman who gives a private or eleemosynary Treat, but rather as one who keeps a public Ordinary, at which all Persons are welcome for their Money. In the former Case, it is well known, that the Entertainer provides what Fare he pleases; and tho' this should be very indifferent, and utterly disagreeable to the Taste of his Company, they must not find any Fault; nay, on the contrary, Good-Breeding forces them outwardly to approve and to commend whatever is set before them. Now the contrary of this happens to the Master of an Ordinary. Men who pay for what they eat, will insist on gratifying their Palates, however nice and whimsical these may prove; and if every Thing is not agreeable to their Taste, will challenge a Right to censure, to abuse, and to d—n their Dinner without Controul.[23]

With his first sentence, Fielding casts a somewhat jaundiced eye back towards a patronage system in which authors had no need to make a case for the "Entertainments" they provided, even if those efforts proved "indifferent, and utterly disagreeable to the Taste" of their readers. By contrast, authors now needed to "welcome" all paying customers—and had compelling economic reasons to attract as many of those as possible. However ironic the tone Fielding frequently adopts, his underlying point is serious—and a nervousness about the viability of his writerly enterprise ultimately outweighs any possible satirical intent. The bill-of-fare, "which all Persons may peruse at their first Entrance," so as to acquaint themselves "with the Entertainment which they may expect," occurs as a natural metaphor for the quasi-contractual relationship Fielding sees himself entering into with his readers—readers who may "either stay and regale with what is provided for them," or "depart" and take their business elsewhere (31).

Something like the contrapositive of this deal is also implicitly in effect: namely, that if the reader, having been provided a full account of what to expect, still purchases the book, or attends the play, and nevertheless does not find the results pleasing, then that consumer only has him- or herself to blame, and the author is in the clear. Perhaps because she is writing from a much more precarious position than Fielding—as a woman, but also at an earlier moment, when the modern literary profession was still coming into being—Aphra Behn is particularly clear about this quality of mutual obligation. In stark contrast to Fielding's geniality, Behn begins *The Dutch Lover* by almost taunting the "Good, Sweet, Honey, Sugar-candied READER."[24] Her opening epistle, whose logic (if not tone) Fielding largely adopts, is far less interested in welcoming the prospective reader than in defending the author from that reader's displeasure. Refusing to "*beg your pardon for diverting you from your affairs, by such an idle Pamphlet as this*," Behn carefully tries to imagine her addressee as, at once, a member of the leisured class ("*I presume you have not much to do, and therefore are to be obliged to me for keeping you from worse imployment*") and as a paying customer, rather than an aristocratic patron (5:160). In such a situation, she can only request that the reader peruse her Terms of Use carefully ... and keep quiet if his expectations are not met: "*if you will misspend your time, pray lay the fault upon your self; for I have dealt pretty fairly in the matter, and told you in the Title Page what you are to expect within. ... Having inscrib'd Comedy on the beginning of my Book, you may guess pretty near what peny-worths you are like to have, and ware your money and your time accordingly*" (5:160). To reiterate: neither Behn nor Dryden could be called a liberal. Nevertheless, these writers' willingness, economically motivated though it may have been, to reflect on their work using the language of contracts, indicates a certain thinking along with the political contractarianism of Hobbes, Locke, and their followers.[25] Moreover, though this was hardly their intention, these writers were helping to lay the groundwork—as Addison could not—for a liberal *way of reading* and evaluating texts. Almost as an afterthought, Behn takes a hatchet to the aesthetic categories so dear to Addison (or indeed Dryden). In terms that a present-day populist might embrace, she openly mocks "*most of that which bears the name of Learning*" and commends her own "*want of letters*" (5:160), thus undoing the Horatian injunction that literature both instruct and delight.[26] "*None of all our English poets*," she comments, "*can justly be charg'd with too great reformation of mens minds or manners.*" (5:160). Moreover, she is "*sure ... no Play was ever writ with that design*" (5:161). If a paying audience wishes to be delighted and could not care less about being instructed, then a successful play or work of fiction will be judged solely by its capacity to delight. Indeed, the introduction of moral instruction by the author might be seen as tantamount to a betrayal of trust. If plays "*were certainly intended for the exercising of mens passions, not their understandings*," then "*he is infinitely far from wise, that will bestow one moments meditation on such things*" (5:161). However careful Behn might have been to restrict herself, at moments like this, to the idiom of buying and selling, it is clear that her logic had far-reaching ideological and aesthetic implications.

We should clarify that we are by no means the first to notice the ways that the author-reader relationship might be understood along contractual lines—such thinking appearing prominently in the work of late twentieth-century French theorists especially, including Jean-Louis Curtis, Philippe Lejeune, and Gérard Genette. Lejeune, for example, begins his extensive study of autobiography, *Le Pacte autobiographique*, by observing that "the autobiographical genre is a *contractual* genre" (Lejeune's italics); Curtis contends that "to read a novel is in effect to have made a tacit pact with the novelist. A pact assumes agreement with two parties, mutual consent."[27] It is Genette, however, whose study of the "paratext"—his term for those elements (prefaces, epilogues, titles, interviews, etc.) that "surround ... and extend [a text], precisely in order to *present* it, ... to ensure the text's 'reception' and consumption" (Genette's italics)—remains the single most influential and extensive account of author-reader bargaining, who comes closest to our own concerns.[28] For Genette, who devotes three chapters of *Paratexts* just to the study of prefaces, such authorial statements often carry a "binding contractual force," locking both writer and reader into a certain understanding of how the text is to be received.

While we don't disagree with any of these observations, we would nevertheless suggest that Genette and his contemporaries take a far more restrictive view of authorial contracts than what we see in the work of many eighteenth-century writers. For Genette, the "original assumptive authorial preface ... has as its chief function *to ensure that the text is read properly*" (Genette's italics), and, in much the same spirit, Lejeune comments that the paratext is "a fringe of the printed text which in reality *controls* one's whole reading of the text" (our italics).[29] For both critics, the authorial contract is ultimately rule-establishing: it governs the procedures by which a text is to be "properly" apprehended by the reader. In short, this particular view of the contract aligns neatly with some theories of *genre*, "mold[ing] the reader," as Wayne Booth puts it in *The Rhetoric of Fiction,* "into the kind of person suited to appreciate ... the book [the author] is writing."[30] Indeed, in some moods, eighteenth-century writers extend their "contracts" in precisely this spirit; once again, Henry Fielding:

> as I am, in reality, the Founder of a new Province of Writing, so I am at liberty to make what Laws I please therein. And these Laws, my Readers, whom I consider as my Subjects, are bound to believe in and to obey; with which that they may readily and cheerfully comply, I do hereby assure them that I shall principally regard their Ease and Advantage in all such Institutions: For I do not, like a *jure divino* Tyrant, imagine that they are my Slaves, or my Commodity. I am, indeed, set over them for their own Good only, and was created for their Use, and not they for mine. (77–78)

In Fielding's elegant parody of Locke, the work of the author entails establishing the parameters of proper reading ("readily and cheerfully" complied with by his happy subjects). By the same token, the proper task of the literary critic is to examine carefully the extent to which any new novel or poem meets or somehow violates those generic strictures—a task that came naturally to masters of "propriety," such as John Dennis and Samuel Johnson.

And yet it bears pointing out how distant the rule-setting gestures of the opening chapter of Book II of *Tom Jones*, just quoted, feel from Fielding's "Bill of Fare" for the novel as a whole, or, for that matter, from Behn's epistle, which openly mocks the fetishization of rules for their own sake: "*I think a Play the best divertisement that wise men have; but I do also think them nothing so, who do discourse as formallie about the rules of it, as if 'twere the grand affair of humane life*" (5:162). Contracts may certainly be understood as rule-establishing (as salvos in the rhetoric of genre), but they may equally be understood as *promises*, as gestures with complex implications. What promises, we might ask, does an author make to his or her readers? "Buy my book, and read it in a certain way, and in return, I will provide you with X" (where "X" could mean "entertainment," or "emotional stimulation," or "the sensation of unfettered access to another's mind," or countless other things). What happens, in turn, when an author finds it impossible or inconvenient to abide by the promises that she or he has made? Perusing Dryden, Behn, and Fielding, we might well wonder to what extent a contract may be attenuated while still remaining "in effect" and what tactics an author might employ to break an agreement. Overtly or covertly? With the full knowledge of the reader, or in the hopes that the reader might not notice, and so on? Far from establishing the rules of a genre, eighteenth-century paratexts often point towards the subtle, complex, often unspoken, instrumental agreements that underlie the production and reception of literature—agreements that ultimately push far beyond economic bargaining and into the sphere of ethics—and suggest, in turn, avenues for both criticism and theory to pursue.

Towards an Ethics of Reading

We began this essay by suggesting that eighteenth-century literature frequently indicates, or invites, ways of reading that feel significantly different from both the hermeneutics of suspicion and its near-synonyms (paranoid reading, critique, etc.) and the various forms of weak theory that seem to find a natural home in the age. What we did not suggest, however, is that any of the major period authors, let alone any of the countless less prominent ones, Whig or Tory, ever came close to articulating a systematic metalanguage, rooted in liberal-contractarian ideas, about how to understand or analyze literature as a whole. In short, whatever the implications of Fielding's or Behn's prefaces and introductions, the concerns of those writers are always local and specific, concerned with the reception of this particular novel or that particular play. Though we may well notice theoretical implications in these paratexts, the authors themselves are ultimately focused on the pragmatics of writing and reading. To the extent that these writers were in conversation with "literary theory," it was, as we have already seen, with the dominant theories of the day: neoclassicism, the discourses of sentiment and affect, the sublime and the beautiful, and so on.

It is only at the very end of the eighteenth century that we begin to see the glimmers of a theoretical self-awareness begin to arise out of the rich discourse of authorial bargaining. When Mary Wollstonecraft, for example, prefaces her final novel, *Maria; or The Wrongs of Woman*, by commenting that "in many instances I *could* have made the incidents more dramatic, would I have sacrificed my main object" (our italics), she is admitting that a contract of sorts has been thrown into abeyance.[31] Her central moral concern, "exhibiting the misery and oppression, peculiar to women, that arise out of the partial laws and customs of society," has led her not to write the "dramatic" novel of manners that her readers might reasonably have expected on opening her volume: "in the invention of the story, this view restrained my fancy." Undoubtedly the closest we come, however, to a fully contract-centered theoretical statement is in a relatively little-studied section of William Wordsworth's 1800 preface to *Lyrical Ballads* (little-studied because it does not treat his poetics directly), which we must quote in full:

> It is supposed, that by the act of writing in verse an Author makes a formal engagement that he will gratify certain known habits of association, that he not only thus apprizes the Reader that certain classes of ideas and expressions will be found in his book, but that others will be carefully excluded. This exponent or symbol held forth by metrical language must in different æras of literature have excited very different expectations: for example, in the age of Catullus Terence and Lucretius, and that of Statius or Claudian, and in our own country, in the age of Shakespeare and Beaumont and Fletcher, and that of Donne and Cowley, or Dryden, or Pope. I will not take upon me to determine the exact import of the promise which by the act of writing in verse an Author in the present day makes to his Reader; but I am certain it will appear to many persons that I have not fulfilled the terms of an engagement thus voluntarily contracted. They who have been accustomed to the gaudiness and inane phraseology of many modern writers, if they persist in reading this book to its conclusion, will, no doubt, frequently have to struggle with feelings of strangeness and aukwardness: they will look round for poetry, and will be induced to enquire by what species of courtesy these attempts can be permitted to assume that title. I

hope therefore the Reader will not censure me, if I attempt to
state what I have proposed to myself to perform, and also, (as
far as the limits of a preface will permit) to explain some of the
chief reasons which have determined me in the choice of my
purpose: that at least he may be spared any unpleasant feeling
of disappointment, and that I myself may be protected from the
most dishonorable accusation which can be brought against an
Author, namely, that of an indolence which prevents him from
endeavouring to ascertain what is his duty, or, when his duty is
ascertained, prevents him from performing it.[32]

In the course of Wordsworth's self-defense, a whole way of reading, or
method of analysis, begins to round into view. Even more than Wollstonecraft,
Wordsworth has absorbed the language of "promise[s] ... an Author ... makes
to his Reader" and that of covenants more generally; like Wollstonecraft,
he is acutely aware that *Lyrical Ballads*, through his very gesture of calling
it a book of "verse," may appear not to have "fulfilled the terms of an
engagement ... voluntarily contracted." What ensues, for the remainder of
the preface, is very much a negotiation regarding genre (what gets to count
as poetry and what doesn't)—a negotiation, importantly, that is carried out
in explicitly moral terms: Wordsworth is less concerned by the accusation
of having violated a trust, a "formal engagement" with the reader, than with
explaining why he has done so. If his "duty" has been to conform to certain
"expectations" (e.g., for elevated poetic diction), then the remainder of the
preface will detail, at length, why a higher consideration has "prevent[ed]
him from performing" that duty. Sometimes, it would appear, the breaking
of a trust is preferable to the keeping of it—and by thinking through the
implications of this seeming paradox, Wordsworth begins to unite two
strands of post-Lockean thought that we have so far observed operating in
isolation: on the one hand, an economically motivated contractarianism, and
on the other, a set of values that Addison, and Addison's successors, saw as
consonant with liberal ideology. It is important, moreover, that Wordsworth
is making no effort to conceal his apparent betrayal of trust from the reader—
quite pointedly the opposite: it is part-and-parcel of his liberalism that he
conceives of the reader as a full partner in establishing the consequences of
his choices as an author. Most significantly, perhaps, Wordsworth emphasizes
that his breaking of the pact is occurring at a particular moment, for reasons
peculiar to that moment. Readerly expectations would have been different
in the age of Pope, let alone the age of Shakespeare or of Catullus.[33] It is
unreasonable, and perhaps immoral, Wordsworth implies, to think that poets
will adhere to bargains struck a century or millennium—or even a decade—
previously. Rather, the author-reader relationship must entail a process of

continuous re-negotiation—an insight with profound consequences for how one conceives of "literary history," writ large—of which the preface itself is, of course, a signal example.

Wordsworth's purpose in the preface was to articulate a poetics, not a systematic theory of literature; however effectively he summarized, reconciled, or made explicit lines of thinking that had been ramifying over the course of the long eighteenth century, he finally exercised little influence on the professional study of literature as it subsequently developed. That work fell ultimately to the hermeneuticists—first in Germany, but soon enough in England and the United States—to the point where "hermeneutics" and "literary criticism" have at times seemed nearly synonymous.[34] In contrast to the hermeneutic emphasis on decoding, uncovering, or revealing, the strand of eighteenth-century criticism we have been discussing invites us to see literature as a kind of force field, in which contractual gestures—promises—interact, morph, grow, or wane in strength over time. A full explication of such a view of literature—both its theoretical/ideological implications and its consequences for practical criticism and analysis—would far exceed the scope of this essay and take us well beyond the eighteenth century. Instead, we will end with a brief reading, or at least an examination, of such a force field in action. To this point we have looked mainly at "paratexts," in which the author's critical activity has been inseparable from the need to defend or explain a specific literary work. In closing, we will turn to a work of pure criticism—a work unhampered, as it were, by the requirements of self-justification—in which the labor of contractual bargaining nonetheless comes across with particular vividness: Samuel Johnson's *Rambler* number 4. As Johnson discusses the nature of fiction (especially what we would now term "the novel"), his typical confidence as a critic wavers ever so slightly. Trying to account for a genre at once new and overwhelmingly popular, and of which he largely disapproves, Johnson engages in some energetic negotiations in order to square the virtues of the form with his broader aesthetic and civic priorities.

The great strength of the novel, self-evidently for Johnson, is its realism. In more or less the same terms as Ian Watt would lay out two centuries later, Johnson contrasts the previously dominant form of prose fiction, romance, with a new genre dedicated to exhibiting "life in its true state, diversified only by accidents that daily happen in the world."[35] In drawing this distinction, Johnson plants his feet squarely in two camps. He has absorbed enough of the economic-contractual spirit of the age to ascribe the decline of romance to a waning market: why romance "found reception so long, in polite and learned ages, it is not easy to conceive; but we cannot wonder that, while readers could be procured, the authors were willing to continue it" (10). At the same time, Johnson the policer of generic rules is also fully present. Having determined that the novel "is to be conducted nearly by the rules of comic poetry" (9), he spends the first pages of the essay briskly establishing what the novel may or may not do, when it comes to plot and characterization.[36] Since its "province is to bring about natural events by easy means" (9) and "must arise from general converse, and accurate observation of the living world" (10), it is "therefore precluded from the machines and expedients of the heroic romance"—for example, "employ[ing] giants to snatch away a lady from the nuptial rites" (9).

The chief distinction, however, that concerns Johnson—and that, it transpires, is the motivating worry of the essay—centers on the differing powers of romance and the novel to command readerly belief. Because the plots of romance were so preposterous, "the reader was in very little danger of making any applications to himself" (11). Not so the novel, especially when it comes to the "young, the ignorant, and the idle," who comprise (according to Johnson) the genre's primary consumers and to whom novels "serve as lectures of conduct, and introductions into life" (11). Here, the very verisimilitude that gives the novel its extraordinary power (and accounts for its popularity) comes into direct conflict with Johnson's conservatism and, still more, his Horatian insistence that literature be an instructive tool. If "the power" of realism "is so great, as to take possession of the memory by a kind of violence, and produce effects *almost without the intervention of the will*, care ought to be taken" by authors that the novel do no harm (12; our italics). The remainder of *Rambler* 4 is at once an acute examination of the psychology of reading and—more important for our purposes—a furious effort to establish, in an increasingly hostile literary environment, the very nature and boundaries of realism. Thus authors, though constrained by emerging canons of representation "to imitate nature" (12), should still exercise some restraint over what they represent:

> The chief advantage which these fictions have over real life is, that their authors are at liberty, tho' not to invent, yet to *select* objects, and to cull from the mass of mankind, those individuals *upon which the attention ought most to be employ'd*. ... It may not be ... safe to ... show ... all that presents itself without *discrimination* ... that observation which is called knowledge of the world, will be found much more frequently to make men cunning than good. The purpose of these writings is surely not only to show mankind, but to provide that they may be seen hereafter with less hazard; to teach the means of avoiding the snares which are laid by Treachery for Innocence (12–13; our italics).

By the end of his account, Johnson has talked himself into allegory—a long way, we might observe, from the "realism" with which he began. Indeed, if "vice, for vice is necessary to be shewn, should always disgust" (15), and if virtue should invariably be rewarded and evil punished, it is hard to say what remains of realism once Johnson's process of "selection" has concluded.

Before drawing our own conclusions, we will pause to note how ripe *Rambler* 4 is for a "suspicious" or "paranoid" reading; indeed, we would be the last to suggest that such a reading of Johnson's essay is unjustified. With no subtlety at all, Johnson attempts to steer the anarchic energies of an emerging genre into ideologically acceptable territory—providing an almost textbook demonstration of the ways in which the discourses of power extend their reach over unclaimed spaces of the human mind. Whatever threat early novels might have posed to the "Innocen[t]," texts composed within the discursive boundaries specified by Johnson might reliably be expected to produce well-disciplined subjects. Novels that "confound the colours of right and wrong, and instead of helping to settle their boundaries, mix them with so much art, that *no common mind* is able to disunite them" (14; our italics), are thus banished from Johnson's Republic. Such a reading is more than plausible and also gives us (critics of the present day) the pleasant sensation of having caught the good doctor at his game and, most likely, of knowing quite a bit more about that game than he did—Johnson himself, after all, being a well-disciplined subject. And yet, without any of these conclusions being falsifiable, how far from the spirit of *Rambler* 4 those conclusions actually seem. With only the slightest shift of frame, it becomes possible to view Johnson as energetically (and quite consciously) engaging in the contractual bargaining typical of the age. If we take "realism" to consist of a kind of contract—in which the author promises to provide a view of the world as it "really" is, of "life in its true state" (9)—then *Rambler* 4 vividly shows us Johnson trying to imagine how far that contract might be extended, or tampered with, or modified, without explicitly violating those initial terms. Verisimilitude, yes—but need one represent *everything*? Surely, one might select some things to represent, and ignore all else—in order to preserve a role for literature that Johnson is unwilling to surrender? Would that not still be "realism"? That subsequent novelists in the "realistic" tradition would call Johnson out on his bad faith, and reject his particular bargain, is entirely the point; it would be unreasonable for a Dickens, or a Poe, or a Conrad—or, indeed, one of Johnson's own less timorous contemporaries, like Fielding—to accept his terms.[37]

That Johnson was no liberal in no way negates the essentially liberal dynamics at play in *Rambler* 4; inevitably, Johnson's need to grapple with a new and "unsafe" genre draws him out of his usual and relatively comfortable task of assessment into something far less stable: an intense contest with rivals over what constitutes an acceptable literature—a contest that, in the fullness of time, he eventually loses. It is to our point, finally, that Johnson's bargaining occurs entirely within the bounds of the practical criticism native to the age; the vital link we have perceived between liberal-contractarianism and the bargaining evident in paratexts, in critical essays, and perhaps most of all (though we lack the space to pursue this idea) in literary texts themselves never achieved anything approaching theoretical self-awareness during the eighteenth century—not until a glimmering awareness in Wordsworth, anyway. It was only at the very end of the century that something like a liberal theory of reading and analyzing texts became plausible—at precisely the moment when criticism began its turn towards hermeneutics, and "literary theory" began to take the form with which we are all familiar. In the twenty-first century, we have begun to grapple with the costs of this turn, alongside its innumerable benefits, to the profession. As we begin to explore new ways of reading and thinking about literature, the loss to hermeneutics may finally be a gain for ethics.

Notes

1. Sedgwick, *Touching Feeling: Affect, Pedagogy, Performativity* (Durham: Duke University Press, 2003), 133 et passim. For Sedgwick, a hallmark of "strong theory" is its tendency to assert a primacy over the text under examination, usually by hermeneutic means. For this reason, "strong theory" ranges from the highly politicized (e.g., theories derived from Marx or Foucault) to the purportedly apolitical (post-Freudian theories or poststructuralism).

2. We might take the foci of recent "special issues" of the leading eighteenth-century journals as indicative of the continuing predominance of historicist and archival scholarship, as well as of the various species of "weak theory," in the discipline. Thus we note special issues on "Thing Theory," "Easts and Wests," and "The Maritime Eighteenth Century" (all in *Eighteenth-Century Studies*); "Form and Formalism," "The Senses of Humor," "Material Fictions," and "Ecological Footprints" (all in *Eighteenth-Century Fiction*); and "Historical Criticism and Eighteenth-Century Studies," "New Findings from the Digital Miscellanies Index," and "Literary Ephemera" (all in *Eighteenth-Century Life*).

3. In his early work on the "post-critical," Michael Polanyi defined it against the "critical mode" he imagined as born in the Enlightenment. Kant, Preface to *Critique of Pure Reason*, trans. Paul Guyer and Allen Wood (Cambridge: Cambridge University Press, 1998), 100–1. See Elizabeth S. Anker and Rita Felski, Introduction to *Critique and Postcritique* (Durham: Duke University Press, 2017), 1–25.

4. Sedgwick, *Touching Feeling,* 138, 141. Felski's work on "critique" borrows heavily from Sedgwick's work on paranoid reading and "strong theory." Felski discusses the destructiveness of critique in several places; see especially her claim that "Critique is Negative" in "Critique and the Hermeneutics of Suspicion," *M/C Journal* 15, no. 1 (March 2012).

5. Lest the language of "professional suicide" seem overly dramatic, we would note that recent debates over the merits of "postcritique" have often taken that exact tone. See, for example, Bruce Robbins's response to Rita Felski's attack on "suspicious reading" and "fault-finding" in *The Limits of Critique,* in which he argues that critique is the only thing that "distinguishes us as academics from fans as well as from most reviewers, belletrists, and other adjuncts to the publishing industry." Robbins goes on to imagine what would happen to the field if it adopted Felski's vision of postcritique:

> [We would be left with] a criticism that is closer to fandom, a profession that is closer to the industry's dollars-and-cents metric and its rhetoric of helpful and largely positive advice to the would-be consumer ... Felski might have paid more heed to this question, considering possible disadvantages of putting the discipline through what looks to me like a corporate re-structuring. ("Not So Well Attached," *PMLA* 132, no. 2 [2017], 372).

6. Cf. Karen Collis, "Shaftesbury and Literary Criticism: Philosophers and Critics in Early Eighteenth-Century England," *The Review of English Studies,* n.s., 67, no. 279 (April 2016): 294–315. Collis argues that Anthony Ashley Cooper, the Third Earl of Shaftesbury, was able to reconcile his aesthetics and his Whig politics by essentially ignoring Locke's epistemology, while Joseph Addison's acceptance of the *Essay* led necessarily to his perceiving a diminished role for literature.

7. *The Free-Holder* 2 (26 December 1715).

8. *The Spectator* 291 (2 February 1712).

9. For the discussion of "figurative language" as an "abuse," see Locke, *An Essay Concerning Human Understanding,* Book III, chapter X (Amherst: Prometheus Books, 1995). Needless to say, subsequent philosophers of language have problematized Locke's seemingly straightforward distinction between philosophical and imaginative discourse. For a reading of the *Essay* that examines the inexorably figurative nature of *all* language, see Paul de Man, "The Epistemology of Metaphor," *Critical Inquiry* 5, no.1 (Autumn 1978): 13–30.

10. *The Spectator* 297 (9 February 1712).

11. On those few occasions that Locke discusses questions of taste, he, too, can show a surprisingly high-handed side, claiming that only some people are born with minds well suited to "judgment" and that artistic discrimination is only "natural to some tempers." Politically, Locke believes that every individual has rights that must be respected; in terms of critical judgment, he thinks that "brutes" and "idiots" can distinguish between and compare ideas and sentiments "to no great degree" and that those who perceive or retain ideas "dully" cannot "judge or reason to any

tolerable degree; but only a little and imperfectly" (*An Essay Concerning Human Understanding,* Book II, chapter XI, 105). For Addison on "Mob Readers" see *The Spectator* 62 (11 May 1711).

12. Locke, "The Epistle to the Reader," *An Essay Concerning Human Understanding,* xiii; *The Spectator* 111 (7 July 1711).

13. The *Spectator* 291 (2 February 1712).

14. Abigail Williams, in *Poetry and the Creation of a Whig Literary Culture, 1681–1714* (Oxford: Oxford University Press, 2005), argues for a "Whiggish vision of literary aesthetics" (18), with Whig poets drawing on a particular store of tropes and rhetoric. Yet, as Williams recognizes, the majority of those tropes were themselves drawn from classical models, as they were in Tory poems. Whig and Tory poems may have had different philosophical and ideological foundations, but, as far as questions of structure and decorum were concerned, there was no vast difference between the neoclassicist judgments put forward by Whigs, like Thomas Rymer or Charles Gildon, and those of a Tory critic, like George Granville—or for that matter, those of a less avowedly political publisher, like John Newbery, who, a century after Rymer, was still publishing criticism urging adherence to the classical unities (*The Art of Poetry on a New Plan* [London, 1762]).

15. Dryden, "Absalom and Achitophel," in *The Works of John Dryden*, ed. Edward Niles Hooker and H. T. Swedenberg, Jr., et al., 20 vols. (Berkeley: University of California Press, 1956–2002), 2:17.

16. Dryden, "Absalom and Achitophel," 2:28. The *Second Treatise* is sometimes dated to 1689, the year of its publication—well after the appearance of "Absalom and Achitophel." Richard Ashcraft has persuasively argued, however, that it was written during the Exclusion Crisis of 1678–81, making it contemporary with Dryden's poem. It's still highly unlikely, however, that Dryden would have been aware of Locke's text. See Richard Ashcraft, "Revolutionary Politics and Locke's *Two Treatises of Government*: Radicalism and Lockean Political Theory," *Political Theory* 8 (1980): 429–86.

17. For an expansion of these ideas, see our *The Watchman in Pieces: Surveillance, Literature, and Liberal Personhood* (New Haven: Yale University Press, 2013), 70ff.

18. Locke, "An Essay on Toleration," in *Political Essays*, ed. Mark Goldie (Cambridge: Cambridge University Press, 1997), 136.

19. Dryden, *Discourse Concerning the Original and Progress of Satire*, in *The Works of John Dryden*, 4:63, 4:87.

20. Addison was not the only Whig who was, when it came to aesthetics, completely invested in aristocratic and traditional canons of value. Samuel Garth scorned the taste of the "vulgar throng" and the conclusion of Thomas Tickell's "Prologue to the University of Oxford" is virtually a compendium of elitist sentiments:

> None should presume to dictate for the Stage,
> But such as boast a great Extensive Mind,
> Enrich'd by Nature, and by Art refined;

> Whom from the *Antient* Stores their Knowledge bring,
> And tasted Early of the Muse's Spring.
> May none pretend upon her Throne to sit
> But such, as sprung from you, are Born to Wit:
> Chos'n by the *Mob,* their lawless *Claim* we slight:
> Yours is the *Old Hereditary Right.*

—Garth, *The Dispensary; A Poem* (London, 1699), 45; Tickell, "Prologue to the University of Oxford," in *Poetical Miscellanies, Consisting of Original Poems and Translations. By the Best Hands* (London, 1714), 71.

21. The relatively new and utterly inaccurate habit of conflating "liberalism" with "neoliberalism" has been adopted enthusiastically by the socialist and progressive left press. See, for example, the dismissal of Paul Krugman as a "neoliberal" in Paul Heideman, "Bulletproof Neoliberalism," *Jacobin,* 1 June 2014. See also Bruce Robbins, "Everything is not Neoliberalism," *American Literary History* 31, no. 4 (2019): 840–49.

22. This sort of language can be found in the prefatory materials offered up by Tory authors for the remainder of the century (e.g., Maria Edgeworth's "Preface" to *Castle Rackrent*: "the author of the following memoirs has upon these grounds fair claims to the public favor and attention"). Henry Brooke, another Tory, went so far as to parody the fashion in his dedication to *The Fool of Quality* ("To the Right Respectable My Ancient and Well-Beloved Patron, The Public").

23. Fielding, *The History of Tom Jones, A Foundling*, ed. Fredson Bowers (Middletown: Wesleyan University Press, 1975), 31. Subsequent citations of *Tom Jones* will be made parenthetically.

24. Behn, epistle to the "Good, Sweet, Honey, Sugar-candied READER," *The Dutch Lover,* in *The Works of Aphra Behn*, ed. Janet Todd, 7 vols. (Columbus: Ohio State University Press, 1996), 5:160. Subsequent citations of this epistle will be made parenthetically.

25. The fact that this thinking along often happened in works of satire is particularly notable: as in *Absalom and Achitophel*, a genuine engagement with contractarian politics could and often did occur more or less independently of the main satiric thrust of a work.

26. Behn also anticipates Locke's dismissal of "*scraps*" of received wisdom by more than a decade, expressing scorn for "*Creatures* [who believe] *such scraps as they pick up from other folks*" (*Works*, 5:162).

27. Lejeune, *On Autobiography*, ed. Paul John Eaken, trans. Katherine M. Leary (Minneapolis: University of Minnesota Press, 1988), 29; Curtis, *Haute Ecole: Essai* (Paris: Rene Juilliard, 1950), 171. Our thanks to Steven Monte for the translation of Curtis.

28. Genette, *Paratexts: Thresholds of Interpretation*, trans. Jane E. Lewin (Cambridge: Cambridge University Press, 1997), 1.

29. Genette, *Paratexts*, 197; Lejeune, *On Autobiography*, 29.

30. Booth, *The Rhetoric of Fiction*, 2nd ed. (Chicago: University of Chicago Press, 1983), 89.

31. Wollstonecraft, *Maria or The Wrongs of Woman* (New York: W. W. Norton, 1975), 5.

32. Wordsworth and Samuel Taylor Coleridge, *Lyrical Ballads: The Text of the 1798 Edition with the Additional 1800 Poems and the Prefaces,* 2nd ed., ed. R. L. Brett and A. R. Jones (London: Routledge, 1991), 235.

33. Wordsworth's very word, "expectations," seems to anticipate the language of Hans Robert Jauss, whose work on reception history approaches the same insight. Cf. Jauss, *Toward an Aesthetic of Reception*, trans. Timothy Bahn (Minneapolis: University of Minnesota Press, 1982).

34. Felski quotes several times Stanley Fish's line: "like it or not, interpretation is the only game in town" (*Is There a Text in this Class? The Authority of Interpretive Communities* [Cambridge: Harvard University Press, 1980], 355).

35. Johnson, *The Rambler* 4 (31 March 1750), in *Selected Essays from the Rambler, Adventurer, and Idler*, ed. W. J. Bate (New Haven: Yale University Press, 1968), 9. Subsequent citations of this essay will be made parenthetically.

36. Johnson is here likely alluding to Fielding's declaration in the "Preface" to *Joseph Andrews* that the novel, or "comic Romance," is a "comic Epic-Poem in Prose" (Fielding, *Joseph Andrews*, ed. Martin C. Battestin [Middletown: Wesleyan University Press, 1967], 4).

37. Indeed, Johnson, in the more conversational mode captured in Boswell's *Life,* takes Fielding repeatedly to task in exactly these terms: "Fielding, being mentioned, Johnson exclaimed, ... 'he was a barren rascal.' BOSWELL. 'Will you not allow, Sir, that he draws very natural pictures of human life?' JOHNSON. 'Why, Sir, it is of very low life. Richardson used to say, that had he not known who Fielding was, he should have believed he was an ostler.'" (Boswell, *Life of Johnson*, ed. R. W. Chapman [Oxford: Oxford University Press, 1989], 480).

Novel Paintings:
Learning to Read Art through Joseph Highmore's *Adventures of Pamela*

AARON GABRIEL MONTALVO

In 1744, the portrait painter Joseph Highmore announced the completion of a possibly unprecedented project: adapting a contemporary English novel into painting.[1] Highmore had transformed Samuel Richardson's *Pamela: Or, Virtue Rewarded* into a grand series of twelve oil paintings, subsequently reproduced in a series of engravings. Highmore's *Adventures of Pamela* series marks a significant moment in the development of literary-artistic relations.[2] Adapting a novel was itself novel. Though the field of history painting had long been centered on literary subjects such as religion, mythology, and classical poetry, English fiction was a newer, more controversial genre that artists had previously avoided.[3] Highmore drew his subject matter from one of the most contentious and popular novels of the era. *Pamela* had attracted controversy from the moment of its publication in 1740 with its account of a virtuous servant first harassed and later married by her aristocratic employer, which awakened eighteenth-century anxieties about the growing bourgeoisie's challenge to traditional hierarchies, including those of morals, class, and art.[4] With his adaptation, Highmore would draw upon this controversy to both bolster his own reputation and promote his own perspective on these changes.

Despite its originality, Highmore's project has received little attention in eighteenth-century scholarship. T. C. Duncan Eaves, the first scholar to examine visual representations of *Pamela*, argued that Highmore's paintings were true to the spirit of Richardson's novel and thus a worthy adaptation.[5] Subsequent scholarship has shifted from questions of fidelity to the text to efforts to contextualize Highmore's paintings in the debates over class struggle and virtuous womanhood that surrounded the reception of the novel.[6] This essay examines Highmore's *Adventures of Pamela* in relation to eighteenth-century debates about art and the development of visual culture. A critical engagement with Highmore's paintings in relation to, but not in service of, Richardson's *Pamela* reveals the paintings' engagement with issues of spectatorship in the era, when questions of who could properly claim to understand images and how one should assert that knowledge abounded. Rather than follow aristocratic claims for epistemological superiority based upon education, Highmore advocated for a distributed form of recognition based upon an experiential, responsive approach to spectatorship, a viewing practice that carried beyond artworks into the wider social sphere. Highmore's *Adventures of Pamela* series depicts spectatorship for its audience in order to argue for a form of viewership based upon interactive, sentimental responses to paintings as a means of better understanding people.

Picturing the Market

Both Richardson's text and Highmore's paintings were the products of broad cultural shifts underway in the era. In their study of the *Pamela* debates, Thomas Keymer and Peter Sabor assert that the controversy represents a "market phenomenon: ... the product, agent, and uniquely visible trace of the new consumer culture that was taking hold, in which the novel genre was becoming an increasingly important commercial and literary mode and object of fashionable attention."[7] Keymer and Sabor's argument is instructive for the way it situates *Pamela* and its progeny in a dynamic cultural context that allows the visual art based on *Pamela* to be analyzed in relation to the development of new commercial and cultural spheres, rather than as mere commentary on the novel. *Pamela* has long been understood as a milestone in the developing literary market.[8] Highmore's paintings can be similarly seen as participating in the contemporary art market. They were a speculative enterprise, undertaken in the hope of commercial success. Highmore's decision to have the series engraved and advertised in newspapers demonstrates his use of the market's apparatuses to produce and market his works to a wide swathe of consumers.[9] Although a response to *Pamela*, Highmore's paintings were created independently of Richardson, which allowed Highmore to exercise considerable agency over their subject matter and composition.[10] In this respect, they differ from the twenty-nine engravings Richardson commissioned from Hubert Gravelot and Francis Hayman for the sixth edition of the novel, published in 1742. The latter engravings have been interpreted as Richardson's attempt to control the meaning of his novel.[11] In contrast, Highmore's status as an innovative, independent artist provides an opportunity for approaching these artworks not as a mere extension of the *Pamela* debates, but instead as evidence of the era's burgeoning discourses around art and spectatorship.

To understand Highmore's work, it is useful to consider the social anxieties associated with the eighteenth-century rise of consumer culture, particularly regarding the art market. The numbers are astounding. Over the course of the century, Britain imported nearly 50,000 paintings and half a million prints from the continent, especially Italy, France, and the Netherlands. Meanwhile its auction houses (themselves a new kind of business) transferred over 100,000 paintings to or between collectors.[12] Britain not only imported artworks but also artists. Painters, engravers, and sculptors flocked to London to take advantage of the expanding art market.[13] Highmore was a product of this new market, working primarily as a portrait artist, the most popular genre of the era.[14]

This art market grew not only in the sheer number of art objects, but also in the availability of those objects to a broader array of middle-class consumers. Regarding this dissemination, Robert D. Hume persuasively claims that the principal cultural consumers were an elite audience of approximately three percent of the families in Britain.[15] However, although these elites were the primary market for art, access to the market was not limited to them.[16] Prints, for example, were affordable to a much wider range of buyers than paintings. Print prices averaged between one and two shillings, a price equivalent to two to four days of labor for the average worker, yet within reach for many consumers of "the middling sort."[17] Selling prints by subscription allowed artists to fund projects outside of conventional patronage structures. Highmore took advantage of this strategy, selling his series by subscription for two guineas.[18] Though expensive, these prints made the series far more available than any single painting and did so in a way that allowed the series's narrative to be preserved. Further, the subscription helped Highmore attract clients for his paintings, demonstrating how artists could utilize various levels of the market. Though much of this developing market was concentrated in a high social stratum, the market was not confined there, and this high stratum had its own internal divisions. Highmore himself could be classed among the "middling sort." His practice was successful enough to leave his family £550 at his death.[19] Yet, Highmore almost certainly could not afford the £500 per annum Jacob Vanderlint gave as the cost to live as a gentleman.[20] The growing presence of men of Highmore's status not only changed the art market, but also ideas about how art should be understood.

Just as the rise of the novel provoked concerns among the literati, so too did the growth of the art market provoke concerns about the proper audience for and reception of art.[21] These concerns inspired the development of the pedagogy of polite culture, which linked aesthetic taste to moral judgment.[22] Aesthetic considerations typically operated on two levels. The first concerned a combination of artistic skill and an image's relation to "nature," however the latter was defined. The second level consisted of the moral lesson evoked by the art. A representation of a noble or heroic deed in painting, for example, was said to inspire audiences to behave in a similar manner.[23] The value of an object was not only a function of its appearance but also of its utility as an object of social education. A proper taste was as much a function of moral responsiveness as it was of a discerning eye.

The training of a discerning eye prompted its own debates, a topic provocatively explored by Peter de Bolla. Though de Bolla's work focuses on the 1760s, his comments are significant for the ways in which they highlight how differences in perception were linked to class affiliation, considerations evident in Highmore's writing from that same period. De Bolla argues that artistic discernments can be organized into roughly two camps: the "regime of the picture" and the "regime of the eye."[24] The first contended that discernment was based upon knowledge already possessed by the viewer. When viewers approached an image, they used knowledge they had already acquired in order to understand the image before them and make an aesthetic evaluation. This approach relied upon an understanding of history, mythology, religious doctrines, and artistic traditions gained from a strong educational foundation. As such, it was primarily associated with the aristocracy. The other camp, "the regime of the eye," proposed a method of viewership in which discernment was developed based upon the internal form and qualities of object(s) under study, rather than preexisting external knowledge. Daniel Webb, whose writing on aesthetics Highmore commended, proclaimed that "we have all within us the seeds of taste, and are capable, if we exercise our powers, of improving them into a sufficient knowledge of the polite arts."[25] Knowledge could come either through a form of liberal education, in which audiences might recognize and grasp the significance of the subject of a history painting, or from the image itself via a proper perception of the underlying principles of sight. These regimes were not mutually exclusive and found shared ground and shared difficulty in portraiture.[26]

Portraiture constituted an aesthetic problem in the eighteenth century because its popularity did not accord with the conventional hierarchy of artistic genres, which established history painting—a category that included mythological and religious subjects—as the intellectual and moral ideal.[27] Where history paintings were said to promote universal ideals, portraits were regarded as documentary at best and risked being rejected as mere vanity.[28] While this hierarchy was not as influential in Britain as on the continent, it limited the value both of works of art and of artists themselves. Portraits could be classed as mere imitation, a craft carried out by artisans who might be skillful, but who were not on a level with the producers of true fine art. Though a few portrait artists, such as Anthony Van Dyck and Godfrey Kneller, attained wealth and social prominence, most portrait artists were relegated to lower stature, especially in the first half of the eighteenth century. Ambitious painters promoted history painting as a means of highlighting the intellectual status of their art. Highmore embodied this trend in his own career, transitioning to history painting in the 1740s after working as a portraitist for approximately twenty-five years.[29] This move helped Highmore raise his profile, expand his market, and demonstrate the relevancy of his work to a wider social sphere.[30]

Highmore's attempts to elevate his practice coincided with the growth of the market for portraiture beyond its traditional, aristocratic audience. By the 1740s, sitters for portraits were increasingly members of the developing mercantile and professional classes.[31] The earliest portrait of Samuel Richardson, for instance, dates to c. 1740–41.[32] This clientele would constitute the primary market for the group portraits and conversation pieces painted in the 1740s and 1750s. During these decades, portrait artists were well positioned to observe the tensions associated with the depiction of modern figures, as members of "the middling sort" appropriated the tropes of aristocratic portraiture—to the consternation of the aristocracy. The interrelation of the aesthetic and the social in the portrait reflects its significance for polite culture and influenced the meaning of portraits for sitters, painters, and viewers.

Because portraits depicted members of society, they provided a notable window for analyzing both social deportment and painting's influence upon it.[33] Sitters demonstrated their status by a series of carefully codified gestures and poses intended to convey their good manners and polite sensibility.[34] This is especially true of the genre of painting known as the "conversation piece." Conversation pieces portray friends, families, clubs, and other social units in ways that highlight their group dynamics and demonstrate the good-natured relationships between the sitters. Though these poses might look stilted to modern audiences, they were crafted as a public performance of personal sentimentality. This inner/outer dynamic was one of the primary means of defending portraiture's status against its critics, foregrounding the idea that portraits could make visible an exemplary inner character that could provide a useful role model. The painter Jonathan Richardson, for instance, claimed that "upon the sight of a Portrait the Character, and Master-strokes of the History of the Person it represents, are apt to flow in upon the Mind and to be the Subject of Conversation" and that "Men are excited to imitate the Good Actions, and persuaded to shun the Vices of those whose Examples are thus set before them."[35] Understanding portraits required audiences to look beyond the surface level of resemblance in order to discern the character of the person before them. Richardson's use of the term "conversation" is notable for the way it reinforces the social dynamics inherent in viewing portraits. As Kate Retford explains, "conversation" in the eighteenth century involved much more than just talk; it was a proxy for one's social circle and one's social conduct.[36] Thus, portraits provided a means of reflecting on one's own character.[37] Portraits were a useful tool for apprehending the didactic possibilities of painting.

The interrelation of painting and knowledge is a primary theme of Highmore's essay, "Whether ARTISTS only are proper Judges of WORKS OF ART," which demonstrates his respect for the new audiences for art.[38] Highmore does not relegate proper judgment of art to artists, nor limit it to the aristocracy, but instead recognizes all viewers as capable of perceiving an artwork's value through their relation to the image under study. Highmore argued that "every man is a judge of the representation, in proportion as he is of the original subject; a sailor, for instance, is a better judge of the principal circumstances which enter into the composition of a sea-piece, than the best painter in the world, who was never at sea."[39] While artistic judgment is connected to knowledge, valuable knowledge is derived not only from a formal education but also from personal experience. The quality of a work of art is thus potentially subject to interpretation from a broad range of audiences.

Highmore utilizes the interpretive possibilities of painting to underscore its epistemic possibilities. According to Highmore, "a poet, historian, philosopher, or (in general) any man of genius and taste, will conceive of an extraordinary fact or event, just as a great painter would, and may have within him all the requisites of such painter, except the mere mechanical part; and therefore, must necessarily be a good judge of such a subject executed."[40] Highmore's arguments echo those of Jonathan Richardson, who contended that painters must possess the knowledge of these various spheres in order to execute their art and thereby should be afforded the same respect.[41] Writing decades after Richardson, Highmore did not need to argue so strongly for the social status of painters. Rather, Highmore advocated for the intellectual status of paintings. Highmore's claim that these other practitioners can interpret art just as a painter can indicates that understanding a painting involves more than just the evaluation of its "mechanical" qualities. Understanding a painting might involve the skills of the poet or philosopher, demonstrating that paintings were interrelated with other, complementary disciplines and could serve as their own form of knowledge. The interrelation of these disciplines grants authors and artists equal status in providing insight into the subject under study.

Highmore's essay provides insight into his intellectual considerations during the composition of his *Pamela* paintings and suggests how he imagined his audience would interpret his visualizations. Rather than subordinating his series of paintings to Richardson's novel, Highmore considered his series as its own project, a chance to bring Pamela's story to life in a visual medium. Highmore himself made these ideas clear in his advertisement for the engraved version of the series, explaining that his work not only "endeavoured to comprehend her whole Story" but that it also would be accompanied by a "printed Account given to the Subscribers, wherein all the twelve Pictures are described and their respective Connexion shewn."[42] Audiences viewing the images were thus prompted to consider the ways that Highmore's series constitutes its own narrative. While the audience for Highmore's series would likely have also read the novel, that prior knowledge was not the sole criterion for judging the art. Rather than simply treating the images as illustrations of the novel, viewers were prompted to use their knowledge of *Pamela* as a starting point to understand the inner nature of Highmore's images. This method is akin to the painterly ideas of character that Highmore endorsed in his essay. Highmore stated that the value of an image was not based on the "the mere effect of manual operation, or mechanical practice, but depend[s] on … general understanding, judgement, learning, and knowledge of the human heart."[43] Discernment of the value of a painting rests on an understanding of painting not as an exercise of technical skill, but as an appreciation of the representation of human character. Although Highmore's formulation may seem overly ambitious (who can truly possess knowledge of the human heart?), his belief reflects the era's idealization of both knowledge and sentimental connection. It also relates to his interest in *Pamela* as a subject, for the novel is nothing if not an exploration of its heroine's emotional core.

This is the background of Highmore's *Adventures of Pamela*. The series was a commercial enterprise in a growing art market that gave rise to new understandings of visual culture in general and painting in particular. Highmore's career followed these developments, and he participated in the new discourse revolving around modes of spectatorship for art. With this framing in mind, I now turn to the paintings themselves, analyzing the ways in which they participate in this conversation, educating their audience in the proper mode of viewing.

Mr. B. and Improper Spectatorship

Highmore's *Adventures of Pamela* presents its audience with a lesson in spectatorship. As a series of paintings of the fictional heroine, the paintings are akin to portraits of Pamela and her world. They transform the interiority of the novel into external appearances. Indeed, appearances and how they are received are a key theme of the series as a whole and of each painting, as Pamela is always being watched in some way or another. While the figures in the paintings never directly acknowledge the audience by breaking the fourth wall, they implicate viewers in their interrogations of viewing practices by placing Pamela at the center of a series of onlookers among whom viewers can take their places. By watching the watching of others, viewers may learn something about their own methods of spectatorship. These lessons are primarily focalized through the character of Mr. B., who changes from an improper spectator to a respectful, moral viewer over the course of the series. The *Adventures of Pamela* serves as a lesson in how to view both paintings and people.

Highmore drew on the power of earlier pictorial narrative to reinforce his series's conception of the moral possibilities of painting. William Hogarth had introduced this narrative structure to recent painting with *A Harlot's Progress* (1731–32) and *A Rake's Progress* (1734–35) and later bolstered its recognition through his *Marriage A-La-Mode*, in production at the same time as Highmore's series. Hogarth's work was an important influence on the series's conception and on aspects of its composition, as Jacqueline Riding has demonstrated.[44] For the purposes of this discussion, two points should be recognized. First, Hogarth's "modern moral subjects" prepared audiences to analyze Highmore's series as moral commentary, prompting viewers to analyze behavior and to look for signs of impropriety, thus engaging with Highmore's visual arguments about moral viewership. Second, and in contrast, Highmore's genteel stylings are operating far from Hogarth's caricature and social satire. Though it is possible to assess this difference as a polite diminishment of the violence of Richardson's narrative, as David Solkin suggests, I would argue that the significance here is that Highmore's stylings offer a redemptive possibility that Hogarth's works eschew.[45] Hogarth's characters are invariably bound to fall, their outward appearances proof of their moral failures. Highmore, in contrast, carefully plays with the distinction between inner character and outward appearance and attempts to use the moral improvement of Mr. B. as a model. Hogarth's paintings, like Richardson's novel, provided Highmore with a form he could adapt for his own purposes.

While Highmore's paintings call for comparisons with Richardson's novel, Highmore was not striving for imitation. Highmore distanced himself from Richardson with both visual and verbal cues. Regarding the former, Highmore's paintings are notably small, approximately 65 x 76 cm each. This small size made hanging the paintings together easier, allowing for a greater narrativity to develop between the works. This narrativity was enhanced in the engraved versions, each approximately 30 x 36 cm. These engravings might be displayed together on a wall, guiding the eye through the sequence, or, alternately, they might be pasted in an album, in which case the narrative would unfold on successive leaves, as if one were reading a novel. The presentation of the series as a narrative was further reinforced by the descriptions located at the bottom of each plate (see, for example, Figure 5). With these captions, Highmore provided his audience with an immediate alternative to Richardson's novel.[46] The first caption reinforces this point, stating that "Pamela is represented in this first Piece, writing in her late Lady's dressing room, her history being known only by her letters."[47] By making her supposedly real letters, rather than Richardson's novel, his source, Highmore develops the claim that this work is a distinct presentation of the story with its own concerns.

From the start of the series, Highmore makes the point that, while knowledge of the novel can be assumed, and in some cases might bolster the meaning of a painting, analyses should not stop there. The first painting in the series, *Mr B. Finds Pamela Writing* (see Figure 1), highlights the series's relation to the novel and to the larger concerns of pictorial representation that it will teach its audience to understand. Here, Pamela writes the first of the many letters that will comprise her story. This scene, the only one of the paintings that presents Pamela writing, plays with Highmore's conception of art's interpretive possibilities. The letters that constitute the novel are here displayed for the viewer, who then recognizes their new presentation in the painting. Highmore posits the imagined history that inspired the novel as the primary source for his own work, rather than the text published by Richardson. Janet Aikins, writing of the same scene in the Hayman/Gravelot engravings commissioned by Richardson, observes that viewing "the actual letter in its manifestation as a physical object ... remind[s] us that the printer of the novel has served as intermediary between us and Pamela's words as they were hypothetically penned."[48] Highmore's work operates in this same manner. By calling to mind the mediation of Richardson's text, Highmore

Figure 1. Joseph Highmore, *Mr. B. Finds Pamela Writing,* 1743-44, oil on canvas, 65.1 x 75.9 cm, Tate. Photo: Tate.

demonstrates the capacities of his own work, depicting what Richardson could only describe. Highmore illustrates this distinction in order to demonstrate the way his narrative will operate at a visual level. The audience is encouraged to view the series as a commentary on viewing, much as the novel concerned itself with the practice of reading.

In this opening scene, the importance of developing a careful viewing practice is personified by Pamela. As Highmore's caption on the engraved version informs the audience, Pamela "is here surprised by Mr B. who improves this occasion to further his designs."[49] This danger is not immediately apparent in the image, where Mr. B. appears with outstretched arm in an apparent display of generosity. Rather, Mr. B.'s deception is only apparent retrospectively, after viewers see his rakish behavior, prompting a reconsideration of this seeming generosity. In this way, viewers of the painting replicate the misreading of Mr. B's intention that Pamela makes in this scene. Readers of the novel would recognize the books on display as those of Pamela's former mistress, offered by Mr. B. as a sign of charity that is actually the first step of his seduction.[50] It is only after Pamela's parents question Mr. B.'s motives that she recognizes his deceptiveness (12). The viewer of the painting, likely cognizant of these later developments from having read the novel, recognizes this moment for what it is and reexamines the picture in light of this knowledge, much as Pamela does upon reading the admonitions of her parents. Perception is revealed as a continuous learning process, in which what one knows and what one sees combine to create new formations of knowledge and vision in a recursive cycle. It is a cycle that prompts a move from sight to insight, a mode of viewing that begins with surface appearances but extends to understand what lies beneath.

This form of spectatorship, in which one moves from outward appearances to inner recognition, is contrasted with Mr. B., who claims to know Pamela by her appearance as a waiting-maid. As the bulge in his breeches indicates, Mr. B. sees in Pamela the social type of a sexually available servant, rather than recognizing her virtuous interiority. As William Sale Jr. phrased it, Mr. B. views her "as part of his goods and chattels and exercises over her a conventional prerogative."[51] As a wealthy, educated man, Mr. B. engages in a spectatorship in which what he believes he knows, the convention, takes precedent over the particularity of what he sees. While Pamela is writing her own story, Mr. B. thinks he already knows its end, the closed book beside him a metaphor for his closed perception. Mr. B.'s lustful gaze overrides all other views, rendering Pamela the object of vice it wishes to see. This is apparent in the composition of the painting. Pamela sits in a harmonious triangle, rising from the bottom corners to the top center. Mr. B.'s gaze breaks this triangle at an obtuse angle, disturbing this harmony in favor of his own view. Conflicting perceptions continue in their dress. Mr. B. believes Pamela's lowly outfit signifies an equally low morality, while sympathetic viewers recognize that her servant's clothing conceals her virtuous nature. Her appearance is an inversion of Mr. B.'s appearance as a respectably dressed rake. Each of these perspectives remains in play, however. To properly understand this scene, viewers cannot rely on the novel alone. The picture tells its own story in its own visual terms.

The conflict between these forms of viewing is reflected in the painting that hangs behind Pamela, which, as other critics have indicated, illustrates the story of the Good Samaritan.[52] This painting within a painting creates a metapictorial moment that demonstrates the ability of painting-as-adaptation to go beyond the mere imitation of text.[53] Highmore's metapicture serves as commentary, interpreting the scene below. Warren Mild analyzes this image as a metaphor for Mr. B. and Pamela's relationship, viewing the Pharisee in the background as a reflection of Mr. B.'s inhumanity toward Pamela.[54] His contention is bolstered by the similarity of their poses, as each travel through the painting from left to right. Miriam Dick sees the inset painting rather differently, arguing that it represents Mr. B. as a good Samaritan come to improve the life of his servant.[55] Highmore's visual commentary thus opens new possibilities of interpretation for the audience. Placing these differing views alongside one another suggests the conversational possibilities of painting. The dialogue created by these readings produces yet another reading. At first, Mr. B. imitates the Pharisee by appearing as an ally, but acting with callousness. When Mr. B. comes to respect Pamela and recognize her for who she is, however, he becomes the good Samaritan. Viewers, like Mr. B., must dissuade themselves from relying on preordered, conventional views in order to achieve a more clear-eyed, virtuous point of view. The Good Samaritan story is an apt one, for despite the expectation the traveler had of the Samaritan, a judgment based upon his looks, he found in him an unlikely friend.

The dangers of improper spectatorship, whereby viewers wrongly assert a possessive knowledge of those they see, are apparent in several of the subsequent images in the series, such as the second painting, *Pamela and Mr B. in the Summer House* (in which Mr. B. grasps Pamela against her will, staring at her as she averts her gaze), or the fourth painting, *Pamela Leaves Mr B.'s House in Bedfordshire,* in which he spies on her as she attempts to leave him, knowing she is to be kidnapped and taken to his Lincolnshire estate (93–101).[56] This trajectory of improper looking culminates in the seventh painting in the series, *Pamela in the Bedroom with Mrs. Jewkes and Mr B.* (see Figure 2), which depicts his gaze in its most lustful, reprehensible form in order to teach the dangers of such viewing.[57] This painting presents the audience with a prurient scene of Pamela undressing. Viewers are invited to gaze on Pamela, their eyes drawn to her luminous figure from the darker space around it. Richardson, sensitive to any charges against Pamela's morality, would certainly have preferred Highmore to avoid this "warm scene," but Highmore's independence allowed him to fulfill Richardson's stated plan to "*paint* VICE *in its proper Colours, to make it* deservedly odious; *and to set* VIRTUE *in its own amiable Light, to make it* truly Lovely" (3). Although Pamela unknowingly captures the audience's initial attention, this focal point is balanced with another to convey the painting's moral. This is revealed when audiences shift their gaze to Mr. B., who is again engaged in an act of improper spectatorship. Unlike the first painting in the series, however, Mr. B. is now engaged in a surreptitious mode of viewing, hiding in the corner while staring at Pamela in a fit of lust, his body veiled under the clothes of another maidservant, leaving only his hands and face visible. Following Highmore's visual cues, the audience, for whom Pamela's body is much more directly visible than it is for Mr. B., is powerfully implicated in his act of voyeurism.

Figure 2. Joseph Highmore, *Pamela in the Bedroom with Mrs. Jewkes and Mr. B,* 1743-44, oil on canvas, 62.7 x 75.7 cm, Tate. Photo: Tate.

The immorality of this voyeurism is not confined to viewing but also extends to the actions that follow this violation. As the plate explains, "Mr B. ... is impatiently waiting for the execution of his plot."[58] Readers of the novel would know that this "plot" is the attempted rape of Pamela (187–88). Audiences could thus scrutinize this moment for its intimations of sexual violence. Viewers who looked at Pamela in the same manner as Mr. B. might realize they too are implicated in his behavior; they too were attempting to destroy Pamela's virtue by stripping her of an inner being in favor of a focus upon her outward form. Viewers must reconsider their actions and review the painting in order to recognize Pamela's luminosity not as an enticement, but rather a sign of her purity. This dynamic also offers a lesson to those who would dismiss the painting as mere lechery. Audiences who view the painting in this manner inadvertently repeat Mr. B.'s lustful gaze by concentrating solely on the image they claim to find offensive. As Riding argues, Highmore does not indicate that Mr. B.'s desire is inherently immoral, but the way he acts on that desire is.[59] Viewers must be cognizant of the nature of their perception and what that perception will lead to. Even an image that first appears immoral may have something to teach spectators, if they are willing to look beyond initial appearances.

The Moral Spectator

Thus far in the series, Highmore's paintings have engaged with the issue of improper spectatorship. Mr. B.'s gaze is shown as improper both in the sense of social impropriety and in the sense that he fails to see what is before him: not the caricature of a sexually available servant, but a living, feeling human being. In the eighth painting in the series, *Pamela Greets Her Father* (see Figure 3), Highmore shifts to depicting a moral spectatorship based on recognizing the relation between the viewer and the viewed. Rather than imposing meaning based on what they think they know, moral spectators learn from what they see and remain open to a sentimental affect that allows them to recognize the human interiority beneath surface appearances.

In this painting, Mr. B. represents this moral spectatorship for the audience. Readers of the novel would recognize that, in the intervening time between this painting and the last, Mr. B. has undergone a profound moral education, as Pamela's virtue inspired him to forsake his rakish behavior and to promise to marry her (242). Indeed, Mr. B.'s moral shift is underscored in Highmore's series by the ninth painting, which depicts their marriage.[60] Here in the eighth painting, we again see Mr. B. staring at Pamela, but his attitude is changed as he clutches his heart and looks on with a measure of surprise.[61] The depicted scene, in which Pamela overturns the card table in rushing to greet her father, is certainly cause for surprise, but Mr. B.'s response is not the shock of the fashionable people behind him. Rather, Mr. B.'s attention is focused on the loving exchange before him, the first time in the series in which his eyes are not trained solely on Pamela. Here, Mr. B.'s viewership is not an instance of attempted control, but a sympathetic response to the scene before him. He is caught off-guard and must reassess what he believes he knows; Pamela can surprise him even now. In viewing the relationship between Pamela and her father, Mr. B. is overcome not by lustful passion, but by heartfelt sentiment.

Spectatorship does not merely occur on an individual level, however, but rather is an interaction among viewers. Viewing should not be a looking at but a looking into, as Pamela and her father demonstrate. Highmore chose as his subject the moment before Pamela and her father embrace, as they stare into one another's eyes. Their familial bond is presented as a relationship in which sight is a medium of social exchange. Pamela's visual exchange with her father is one of recognition: they know one another. But

Figure 3. Joseph Highmore, *Pamela Greets Her Father*, 1743-44, oil on canvas, 63.5 x 76.2 cm, National Gallery of Victoria, Melbourne.

it is also an exchange of responsiveness: they are surprised by each other's presence. Their gaze is like Mr. B.'s, but is also the cause of it because they connect emotionally to one another through sight. Highmore positions this exchange against a social backdrop created by the audience in the painting's background, which includes Parson Peters, the Darnford family (Simon, Lady, and Miss), and five other anonymous women.[62] Pamela and her father are an object of study for these other viewers, who do not look upon them in the same way as Mr. B. does. They may appear curious and surprised, but they lack an empathetic response to the scene before them.[63] Pamela has upended the social conventions of the card table as well as those of class distinction; her actions disrupt the order they expect. Pamela will contend with such views from Mr. B.'s disapproving family later in the series, evidence of the difficulties surrounding her change in station.[64] Like Mr. B. earlier in the narrative, these figures assume that they know Pamela through their own superficial observation and so must reform their view of her .

In addition to depicting spectators, Highmore reinforces the social function of painting by showing more paintings within paintings, in this case, the portraits lining the wall. These portraits constitute a family gallery, a traditional mode of display that showed off a family's history and lineage.[65] The inclusion of the family gallery was a convention of conversation pieces, linking current and previous generations in a way that implied the approval of the sitters' forebears.[66] In placing Pamela in this context just before her wedding day, Highmore signals Pamela's social ascendance and the virtue of her marriage to Mr. B., whose spectatorial reform is sanctioned by his ancestors. The cross-generational conversation implied by this painting also connects to considerations of the relation of conversation to art. Three of the women in the background look not at Pamela or her father, but rather at a painting above them. Highmore underscores the social nature of viewing art, which brings these women together. Further, two of the women are engaged in discussion, one of them gesturing toward the painting. Highmore shows his audience how they should engage with the works before them, interpreting their meanings while conversing with companions. Perhaps the women are considering where Pamela will fit in this family history, conversing not only with each other but also with the portraits before them. Perception is here depicted as both socially mediated and socially bonding.

By staging Pamela's scene of familial bonding in the context of familial portraiture, Highmore points to a relation between viewing art and viewing people. Pamela and her father are portrayed in the painting for Highmore's audience, but they are also the living subjects of the viewers of Mr. B.'s social circle. Pamela and her father are like the portraits discussed earlier, paintings with a life of their own. But Highmore's series moves beyond static portraiture by painting the exhilarating life story of Pamela, her adventures provoking a multiplicity of emotions for both her and her viewers. The psychological realism attributed to Richardson's novel can thus be glimpsed in the paintings' narrative. How one views an artwork affects how one views other people. If viewers learn to see like Mr. B. (from this particular painting on), they can be sentimentally affected in the same manner that he is, or that Pamela and her father are. Highmore claimed that a proper judgment of painting required a proper understanding of the human heart, and here that understanding has been made visible.

The value of this new-formed understanding is evident in the next painting in the series, in which Mr. B. and Pamela are married, but it is most apparent in the series's final painting, *Pamela Tells a Nursery Tale* (see Figure 4). Here, the bed appears not as a site of terror, as it did in the painting of Mr. B.'s voyeurism, but rather a site of marriage and domestic bliss.[67] Pamela is again the center of attention, but now her viewers' faces are full of delight

Figure 4. Joseph Highmore, *Pamela Tells a Nursery Tale,* c. 1744, oil on canvas, 62.9 x 74.7 cm, The Fitzwilliam Museum, Cambridge. Reproduction by permission of the Syndics of the Fitzwilliam Museum, Cambridge.

and wonder as she is surrounded by her children. Pamela's children watch her intently, their wide eyes signaling an openness to the lessons she will teach them as she weaves a tale anew.

Pamela's children are described by Highmore in the caption to the engraved version of this image as the "peaceable fruits of her Virtue long after having surmounted all the difficulties it had been exposed to."[68] Pamela's children, however, are more than her personal reward for virtue, for they symbolize societal progress as well. Children here represent the result of the bonds of a loving marriage and thus may be read as symbols of harmonious social interactions.[69] New ideas about the influence of motherhood on the development of children were tied to beliefs concerning women's supposed greater sentimentality. Women could pass on their intellectual and emotional responsiveness to future generations in the form of ingrained standards of behavior. This generational progress was likened to a national moral development, as each generation was imagined as improving upon the last.

Pamela's children represent this moral improvement in their newly learned modes of viewing, seeing Pamela in a proper manner that will ideally be instilled in others of their generation.

The hope for this new generation is reinforced by the painting hanging over the fireplace, which is more visible in the engraved version (see Figure 5). The first metapicture of the series, the Good Samaritan, reinforced the moral considerations at stake by sending Mr. B. on the path to learn proper judgement. This final metapicture, on the other hand, depicts a naked babe held from behind by its mother, reaching out to touch another young child. This composition echoes images of the Madonna and Child with an infant St. John the Baptist. Highmore thus connects Pamela to Mary and her children to Jesus and St. John and the themes of innocence and virtuous motherhood that those paintings traditionally represented.[70] Portraitists often drew upon this iconography in paintings of mothers and children in order to universalize their subjects, demonstrating the moral possibilities of contemporary motherhood. Recognizing this classic iconography helps viewers understand how Highmore's painting are not just about Pamela, but also about the nature of people more generally. The virtue they aim to instill is one of a societal moral redemption. Societal progress is presented as an improvement of vision, each new iteration refining what viewers can see until they reach an understanding of the human heart.

Viewing Highmore and Richardson Anew

The *Adventures of Pamela* remained on display in Highmore's studio until his retirement to the country in 1762, when it was almost certainly sold at auction, along with the rest of Highmore's collection.[71] In 1920, the set appeared at auction at Christies. It was subsequently donated to the National Gallery, London, and was divided between that institution, the Fitzwilliam Museum, and the National Gallery of Victoria, Melbourne.[72] The dispersal of the series has undoubtedly contributed to its lack of recognition. Separated from one another, these paintings lose the coherence essential to their work as a pictorial equivalent of a novel. Viewing them as singular pieces or in small, random groupings reduces the paintings to scattered bits of *Pamela* ephemera and forces audiences to turn to Richardson's text to bind the pieces back together. This essay offers a way to understand this series without relying first and foremost on Richardson's novel.

However, this essay would be remiss if it did not return to Richardson one final time, for he was quite taken with Highmore's work and, as a result, the two became lifelong friends.[73] Ultimately, Highmore claimed Richardson as his closest friend and was with Richardson just before he died in 1761.[74]

Figure 5. Antoine Benoist after Joseph Highmore, *Pamela Tells a Nursery Tale,* 1745, engraving, 26.7 x 37.3 cm, National Gallery of Victoria, Melbourne.

In the years before his passing, Highmore painted several portraits of Richardson, including one that hangs in the National Portrait Gallery (see Figure 6), which was commissioned by Richardson's friend and admirer, Lady Bradshaigh.[75] The social function of novels and paintings is on full display in Richardson's portrait. Highmore depicts Richardson with the signs of his professional accomplishments, pen and paper in hand, while behind him a bookshelf stands housing the results of those tools. Richardson's own virtue is here visible for all to see. Underneath the public aspect of this portrait, however, is a further personal meaning. Lady Bradshaigh, writing to Richardson, stated she "would chuse you drawn in your study, a table or desk by you, with pen, ink, and paper; one letter just sealed, which I shall fancy is to me."[76] Understood in this light, the painting juxtaposes Richardson as both the brilliant epistolary novelist and a faithful, personal friend.

There is one final touch that makes this portrait a monument to sociability: its collaborative composition. While Highmore was working on Lady Bradshaigh's commission, Richardson asked him to reproduce a painting of Lady Bradshaigh and her husband done by Edward Haytley. Richardson

Figure 6. Joseph Highmore, *Samuel Richardson*, 1750, oil on canvas, 52.7 x 36.8 cm, National Portrait Gallery, London.

wanted more than a mere copy, however, and asked Highmore to make the work more personal. Highmore complied by dressing the two in the Van Dyck style and replacing Lord Bradshaigh's dog with Lady Bradshaigh's tame fawn, Fanny. When Highmore painted his portrait of Richardson, he inserted this image into the background, building on Richardson's ideas to add another level of intimate depth to this piece. Highmore's portrait of Richardson is thus layered with personal, sentimental meaning derived from both of these eighteenth-century masters. The accomplishment of this portrait derives from the same source that make Highmore's *Adventures of Pamela* such a success. It is a work made not in imitation, but in sympathy.

Notes

For their suggestions, critiques, and edits across the numerous drafts of this essay, I would like to thank my advisors Carla J. Mulford and Christopher Reed.

1. Brian Allen, *Francis Hayman* (New Haven: Yale University Press, 1987), 180–82; Richard D. Altick, *Painting From Books: Art and Literature in Britain, 1760–1900* (Columbus: Ohio State University Press, 1985), 15; *The Pamela Controversy: Criticisms and Adaptations of Samuel Richardson's* Pamela, *1740–1750,* ed. Thomas Keymer and Peter Sabor, 6 vols. (London: Pickering & Chatto, 2001), 2:xlii. Highmore may have been preceded by Francis Hayman and members of his studio, whose paintings for Vauxhall Gardens included two scenes adapted from Hayman's engravings for the illustrated sixth edition of *Pamela,* discussed below. Allen gives these paintings a date of c. 1741–42, while Altick states that the dating is unclear. Keymer and Sabor think Highmore was the first.

2. Warren Mild, *Joseph Highmore of Holborn Row* (Ardmore: Kingswood, 1990), 259. The paintings do not have an official title and are often referred to by nondescript titles like the *Pamela* paintings. Here I deploy the name used by Mild in the attempt to recognize the paintings as an independent production. Mild's title is drawn from advertisements for the engravings made after the paintings, which open, "Mr. Highmore Proposes to Publish by SUBSCRIPTION, TWELVE PRINTS by the best French Engravers, after his own PAINTINGS, representing the most remarkable ADVENTURES OF PAMELA." Titles for individual paintings will follow the title given in the catalogues of the museums in which they currently reside. The titles given to the prints in the engraved version vary by the institution holding them but often follow the titles for their corresponding paintings.

3. Altick, *Painting from Books,* 17–21.

4. Thomas Keymer and Peter Sabor, *Pamela in the Marketplace: Literary Controversy and Print Culture in Eighteenth-Century Britain and Ireland* (New York: Cambridge University Press, 2005), 1–10.

5. Eaves, "Graphic Illustrations of the Novels of Samuel Richardson, 1740–1810," *Huntington Library Quarterly* 14, no. 4 (August 1951): 358–62. For a different take, see Marcia Epstein Allentuck, "Narration and Illustration: The Problem of Richardson's *Pamela*," *Philological Quarterly* 51, no. 4 (October 1971): 874–86.

6. Miriam Dick, "Joseph Highmore's Vision of *Pamela*," *English Language Notes* 24, no. 4 (June 1987): 41–42; Louise M. Miller, "Author, Artist, Reader: 'The Spirit of the Passages' and the Illustrations to *Pamela*," *Q/W/E/R/T/Y: Arts, Littératures & Civilisations du Monde Anglophone* 4 (October 1994): 123–30; James Grantham Turner, "Novel Panic: Picture and Performance in the Reception of Richardson's *Pamela*," *Representations* 48 (Autumn 1994): 73, 83–86.

7. Keymer and Sabor, *Pamela in the Marketplace,* 15.

8. Keymer and Sabor, *Pamela in the Marketplace,* 3–6.

9. Highmore's advertisements ran in the *London Daily Post and General Advertiser*, the *General Evening Post,* and the *Daily Advertiser* from 16 February 1744 through 20 July 1745. An initial series of eight announcements ran simultaneously in the publications in February 1744, with an additional notice appearing on 10 May. As the engraving series neared completion, Highmore resumed advertising, starting on 13 March 1745 and continuing until 1 May, when the subscription was declared closed. On 13 July, Highmore announced the completion of the prints and would repeat this notice through 20 July. See Mild, *Joseph Highmore,* 258–62; Jacqueline Riding, *Basic Instincts: Love, Passion, and Violence in the Art of Joseph Highmore* (Andoain: Paul Hoberton Publishing), 57–59.

10. Mild, *Joseph Highmore,* 257.

11. Gravelot and Hayman's engravings have been examined by numerous scholars, including Eaves, "Graphic Illustrations," 352–57, and Miller, "Author, Artist, Reader," 123–30, both of whom compare them to Highmore's paintings. The most comprehensive work on the engravings is Janet E. Aikins, "Picturing 'Samuel Richardson': Francis Hayman and the Intersections of Word and Image," *Eighteenth-Century Fiction* 14, no. 3–4 (2002): 465–505, where she argues that the engravings highlight the intermedial possibilities of eighteenth-century fiction and visual art as well as Richardson's collaborative approach to fiction. For a subversive reading of these engravings, see Stephen A. Raynie, "Hayman and Gravelot's Anti-*Pamela* Designs for Richardson's Octavo Edition of *Pamela I* and *II*," *Eighteenth-Century Life* 23, no. 3 (November 1999): 77–93.

12. John Brewer, "Cultural Production, Consumption, and the Place of the Artist in Eighteenth-Century England," in *Towards a Modern Art World*, ed. Brian Allen (London: Yale University Press, 1995), 8. For a history of English art importation and auction houses, see Iain Pears, *The Discovery of Painting: The Growth of Interest in the Arts in England, 1680–1768* (London: Yale University Press, 1988), 51–75.

13. Brewer, "Cultural Production," 8.

14. Riding, *Basic Instincts,* 17.

15. Hume, "The Value of Money in Eighteenth-Century England: Incomes, Prices, Buying Power—and Some Problems in Cultural Economics," *Huntington Library Quarterly* 77, no. 4, (Winter 2014): 377.

16. Hume acknowledges that access is a significant but incalculable consideration. See Hume, "The Value of Money," 378–79.

17. For print prices, see Timothy Clayton, *The English Print, 1688–1802* (New Haven: Yale University Press, 1997), 22, 52, 57, 82. For wages, see Hume, "The Value of Money," 412.

18. Riding, *Basic Instincts*, 57.

19. Hume, "The Value of Money," 406.

20. Hume, "The Value of Money," 377.

21. For a comparison of the novel and visual art and the debates they each elicited, see Alison Conway, *Private Interests: Women, Portraiture, and the Visual Culture of the English Novel, 1709–1791* (Toronto: University of Toronto Press, 2001), esp. 14–32.

22. Information in this paragraph is drawn from Stephen Copley, "The Fine Arts in Eighteenth Century Polite Culture," in *Painting and the Politics of Culture: New Essays on British Art, 1700–1850,* ed. John Barrell (New York: Oxford University Press, 1992), 13–39, esp. 15–16. See also Pears, *Discovery of Painting,* 27–50.

23. Pears, *Discovery of Painting,* 39. See also John Brewer, *The Pleasures of the Imagination: English Culture in the Eighteenth Century* (New York: Farrar Straus Giroux, 1997), 206.

24. De Bolla, *The Education of the Eye: Painting, Landscape, and Architecture in Eighteenth-Century Britain* (Stanford: Stanford University Press, 2003), 9–10.

25. Webb, *An Inquiry into the Beauties of Painting; and into the Merits of the Most Celebrated Painters, Ancient and Modern,* 2nd ed. (London, 1761), 18; Joseph Highmore, "Remarks on some Passages in Mr Webb's 'Enquiry into the Beauties of Painting, &c.,'" *Gentleman's Magazine* 36 (1766): 353-56. See also De Bolla, *Education of the Eye,* 15–16.

26. See De Bolla, *Education of the Eye,* 28–31.

27. My discussion of portraiture and the hierarchy of genres draws upon David H. Solkin, *Art in Britain, 1660–1815* (New Haven: Yale University Press, 2015), 61–62, 80–81.

28. Conway, *Private Interests,* 18.

29. Riding, *Basic Instincts,* 17. Riding does not give a firm date for Highmore's first history works, but the earliest surviving works date to 1744, when Highmore was wrapping up the *Adventures of Pamela* (*Basic Instincts,* 93).

30. Riding, *Basic Instincts,* 93.

31. This paragraph draws on Solkin, *Art in Britain,* 111–12, 131–33.

32. Francis Hayman painted the piece, which Aikins analyzes as an attempt to represent Richardson's professional and familial status ("Picturing 'Samuel Richardson,'" 484–92).

33. This paragraph draws on Kate Retford, *The Conversation Piece: Making Modern Art in Eighteenth-Century Britain* (New Haven: Yale University Press, 2017), 11, 65–93, esp. 65–74, and Retford, *The Art of Domestic Life: Family Portraiture in Eighteenth-Century England* (New Haven: Yale University Press, 2006), 7–12. See also De Bolla, *Education of the Eye,* 36–54.

34. Lynn Shepherd, for example, notes that Hubert and Gravelot's first engraving for Richardson puts Pamela in a pose outlined in one of the era's conduct books, thereby demonstrating her gentility despite her station (*Clarissa's Painter: Portraiture, Illustration, and Representation in the Novels of Samuel Richardson* [New York: Oxford University Press, 2009], 79–82).

35. Richardson, *An Essay on the Theory of Painting* (London, 1715), 16. Cf. Brewer, *Pleasures of the Imagination*, 311.

36. Retford, *Conversation Piece*, 28.

37. Indeed, Louise Lippincott suggests that while academic theory held history painting to be the height of moral instruction, in practice this role was primarily performed by portraits, which were both more common and more directly tied to public life. See Louise Lippincott, "Expanding on Portraiture: The Market, the Public, and the Hierarchy of Genres in Eighteenth-Century Britain," in *The Consumption of Culture, 1600-1800,* ed. Ann Bermingham and John Brewer (New York: Routledge, 1995), 75–88, esp. 82.

38. Though this essay was published in 1766, after Highmore's retirement to the country, its arguments reflect concerns about the standing of both audiences and painters already underway in the preceding decades.

39. Joseph Highmore, "Whether Artists Only Are Proper Judges of Works of Art," in *Essays, Moral, Religious, and Miscellaneous,* 2 vols. (London, 1766), 2:87.

40. Highmore, "Whether Artists Only Are Proper Judges," 2:87.

41. Richardson, *Essay on the Theory of Painting*, 19–23.

42. *The General Evening Post*, 16 February 1744. Riding uses the line quoted to make a similar argument and notes that no copy of this "printed Account" has come to light (*Basic Instincts*, 62).

43. Highmore, "Whether Artists Only Are Proper Judges," 2:85.

44. Riding, *Basic Instincts*, 68–75.

45. Solkin, *Art in Britain*, 111. Mild makes a similar point to my own (*Joseph Highmore*, 281–83).

46. Captions were not included with the paintings. However, since they were displayed in his studio, Highmore would have been present to guide the audience through the narrative.

47. Quoted in Mild, *Joseph Highmore*, 264.

48. Aikins, "Picturing 'Samuel Richardson,'" 479.

49. Quoted in Mild, *Joseph Highmore*, 264. Timothy Erwin argues that "design" is significant for the way it echoes "design" in artistic composition, which he links to classically oriented artistic rhetoric. This is contrasted with a modern interest in color that he associates with Highmore. See his *Augustan Design and the Invention of Eighteenth-Century British Culture* (Lewisburg: Bucknell University Press, 2015), 1–15, 147–51.

50. Samuel Richardson, *Pamela: or, Virtue Rewarded,* ed. Thomas Keymer and Peter Sabor, *The Cambridge Edition of the Works of Samuel Richardson,* 12 vols. planned (New York: Cambridge University Press, 2011–), 2:10. Subsequent references to *Pamela* will use this edition and will be made parenthetically.

51. Sale, Introduction to Samuel Richardson, *Pamela, or Virtue Rewarded* (New York: W.W. Norton, 1993), ix.

52. Mild, *Joseph Highmore*, 283; Dick, "Joseph Highmore's Vision," 42; Riding, *Basic Instincts*, 71. Highmore painted the Good Samaritan story during the same years as the series, though with a different composition than the painting discussed here. See Highmore, *The Good Samaritan*, 1744, oil on canvas, 159.5 x 144.8 cm, Tate Gallery, London. *https://www.tate.org.uk/art/artworks/highmore-the-good-samaritan-t00076*.

53. Hogarth used a similar trick in his modern moral subjects. See Solkin, *Art in Britain*, 94–97, 105–6.

54. Mild, *Joseph Highmore*, 283–84.

55. Dick, "Joseph Highmore's Vision," 42. Riding concurs that the image represents the choice of behavior that Mr. B. can make in relation to Pamela, but focuses on Mr. B.'s lecherous character, rather than the way Mr. B. comes to embody both these roles (*Basic Instincts*, 71).

56. Highmore, *Pamela and Mr B. in the Summer House*, c. 1744, oil on canvas, 62.9 x 75.6 cm, Fitzwilliam Museum, Cambridge. *https://collection.beta.fitz.ms/id/object/3341*. The third image in the sequence is a notable exception, as Mr. B. attempts to revive Pamela after his first assault causes her to faint. His concern, however, is only temporary, as his second assault makes clear. See Highmore, *Pamela Fainting*, 1743–44, oil on canvas, 63.5 x 76.2 cm, National Gallery of Victoria, Melbourne. *https://www.ngv.vic.gov.au/explore/collection/work/4040/*.

57. Pears discusses a similarly didactic print about the relation between viewership and lust (*Discovery of Painting*, 40–41).

58. Quoted in Mild, *Joseph Highmore*, 273. The full caption reads "Pamela undressing herself (Mrs. Jewkes being first got to bed) while Mr B. disguised in the maid's clothing, with the apron thrown over his face, is impatiently waiting for the execution of his plot."

59. Riding, *Basic Instincts*, 79.

60. Highmore, *Pamela is Married*, oil on canvas, 62.8 x 76 cm, Tate Gallery, London. *https://www.tate.org.uk/art/artworks/highmore-ix-pamela-is-married-n03575*.

61. The caption reads "Pamela on her knees before her Father, whom she had discovered behind the door, having over turn'd the card-table in her way. Sir Simon Darnford, his lady &c. observing her with eagerness and admiration. Mr. B struck with this scene is waiting the issue." Quoted in Mild, *Joseph Highmore*, 274.

62. Mild, *Joseph Highmore*, 275.

63. Riding makes a similar point regarding the disconnect between Mr. B. and the other spectators (*Basic Instincts*, 64).

64. Highmore, *Pamela and Lady Davers*, 1743–44, oil on canvas, 63.5 x 76.2 cm, National Gallery of Victoria, Melbourne. *https://www.ngv.vic.gov.au/explore/collection/work/4043/*; Highmore, *Pamela Asks Sir Jacob Swinford's Blessing*, 1743–44, oil on canvas, 63.2 x 75 cm, Tate Gallery, London. *https://www.tate.org.uk/art/artworks/highmore-xi-pamela-asks-sir-jacob-swinfords-blessing-n03576*.

65. Marcia Pointon, *Hanging the Head: Portraiture and Social Formation in Eighteenth-Century England* (New Haven: Yale University Press, 1993), 23.

66. Retford, *Conversation Piece*, 234–39. Riding argues that the painting's display of only the legs of these ancestors signals the way in which Pamela will remain apart from the landed gentry due to her background and virtue (*Basic Instincts*, 64–65).

67. Riding, *Basic Instincts*, 66.

68. Quoted in Mild, *Joseph Highmore*, 278.

69. See Retford, *Art of Domestic Life*, 83–114.

70. Retford, *Art of Domestic Life*, 91–95.

71. Elizabeth Einberg, *Manners & Morals: Hogarth and British Painting, 1700–1760* (London: Tate Gallery Publications, 1987), 157. Mild discusses the sale of the *Adventures of Pamela* plates to John Boydell but does not describe the sale of the paintings themselves (*Joseph Highmore*, 379–86).

72. See the Tate's "Catalogue Entry" for Highmore, *Mr B. Finds Pamela Writing*. *https://www.tate.org.uk/art/artworks/highmore-i-mr-b-finds-pamela-writing-n03573*.

73. Mild, *Joseph Highmore*, 254.

74. Mild, *Joseph Highmore*, 254.

75. See Mild, *Joseph Highmore*, 293–300.

76. Quoted in Mild, *Joseph Highmore*, 299–300.

"A tedious accumulation of nothing": Christopher Smart, Imperialist Archives, and Mechanical Poetry in the Eighteenth Century

JESSLYN WHITTELL

> Knowest thou that trees and fruits flourish upon the earth
> To gratify senses unknown—trees, beasts, and birds unknown;
> Unknown, not unperceivd, spread in the infinite microscope.[1]

> Let Dawn, house of Dawn rejoice with the Frigate Bird which is
> found upon the coasts of India.[2]

This essay begins with a trick question: is Christopher Smart's *Jubilate Agno* a twentieth-century poem? Smart wrote *Jubilate Agno* during what he called his "jeopardy," a six-year confinement in St. Luke's asylum from 1757–63, but the work remained unpublished until W. F. Stead released a version as *Rejoice in the Lamb* in 1939.[3] After its publication, *Jubilate Agno* was popularized by twentieth-century experimental poets and literary scholars. It is now one of the few works by Smart consistently taken up in scholarship. Given Smart's background and the poem's bizarre formal experiments, the almost-two-hundred-year delay between *Jubilate Agno*'s production and principal reception is not surprising. Smart's contemporaries regarded him as a commercial hack, a winner of Cambridge-sponsored competitions, but no prophetic luminary: when Samuel Johnson was asked whether he considered Samuel Derrick or Smart the better poet, he reportedly declared, "there is no settling the point of precedency between a louse and a flea."[4]

But *Jubilate Agno* is a poem utterly unlike the odes, classical translations, and children's verses that Smart churned out to support himself. Part Magnificat, part diary, and part annotations to Pliny's *Natural History*, the poem cycles through paratactic exclamations along the lines of "Let Ishmael dedicate a Tyger, and give praise for the liberty, in which the Lord has let him at large," which are populated by a rotating cast of biblical heroes, animals, institutions, nations, places, and even the alphabet (*JA,* A.10). If this formal experimentation was uncongenial to the eighteenth century, it made *Jubilate Agno* the darling of a twentieth-century modernist cohort that included Marianne Moore and possibly Countee Cullen.[5] *Jubilate Agno* remains something of a cult classic, with "For I will consider my cat Jeoffry"—an extended meditation on Smart's cat in Fragment B—receiving the most airtime (*JA,* B.695–713). More recent citations of the poem include Chen Chen's "For I will consider my boyfriend Jeffrey," Mac Wellman's *Awe,* Geoffrey G. O'Brien's "Christopher Smart," and the inclusion of several lines from Fragment B in *Imagining Language,* an anthology of experimental poetry.[6] More broadly, Smart's work is at home among texts like John Barton Wolgamot's *In Sara Mencken, Christ, and Beethoven There Were Men and Women* (1944), Gertrude Stein's *The Making of Americans* (1925), even Louis Zukofsky's "*A.*"[7] These works share *Jubilate Agno*'s fixation on repetition, wordplay, and reference being done to death. Wolgamot, for example, takes the same sentence and repeats it, with incremental changes, for several pages, swapping out the names of canonical big wigs and replacing the many adverbs with synonyms that creep into new meanings.[8]

I'm setting *Jubilate Agno* among these much later texts because I believe the resonance between Smart's poem and its (post)modern counterparts can show us how eighteenth-century poetic experimentation was predicated on the existence of imperial archives and how this history continues to shape the poetic function of information and mechanism in contemporary poetry. Saidiya Hartman reminds us of the psychological and physical weight of these archives and cautions that inhabiting them often results in the experience of violence or its recapitulation.[9] At what point does literary scholarship become an invoice of violence, recapitulating the harms that it recites without offering a meaningful remedy? How can eighteenth-century studies better inhabit its archives and texts, and how do we narrate history without developing an acquisitive relation to violence, without making it a commodity within the academy? Rather than answering these questions, this essay will consider how Smart's formal choices, read through an avant-garde approach to information, confront us with them.

Smart's writing has been consistently characterized as part of the visionary tradition, as prophetic madness, despite his biographer's dismissal of "the construction of a mad poet."[10] I am advocating, however, for a different understanding of Smart's poetic labor and of his relation to *Jubilate Agno*'s source texts and archives. At one point in *Jubilate Agno*, Smart observes "For the relations of words are in pairs first" (*JA*, B.598). "Pairs" becomes the poem's modus operandi, allowing Smart to match vastly different archives, like gems to English surnames or biblical characters to various flora and fauna. Smart calls this pairwise repetition a "cipher." In my reading, the programmatic, almost-algorithmic cipher becomes a means of working with broken materials.

Given this mechanism, a more productive description of the affect of *Jubilate Agno* might be what Sianne Ngai calls "stuplimity," which combines shock and awe with boredom; the word is a portmanteau of "stupid" and "sublime."[11] The stuplime anticipates Ngai's later focus on the "overarching habitualization of aesthetic novelty" in the twentieth century and on art's attendant failure to "produc[e] perceptual shocks," but the stuplime is particularly useful as a concept because it acknowledges the "stupefaction" of the reader and the ways in which "thick" language "challenges [their] own capacity to read, interpret, or critically respond to the stuplime in conventional ways."[12] Stuplimity signals a failure in which criticism fumbles the obvious precisely because it is obvious. The stuplime outsmarts us in its absolute availability; its coy sincerity or concussive directness is what stops us in our tracks, not its obfuscations. Ngai locates this bang-clash, high-cost, low-reward artistic aesthetic—one that anticipates her more recent engagement with the gimmick—in modernist poetry, like the writing of Gertrude Stein, but this system is also precisely how Smart's ciphers operate.[13]

Reading *Jubilate Agno* as a "stuplime" forerunner to experimental poetry can help us better situate the text between archive and poem and understand how Smart's ciphers highlight the labor of shifting between the two. As I will argue in the final section of this essay, the "stupefaction" generated by the obvious, but inarticulable, shock of Smart's labor shifts information in *Jubilate Agno* from mere textual data to a form of weak affect. In other words, the poem raises the problem of how to *feel* information, or how we fail to feel it.[14] Not quite an archive but yet not quite a poem (at least, not by eighteenth-century standards), *Jubilate Agno* makes us sensible of the formal challenges that define a poetic relationship to the archive, challenges that, for Smart, are frequently both material and affective.

One major goal of this essay is to unpack *Jubilate Agno*'s peculiar relationship to its source texts. I examine ciphers, citations, translations, wordplay, and repetition in Smart's work as an experimental form that deploys stuplimity in response to a glut of imperial information. As I see it, Smart's goal is the ciphering of archives, the transcription of natural histories and encyclopedias in a process that Kevis Goodman calls "georgic cultivation."[15] These ciphers share the cataloguing impulse of Smart's source texts, marshalling a global panoply of plants, animals, and minerals into the poem. Academic readings of the poem, including those of Geoffrey Hartman and Tobias Menely, tend to equate the sheer number of listed species with a reaffirmation of multispecies spiritual vitality: "For Man and Earth suffer together" (*JA,* C.155).[16] These scholars make *Jubilate Agno* a case-study in the "comforting of creatureliness," a celebration of the shared dignity of material and animal beings.[17]

Yet the final product of this stuplime ciphering is less poem than encyclopedia, what Scott M. Cleary describes as "a master system seeking totalizing knowledge of nature in its multiple manifestations."[18] This isn't a coincidence. Smart seems to have supported imperialism or, at the minimum, espoused an almost-jingoistic investment in Britain's affairs abroad, and while he suffered extensively at the hands of the British carceral state, his commitment to building up imperial archives is reflected in his ciphers.[19] The role of encyclopedias and natural histories in the British empire has been well-documented, and even Pliny's *Natural History* participated in what Elizabeth Ann Pollard calls "imperialism by plant."[20] As Edward Said explains in *Orientalism,* the eighteenth century—particularly the pivot toward totalizing knowledge, Linnaean classification of the natural world, and the explosion of encyclopedias, histories, and travel accounts—consolidated orientalism and broader imperial attitudes into "systematic discipline[s]." In other words, eighteenth-century natural histories gave institutional "precision" to the violence of empire.[21] This essay goes further by arguing that Smart's fixation on archival labor and ciphering makes imperialist catalogues and taxonomies a formal problem. Here, I'm picking up where Clement Hawes leaves off in *Mania and Literary Style.* Hawes looks to strike a balance between the leveling impulse of Smart's "rhetoric of mania" and "ADD+oration," a pun Hawes borrows from Hartman to link the additive repetition of Smart's verse-ark to imperialist "appropriation and possession."[22]

Toward that end, I want to emphasize that *Jubilate Agno*, despite its off-the-wall experimental form, is a deeply nationalistic text. Smart openly espouses a desire to be the "reviver of Adoration amongst ENGLISH-MEN" and prophesies that "the ENGLISH tongue shall be the language of the

WEST" (*JA*, B.332, B.127). This nationalism even emerges in his work as a translator: Leah Orr gives an excellent account of how Smart's translations of Horace impose Christian values on the original text.[23] I don't want to reductively compare translation to the transcription and bricolage that Smart employed in forklifting chunks of natural history into *Jubilate Agno*, but Orr's account illuminates how completely Smart's ideological investments imbued his practice as a creator. Orr and Hawes are among the few scholars to discuss seriously the nationalism that complements Smart's rhetoric of mania, but Hawes in particular moves rather quickly from a discussion of the imperialist aesthetics of *Jubilate Agno* to its redemptive sincerity.[24] My essay will take a less comforting approach.

Starting with the verse "Let Dawn, house of Dawn with the Frigate Bird which is found upon the coasts of India," I examine *Jubilate Agno*'s formal accumulation, networks, and patterns as an archival aesthetics that treats the *idea* of biodiversity as a formal commodity, while also extracting and adapting ecological data in service of empire. This understanding of the relationship between literary form and information is heavily indebted to Tita Chico's claim that "early science formulated itself through literary knowledge" and that "science is a literary trope."[25] Goodman has also traced the historical relationship between scientific perception and literature, with an extended discussion of how literature, specifically Virgil's *Georgics*, "were understood to *be* a kind of artificial organ."[26]

But the through-lines between poetry and scientific inquiry only partially account for the affective, as well as formal, function of Smart's citations. Cleary tacitly links Smart's systematized methods to technology, pointing briefly to what he terms "mechanisms of automation, control, and correction."[27] Within the context of mechanism, the twentieth-century avant-garde offers another framework for reading systematized knowledge in *Jubilate Agno*. We might start with Craig Dworkin's account of definitional literature (an Oulipo method) in "The Potential Energy of Texts [$\Delta U = -P\Delta V$]."[28] Definitional poetics, like the georgic mode, uses information as a trope to relentlessly inhabit the space between texts. As Dworkin's performatively mathematical title demonstrates, information, even a potentially useless formula, comes with its own aesthetic pleasures and cachet. For Dworkin, as for Smart, even when information isn't explicitly mechanical, it evokes mechanism, and mechanism has baggage.[29]

I believe that the avant-garde and its fraught relationship to systems of information can help us situate *Jubilate Agno* as an archival project that explores the formal processes of reducing information to data, where data allows for both imperialist commodification and, potentially, more productive disidentifications and "failures of feeling." By a reduction to data, I mean that the ciphers in *Jubilate Agno* suspend the poem between being a useful database and a stuplime information overload. This suspension distorts the familiar proportions between radical form and reactionary jingoism and between an imperial agenda and antinomian spirituality. This is not to give Smart a pass, but rather to say that the usual language for criticizing empire corrodes in the toxic slurry of *Jubilate Agno*. By zooming in on these ciphers, I hope to account for how the poem reinvents information as affect in the age of imperialism.

Smart's Georgic of the Frigatebird

In this first section, by tracing the networks of information behind *Jubilate Agno,* I argue that the poem defines its formal choices in terms of its relation to archives. The form makes readers sensible of the labor of transcription and "georgic cultivation." Goodman uses "cultivation" to describe the ways in which georgic poetry "obsessively tests its mediating power, and even when it attempts to narrate or otherwise contain history, something else—an affective residue—will out."[30] While the term "georgic" might threaten to restrict our discussion of poetic mediation and the "affective residue" of "an otherwise unknowable history" to gardening manuals, Goodman helpfully expands the definition of the georgic: for example, reading William Cowper's *The Task* as a georgic of the news.[31] As she argues, the same labor of cultivation that goes into tilling the soil or writing a poem about how to till the soil goes into Cowper's working of prosaic newspaper clippings into *The Task*'s iambic pentameter. This more capacious model of georgic cultivation, the shepherding of prose into verse, holds for Smart's project.

But unlike *The Task*—or perhaps just to a greater extent than that poem, *Jubilate Agno* dumps the responsibility for this cultivation into the reader's lap. Smart's georgic exists not as a finished poetic product, but as a process of moving between an archive and a poem that, in order to be read, requires a reader to treat the poem as an archive, one that requires precisely the kinds of cultivation and mechanical unpacking that Smart teaches us to execute. I am here beginning to engage in that labor. Taking my cue in part from Karina Williamson's "Surfing the Intertext," which traces various uses of *Jubilate Agno* through the twentieth century, I focus on the background of one line: "Let Dawn, house of Dawn rejoice with the Frigate Bird which is found upon the coasts of India" (*JA,* D.194).[32] My selection of this line was arbitrary. Part of the stuplime tragedy of *Jubilate Agno* is that most lines would yield a history as extensive and cruel as the one I trace here.

The Magnificent Frigatebird (*Fregata magnificens*) is one of five species of the genus *Fregata*.[33] It lives on the coasts of the Caribbean, the Gulf of Mexico, and the Gulf of California, where it builds rookeries in rocky outcroppings or on small islands. The frigatebird is an unusual seabird in that its wings are not naturally waterproof, so despite its coastal habitat and fish-based diet, it can't land on or dive into water. This condemns the frigatebird to a life of poaching: it skims fish off the surface or steals food from larger and more impermeable species who can reach below the surface.[34]

The *OED* cites Eleazar Albin's *A Natural History of the Birds* (1738) as the earliest use of "Frigate Bird" in English, and it was through Albin's *Natural History*, a copy of which Smart retained in his time at St. Luke's and Mr. Potter's asylums, that the frigatebird arrived in *Jubilate Agno*.[35] The entry for frigatebird in *A Natural History of the Birds* reads:

> THE Indians call it so, because of the Swiftness of its Flight; its Body is no bigger than a *Pullet*'s, but the Stomach is very fleshy; the Males are as black as Ravens, the Neck long, the Head small, with great black Eyes, and the Sight more piercing than the Eagle's; the Bill is thick and intirely black, about seven Inches long; the upper Beak at the end crooked like a Hook; the Toes are short, armed with strong black Talons, and divided as the Vulture's, the Wings of this Bird are very large and long, reaching beyond the Tail, and not without a provident Design of Nature, since the Wings are sometimes employed to carry him above a hundred Leagues from Land: It is with a great deal of Trouble that he can raise himself upon the Branches, because of the extraordinary length of his Wings; but when he has once taken his Flight, he keeps his Wings extended almost without Motion or Fatigue; if sometimes the Weight of the Rain or Violence of the Winds force him, he mounts above the Clouds beyond Sight, in the middle Region of the Air; and when he is at the highest he does not forget where he is, but remembers the place where the Dolphin gives chafe to the flying Fish, and then he throws himself down like Lightning; not so as to strike upon the Water, for then it would be difficult for him to rise again; but when he comes within twelve or fourteen Paces he makes a large Turn, and lowering himself, as it were insensibly, till he comes to skim the Waters where the Chace is given; in passing he takes up the little Fish, either with his Bill or Talons.[36]

Albin's entry for the frigatebird hews closely to Chico's argument that literary methods influenced scientific knowledge in the eighteenth century. His description of the species relies almost entirely on comparisons: "no bigger than a *Pullet*'s," "as black as Ravens," "more piercing than the Eagle's," "down like Lightning." Yet much of the work of literary comparison here is to make these birds palatable to an English audience of the 1730s. Or rather to a French one, since Albin's text is an almost exact translation of Jean Baptise Du Tertre's *Histoire générale des Antilles habitées par les François* (1667–71).[37] Du Tertre was himself a French colonizer and missionary who wrote a natural history of the West Indies during his residence there in the seventeenth century. The literary style that Albin and Du Tertre use to make the frigatebird visualizable becomes a means of consuming it.

The same ethos governs Smart's work. In "Fragment D," animals, vegetables, and minerals are paired with English family names. Most lines in the fragment have the form: "Let X, house of X, rejoice with Y." By pairing English houses with global creatures and commodities, *Jubilate Agno* aligns itself with the imperial appropriation of plundered goods. And make no mistake, the frigatebird was a literal commodity. Thomas Boreman, who cribbed huge blocks of Albin's *Natural History* for his 1769 *A Description of Three Hundred Animals*, adds to Albin's original entry on the frigatebird a graphic description of the birds being hunted for their oil:

> Father *du Tertre*, Apostolical Missionary in the *Antillees*, mov'd by the large Commendations give[n] of the Oil drawn from these Fowls, with the Assistance of two or three more Persons, took above one hundred of them in less than two hours time. They surpriz'd the old ones upon the Branches of the Trees, or in the Nests; and as they rise with a great deal of Difficulty to take Wing, it was an easy matter to beat them down with long Sticks. The Oil, or Fat of these Birds, is a sovereign Remedy for *Sciatica* Pains; and for all others proceeding from a cold Cause.[38]

Boreman goes on to explain that the birds were hunted so exhaustively that they became extinct on the Isle of Frigates, an island initially named after them.

For Goodman, an unknowable history is perceived as interface or interference, "the clash between rival mediations."[39] In this nesting doll of natural histories, we perceive these rival mediations both in the authorial choices made by Albin and Smart and in their misapprehensions as readers. For both Albin and Smart, this middle-man position was the site of critical, violent work. One alteration made by Albin is the insertion of "Providential design" to Du Tertre's account. In his account of the frigatebird's enormous wings, Du Tertre writes that their size is not "*sans sujet*," which Albin swaps for "without a provident Design of Nature." It's one of few alterations to Du Tertre's language, and one that glaringly slaps Christian theology over natural history. As with the comparisons between the frigatebird and the pullet, or the pairing of names and creatures that occurs in Smart's poem, the insertion of "provident Design of Nature" demonstrates how Albin's role as translator allows him to superimpose a Western—and here specifically Protestant—logic onto his subject matter.

But all these layers of information lead to literary errors. Albin writes of the word "frigate bird," "the Indians call it so" (seemingly referring to Indigenous people in the West Indies), but he gets here by translating Du Tertre, whose entry reads, "L'Oyseau que les habitans de Indes appellant Fregate." For Du Tertre "habitans" seems to mean "French inhabitants," since the title of his book promises a history of the Antilles *habitées par les François,* that is, "inhabited by the French." In turn, Albin's mistranslated text leads Smart to confuse "the coasts of India" with the West Indies, collapsing one nation into another with the indifference of someone for whom the world can, in Edward Said's terms, be divided into the West and everywhere else.[40]

Even the bird's name is bound up with this colonial imagery, being named after a warship used in maritime conquest. Frigates were battleships designed for maneuverability and speed, the first modern version of which was developed by the Dutch in the 1590s.[41] The English adopted the frigate in the early seventeenth century, after encountering the Dutch ships in the war with Spain, and frigates quickly became one of the principal weapons used in confrontations between rival colonial powers.[42] Smart, in his transcription, makes this pun explicit: "Let Dawn, house of Dawn rejoice with the Frigate Bird which is found upon the coasts of India" (*JA,* D.194) By referencing the "coasts of India," Smart highlights that the frigate is both a warship and a bird. In fact, the act of naming the bird becomes a weapon, like a frigate, in the British imperialist project. Smart was writing *Jubilate Agno* during a period that scholars recognize as a major escalation of British imperial aggression in both India and the West Indies.[43] If Smart acknowledges this history with a pun, he does so less with critique than enthusiasm; pairing the frigate (bird) with "Dawn" doubles down by invoking the sun, an image often employed in justifications for British imperialism.

Although other authors have acknowledged Smart's cheerful complicity with empire, their discussions tend to take his poetry at face value, rather than positioning these texts within the longer history of their archives. I chose the frigatebird almost at random, and it's entirely possible that every line in the poem could be peeled back to reveal layers of imperialist acquisition. Even when this history isn't immediately visible, *Jubilate Agno* works by evoking, by gesturing to, the possibility of these archival layers. In other words, the promise of archival depth is built into the poem's form. There's evidence that Smart saw this transcription—and all of what Cleary calls "technologies of writing"—as inseparable from his poetics.[44] Not once, not twice, but upwards of two and a half times, *Jubilate Agno*'s catalogue even veers into a sequence on the alphabet: we get "A–Z" twice in Fragment B and a bonus "H–Z" in Fragment C. Effectively, Smart approaches technologies of writing with the same cataloguing impulse that he applies to plants, animals, and minerals. The result is a text structured around a relationship to archives, one that presents information as a formal and affective problem in a way that anticipates twentieth- and twenty-first-century art.

In the next section, I discuss this systematic wordplay, what Smart called his "ciphers," as an algorithmic form, but before we get there, I want to start with a fairly well-contained example of how information shapes Smart's poetics and what the frigatebird can tell us about them. This excerpt comes at the beginning of Fragment D, and Smart uses these lines to establish the *modus operandi* for that section of the poem:

> Let Hook, house of Hook rejoice with Sarda a Cornelian—blessed
>   be the name of Jesus by hook.
> Let Crook house of Crook rejoice with Ophites black spotted
>   marble—Blessed be the name of the Lord Jesus by crook. The
> Lord enable me to shift. (*JA,* D.4–5)

I'll just say it: these lines are funny. "The Lord enable me to shift" comes like a wink to remind us that, while "Hook" and "Crook" might be two houses, they're also constitutive of the phrase "by hook or by crook." That idiom seems to have guided and justified the juxtaposition of house Hook with house Crook, and Smart is making sure we notice. But this clever pun is just the first of an intricate web of associations. Sarda (now Sard) names a kind of gemstone similar to carnelian, but it's also a kind of fish, making that "hook" extra useful.[45] Similarly, while Ophite is indeed a "black spotted marble," it's more familiarly associated with a Gnostic sect that worshipped the snake as the source of all wisdom. Such "heresy" might have been "crooked" to Smart, but the connection works doubly well given the Ophites' symbolic interest in the Nehushtan staff (the brass serpent affixed to a pole by Moses in Numbers 21:9, and so an analog to a shepherd's hook [or crook] as a staff with something added to it to help protect the flock).

The use of associative (or dissociative) connections between words to structure the poem speaks to the poem's desire to "shift," which doubles down on the relationship between transferring (shifting references) and making do (shifting for oneself). There's an element of desperation here. The ghost of the phrase "blessed be the name of the Lord Jesus by hook or by crook" suggests that these shifty puns, wordplay, and ciphering are simply part of getting to the next line. When Hartman zooms in on Smart's morphemes, translation, and puns across multiple languages, a form of "promiscuous" and productive excess, he presents Smart's excessive, literalist wordplay as a method of dealing with "depletion anxieties" and a suspicion "that visionary language has lost its effectiveness."[46] As Hartman reads it, depletion anxiety inspires both excess and greater thrift, a turn toward punning, double-entendre and other forms of "classical restraint."[47] This zero-sum approach to language frames poetic "shifting" as an extension of resource acquisition. Here, the shifting, ciphering movement through chains of association happens as a last resort, a last-ditch effort that will accomplish its goal however it can. Language becomes the hook or crook by which the poem gets finished; equally, it becomes the hook or crook through which Smart will proselytize.

While this analysis of "shifting" and associative logic will be expanded in the third section, where I detail Smart's relationship to "ciphering" and transcription, there's one further latent association here that I want to foreground. If we glance back at the frigatebird, "hook" and "crook" have been with us since Albin's description of "the upper Beak at the end crooked like a Hook." The link here is tenuous. Although we have no way to rule out the possibilities that Smart deliberately echoed Albin or that Albin had the phrase in the back of his mind when he transcribed Du Tertre's "Mais le dessus est recourbé par l'extremité, en forme de crochet," the parallel could be purely coincidental. [48] But this circumstantial echo evokes what I will discuss throughout the rest of this essay, which is the dependence of Smart's desperate ciphers ("by hook" or "by crook") on imperialist archives. The cipher, like a beak, is a site of acquisition and consumption; if we read it as such, poetic "shifting" allows us to examine biodiversity and infinity as formal tropes that were invoked in the service of empire. Beyond the acquisitive listing of flora and fauna, "shifting" positions Smart and his readers not as consumers of imperial commodities, but as transcribers within that supply chain, actively writing archival information into poetry.

Smart in the Avant-garde Tradition

In his description of Smart's promiscuous "pairing" of words, Hartman concludes that "the ark into which these pairs enter" might not be "that of generation," but merely "regeneration," an artificial heartbeat that might or might not be enough to elevate Smart's poetry beyond the "creaturely," literal, and "speckled language" out of which Smart creates a "poetics of relation." This "relation," which Hartman uses to name Smart's puns across fields and languages, gets stranded in a haze of associative logic that does not produce ("generate") new knowledge. While this distinction might seem to malign the work of "regeneration," Hartman's characterization implicitly links Smart's work to the mechanical and computational methods of the experimental tradition.[49] Borrowing the formalism of the avant-garde—and in particular its investment in algorithmic or mechanical form—can help us better situate the poem's unusual style within the affective and aesthetic protocols of empire. A working definition of the avant-garde far exceeds the scope of this project, but I want to highlight two features of twentieth-century avant-garde poetry that can help us situate *Jubilate Agno* in a transhistorical context. These are its formal deployment of algorithms, data, and digitization, and, relatedly, its tendency to center and default to whiteness. As Cathy Park Hong explains: "The avant-garde's 'delusion of whiteness' is the luxurious opinion that anyone can be 'post-identity' and can casually slip in and out of identities like a video game avatar, when there are those who are consistently harassed, surveilled, profiled, or deported for whom they are."[50] This critique, especially the unacknowledged whiteness of the notion of "post-identity," is particularly applicable to mechanical form, which explores what it considers calculated, impersonal, or "objective" models of writing.

Let's start with algorithmic form. Recent stabs at algorithmic or mechanical writing range from the constraints of Oulipo to more recent experiments with digital information in Stephanie Strickland's *Zone: Zero,* but no better example exists than John Cage.[51] Cage's work relied on the *I Ching* to randomly incorporate material from source texts into "empty words."[52] Depending upon whom you ask, this emptiness could be "plant-like" and apolitical, as Yoko Ono described it, or radical and anti-imperialist, at least to the extent that Cage aligned his work with non-interventionalist policy during the Cold War.[53] I'm inclined to favor the first reading, but I think Cage's work epitomizes algorithmic form as a relationship to history. In works like *Europeras*, a randomized redux of famous arias, and the reworking of Thoreau in *Empty Words*, algorithmic form digests (and regurgitates) historical material and alters it past recognition.[54] In other words, algorithmic form enables a particular relation to history that positions itself within its source material while performing affective detachment. One word for naming the exhaustive, mechanical overwhelm of projects like Cage's, and the disaffected or distanced sense of history that these texts invoke, might be stuplime.

This avant-garde relation to history matters for eighteenth-century scholars because these texts reinvent the history that they define themselves against; or at the very least, they lend themselves to reductive reinventions. Marjorie Perloff, one of Cage's most vocal champions, argues that Cage and similar twentieth-century poets abandoned mimetic lyricism for an advertised artifice.[55] It's an argument that belongs to a long tradition of marketing experimentalism as a break from eighteenth-century and Romantic lyricism, but as Anahid Nersessian reminds us in "Romantic Difficulty," "the whole contest over what counts as experimental in the present tends to produce heavily edited and astonishingly monotonous archives of a thing we call the past."[56]

I am suspicious of the tendency to pit lyric affect against avant-garde mechanism for several reasons. First, the overlap between lyricism and mechanism sat much farther forward in the work of eighteenth-century poets than this narrative suggests.[57] Second, the use of mechanism as a break from subjective, affective, or creative writing has been widely critiqued for the implied whiteness of post-lyric work, an issue unpacked by Evie Shockley in *Renegade Poetics* and Timothy Yu in *Race and the Avant-garde*.[58] As Shockley and Yu remind us, the white avant-garde has built an industry out of a performed non-subjectivity that runs to its logical conclusions in Kenneth Goldsmith's "uncreative writing."[59] Shockley's thesis challenges the assumption that avant-garde aesthetics are categorically distinct from the aesthetic developments informed by race and identity, including the Black Arts Movement. As Shockley reminds us, an explicit poetic engagement with race and the "racist baggage of language" lends itself to experimentalism.[60] Meanwhile, the notion of an "uncreative writing" divorced from subject positionality is used to reinscribe what Cathy Park Hong, talking about Goldsmith in "Delusions of the Avant-Garde," calls "the expired snake oil that poetry should be 'against expression' and 'post-identity.'"[61]

I've broached the whiteness of the avant-garde here because the ciphers I discuss in the next section operate via a similarly mechanical process of verbal and historical regurgitation. An experimental poetics built around the mechanical and the archival threatens to become an extension of what the archive is to Saidiya Hartman: "the archive is, in this case, a death sentence, a tomb, a display of the violated body, an inventory of property, a medical treatise on gonorrhea, a few lines about a whore's life, an asterisk in the grand narrative of history."[62] While Smart's project was enthusiastically, not reluctantly, complicit in the imperial consolidation of the information that he recycles, *Jubilate Agno* demonstrates that there is no neutral transcription, that the act of "accumulating" information, however scientific, "tedious," or mechanical that information may be, extends the violence of colonial acquisition. Smart's ciphers toe the line between mechanical repetition and aggressive mediation. As I describe in the next section, *Jubilate Agno* insists, loudly, on the labor of transcription that goes into its production and, as a result, draws its readers into the middle ground between recitation and adaptation, between archive and poem.

The Cipher, or, Making Information Useless

In this section, I examine *Jubilate Agno's* "ciphers," Smart's term for the repetitive and patterned structure of his text. This is an elaborate way of saying *Jubilate Agno* is an absolutely exhausting text to read. Smart churns out line after line of formally identical and linguistically intricate poetry that lacks any coherent narrative or organizing principle. Certainly, some lines, such as those unpacked by Geoffrey Hartman in "Christopher Smart's Magnificat," reward a reader's attention to the myths, allusions, histories, etymology, natural history, puns, dirty jokes, and all the other references that Smart interlaced less purposively than compulsively. Other lines are more reticent. They seem to mark time or fill the page, and the verses keep piling up. Smart calls it "*a tedious accumulation of nothing*":

> Let Tel-harsa rejoice with Aparine Clivers.
> For Cipher is a note of augmentation very good.
>
> Let Rehoboam rejoice with Polium Montanum. God give grace
> to the Young King.
> *For innumerable ciphers will amount to something.*
>
> Let Hanan rejoice with Poley of Crete.
> *For the mind of man cannot bear a tedious accumulation of*
> *nothing without effort.*
>
> Let Sheshbazzar rejoice with Polygonatum Solomon's seal.
> *For infinite upon infinite they make a chain.* (*JA,* C.34–37)

In these lines, which come hard on the heels of a section about the numbers, Smart characterizes his list-based process as a cipher, a word that plugs his project into eighteenth-century notions of algorithmic logic, counting, and arithmetic. This mechanical ciphering allows Smart to engage with his botanical archive. An algorithmic literalism dominates this passage, especially in the wordplay between "Polium Montanum" and "amount" and in the flow from "Polium" to "Poley" to "Polygonatum." Likewise, two of the plants Smart chooses in this passage seem to perform the behavior that Smart attributes to ciphers. Clivers (Galium aparine) takes its name from the same Greek root as "cleave," after the sticky burrs with which it clings to climbing surfaces. Meanwhile, the intricate buds on Solomon's Seal (Polygonatum odoratum) resemble the chain described in C.37. If the form of the poem is a cipher, Smart initially judges this a "*very good*" one that accumulates over time.

However, other lines in the passage complicate the utility of all this augmentation. First comes the wishy-washy shrug of "*innumerable ciphers will amount to something*"—ok, great, but what?—after which Smart elaborates, "*For the mind of man cannot bear a tedious accumulation of nothing without effort.*" The conjunction "for," which positions each subsequent new statement in a causal or explanatory relationship to its precursor, invites us to read all three lines as one long argument: all ciphers must produce augmentation because even innumerable ciphers have to add up to something because people can't be bored for too long. In other words, the high rate of return promised by that *"note of augmentation very good"* turns out to be a readerly coping mechanism for rationalizing a stuplimly empty infinity. Moreover, by effectively rewriting the previous verses—*"innumerable"* anticipates *"tedious*[ness]*,"* and *"accumulation"* follows up on *"augmentation"* and *"amount"*—this line presents *"a tedious accumulation of nothing"* as the flip side of *"a note of augmentation very good,"* thereby collapsing any easy distinction between productive and unproductive repetition, between a text that builds upon itself and one that spins its wheels.

If we turn back to the line *"for Cipher is a note of augmentation very good,"* we can start to locate fissures in its cheerful promise about the usefulness of the cipher. For starters, what is *"a note of augmentation?"* Is the note being augmented or doing the augmenting? We could gloss "note" as a letter or banknote, a small textual maker of a fact. Then there's "musical note," a bit of a red herring but not a huge stretch given Smart's preoccupation with the musicality of text. Or we could go with "linguistic particle," also not far out of Smart's wheelhouse.[63] Finally, the proximity of "note" to "not," especially so close to the phrase *"tedious accumulation of nothing,"* reminds us of the fine line between a positive slightness and nonexistence. Here, it might be useful to point out that "cipher" used to be synonymous with "zero" and only later gained its equivalencies with "arithmetic" and "encryption." Historically, cipher also meant, "a person who fills a place, but is of no importance or worth, a nonentity, a 'mere nothing.'"[64] My goal here is to emphasize how Smart's deviously unintuitive construction makes it impossible to reconstruct the relationship of augmentation to cipher. These conflicted descriptions of augmentation compel Smart's reader to take note of a process that's impossible to catch in action. The cipher becomes a notation for both augmentation and emptiness, and this tension is illustrative of the cipher's relationship to meaning and information.

Before we get too far away from the "zero" built into "cipher," I want to briefly invoke Brian Rotman's *Signifying Nothing*, in which Rotman traces the introduction of zero—as both a number and a concept—into Western mathematics.[65] Zero shifted mathematics away from the premise that numbers were signs for *things* toward a system of relationships and rules *between* signs. As Rotman puts it, "zero is a sign about names, a meta-numeral; and as a number declaring itself to be the origin of counting, the trace of the one-who-counts and produces the number sequence, zero is a meta-number, a sign indicating the whole potentially infinite progression of integers."[66] I am interested in Rotman's articulation of infinity as a conceptual counterpart to zero, because Smart's "cipher" yokes the emptiness of zero, tedious "*note*[s]" of "*nothing*," to the mechanical repetition that "*infinite upon infinite ... make*[s] *a chain.*" In other words, *Jubilate Agno*'s poetics structures themselves around the interplay between—or codependence of—emptiness and excess.

In fact, the structure of *Jubilate Agno* deliberately problematizes the relationship between information and receptivity. These lines exist in an equilibrium between emptiness and information overload: the "For" sequence takes up abstractions of mind and infinity, while the "Let" sequence maps four esoteric biblical figures onto four equally niche plants. Harriet Guest has already documented the call-and-response relationship between the "Let" and "For" sequences of Smart's poem.[67] Here, the see-saw effect exaggerates the poem's investment in toggling between data and theories of data, between the particularities of "Tel-Harsa," Aparaine Clivers, Poley of Crete, Rehoboam, et al., and a generalized infinity. Instead, Smart pushes the text into a kind of embodied attention, where nuggets of "information" are less important than the uncompromising fact of the text's continuation. We're faced here with an extension of what Alan Liu—perhaps the first scholar to find digital and data-bent themes in eighteenth-century poetry—calls the "Romanticism of detail," or the construction of a literary paradigm for recognizing details as significant in the abstract, as the *idea of detail.*[68]

Rotman is on to something similar when he links the rise of zero to the development of "a semiotic closure of itself, namely the algebraic variable."[69] He adds that the concept of a variable, an absence that can be filled by infinite possibilities, precipitates the use of the vanishing point in art and the replacement of specie with paper money. Each of these developments shifted specific and particular modes of viewing or possessing to modes that "de-deictified" and "depersonalised," that "freed" objects "from the attachment to a spatially particularised viewer or owner."[70] The variable is a useful term for approaching the fate of individual entries in *Jubilate Agno*, which are ciphered from individually specific bits of information—here, the names of plants sourced from Pliny—into placeholders for a pattern. The individual relevance of Polygonatum, for example, takes second fiddle to the idea of a botanical archive constructed in the resonance between Polium, Poley, and Polygonatum. In fact, with everything going on between the archival "Let" sequence and the theoretical "For" sequence, it becomes difficult to pay real attention to any of Smart's references, even if, as with the frigatebird, each slight reference may open onto exhaustive histories of its own. As Smart indicates, this transformation of fact into variable is not an unfortunate byproduct of his ciphering, but rather its direct and intended consequence: for Smart, ciphers produce "meaning" through "meaningless" repetition—indeed, they make repetition meaningless.

While there is a certain pleasure in abstractions like "nothing" and "infinity," the stuplime can once again help us link these semiotic broad strokes to the grittiness of Smart's work and to the problem of tedium that Smart himself raises. As Ngai explains, the Burkean and Kantian sublime from which the stuplime takes half of its name "was typically invoked in response to things overwhelmingly vast or massive and large (mountains, seas, the infinite, and so forth)," but, for Ngai, such vastness doesn't quite capture the attendant boredom of *The Making of Americans* or, in our case, *Jubilate Agno*.[71] Ngai's answer is the stuplime, which "call[s] attention to the affinity between exhaustion and the astonishment particular to the sublime, invoking the latter while detaching it from its previous romantic affiliations."[72]

As I have already indicated at a few points, discussions of *Jubilate Agno* tend toward generalized discussions of its formal choices and the romanticized sublime of its length and scope. In Ngai's reading, it is weak affect—sometimes, boredom; other times, exhaustion—that can point us to the exit from these generalizations. What we're left with, the "affective residue" of this text, is the sliding scale of slightness between all or nothing. Tedious accumulation raises the problem of slightness ("notes" vs. "nots") and whether it can be summed together, collected, or accumulated. To call Smart's ciphers stuplime is to acknowledge their investment in infinity and the cosmic without losing sight of the details, histories, and barbs in its archival layers and to admit to ourselves that our vocabulary for those details, histories, and layers is critically limited by that investment.

Ultimately, Smart's ciphering transforms natural history into "*a tedious accumulation of nothing*" that "*amount*[s] *to something*" only after sufficiently taxing the reader's focus. This meaning-in-boredom (tedium) is a response to the affective and attentive failures triggered by too much information. Because its relentless ciphering affords very little time to comprehend the information that is being transcribed, we are left with the tension between the poem's parts and the whole, its hyperspecific references and the generalized "infinities" or "nothings" into which Smart imagines them summed. Goodman says it best: the georgic mode advertises a "teeming historical presentness that is 'not yet' fully formed as knowledge."[73] In other words, georgic cultivation doesn't recover history, but openly admits its own failure to perceive it. In *Jubilate Agno,* the cipher compresses books of natural history into their ongoing transcription (cultivation à la Cowper), stranding the reader in the moment when that transcription happens.

Violent Infinities and the Insensible

As Smart's language suggests, the problem of ciphering is also the problem of representing infinity in form. Another way to frame the formal problem of infinity—how we can thread a reader's focus through the eye of vastness-as-particularity—would be to allow the infinite to emphasize, rather than erase, more ordinary feelings of labor and exhaustion. The problem is best identified by Chris Nealon in "Infinity for Marxists," where he offers a searing critique of literary gestures with respect to scale as reductive and entrenched in Christian liturgical mystery.[74] Nealon puts it, "items in [an] array are not dignified by "autonomy" from us, or from each other. They are routed *through* each other; they are mediations *of* each other."[75] Effectively, gestures to infinity that rely on lists or arrays work by reducing details to, as Liu might call it, romanticized abstraction. Nealon calls for a formal practice that refuses to theorize what it cannot feel, that never loses sight of the critical challenges posed by literalism, precision, and the obvious.

The aesthetic stakes of this infinity align with what Rachel Feder describes in "The Poetic Limit" as the Romantic project of "excavating the crisis of infinity as an intellectual-historical phenomenon … in which enlightenment models of infinity are remade with poetic ends."[76] Feder's work reminds us that questions of "infinity" and its aesthetic function weighed heavily on eighteenth-century authors. Feder's go-to is David Hume, but we could equally turn to Edmund Burke, who, in the later sections of *A Philosophical Inquiry into the Origin of Our Ideas of the Sublime and Beautiful* offers step-by-step instructions for approximating the sublime. One such strategy is mechanical repetition: "Succession and *uniformity* of parts are what constitute the artificial infinite."[77] These are necessary because "uninterrupted progression … alone can stamp on bounded objects the character of infinity."[78] Burke's cheat sheet points to the role of artificial, good enough infinities, something Smart also seems to understand: his description of the infinite chain of ciphers comes hard on the heels of his reference to "Polygonatum Solomon's seal," a plant whose flowers *do* approximate chains. The plant isn't infinity; it's a gesture towards a garden-variety pattern that repeats in human-sized proportions. Similarly, the cipher becomes a gesture toward infinity that operates by artificial repetition. This poetic making-do, this infinity "by hook or by crook," certainly acknowledges its material limits, but this infinity and those limits also had purchase for an imperialist discourse. In what follows, I will discuss the limits of a poetic approach to information that cultivates insensibility by examining the historical function of infinity as a colonial trope.

In *Visions of the Daughters of Albion,* the poem that this essay took for an epigraph, William Blake expresses an uncharacteristically pessimistic view of infinity. Bromion—often read as a figure for empire and empiricism in the eighteenth century—converts all experience to a zero-sum struggle over material resources:

> Knowest thou that trees and fruits flourish upon the earth
> To gratify senses unknown—trees, beasts, and birds unknown;
> Unknown, not unperceivd, spread in the infinite microscope.[79]

Here, the "infinite microscope" names a sensory experience in which perception outruns comprehension. Under the lens of infinity, creatures and senses that would otherwise be "unknown" are at least "not unperceivd." Strangely, even perception gets lost in this empirical reality when Bromion merges "senses unknown" into the very things ("trees, beasts, and birds") that these senses ought to perceive. As a result, the "infinite microscope" reveals the stuplime's tension between vastness and slightness, the raw contradiction of a fantasy of indefinitely zooming in on some nonexistent, insensible particularity in which this imperceptible contradiction is itself the tool ("microscope") of perceiving. In Blake's formulation, Bromion's fantasy of colonial plunder—"trees, beasts, and birds"—ends with its objects "spread in the infinite microscope," an empiricist endgame that links the infinite microscope to material conquest. More importantly, this passage makes it abundantly clear that the insensible—i.e., the idea that there exist senses that haven't yet been gratified—is a tool of empire. The insensible and the infinite function not as sites of radical potentiality, but as means of reducing real circumstances to remote concepts. In fact, infinity fuels the fantasy of imperialist expansion by converting the contradictions of scarcity and excess into identical abstractions.

Fredric Jameson has long discussed the role of infinity in modernist tropes of empire. However, it's worth noting that as he explored "the contradiction between the contingency of physical objects and the demand for an impossible meaning, here marked by dead philosophical abstraction," the latter became equated with Immanuel Kant and eighteenth-century notions of the sublime.[80] In this characterization of imperialism, the eighteenth century functions *as a concept,* a "dead abstraction" that exists on the periphery of modernism's aesthetic arsenal. Jameson's stand-in for "dead philosophical abstraction" is Kant, but Burke provides equal insights into infinity as an imperial trope. In *A Philosophical Inquiry,* immediately on the heels of the passage quoted earlier, Burke offers the rotund as an example of "artificial infinity" and argues:

> For in a rotund, whether it be a building or a plantation, you can
> no where fix a boundary; turn which way you will, the same
> object still seems to continue, and the imagination has no rest.
> But the parts must be uniform as well as circularly disposed, to
> give this figure its full force; because any difference, whether
> it be in the disposition, or in the figure, or even in the colour of
> the parts, is highly prejudicial to the idea of infinity, which every
> change must check and interrupt, at every alteration commencing
> a new series.[81]

Burke, like E. M. Forster in Jameson's analysis, uses infinity to set finite
material space in uncomfortable proximity to a space without boundaries
and the fantasy of continual expansion. Burke's example here enumerates
some literal architectural qualities that don't quite track for poetry, including
uniformity and circularity, but the role of "artificial infinity" in evoking
unbounded expansion applies to Smart's poem in the ways described earlier.
Moreover, Burke's choice of the plantation as a figure for the rotund explicitly
connects the language of unbounded expansion to empire.

This thread plays out more fully in Burke's *Observations on a Late
Publication, Intituled 'The Present State of the Nation,'* a response to a
pamphlet by William Knox. Burke here uses infinity almost interchangeably
with the language of material austerity that governs imperialist discourse.
He writes that Knox:

> talks of his union, just as he does of his taxes and his savings, with
> as much *sang froid* and ease as if his wish and the enjoyment were
> exactly the same thing. He appears not to have troubled his head
> with the *infinite difficulty* of settling that representation on a fair
> balance of wealth and numbers throughout the several provinces
> of America and the West Indies, *under such an infinite variety of
> circumstances*. It costs him nothing to fight with nature, and to
> conquer the order of Providence, which manifestly opposes itself
> to the possibility of such a Parliamentary union.[82]

Burke uses "infinite" twice in a single sentence—and several more times
throughout the "Observations." That redundancy seems deliberate, an
attempt to emphasize the *"infinite variety of circumstances"* produced by
the sheer number of colonial holdings to which Knox is referring.[83] Here,
the use of infinity allows Burke to rework Knox's investment in political
representation (and let's be clear, this would be representation of the white
settlers, so neither author is precisely on the side of the angels) as a circular
problem, such that "representation" distributed fairly along the lines of
"wealth and numbers" could not be attained without first ascertaining what

those numbers were, which runs counter to the designs of Providence. Meanwhile, Burke is quick to emphasize the comparative lack of labor involved in desiring a solution to this issue: it "costs [Knox] nothing," even as the infinite variety of the situation is equated with "infinite difficulty." Any attempt at either is, for Burke, both unnatural and heretical. These hyperbolic turns in Burke's language are at odds with the function of an "infinite variety of circumstances" later in the text, where Burke uses the idea of heterogeneity to argue that British imperialism is unprecedented and cannot be held accountable to other moral or ethical standards. Effectively, infinity is a trope for creating a dangerous lack of precedent that necessitates, for Burke, a totalizing system of control. This abstract threat is key to justifying the austerity measures and colonial violence that Burke calls for in the *Observations*. Smart's poem exists between excess and absence, advertising the relative ease with which one can blur into the other and so turn real information into a generalized, insensible abstraction. For Dworkin, that tension becomes a "textual engine" generating "potential energy," but that same potentiality underlies the abstract and insensible infinities that Burke used to justify colonial governance.[84]

At the same time, Smart's ciphers strain notions of productivity and thwart the carceral practices of close reading against which Nan Z. Da has cautioned us.[85] Within the repetitive patterns of *Jubilate Agno*, the reality of Smart's life in the asylum becomes almost unrecognizable. Instead, the disciplinary structures that marked Smart's day-to-day existence flash up only briefly against a repetitive and highly abstract backdrop, as, for example, in a passing reference to his arrest: "For the officers of the peace are at variance with me, and the watchman smites me with his staff" (*JA*, B.91). The line refers to Smart's arrest in 1757, ostensibly for "religious mania," although Chris Mounsey adds financial debt, homophobia, a possible dispute with his father-in-law, and political tensions as ulterior causes behind Smart's imprisonment.[86] In moments like this, the poem lurches from a smorgasbord of scientific factuality to a crumb of biographical specificity, a turn that lasts hardly more than a second. By the next line, we're dragged back into the general flow: "Let Ziba rejoice with Glottis whose tongue is wreathed in his throat" (*JA*, B.92).

The formal relevance of this passage hinges on Smart's use of "variance" (as in infinite variety) to describe his assault by the watchman. While variance describes a sense of being at odds with someone, it also captures the ciphering differences between each of the individual verses. The slightness of the references in *Jubilate Agno* makes larger events, about which we might have more distinct and obvious feelings, into mere gestures. Smart's ciphers confront us with the challenge of how to react when familiar proportions break down, and while "variance" seems to contrast this loss of proportional feelings with systematized control, the net effect strands the reader between indifference and attentiveness and reminds us that, for a text like this, both can be complicit.[87] In fact, the cipher confronts us with the problem of not feeling these distinctions quite enough, or not in the right way. If we consider the text as a whole, we're left with what Anne-Lise François calls "the feel of not to feel it."[88] This poetic disidentification, which François brilliantly borrows from Keats's lyricism, is also part and parcel of a stuplime poetics: as Stephanie Strickland puts it, "mathematical ideas ... the form that no one has ever felt."[89]

Jubilate Agno has limits, as do the conversations that it enables. Rather than offer an easy out, the poem is an archival project that develops a relationship to information as a formal feeling—or really, a lack thereof, "*a tedious accumulation of nothing.*" Within Smart's cipher logic, excess ("accumulation") starts to work like scarcity ("nothing"). The cipher draws our attention to the process of navigating fragmented archives, something that accounts for both Smart's poetic process and the experience of reading the poem. In other words, the insensibility built into *Jubilate Agno*'s form can also help us account for the difficulty of reconciling the scope of the violent history that the text registers to its reductive or boring repetition—to the problem of proportioning out our feelings within a grammar of scarcity or propriety. By highlighting the transcription of information, the poem reminds us that scholarship on the eighteenth century runs the risk of tipping into a gleeful accumulation of tragedy repackaged as "discovery." Unfortunately, and Smart gets here too, the language of generalization with which one might try to talk around violence is equally destructive; Blake would have called it "cold floods of abstraction."[90] Stuck between the violence of precision and the violence of abstraction, the violence of the particular and the violence of the general, *Jubilate Agno* details the absolute necessity of finding another way to survive the archives we have, because the georgic or mechanical labor of transcription is only making do, "by hook or by crook," in the meantime.

Notes

1. William Blake, *Visions of the Daughters of Albion,* The William Blake Archive, *http://www.blakearchive.org/copy/vda.b?descId=vda.b.illbk.07.*

2. Christopher Smart, *Jubilate Agno,* in *Selected Poems*, ed. Karina Williamson and Marcus Walsh (New York: Penguin, 1990), D.194. Hereafter cited parenthetically by fragment (A, B, C, or D) and line number, with the abbreviation *JA*.

3. Smart, *Rejoice in the Lamb: A Song from Bedlam,* ed. W. F. Stead (London: Jonathan Cape, 1939).

4. James Boswell, *Life of Johnson,* ed. G. B. Hill and L. F. Powell (Oxford: Oxford University Press, 2014), 192–93.

5. See Scott M. Cleary, "Castles in the Air: Christopher Smart and the Concept of System," *Eighteenth-Century Studies* 43, no. 2 (2010): 193–206, and Benjamin Kahan, "Antediluvian Sex: Countée Cullen, Christopher Smart, and the Queerness of Uplift," *African American Review* 48, no. 1 (2015): 191–202.

6. Chen, "For I Will Consider My Boyfriend Jeffrey," in *When I Grow Up I Want to Be a List of Further Possibilities* (Rochester: BOA Editions, 2017), 72; Wellman, *Awe* (New York: Ugly Duckling Presse, 2019); O'Brien, "Christopher Smart," in *People on Sunday* (Seattle: Wave Books, 2013), 76–78; *Imagining Language: An Anthology*, ed. Jed Rasula and Steve McCaffery (Boston: MIT Press, 1998).

7. Wolgamot, "In Sara Mencken, Christ, and Beethoven There Were Men and Women," in *J.B.W.,* ed. Robert Ashley and Keith Waldrop (New York: Lovely Music, 2011); Stein, *The Making of Americans: Being a History of a Family's Progress* (Champaign: Dalkey Archive Press, 1995); Zukofsky, *"A"* (Baltimore: Johns Hopkins University Press, 1993).

8. Wolgamot, "In Sara Mencken," 45.

9. Hartman, "Venus in Two Acts," *Small Axe* 26 (2008): 1–14.

10. Chris Mounsey, *Christopher Smart: Clown of God* (Lewisburg: Bucknell University Press, 2001), 273–84.

11. Ngai, "Stuplimity: Shock and Boredom in Twentieth-Century Aesthetics," *Postmodern Culture* 10, no. 2 (2000).

12. Ngai, *Our Aesthetic Categories: Zany, Cute, Interesting* (Cambridge: Harvard University Press, 2012): 1, 21; Ngai, "Stuplimity."

13. Ngai, *Theory of the Gimmick: Aesthetic Judgment and Capitalist Form* (Cambridge: the Belknap Press of Harvard University Press, 2020).

14. See Wendy Anne Lee, *Failures of Feeling: Insensibility and the Novel* (Stanford: Stanford University Press, 2018).

15. Goodman, *Georgic Modernity and British Romanticism: Poetry and the Mediation of History* (Cambridge: Cambridge University Press, 2004).

16. See Hartman, "Christopher Smart's Magnificat: Towards a Theory of Representation," *ELH* 41, no. 3 (1974): 429–54; Tobias Menely, *The Animal Claim: Sensibility and the Creaturely Voice* (Chicago: University of Chicago Press), 2015.

17. Hartman, "Christopher Smart's Magnificat," 451.

18. Cleary, "Castles in the Air," 198.

19. Among many other things, *Jubilate Agno* is a diary in which Smart recorded world news that reached him in confinement. Lines like "Let Wing, house of Wing rejoice with Phlomos a sort of Rush, I give the glory to God, thro' Christ, for taking the Havannah. Septr 30th 1762" (*JA,* D.112) register Smart's enthusiastic response to British victories abroad, in this case, the occupation of Havana by British troops

during the Seven Years' War. Smart's later poems include panegyrics that celebrate military officers who were critical players in British imperial aggression. See the "Ode to Admiral Sir George Peacock" and the "Ode to General Draper," in *Selected Poems*, 256–62.

20. Edward Said's *Culture and Imperialism* (London: Chatto and Windus, 1993) has been indispensable in making the connections between literary production and British imperialism, but see too Yota Batsaki, Sarah Burke Cahalan, and Anatole Tchikine, *The Botany of Empire in the Long Eighteenth Century* (Washington: Dumbarton Oaks Research Library and Collection, 2016); Pollard, "Pliny's *Natural History* and the Flavian *Templum Pacis*: Botanical Imperialism in First-Century C. E. Rome," *Journal of World History* 20, no. 3 (2009): 309–38.

21. Said, *Orientalism* (New York: Vintage Books, 1994), 119, 123.

22. Hawes, *Mania and Literary Style: The Rhetoric of Enthusiasm from the Ranters to Christopher Smart* (Cambridge: Cambridge University Press, 1996), 215.

23. Orr, "Christopher Smart as a Christian Translator: The Verse Horace of 1767," *Studies in Philology* 108, no. 3 (2011): 439–67.

24. "Hawes, *Mania and Literary Style,* 223–24; Orr, "Smart as a Christian Translator," 228.

25. Chico, *The Experimental Imagination: Literary Knowledge and Science in the British Enlightenment* (Stanford: Stanford University Press, 2018), 17, 7.

26. Goodman, *Georgic Modernity,* 11, 29.

27. Cleary, "Castles in the Air," 200.

28. Dworkin, "The Potential Energy of Texts [$\Delta U = -P\Delta V$]," *Iowa Review* 44, no. 3 (2014–15): 133–48.

29. Dworkin, "Potential Energy," 139.

30. Goodman, *Georgic Modernity,* 8–9.

31. Goodman, *Georgic Modernity,* 9.

32. Williamson, "Surfing the Intertext: Smart among the Moderns," in *Christopher Smart and the Enlightenment*, ed. Clement Hawes (New York: St. Martin's Press, 1999), 235–71.

33. "Fregata magnificens," in *Integrated Taxonomic Information System, https://www.itis.gov/*.

34. Magnificent Frigatebird," in *Audubon Guide to North American Birds*, *https://www.audubon.org/field-guide/bird/magnificent-frigatebird*.

35. s.v. "frigate-bird," *OED*; Menely, *The Animal Claim,* 138.

36. Eleazer Albin and W. Derham, *A Natural History of Birds,* 3 vols. (London, 1731–38), 3:75.

37. For the entry "De la fregate," see Du Tertre, *Histoire générale des Antilles habitées par les François, https://gallica.bnf.fr/ark:/12148/bpt6k114021k/f297. image*.

38. Boreman, *A Description of a Great Variety of Animals and Vegetables: viz. Beasts, Birds, Fishes, Insects, Plants, Fruits, and Flowers. Extracted from the Most Considerable writers of Natural History* (London, 1736), 10.

39. Goodman, *Georgic Modernity,* 71.

40. Said writes that "it should be evident that no one overarching theoretical principle governs the whole imperialist ensemble, and it should be just as evident that the principle of domination and resistance based on the division between the West and the rest of the world—to adapt freely from the African critic Chinweizu—runs like a fissure throughout." *Culture and Imperialism* (New York: Vintage Books, 1994): 51.

41. Robert Gardiner, *The Sailing Frigate: A History in Ship Models* (Barnsley: Seaforth Publishing, 2012): 10.

42. Gardiner, *Sailing Frigate,* 13.

43. At the time, Britain was enmired in the Seven Years' War, fighting Spain and France for dominance in the Atlantic. Smart references the "taking of the Havana" in 1762 as part of this conflict. After the Battle of Plassey in 1757 (also the year of Smart's first confinement for "lunacy"), the East India Company imposed itself in Bengal, laying the foundation for the formal occupation of India by the British state in the nineteenth century. See Philip J. Stern, "Early Eighteenth-Century British India: Antimeridian or antemeridiem?" *Journal of Colonialism and Colonial History,* 21, no. 2 (2020).

44. Cleary, "Castles in the Air," 198.

45. Susan M. Luna and Kathleen Kesner-Reyes, "Sarda sarda." *https://www.fishbase.se/summary/115*

46. Hartman, "Smart's Magnificat," 433. Hawes also discusses translation in Smart, albeit with a more generous eye; see *Mania and Literary Style,* 170.

47. Hartman, "Smart's Magnificat," 433–34.

48. Here, I'll add that *recourbé* could more readily be translated as "curved."

49. Hartman, "Smart's Magnificat," 451.

50. Hong, "Delusions of Whiteness in the Avant-Garde," *Lana Turner Journal* 7 (3 November 2014), *https://arcade.stanford.edu/content/delusions-whiteness-avant-garde.*

51. Stephanie Strickland, *Zone: Zero* (Boise: Ahsahta Press, 2008).

52. John Cage, *Empty Words: Writings '73–'78* (Middletown: Wesleyan University Press, 1979).

53. Ono, "The Word of a Fabricator," trans. Yoko Ono, in *Imagine Yoko* (Lund: Bakhall, 2015), 115; Vaughn Anderson, "'Revision of the Golden Rule': John Cage, Latin America, and the Poetics of Non-Interventionism," *Journal of Modern Literature,* 41, no. 1 (2017): 58–80. I am also indebted to Brigid Cohen's discussion of Ono and Cage in "Ono in Opera: A Politics of Art and Action, 1960–1962," *ASAP/Journal* 3, No. 1 (2018): 41–62.

54. Cage, *Empty Words,* 11.

55. Perloff, *Radical Artifice: Poetry in the Age of Media* (Chicago: University of Chicago Press, 1991).

56. Nersessian, "Romantic Difficulty," *New Literary History* 49, no. 4 (2018): 459.

57. See Steven Goldsmith, *Blake's Agitation: Criticism and the Emotions* (Baltimore: Johns Hopkins University Press, 2013), especially the chapter "Strange Pulse"; and Lily Gurton-Wachter, "Blake's 'Little Black Thing:' Happiness and Injury in the Age of Slavery," *ELH* 87, No. 2 (2020): 519–52.

58. Shockley, *Renegade Poetics: Black Aesthetics and Formal Innovation in African American Poetry* (Iowa City: University of Iowa Press, 2011); Yu, *Race and the Avant-garde: Experimental and Asian American Poetry Since 1965* (Stanford: Stanford University Press, 2009).

59. Goldsmith, *Uncreative Writing: Managing Language in the Digital Age* (New York: Columbia University Press, 2011).

60. Shockley takes up avant-garde poetry most directly in the chapters of *Renegade Poetics* on Harryette Mullen's *Recyclopedia* and *Sleeping with the Dictionary* and M. NourbeSe Philip's *Zong!*

61. Hong, "Delusions of Whiteness in the Avant-Garde."

62. Hartman, "Venus in Two Acts," 2.

63. s.v. "note, n.2," *OED Online*, Oxford University Press.

64. s.v. "cipher, n," *OED Online*, Oxford University Press.

65. Rotman, *Signifying Nothing: The Semiotics of Zero* (London: Macmillan Press, 1987).

66. Rotman, *Signifying Nothing,* 14.

67. Guest, *A Form of Sound and Words: The Religious Poetry of Christopher Smart* (Oxford: Clarendon Press, 1989), 142–45.

68. Liu, *Local Transcendence: Essays on Postmodern Historicism and the Database* (Chicago: University of Chicago Press, 2008), 109–39.

69. Rotman, *Signifying Nothing,* 4.

70. Rotman, *Signifying Nothing,* 47.

71. Ngai, "Stuplimity."

72. Ngai, "Stuplimity."

73. Goodman, *Georgic Modernity,* 105.

74. Nealon, "Infinity for Marxists," *Mediations* 28, no. 2 (2015): 47–63.

75. Nealon, "Infinity for Marxists," 57.

76. Feder, "The Poetic Limit: Mathematics, Aesthetics, and the Crisis of Infinity," *ELH* 81, no. 1 (2014): 189.

77. Burke, *A Philosophical Inquiry into the Origin of our Ideas of the Sublime and Beautiful,* ed. Adam Phillips (Oxford: Oxford University Press, 1990), 68.

78. Burke, *Philosophical Inquiry,* 68.

79. See David V. Erdman, "Blake's Vision of Slavery," *Journal of the Warburg and Courtauld Institutes* 15, no. 3/4 (1952): 242–52; and Saree Makdisi, *William Blake and the Impossible History of the 1790s,* especially chapter 4; Blake, *Visions of the Daughters of Albion,* The William Blake Archive, *http://www.blakearchive.org/copy/vda.b?descId=vda.b.illbk.07.*

80. Jameson, "Modernism and Imperialism," in *The Modernist Papers* (London: Verso, 2007), 160.

81. Burke, *A Philosophical Inquiry,* 68.

82. Burke, *Observations on a Late Publication Intituled "The Present State of the Nation,"* in *The Works of the Right Honourable Edmund Burke,* 12 vols. (London, 1887), 1:373.

83. Burke used "infinite variety" earlier in the *Observations* to describe "that infinite variety of admirable manufactures that grow and extend every year among the spirited, inventive, and enterprising traders of Manchester" (*Observations*, 1:313).

84. Dworkin, "Potential Energy," 144.

85. Da, "Decoy Vices" (lecture, UCLA Department of English, Los Angeles, California, 18 February 2020).

86. Mounsey, *Clown of God,* 200.

87. Given the strain these ciphers place on our attention, it's also worth mentioning Lily Gurton-Wachter's theory of attention in eighteenth-century poetry as imbricated in wartime surveillance; see her *Watchwords: Romanticism and the Poetics of Attention* (Stanford: Stanford University Press, 2016).

88. François, "'The Feel of Not to Feel It:' or the Pleasures of Enduring Form," in *A Companion to Romantic Poetry,* ed. Charles Mahoney (Hoboken: Blackwell Publishing, 2011), 445–66.

89. Strickland, "Slippingglimpse" in *Zone: Zero,* 91.

90. Blake, *Visions of the Daughters of Albion,* The William Blake Archive, *http://www.blakearchive.org/copy/vda.b?descId=vda.b.illbk.07.*

Robert Burns and the Refashioning of Scottish Identity through Song

STACEY JOCOY

The Scots Musical Museum in six volumes (initiated and published by James Johnson between 1787 and 1803) was a project to which Robert Burns devoted great time and energy toward the end of his life. It was, according to the Introduction, the solution to a perceived problem: "It has long been a just and general Complaint, that among all of the Music Books of Scots Songs that have been hitherto offered to the public, not one, nor even all of them put together, can be said to have merited the name of what may be called A Complete Collection."[1] Certainly the drive toward completeness was in keeping with the philosophical drives of the Scottish Enlightenment. However, what Charles Duffin calls the "creative urgency" that Burns exerted to unite texts with tunes was extreme; many collections throughout the period and well into the nineteenth century still neglected to include the musical notation with the song lyrics. This passion seemingly connects Burns's collecting with Johann Herder's contemporary conception of the Folk (*Volk*) and of folk song as the remnants of the true voice of a nation's people.[2] This is not to suggest that Burns was following Herder, but rather that a proto-Romantic zeitgeist born of Enlightenment ideals affected both of them.[3] To collect these songs and subsequently mediate their texts, as a museum curator would assemble and mount an exhibition, was not merely a hobby or poetical obsession for Burns; it was a conscious effort to refashion the ideological stance of Scotland.

Working half a century or more after the Jacobite Rising of 1745 (the '45), Burns, as the Ploughman Poet speaking as a Scots patriot, had his own agendas, the larger discussion of which lies outside of the scope of this article.[4] With regard to his song collecting, however, it would appear that Burns had found a suitable vehicle with which to navigate the ongoing issues of nationality and how to create a modern Scotland that could be organized neither around the Kirk of the past, nor around the Anglicizing tendencies of the Union-embracing, Edinburgh-based literati, but rather in an imagined space of language and culture. Language always informs culture, and this is especially true for Burns's use of the Scots language in his versions of Scots songs, which changed even well-known tunes into something seemingly exotic. Distinct from both English and Gaelic, Scots, or the "dooble tongue," registered a resistance to the unifying effects of English seen in earlier song collections.[5] Burns was both criticized and praised for his linguistic preference, which has subsequently served as a rallying point for Scottish nationalists. This use of language aligns with an element of Benedict Anderson's theory of nationalism as an imagined community, in that the use of vernacular publications distributed through print capitalism had the power to unify readers separated by space and personally unknown to one another to express a "community consciousness."[6] For Burns, Scots culture could be drawn from songs and ballads because of their newfound status as important cultural artifacts in an age of fashionable antiquarianism.

This stance helps to explain Burns's questionable collecting and editing practices, which lie between those of a ballad maker of the previous century and the more precise archival or ethnographic collectors of the future. Burns was omnivorous in his consideration of all sources that came to his hand, whether from manuscripts or from oral collection.[7] This egalitarian consideration of both written and oral sources distinguished Burns from many of the other collectors of his period who eschewed orality, especially in the wake of the Ossian debates. For other collectors, including Thomas Percy, Joseph Ritson, and even David Herd, orality was likely debased and problematic without corroborating extant, textual sources.[8] Burns's editing, which has received extended analysis in Murray Pittock's edition of *The Scots Musical Museum*, varied greatly depending on the source material.[9] As Carol McGuirk notes, it could be as minimal as "mending"—a changed word or spelling—or as intrusive as "hacking and hewing."[10] This variability, I argue, was at least in part driven by his musicality, the question of which has simmered beneath the largely text-driven scholarship on Burns. Burns's annotation in his copy of *The Scots Musical Museum* (written c. 1790) conveys his respect for tunes and their innate cultural qualities:

> As Music is the language of Nature & Poetry, particularly Songs,
> are always less or more localized (if I may be allowed the verb) by
> some of the modifications of Time & Place, this is the reason why
> so many of our Scots airs have outlived their original & ~~perhaps~~
> many subsequent sets of verses; except perhaps a single name,
> or phrase, or sometimes one or two lines, simply to ~~remember~~
> distinguish the tunes by.[11]

This oft-used quotation has been analyzed in a number of ways over the years to interrogate Burns's idea about music as a part of nature, or as a universalizing agent, to consider the meaning of the term "local," or even as a way to dismiss Burns's usage of tunes.[12] An important point, however, is his recognition of a memorable, distinguishing textuality that clings to the tunes, as he further alludes to in the Riddell annotations concerning songs in his "Z" category (those most changed): "little more than the Chorus is ancient."[13] Even when acknowledging his fierce editing-creation of texts, Burns notes that the "ancient" chorus remains. These textual hints, names, phrases, or surviving lines, as well as the character of the air—its mode and melodic shape, rhythmic qualities, and phrase lengths—help to guide his new editions of these tunes. While it is easy to argue that his point here is regarding textual paucity or decay, what he reveals is quite telling: Burns recognizes an indelible connection between tunes and texts that forms a lasting resonance with uses of the tune in the past. This indexes not only an "archaeology of tunes," as Pittock has suggested, but also a network of tune topoi—not merely linguistic fragments, but tunes read as texts that recall, evoke, and even demand the application of specific themes (such as deserved death by hanging, a father saved by his devoted daughter, or betrayal of a sibling, for example).[14]

Burns's refashioning of tunes shows a complexity born of his ability to stand at the historical nexus between balladeer and collector, manipulating texts, both musical and linguistic, to convey his altered messages.[15] Herein lies the power of Burns's Scots Songs for their placement within a cultural reimagining of Scotland: these tunes were rooted in a traditional performativity that Burns both recognized and employed when creating his new lyrics. Karen McAuley notes that while Burns was not able to take down the actual music when collecting, he took care to have someone else with him who could do so.[16] With this connection to the past, Burns's Scots songs speak more powerfully than Allan Ramsay's gentrified versions or John Home's bowdlerized texts because they use the Scots language, a resistant linguistic choice that helps seamlessly integrate these texts with the long cultural memory embedded within the tunes themselves.

Studies of period collections of Scots songs typically attempt to consider the larger opus, asking important questions about their authorship, collecting methods, and ideological purpose. *The Scots Musical Museum* and other collections of the period with which Burns was involved, including George Thomson's *Select Collection of Original Scotish Airs* and even the bawdy *Merry Muses of Caledonia*, include an enormous number of pieces, many with questionable, non-Scottish tune origins. A sharper focus on specific pieces can help address these origins, offering important details about Burns's collecting habits, editing, word or phrase substitution, and re-texting practices—in short, an "archeology of Burns's songs."[17]

In some cases, such as the tunes "Killiecrankie" or "Highland Laddie," Burns's choice to collect and include the piece as representative of Scottish heritage is quite obvious. The rationale behind the inclusion of other works, however, is less clear. While the discourse around Burns's song collecting has primarily focused on his textual editing or authorship, this study interrogates the tunes and musical choices, secondarily reflecting on how Burns fit texts to them. Although it has been argued that tunes and texts are by their nature separable, tune choice was not arbitrary for Burns.[18] At the tail-end of a centuries-long ballad tradition, Burns could still hear the resonances that allowed earlier ballad makers to choose tunes that complemented their texts, not merely as pitched or rhythmic decoration, but to convey semiotic, sociopolitical meaning embedded within the aurality of each tune. Burns knew this, likely through the lively ballad opera tradition, aural collecting, and the written efforts of earlier collectors, such as Herd, Percy, and Ritson.[19] Unlike these other collectors, however, Burns's collecting did not prioritize the manuscript as the main means of historical transmission. Pittock notes that Burns commented on the national purity of songs (i.e., he thought some tunes were intrinsically linked to their Scottish origins), but he also allowed for a contemporary musical fusion.[20] Hearing the songs as part of an embodied sonic tradition, rather than focusing on their textual antiquity or authenticity, allowed Burns a unique aural perspective that he connected with textual fragments and earlier versions to order to achieve his own fusion.

"Greensleeves" for instance, could be seen as an unusual Scots song as it had direct historical ties to England.[21] By the later eighteenth century, the tune had gone through many title changes, including "The Blacksmith" with its well-known refrain "Which nobody can deny," made famous by the Civil Wars of the mid-seventeenth century, and "Upon Tyburn Tree," which was created for John Gay's wildly popular *The Beggar's Opera* (1728).[22] Burns may have been following Herd's earlier inclusion of the tune with the text "As I walk'd by mysel," but this older text is neither mentioned, nor cited.[23] Burns's version of "Greensleeves," which appears in *The Merry Muses of*

Caledonia (1799) and also exists in an autograph manuscript, is interesting not so much for its bawdiness as for its reference to clothing: "Greensleeves and tartan ties / Mark my true love where she lies; / I'll be at her or she rise, / My fiddle and I thegither."[24] In an age in which tartans were officially illegal, "tartan ties" were perhaps a minor detail intended just for the titillation of the Crochallan Fencibles (an Edinburgh club that Burns frequented), but they are nonetheless an important inclusion that subtly changed a version of a tune that had strong Jacobite connections earlier in the century.

"Ye Jacobites by Name" (which appears as no. 371 in Volume 4 of *The Scots Musical Museum*) is another tune that Burns may well have described as "querulous."[25] The lyrics and tune had a contested heritage of both pro- and anti-Jacobite use before Burns significantly changed the text. James Hogg, who included the tune as no. 34 in his *Jacobite Reliques* (1817), mentions its antiquity, which, through hymn tunes, reaches back several centuries. However, it rose to secular prominence c. 1700, when it was connected to the notorious pirate, Captain Kidd. Including a fraught Jacobite text in *The Scots Musical Museum* may reflect the holistic approach to collecting implicit in its self-description as a "museum." As Steve Newman notes in his study of ballad collecting, the act of "collection faces both ways," both toward the organizing taxonomies of the modern and the valuation of the culture of the past. This, Newman suggests, "tends to raise authors' and readers' consciousness of the insufficiencies of the modern and universalizing culture of the Enlightenment."[26] More likely, however, the perceived value of the song for Burns lies in the manner in which he changes it textually, altering its original, partisan text into something both anti-war and anti-politics. Fiona Stafford has noted Burns's tendency to consciously quote earlier material as a means of both integrating pre-existing texts and writing back at them, essentially adding his texts to theirs in a lively, often argumentative, discourse.[27] I would add, however, that Burns's dialogue with ballads of the past does not stop with their lyrics, but also extends to their tunes, which he recognized as equally significant.

Drawing on the long-practiced art of changing the text in order to reflect a new, but related, meaning, thus forms a pattern for Burns. Balladeers of the past had known that they were not simply writing new lyrics, but that they were adding to a living, multi-textual tradition that wove together texts and melodies into layered, associative tune families. Ballad tunes held cultural memory and were thus an integral element of *The Scots Musical Museum*. As the Ploughman Poet and effective national laureate of Scotland, Burns had a goal not only to represent his vision of Scotland through his work, but also to use poetry and its sister art, music, to heal the wounds of the past— the lingering angst of Culloden and Jacobite fervor—in order to hasten the arrival of a harmonious, unified Scotland. The humble ballad and Scots song, raised from the streets to the pages of multi-volume collections, was one of the best vehicles for such ideological work. Burns's Scottish imaginary used songs—labeled "Scottish," but potentially taken from all over Europe and even the Middle East—to delocalize Scotland's history of internal strife, weaving together rival clans and regions into a musical tartan that could appeal aesthetically to both the literati of the Scottish Enlightenment and the middling classes with new Broadwood pianos in their parlors.[28]

The balance of this study will consider these two tunes, "Greensleeves" and "Ye Jacobites by Name," and their histories and associations to provide context for Burns's versions of them, which not only bring together pirates, Jacobites, and treachery, but also (and more importantly) tell the story of the long road from centuries of clan warfare to a united, proto-Romantic Scottish culture.

"Greensleeves"

Before Burns encountered it, "Greensleeves" had already appeared, both as a tune title and as a song, in several Scottish collections, including Ramsay's *Tea-Table Miscellany* (1724) and Herd's *Ancient Scottish Songs* (1769). "Greensleeves," however, had long been associated with the English. Its musical structure derives from the Spanish *romanesca*, a form that first appeared in continental publications in the mid-sixteenth century.[29] Though

Figure 1. The "Greensleeves" tune as given in Trinity College, Dublin, ms. 408/2, bound with the Ballet Lute book.

modern audiences generally think of the standardized version of the tune seen in Figure 1, for early modern audiences, the tune was multiform.[30] Communicated through both oral transmission and various printed versions, the tune could be in duple or compound meter and could stretch from a regular 8-bar phrase to a 10-bar phrase in order to accommodate longer texts. These changes could make the piece sound rather different than the now standard form given in Figure 1, but it is likely that most people knew the tune in at least one version, making it possible for them to identify it in others.

The tune "Greensleeves" appears to have become popular in the last quarter of the sixteenth century. Although popular legend has it that the text and tune date back to the court of King Henry VIII, the earliest sources are from the 1580s. Full texts for many of the earliest printings are no longer extant, but their titles or incipits in the Stationers' Register at least imply that there was a central female character who wore a garment with green sleeves.[31] The first entries of the tune into the Register (see Table 1, nos. 1–4) were made within days, or even hours, of each other, implying that there was a fashion or possibly a scandal that motivated the stationers to stake their respective claims. Interestingly, some of the earliest titles, including nos. 1, 2, 5, 6, and 8, indicate that the origins of the tune lie either in "the North" or Scotland specifically.

Table 1. Entries in the Stationers' Register for the "Greensleeves" tune, c. 1580–1660

No.	Title	Registration	Stationer
1*	"A new Northern Dittye of the lady Greene Sleeves"	3 September 1580	Richard Jones
2*	"A ballad being the Ladie Greene Sleeves Answere to Donkyn hir frende"[32]	3 September 1580	Edward White
3*	"Green Sleves moralized"	15 September 1580	Henry Carr
4*	"Greene Sleeves and countenance, in Countenance is Green Sleeves"	18 September 1580	Edward White
5	"It was a worthy Lord of Lorne"[33]	6 October 1580	Jno. Wally
6*	"A merry newe Northerne Songe of Green Sleeves"	14 December 1580	Richard Jones
7*	"Reprehension against Green Sleeves"	13 February 1581	William Elderton
8	"A new Ballad declaring the great treason conspired against the young King of Scots"	30 May 1581	William Elderton
9*	"Green Sleeves is worne awaie, Yellow sleeves come to decaie ..."	24 August 1581	Edward White

10	"A New Courtly Sonet of the Lady Greensleeves"	1584	Richard Jones (in *A Handefull of Pleasant Delites*, 1584)
11	"Good Lord what a wicked world is this"	August 1586	P. B. [Phillip Birch?]
12	"You traitors all that doo deuise, to hurt our Queen in trewcherous wise"	August 1588	Edward Allde
13	"A merry new Ballad, both pleasant and sweete, In praise of the Blacksmith, which is very meete"	21 March 1635	J. Okes
14	"Caroll for New-yeares day"	1642	Francis Coles (in *Good and True Fresh and New Carols*, 1642)
15	"The Blacksmith"	1656	Nathaniel Brook (in *Wit and Drollery*, 1656)
16	"Of all the Sciences under the sunne"	1659[34]	
17	"Much ado about Nothing"	1660	T. Vere
18	"Another for Christmas Day at Night"	1660/1	T. Passinger and W. Thackery (in *New Christmas Carrols*, 1660/1)

* Denotes that full text is no longer extant.

The first few surviving texts, beginning with number 5, do not mention the lady, but instead discuss treachery and disloyalty. Numbers 5 ("It was a worthy Lord of Lorne"), 8 ("A new Ballad declaring the great treason conspired against the young King of Scots"), 11 ("Good Lord what a wicked world is this"), and 12 ("You traitors all that doo deuise, to hurt our Queen in trewcherous wise") all discuss betrayal, whether of a Lord, the monarch, or God.[35] This then, it would seem, is one of the earliest themes attached to the tune. Of the early texts, only number 10, "A New Courtly Sonet of the Lady Greensleeves," seems to bring in the lady at all; this is the text found in the *Handefull of Pleasant Delites* (1584). Here she is featured as the object of a lover's complaint: "Alas my love you do me wrong / To cast me off discourteously." It is not the lady, but her rejection of the lover that is central. This famous text is a courtly-love interpretation of false or dishonorable behavior; the lady's actions do not amount to actual treason, as in numbers 8 or 12, but, in the terms of courtly love, the Lady's behavior is just as heinous.

William Shakespeare seems to confirm the idea that early modern audiences thought of "Greensleeves" as a tune suitable for dark or unhappy subjects. In *The Merry Wives of Windsor*, Mistress Ford claims that Falstaff's disposition and his words "do no more adhere and keep place together than the Hundredth Psalm to the tune of 'Greensleeves.'"[36] Contrasting the main idea of the hundredth psalm, which is that of joyful praise, with the tune of "Greensleeves," strongly suggests that Shakespeare's audience would not have associated such celebration with the tune.[37] Sadly, many of the texts that might help to confirm this are no longer extant.

Though some of the texts from the 1580s were reprinted in the following decades, the next significant text set to "Greensleeves" is "A merry new Ballad, both pleasant and sweete, In praise of the Black-smith" (number 13). This jocular text about ironworking, which begins, "of all the Trades that ever I see, /There's none to the Black-smith compared may be," was the production of a literary, quasi-military fraternity called the Order of the Fancy. Not strictly part of the so-called Tribe of Ben (followers of Ben Jonson), this group included figures such as Sir John Suckling, Sir John Mennes, James Smith, and Philip Massinger. Timothy Raylor, who has studied the Order extensively, believes that the Blacksmith ballad was one of the main communal projects of the group; its title was also a play on Smith's surname.[38] This irreverent text acknowledges the idea of rejection (telling the story of Venus's rebuffing of Vulcan, the blacksmith of the Gods), but then becomes a witty mockery of that idea, summed up in its refrain: "which nobody can deny." Though it is clearly tongue in cheek, this text also rejects high society's contempt for the humble trade of blacksmithing, playing with the tune's earlier associations with betrayal or denial:

> Of all the trades that ever I see,
> Ther's none with the Blacksmith compar'd may be,
> With so many several tools works hee,
> Which nobody can deny.

This ballad was most probably written between the late 1620s and the mid-1630s, when the Order was at its height. It reached print in 1635, when it was registered in the Stationer's Register by J. Okes.[39]

During the 1640s, the members of the Order were separated by the exigencies of the Civil Wars. But the refrain "which nobody can deny" continued to circulate, initially as a reminder of the Order's old fraternity, but later with a new connotation of treachery: reminding the listener that something that should never be denied, the king's right, was in contest, along with many other traditional English ideas. In the aftermath of the execution of Charles I, royalists included "The Blacksmith" in printed works sympathetic to the Stuarts. It became the most popular royalist tune of the period (even surpassing Martin Parker's "When the King enjoys his own again"), and its refrain of "which nobody can deny" was used in many other settings and came to symbolize loyal cavalier values during the Interregnum.[40]

Beginning in this period, scurrilous ballads were written to lambaste the Long or "Rump" Parliament. These scatalogical Rump Songs go far beyond the boundaries of good taste, emphasizing the lower status of the M.P.s by literally equating them with the lower bodily functions and excrement; rump cuts of beef were also burned in bonfires around London at different moments in the 1650s. In the largest contemporary collection of these songs and squibs, *The Rump* (1662), compiled by Henry Brome, there are no less than fifteen pieces that call for "the Blacksmith" tune and another half dozen pieces that either use the "which nobody can deny" refrain or otherwise indicate that they are to be sung to the tune of "the Blacksmith."[41] Several of these texts take a mock-serious tone in defense of Parliament, but the clear royalist associations of the refrain remind the listener that these too are meant as anti-Parliamentary satires. The tune undermines the text, but that is part of the humor. For the rest of the century, *Greensleeves* was most popular in its political guise of "the Blacksmith," or "Which nobody can deny," maintaining its older associations with treachery and falseness, but now as qualities to be countered by loyalty.

In the late 1680s, "Greensleeves" was appropriated by the Whigs for the seemingly innocuous piece, "A New Song of Lulla By." The content of this ballad concerns one of the most controversial events of 1688—the birth of James Francis Edward Stuart or "the Old Pretender," and the controversy over whether he was really the son of James II (the prospect of another Catholic Stuart was one of the principal justifications invoked for the Revolution of 1688–89). The ballad portrays the birth as an elaborate Vatican plot to continue Catholic rule in England and includes a Pope who is irate that the plot has been discovered. Of course, shortly after this James II was deposed and William and Mary assumed the throne, but nevertheless fears of a Jacobite rebellion continued throughout the first half of the eighteenth century.

Allan Ramsay's use of "Greensleeves" as the tune indicated for his pastoral love poem beginning "Ye watchful guardians of the Fair," in his *Tea-Table Miscellany* (1724), bears almost no connection to any of the other contemporary uses of the tune. Of its four stanzas, numbers 1, 2, and 4 are about "Delia," the speaker's affection for her, and concerns that she may be seduced by a rich man: "With Soul sunk in a golden Grave." The third verse takes a different turn, however, in its anger against the corruption of the world—a theme in Ramsay's work:

> Let all the World turn upside down,
> And Fools run an eternal Round,
> In Quest of what can ne'er be found,
> To please their vain Ambition.
> Let little Minds great Charms espy
> In Shadows which at Distance ly,
> Whose hop'd for Pleasures, when come nigh,
> Prove nothing in Fruition.[42]

The "World turn[ed] upside down" was a popular phrase in reference to the turmoil of English Civil War and the more recent Revolution of 1688–89. More conservative voices felt that traditional values were being pushed aside in favor of Whiggish capitalism and monetary speculation—financial risk that had formed the massive South Sea Bubble that burst in 1720. Collapsing his insecurities in love with his insecurities concerning the world in general, the persona professes to believe in Delia, but not in the world, which is filled with corrupt men ready to betray him and his love. Ramsay's "Greensleeves," which is the version in *The Scots Musical Museum*, thus uses the pastoral, as Virgil did before him, as a vehicle for social criticism.

In a similar vein, John Gay used the tune "Greensleeves" in his celebrated *Beggar's Opera* (1728). In his cell on the eve of his hanging, the protagonist Captain Macheath sings his lament; he does so not as a confession of guilt, but in the tradition of "last words" denouncing those responsible for his plight: in this case, an unjust government.[43] Here Gay presents the only medley of the opera: ten songs strung together, highlighted by their placement near the end of the opera. After nine earlier snippets of tunes, in which Macheath revels in his misery and attempts to rally his spirits, the mood changes. Quite angry now with his situation, Macheath sings:

> Since Laws were made for ev'ry Degree,
> To curb vice in others, as well as me,
> I wonder we han't better Company,
> Upon Tyburn Tree![44]

The enormous popularity of *The Beggar's Opera* ensured that the text "Upon Tyburn Tree," more than any other, was the one that audiences associated with the "Greensleeves" tune in the 1730s and 1740s. It argued for Tory patriotism, a reassertion of older values that would redress the indignities suffered by those who held to conservative ideologies; it would restore the "world turned upside down" by the Revolution and right the wrongs of an England corrupted by greed and unchecked by honor.

The original tune title had not entirely faded by the 1770s, when James Boswell recorded what he called "Greensleeves and Puddin' Pies." Boswell made special note, in his *Journal of a Tour to the Hebrides,* of a text supposedly sung by Allan MacDonald, one of the Jacobites who assisted Charles Edward Stuart after the collapse of the '45:

> Green Sleeves and Pudding Pies,
> Tell me where my mistress lies,
> And I'll be with her before she rise,
> Fiddle and aw together.
>
> May our affairs abroad succeed,
> And may our king come home with speed,
> And all Pretenders shake for speed,
> And let his health go round.
>
> To all our injured friends in need,
> This side and beyond the Tweed,
> Let all Pretenders shake for dread,
> And let his health go round.[45]

For MacDonald, the "Pretenders" to the crown were the Hanoverians. Bonnie Prince Charlie himself was said to have sung "Greensleeves" during his (much romanticized) crossing to the Isle of Skye after the Battle of Culloden with Flora MacDonald (Allan's future wife), along with "When the king enjoyes his own again."[46]

Given the variety of all of these versions of "Greensleeves," can the song really be understood to connote anything specifically Scottish for Burns or his audience? Betrayal, the dangers of Catholicism, and support for the Stuart cause clearly emerge as recurrent themes, along with connections to the North or Scotland. Percy noticed in his *Reliques of Ancient English Poetry* (1765) that "it is a received tradition in Scotland that 'Greensleeves and pudding pies' was designed to ridicule the Popish Clergy."[47] Percy does not cite a source for this tradition, although it does accord with the other associations discussed in relation with earlier publications of "Greensleeves." Unfortunately, while the title "Greensleeves and Pudding Pies" existed as early as 1656 when it was mentioned in *Sportive Wit,* there are no extant lyrics from this period. This title is also associated with reprints of "The Lord of Lorne" ballad issued by Francis Coles between 1658 and 1674.[48] As a notated tune, it does not appear in print until the seventh edition of John Playford's *Dancing Master* (1686), where it is accompanied by choreography. While the earliest recorded lyrics appear in Herd's manuscript collection, the source of his text is unclear.[49] The first verse is clearly related to the text later transmitted by Burns and also used by Macdonald:

> Greensleeves and pudden-pyes,
> Come tell me where my true love lyes,
> And I'll be wi' her ere she rise:
> Fidle a' the gither!
> …
> Green sleeves and yellow lace,
> Maids, maids, come, marry apace!
> The batchelors are in a pitiful case
> To fiddle a' the gather

Herd's second verse is related to the cavalier tune "Hey boy, up go we!," which introduces a bawdy element and, while it has been suggested that it is an interpolation, its presence in this text—so seemingly out of place—makes a strong case for a mid-seventeenth-century dating.[50] The third verse starts with the text, "Green sleeves and yellow lace." This also becomes a title of the dance in a later version of the *Dancing Master* (the seventeenth edition of 1721), which further indicates that the lyrics were known in the later seventeenth and early eighteenth centuries.

Herd's text bears a strong resemblance to Burns's verses that were included in the *Merry Muses of Caledonia*:

> Green sleeves and tartan ties
> Mark my true love whare she lies:
> I'll be at her or she rise,
> My fiddle and I thegither.
>
> Be it by the chrystal burn,
> Be it by the milkwhite thorn;
> I shall rouse her in the morn,
> My fiddle and I thegither.[51]

Herd was part of Burns's literary network; he was known as "Greysteil" among his acquaintances.[52] Given the scarcity of this text, it seems plausible that Burns had access to Herd's notes for this piece. Burns's version notably changes "pudding pies" to "tartan ties," emphasizing the tune's Scottish associations and altering its sexual implications.[53] He removes the middle verse, and while he keeps the first verse quite close to Herd, he entirely rewrites the third verse to reflect a proto-Romantic, Scottish, pastoral frolic: a "chrystal burn" being a crystal stream and "milkwhite thorn" a flowering, springtime tree.[54] What may once have been a piece intended to ridicule Catholicism, or in many other versions to decry betrayal and treachery, Burns has turned into a self-conscious, Scottish pastoral, featuring "true love" and a happy, casual attitude toward sexuality, as befits a pastoral.

Burns did not erase the past of "Greensleeves"; he overwrote it as part of a living tradition that changed and adapted texts to current cultural aesthetics and needs. Although Johnson did not include this text in *The Scots Musical Museum*, James Hogg made it part of the *Jacobite Relics of Scotland* (1819).

"Greensleeves" is a fraught musical text throughout the seventeenth and eighteenth centuries. Burns's engagement with it speaks to his collecting habits, indicating a knowledge or use of Herd's unpublished research. Against Ramsay's polite, if somewhat aggrieved pastoral, with its buried political subtext, Burns's "Greensleeves" gives the lady her (sexually acquired) "green dress." Countering the elitism of the Scottish Enlightenment with what Pittock calls his "brand" as the Heaven-taught ploughman, Burns brings Ramsay's pastoral back to the human level, while still managing to insert a political jab against the Union.[55] This ability to use tunes with a wide variety of geographical origins and to enforce their supposed Scottishness through a deft interweaving of earlier thematic associations with his own new or newly edited lyrics is a potent element of Burns's collecting practices, one that links him more to the creative ballad-making traditions of the long seventeenth century than to the emerging curatorial impulses of the nineteenth.

"Ye Jacobites by Name"

The tune "Ye Jacobites by Name," through its alternate title "Coming Down," has a colorful connection to execution songs, as well as to hymn tunes and songs attempting to convey a moral lesson. While its exact tune and therefore tune history is unknown, "Coming Down" is related, at least by rhyme and meter, to the "Chimney song" and from there to a larger complex of Samuel or Jack Hall ballads.[56] Bertrand Harris Bronson has followed this tune family back to the Middle Ages, noting that its use in the early modern period was most likely as a hymn tune related to the tune used for "Wondrous Love."[57] The text and associations of "Wondrous Love" would connote the speaker's redemption through Christ, especially in the last verse: "And while from death I'm free, / I'll sing on." Although this layering effect may have created some cognitive dissonance for contemporary audiences, it aligns well with earlier concepts of Christian redemption—the body and its sins will die, but the spirit, even if it was sinful in life, may yet have hope in Christ. In its connection to morality, this tune gained fame in the early eighteenth century for its relation to the trial and death of the infamous pirate, Captain Kidd.

One of the most sensational legal cases at the beginning of the eighteenth century was that of the Scotsman William Kidd, better known as Captain Kidd, executed at Wapping in 1701—hanged twice, after the first rope broke, with his corpse placed in a cage to rot over the Thames at Tilbury Dock as a warning against piracy. In fact, Kidd was a wealthy, settled citizen of New York, married to one of the richest widows in town (Sarah Bradley Cox Oort), when he was asked in 1695, first by the Earl of Bellomont—the governor of Massachusetts, New Hampshire, and New York—and then by King William III, to rid the seas of pirates. In the end, his primary accuser was the *same* Earl of Bellomont, who pursued him mercilessly (in search of Kidd's supposed treasure) after he was said to have returned from the Indies.[58] Damningly, Bellomont confiscated Kidd's proof that he was operating as a legitimate privateer on instructions from the king and ordered his arrest, interrogation, and transport to London for final trial.[59] Bellomont further claimed that Kidd was a Jacobite and so inherently untrustworthy, using his Scottish origins as an additional reason to damn the so-called pirate. Though Kidd defended himself throughout the trial—famously quoting Hammurabi's code of social equality and fairness—he had become an inconvenience to his former supporters, who repudiated him.

The ballad that sensationalized his life, entitled "Captain Kid's Farewel to the Seas, or the Famous Pirate's Lament," set to the tune "Coming Down," is aggressively unrepentant, focusing on his murderous deeds and sacrilegious behavior:

> My Name is Captain Kid who has sail'd, etc.
> My Name is Captain Kid, who has saild,
> My Name is Captain Kid,
> What the Laws did still forbid,
> Unluckily I did while I sail'd.
>
> Upon the Ocean wide, when I sail'd, etc.
> Upon the Ocean wide, when I sail'd,
> Upon the Ocean wide,
> I robb'd on e'ery side.
> With most Ambitious Pride, when I sail'd,
> …
> Farewel the Ocean main, we must die, etc.
> Farewel the Ocean main, we must die,
> Farewel the Ocean main,
> The Coast of France or Spain
> We ne're shall see again, we must die.[60]

The final stanza finishes with a description of the anticipated crowd at his hanging: "Some thousands they will flock when we die." There is absolutely no sign of repentance here, which is fairly odd for an execution song.[61] Execution songs were part of a larger body of execution literature: songs, poems, chapbooks, and final speeches were eagerly awaited and, like modern true crime stories, often highlighted the more colorful aspects of the crimes in order to feed public interest.[62] Collections of these accounts were avidly consumed. One of the first was *The Tyburn Calendar, or Malefactors Bloody Register* (c. 1705), followed by Captain Alexander Smith's *Compleat History of the Lives and Robberies of the Most Notorious Highwaymen* (1719). This gallows literature—sometimes moralized, sometimes not—glorified criminals for financial gain and was largely responsible for raising the figure of the common highwayman, and even the pirate, in popular esteem.[63] As Hal Gladfelder notes in his study of criminal narratives, "the fiction of sociological value drops away, … [gallows songs] are revealed as compilations of a purely literary language, the accessories of deliberately artificial divertissements."[64] These lyrics were meant to portray Kidd as an irredeemable pirate in order to increase sales of the ballad. Although there is no obvious Scottish brogue in Kidd's farewell, Kidd himself, along with several of his supporters, was famously vilified as Scottish during his trial and his unrepentant language is meant to highlight his Otherness, as most execution ballads prior to this evince the subject's remorse. This accords with a "racializing of deviance," here aimed at the Scottish pirate—a politically profitable stance for both Whigs and Tories in 1701.[65]

A later U.S. ballad version, "The Dying Words of Captain Robert Kidd" is where the song finally takes on a moralistic tone, especially toward the end. Earlier verses note that he had abandoned his faith, leaving his "Bible in the sand" and concluding that "Damnation's my just lot." Even with the speaker's recognition of his wickedness and his formulaic caveat ("Take warning now by me"), this Captain Kidd still blames his end on others:

> Take warning now by me, for I must die, for I must die,
> Take warning now by me, for I must die;
> Take warning now by me, and shun bad company,
> Lest you come to hell with me, for I must die
> Lest you come to hell with me, for I must die.[66]

Note that one should "shun bad company, / Lest you come to hell with me," which implies that it was ultimately Kidd's pirate companions, or possibly even Jacobites, that caused his downfall. This ballad seems to date from no earlier than the 1790s, almost a century after Kidd's death, and crossed the Atlantic to Boston, changing his name from William to Robert in the process.[67] Interestingly, as Burns noted in his 1790 annotation about tunes and their textual remnants, quoted earlier, this American version has retained its tune, its rhyme, and its basic subject matter, though much of the text was altered. Another eighteenth-century use of the tune can be found in the ballad of "Admiral Benbow" (1702):

> Come, all you sailors bold, Lend an ear, lend an ear,
> Come all you sailors bold, lend an ear.
> It's of our Admiral's fame,
> Brave Benbow call'd by name,
> How he fought on the main You shall hear, you shall hear,
> How he fought on the main you shall hear.[68]

Captain Kidd was a notorious pirate and Admiral Benbow was a famous military hero; however, the line between infamy and fame can be quite thin. There are also parallels between the two: like Kidd, Benbow died in a grizzly manner, and they were both sea captains, or "seamen bold," which may have further sealed the association.[69]

While "Admiral Benbow" used the tune for "Captain Kidd" shortly after his execution, within a decade or so, the tune was also adopted by Scottish parodic contrafacta, both positive and negative. "Aikendrum" would appear to date to the period before the battle of Sheriffmuir (1715), a low point for Jacobite morale, and lampoons the Whigs: "Ken you how a Whig can fight, Aikendrum, Aikendrum?" The Scottish forces are told that they need not fight, but that they should simply "prig" (haggle) and "the poor, Worm-eaten Whig" will lose. This speaks to the perceived moral failings of the Whigs, especially their unchecked greed, and so positions this text as a moralistic, political parody. Captain Kidd's tune (Roud #369) next appears as the tune for the anti-Jacobite text, "Ye Jacobites by Name," which was likely chosen by the anonymous ballad maker in order to make a connection in contemporary audiences' minds between the infamous Scottish pirate, who got his "just desserts" and the topic of the new text: a negative view of the (primarily Scottish) Jacobites." Ironically, this was quickly followed by a series of texts to the same tune in praise of supporters of the Stuarts, including "You Jacobites by Name," and finally the text by Burns himself. With a familiar mixture of violence, morality, and death, "You Jacobites by Name" valorizes the efforts of the defeated Jacobites, blaming the war on their opponents' treachery:

> You Jacobites by Name, now give Ear, now give Ear,
> You Jacobites by Name, now give Ear;
> You Jacobites by Name, your Praise I will proclaim,
> Some says you are to blame for this Wear.
> …
> They marched thro' our Land cruelly, cruelly,
> They marched thro' our Land cruelly,
> They marched thro' our Land with a bloody thievish Band
> To Edinburgh then they wan Treachery.
> …
> They ought to hing on high for the same.[70]

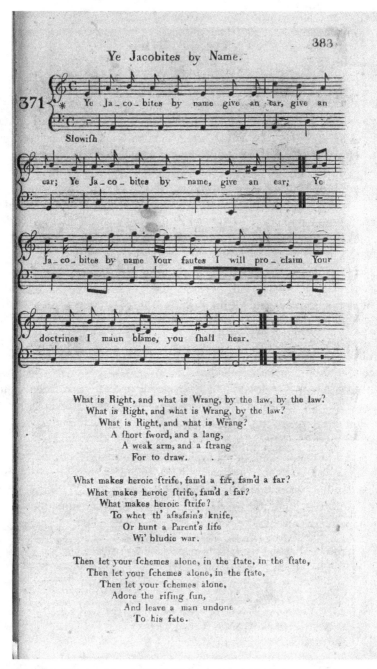

Figure 2. "Ye Jacobites by Name," *Scots Musical Museum*, vol. 4, no. 371 (Edinburgh, 1803). Courtesy of the National Library of Scotland.

As in "Captain Kidd," the opponents of the speaker—here the English and the "Pope and Prelacy"—are incredibly cruel; they are the ones to blame for this tragedy, in a way that could help rally flagging Jacobite hopes, even after the resounding defeat at Culloden.

The fact that the tune had changed sides from anti-Jacobite to Jacobite is important, but note what Burns does with this fraught, militant text (see Figure 2):

> Ye Jacobites by name give an ear, give an ear;
> Ye Jacobites by name give an ear;
> Ye Jacobites by name
> Your faults I will proclaim
> Your doctrines I maun blame,
> You shall hear.
>
> What is Right and what is Wrang, by the law, by the law?
> What is Right and what is Wrang by the law?
> What is Right and what is Wrang?
> A short sword, and a lang,
> A weak arm, and a strang
> For to draw.
>
> What makes heroic strife, fam'd afar, fam'd afar?
> What makes heroic strife, famed afar?
> What makes heroic strife?
> To whet th' assassin's knife,
> Or hunt a Parent's life
> Wi' bludie war.
>
> Then let your schemes alone, in the state, in the state
> Then leave your schemes alone, in the state
> Then leave your schemes alone,
> Adore the rising sun
> And leave a man undone
> To his fate.[71]

Burns uses this tune, which by his time had strong, pro-Scottish sentiment, and a re-texting of its lyrics to question the very idea of war through a complicated twisting of the earlier positive and negative elements. Pittock notes that the speaker describes "his defeat in the metaphor of victory."[72] Beginning in a vein that sounds markedly anti-Jacobite, Burns considers both "faults" and "blame" and then questions "What is Right and what is Wrang, by the law?," thereby bringing in both the morality traditionally associated with the tune and the law of the land—a land that, after 1707, was considered to be a Union. The speaker next asks "What makes heroic strife, fam'd afar?," which oxymoronically combines the positive connotations of "heroic" with the negative ones of "strife." The description of the "heroic strife" as "fam'd afar" appears to be an allusion to both the Battle of Culloden itself and to the lingering resentments in its wake. Burns emphasizes the phrase "fam'd afar" with its threefold repetition, which seems to present that fame as positive, but then counters that presentation with the mention of "bludie war" at the close of the stanza. In the last verse, the speaker condemns the culture of honor and violence that has plagued his country. "Then let your schemes alone," he pleads, using the negative implications of the word "scheme" as a means of denigrating Jacobite fantasies of further violence, only to twist the narrative yet again with his recognition of the appeal of "the rising sun."

This final positive image of the "rising sun" appears to embrace life through nature and an ethos of "live and let live." With this, Burns skillfully, painfully, and even existentially transforms an older, politicized tune valorizing death into a call for the celebration of life. This is all the more poignant in light of the fact that the last lines suggest that the speaker is either a Jacobite or Jacobite sympathizer: "And leave a man undone / To his fate." This complicated weaving of positive and negative imagery memorializes the cause for which so many died, "perhaps," according to Pittock, "to show that Jacobitism remains an enduring belief, even though it may be pointless to rise in its support."[73] Burns thus brings the earlier resonances of the tune (religion, betrayal, and Jacobitism) to bear on his new message that does not deny past pain, but that recognizes the merits of fraught unity over bloody schism.

Burns's Scottish Imaginary

"Greensleeves" and "Ye Jacobites by Name" are just two tunes out of the hundreds of late eighteenth-century Scots songs that were featured in Scots song collections, but they speak volumes about their past use and about Burns's collecting. The archeology of these tunes, through their succession of texts and their unique musical structures, conveys important layers of meaning, including contested Jacobite and related sociopolitical narratives, that can help us reconstruct what eighteenth-century audiences and Burns himself *heard* when they listened to these tunes. This, in turn, will allow us to better understand what Burns was trying to achieve through his collecting and editing of song collections, including *The Scots Musical Museum*. Burns—like James Macpherson, Sir Walter Scott, and Mrs. Brown of Falkland—was a "creative editor" who understood that while texts were subject to slippage, tunes had a longevity that was preserved in the soundscape of contemporary Scotland.[74]

Unlike other collectors of the period, Burns was not overly concerned about authenticity; rather, he was interested in canon creation. Tunes like "Greensleeves" and "Ye Jacobites by Name" had problematic, non-Scottish histories, but this was no more problematic for Burns than it was for Francis Scott Key to use the tune to "Anacreon in Heaven," a British drinking song, as the tune for "The Star Spangled Banner," effectively co-opting the tune and subverting its original significance in favor of his new, highly politicized meaning. Burns's imaginary allowed him to find a middle space between the popular and the literary, a contentious past and an amnesiac Anglicized future, code-switching between Scots and English as part of working toward a future for a Scotland that had its own identity, national language, and uniting traditions. A variety of Scots songs re-texted and refashioned could help further his vision, which may have included "implant[ing] his version of the Jacobite tradition at the heart of the evolving Scottish national identity."[75] Unlike the militant versions of the past, however, Burns's Jacobitism can be understood as a patriotic call to nationalism.

Part of Burns's creative editing was a sense of what Joshua Swidzinski calls "lyric abstraction" that increased the likelihood that his Scottish audience could identify with these tunes and with a shared sense of their nationality. With "Greensleeves," Burns heightened the song's potential Scottish nationalism from the very first line, simply by replacing "pudden-pyes" with "tartan ties." The "chrystal burn" of the second stanza does not relate to any specific location in Scotland, but rather refers to a Highland stream, a natural feature that all Scots could identify. These lyrics create a nostalgia that looks back at a picturesque, wild version of Scotland and forward to a transformed, proto-Romantic Scotland. In "Ye Jacobites by Name," Burns used the most recent pro-Jacobite text, but redeployed specific words—such as "blame" and "war"—in a way that did not celebrate the Jacobite cause, but memorialized it, while looking forward to a less divisive future. This is not a passive, quiescent vision of the past. Burns famously predicted to Johnson, toward the end of his life, that in "future ages your Publication will be the text book and standard of Scotish Song and Music."[76] In Burns's imaginary, Scots songs are about gathering voices into a national chorus joining together the past and the future under a flag that recognized their shared nostalgic material as a path toward a culturally distinct and unified Scotland.

Notes

1. Burns, *The Scots Musical Museum*, 6 vols. (Edinburgh, 1787–1803), 1:iii; hereafter cited as *SMM*.

2. Herder, *Voices of the Peoples in Their Songs* [*Stimmen der Völker in ihren Liedern*], 1773, in *A Companion to the Works of Johann Gottfried Herder*, ed. Hans Adler and Wulf Köpke (Rochester: Camden House, 2009), 324.

3. Murray Pittock, "Who Wrote *The Scots Musical Museum?* Challenging Editorial Practice in the Presence of Authorial Absence," *Studies in Scottish Literature* 42, no. 1 (2016): 10.

4. See Alex Broadhead, *The Language of Robert Burns: Style, Ideology, and Identity* (Lewisburg: Bucknell University Press, 2013) and Mary Ellen Brown, *Burns and Tradition* (London: Palgrave Macmillan, 1984).

5. Jeffrey Skoblow, *Dooble Tongue: Scots, Burns, Contradiction* (Newark: University of Delaware Press, 2001).

6. Anderson, *Imagined Communities* (London: Verso, 2006), 46.

7. Burns's collecting of texts has been discussed by many scholars. However, Joshua Swidzinski offers a new perspective by showing how Burns's collecting was assisted by his work as an excise collector; see Swidzinski, "Lyric Abstraction: Robert Burns as Editor and Exciseman," *Eighteenth-Century Studies* 54, no. 1 (2020): 169–86. For a more detailed account of Burns's collection of both texts and tunes, see Karen McAulay, *Our Ancient National Airs: Scottish Song Collection from the Enlightenment to the Romantic Era* (Farnham: Ashgate, 2013), 42–44.

8. McAulay, *Our Ancient National Airs,* 160.

9. Burns, *The Scots Musical Museum,* ed. Murray Pittock, vols. 2 and 3 of *The Oxford Edition of the Works of Robert Burns* (Oxford: Oxford University Press, 2018); hereafter cited as *Oxford SMM.*

10. McGuirk, review of the *Oxford SMM, The Wordsworth Circle* 49, no. 4 (Autumn 2018): 194–201.

11. The marginalia Burns added to his copy of *The Scots Musical Museum* was published in Robert H. Cromek, *Reliques of Robert Burns* (London, 1808), 202–3.

12. See Matthew Gelbart, "'The Language of Nature': Music as Historical Crucible for the Methodology of Folkloristics," *Ethnomusicology* 53, no. 3 (Fall 2009): 363–64; Swidzinski, "Lyric Abstraction," 174–75.

13. The Riddell annotations are the manuscript notes made by Burns to interleaved volumes of *The Scots Musical Museum* that he left with his mentor Robert Riddell. Burns used letter annotations such as S, R, X, and Z to indicate the extent to which he had altered his source material, Z being the most extreme changes. See David Purdie, *The Burns Encyclopaedia* (London: Robert Hale, 2013), 171.

14. Though Pittock argues for an "archeology of tunes," he acknowledges that his work is primarily bound to text and further notes that tunes themselves were less important because ballad singers who had communicated tunes *with* texts for centuries were being replaced by non-performing chapmen and hawkers. Burns likely replaced some tunes in his editing process. However, it is important to note

that he still attempted to recognize the tune and its connection to the text as part of a still-living, oral tradition in his lived soundscape of Scotland. Pittock, "Who Wrote *The Scots Musical Museum*," 14.

15. Pittock notes that Burns's editions are considered by many to be products of his "magical reputation"; Pittock "Who Wrote *The Scots Musical Museum*," 11.

16. McAulay, *Our Ancient National Airs,* 43.

17. Burns, *Oxford SMM,* 2:12. Cf. Burns, *Robert Burns's Songs for George Thomson,* ed. Kirsten McCue, vol. 4 of *The Oxford Edition of the Works of Robert Burns* (Oxford: Oxford University Press, 2021).

18. Collectors from the mid-eighteenth century forward who were unaware of associative resonances within tunes and their earlier uses would certainly have believed that tunes and texts were separable. This argument is reflected in modern scholarship, including David Atkinson, *The Anglo-Scottish Ballad and its Imaginary Contexts* (Cambridge: Open Book Publishers, 2014), 19.

19. Herd, *Ancient and Modern Scottish Songs, Heroic Ballads, etc.,* 2 vols. (Edinburgh, 1769); Percy, The *Reliques of Ancient English Poetry,* 3 vols. (London, 1765); and Ritson, *Scotish Songs in Two Volumes* (London, 1794).

20. Pittock, "Who Wrote *The Scots Musical Museum*," 4–5.

21. Greensleeves" is a Romanesca-style piece based upon *passamezzo antico* bass line patterns from Spain and Italy. However, the characteristic "Greensleeves" melody only appeared in English lute manuscripts in the 1580s, as in BL MS Add. 31392, f. 29 ("maister Cuttinge").

22. The refrain "Which nobody can deny" also later became a tune title.

23. Herd, *Ancient and Modern Scottish Songs,* 2:229.

24. The autograph manuscript of "Greensleeves" is in Burns's papers at the National Trust for Scotland (BMT310B).

25. "Querulous" comes from a letter of Burns's, quoted in Steve Newman, *Ballad Collection, Lyric, and the Canon* (Philadelphia: University of Pennsylvania Press, 2007), 86.

26. Newman, *Ballad Collection,* 95.

27. Stafford, *Starting Lines in Scottish, English, and Irish Poetry: From Burns to Heaney* (Oxford: Oxford University Press, 2000), 76–77.

28. Swidzinski, "Lyric Abstraction," 181.

29. See Luys de Narváez, *Los seys libros del delphín* (Valladolid, 1538) and Alonso Mudarra, *Tres libros de musica en cifra para vihuela* (Sevilla, 1546); the latter is the first to use the term "romanesca" (f. 24).

30. The "Greensleeves" tune first began to appear in undated, late sixteenth-century lute manuscripts: William Ballet's MS Lute Book, p. 104; Folger Ms 1610.1, f. 5; BL MS Add. 31392, f. 29 ("maister Cuttinge"); Cambridge University Library MSS Dd.3.18, f. 8v (lute) and Dd.4.23, f. 25 (cittern); and *Het Luitboek van Thysius* (Bibliotheca Thysiana), no. 70. The tune provided in the Ballet Lute book is the now standard version. For detailed information concerning its musical structure and transmission, see John M. Ward, "And Who but Ladie Greensleeves?" in *The Well Enchanting Skill,* ed. John Caldwell, Edward Olleson, and Susan Wollenberg (Oxford: Oxford University Press, 1990): 181–211.

31. Claude Simpson notes that by the turn of the seventeenth century, green sleeves had become a metaphor for a prostitute, which fits with the contemporary slang phrase, "green gown," that implies that the grass stains on a woman's dress stem from an outdoor sexual encounter. See Simpson, *The British Broadside Ballad and its Music* (New Brunswick: Rutgers University Press, 1966), 271.

32. "Donkyn" is an alternate spelling for the Scottish clan name Duncan.

33. "Lorne" is a region in Scotland that had a lord in the fifteenth century, although the story seems to be derived from *Roswall and Lillian*, a medieval Scottish romance about an exiled prince. See Laura Hibberd, *Medieval Romance in England* (New York: Burt Franklin, 1963), 290–91.

34. No known printed edition; the manuscript version is NYP Drexel, Ms. 4257, no. 121.

35. Ballad 11 is incomplete, but mentions pride, the wantonness of women, and religious issues. Ballad 12 is about the English Catholics who aided the Spanish prior to the planned invasion of 1588 (the "Spanish Armada"). For the latter, see "A warning to all false Traitors by example of 14. / Wherof vi. were executed in diuers places neere about / London, and 2. neere Braintford the 28. day of August, 1588. Also at Tyborne / were executed the 30. day vj. namely 5. Men and one Woman"; *https://ebba.english.ucsb.edu/ballad/34359/citation*.

36. Shakespeare, *Mr. William Shakespeares Comedies, Histories, & Tragedies* (London, 1623), 44.

37. The translation of psalms was contentious throughout the early modern period. However, Psalm 100 was always a text of joyful praise. Shakespeare would have had access to the Geneva Bible: "Sing ye loud unto the Lord, all the earth," or different versions of the Sternhold and Hopkins *Book of Psalms*: in John Hopkins's rendering, "In God the Lord be glad and light, / Praise him throughout the earth," and in William Kethe's translation, "All people that on earth do dwell, / Sing to the Lord with cheerful voice."

38. Raylor, *Cavaliers, Clubs, and Literary Culture: Sir John Mennes, James Smith, and the Order of the Fancy* (Newark: University of Delaware Press, 1994), 100, 219.

39. *A Merry New Ballad, both Pleasant and Sweete, in Praise of the Black-Smith, which is very Meete to the Tune of Greene Sleeves, &c* (London, 1635).

40. It was not until the Restoration that this refrain was attached to the completely different tune that we know today as "For he's a jolly good fellow."

41. For an account of the full contents and history of this volume, see H. F. Brooks, "Rump Songs: An Index with Notes," *Oxford Bibliographical Society Proceedings & Papers*, vol. 5 (1936–1939), 283–304.

42. Allan Ramsay, *The Tea-Table Miscellany* (Edinburgh, 1724), 78.

43. During the Commonwealth and into the later portion of the seventeenth century, several highwaymen, including Phillip Stafford and James Hind, used their "dying speeches" to promote royalist agendas denouncing what they saw as an unjust government. This political and non-confessional style also characterizes the repertory of hangman's songs or "last goodnights." See Erin Mackie, *Rakes, Highwaymen, and Pirates* (Baltimore: John Hopkins University Press, 2009), 77–84.

44. Gay, *The Beggar's Opera*, 2nd ed. (London, 1728), 72.

45. *Boswell's Life of Johnson*, ed. George Birkbeck, 6 vols. (New York, 1891), 5:296.

46. For the singing during the flight to Skye, see Ernest George Macdonald, *The White Cockade: The Lives and Adventures of James Francis Edward Stuart and His Sons "Bonnie Prince Charlie" and Cardinal York* (London: Hutchinson & Co., 1949), 234; and Compton Mackenzie, *Prince Charlie and His Ladies* (London: Cassell, 1934), 157–58.

47. Percy, *Reliques of Ancient English Poetry*, ed. Henry B. Wheatley, 3 vols. (London, 1885), 2:131.

48. See Simpson, *British Broadside Ballad*, 268–78.

49. *Songs from David Herd's Manuscripts,* ed. Hans Hecht (Edinburgh: William J. Hay, 1904), 177.

50. The second verse reads: "Hey ho! and about she goes, / She's milk in her breasts, she's none in her toes, / She's a hole in her a---, you may put in your nose, / Sing: hey, boys, up go we!" The "Hey, boys, up go we" refrain was used repeatedly during the second half of the seventeenth century in England with bawdy lyrics that referenced cavalier or royalist perspectives as a challenge to the Puritanical sentiments associated with the Interregnum.

51. There are two holograph copies of Burns's version: the Alloway manuscript, currently in the Burns papers at the National Trust of Scotland (BMT310B, 618), and the Huntington Library manuscript (MssHM13046).

52. *Greysteil* was a medieval poem popular in sixteenth-century Scotland, set to music. See "David Herd," *The Burns Encyclopedia, http://www.robertburns.org/encyclopedia/HerdDavid17321511810.444.shtml.*

53. See Kate Lister, "Spotted Dick: Pudding's Historical links to Genitals," *https://inews.co.uk/light-relief/offbeat/surprisingly-rude-history-pudding-98363.* She notes that "so naughty are puddings that the puritans banned them, along with 'spice cakes, buns, biscuits, or other spice bread' in 1592, declaring Christmas puddings 'lewd,' and 'unfit for God-fearing people.'"

54. Although the thorn has a lovely flower, its use here may also be a literary reference to *Greysteil*, as a covert acknowledgement of Burns's use of Herd's text. In *Greysteil,* there is a central character known as the Lady of the White Thorn tree.

55. *Oxford SMM,* 2:32.

56. "Jack Hall" is sometimes conflated with "Samuel Hall" or "Sam Hall" as part of the same tune family. The main catalog for English traditional songs is the Roud Index, housed in the Vaughan William Memorial Library. "Jack Hall" is Roud #369.

57. See Bronson, *The Ballad as Song* (Berkeley: University of California Press, 1969), 31.

58. See Robert Kinsey, "In Search of Captain Kidd's Lost Treasure," *https://www.amdigital.co.uk/about/blog/item/captain-kidds-lost-treasure.*

59. See Robert C. Ritchie, *Captain Kidd and the War against the Pirates* (Cambridge: Harvard University Press, 1986), 193–95.

60. "Captain Kid's Farewel to the Sea, or the Famous Pirate's Lamentation" (1701?). NLS Crawford.EB.843.

61. This calls into question Ritchie's idea that the Captain Kidd songs were "essentially penitential hymns in which Kidd expressed regret for his evil ways"; see Ritchie, *Captain Kidd,* 237.

62. See Una McIlvenna, "When the News was Sung: Ballads as News Media in Early Modern Europe," *Media History* 22, no. 3–4 (2016): 317.

63. See Ritchie, *Captain Kidd,* 237.

64. Gladfelder, *Criminality and Narrative in Eighteenth-Century England: Beyond the Law* (Baltimore: Johns Hopkins University Press, 2001), 25.

65. Gladfelder discusses the uses and abuses of the myth of Queen Scotia and her husband: namely, that the peoples of both Scotland and Ireland were descended from a stray Egyptian tribe that was exiled from Egypt at the time of Moses and supposedly made its way up to Scotland. This myth was used in eighteenth-century England as means of establishing racial difference by linking Scottish (and Irish) people to Africans. See Gladfelder, *Criminality and Narrative*, 24.

66. "The Dying Words of Captain Robert Kidd" (Boston, c. 1810-14).

67. Captain (William) Kidd was occasionally called Robert Kidd. For example, the letter of marque from the crown that Kidd could not produce at the time of his trial lists him as "Robert." See *https://piratedocuments.com/captain-kidd-1695/*.

68. William Chappell, *Popular Music of Olden Time*, 2 vols. (London, 1855–59), 2:678–79.

69. This connection is commented upon by more than one ballad scholar: Willard Hallam Bonner, "The Ballad of Captain Kidd," *American Literature* 15, no. 4 (1944): 374; and Bronson, *Ballad as Song,* 25–27.

70. "An Excellent new Song on the Jacobites, and the Opression of the Rebels. To the Tune of, Captain Kid," in *The Battle of Falkirk Garland* (1746).

71. *SMM,* 4:383.

72. Murray Pittock, *The Invention of Scotland: The Stuart Myth and Scottish Identity, 1638 to the Present* (Abingdon: Routledge, 1991), 82.

73. Pittock, *Invention of Scotland*, 82.

74. Pittock, "Who Wrote *The Scots Musical Museum*," 11.

75. Pittock, *Invention of Scotland*, 80.

76. Letter from Burns to Johnson, 4 July 1796, in Cromek, *Reliques of Robert Burns*, 184–85.

Animal Domestication and Human-Animal Difference in Buffon's *Histoire Naturelle*

DARIO GALVÃO

One of the first texts of Georges Louis Leclerc, comte de Buffon's *Histoire Naturelle, génerale et particulière*, is the "Initial Discourse" (1749), in which he presents the method one should employ when studying nature. Buffon claims that the first truth one is forced to acknowledge when undertaking a serious study of Natural History is one that is probably humiliating to mankind: that man ought to place himself within the class of animals.[1] In the same text, we also learn that classifications are the fruit of human imagination and science, and so do not belong to nature itself. In other words, when distinguishing classes or species, the result is "more of an order appropriate to our *own* nature than one pertaining to the existence of the things which we are considering."[2] Nature is continuous; we are the ones who introduce discontinuity. In general terms, we see here a nominalist critique of the zoological and botanical classifications proposed by naturalists such as John Ray, Carl von Linné (aka Carl Linnaeus), and Joseph Pitton de Tournefort.[3]

When we consider the *Histoire Naturelle* as a whole, however, we must admit that the presumed humiliation more often seems to work to the disadvantage of animals. A clue to this may be found by reflecting on Linnaeus's *Systema Naturae* published in 1735—almost fifteen years before

Buffon's work began to appear. Here, human beings are placed together with the primates, and thus for the first time in the same class; by contrast, in his long section on quadrupeds, Buffon treats primates last, after all the other animals, and they appear only in the fourteenth and fifteenth volumes of the work, published in 1766 and 1767.[4] The reason for this may be found in his method, as presented in the "Initial Discourse": while all classifications are relative to our own nature, from the perspective of nature itself they are all, ultimately, arbitrary; in that case, if we need to establish an order, we should choose the one that best suits our own purposes. Therefore, Buffon proposes an order that is more natural and comfortable to us: that is, going from what is more interesting—because of its close relation to us—to what is more distant and less useful to our lives.

The obvious consequence is that the human being, to a large extent, is placed at the center of nature. Without losing sight of the philosophical sophistication of Buffon's method, which is intimately related to the great influence of Newtonianism in eighteenth-century France, we may nevertheless perceive a certain moral evaluation standing behind it.[5] There is a "grading of dignity," some would say (most notably, Jacques Roger, one of the leading experts on Buffon's work), wherein humans get the first and highest place, and the nobility of every other species depends upon its proximity, or rather utility, to humankind.[6] As Roger writes, "nature is only worthy of human attention insofar as she is useful to man."[7] Commenting on this grading, Thierry Hoquet draws attention to its underlying epistemological character: priority is given to the more familiar species.[8] In every case, it is human beings who take the first place. After humans come the domestic animals, and after those, the wild animals. According to Buffon, for instance, insects do not deserve as much attention as they are given by some entomologists, among which the most famous is René-Antoine Ferchault de Réaumur, who had published the six volumes of *Mémoires pour servir à l'histoire des insectes* (1734–42). The quarrel between these two naturalists is well known. Among his several attacks, Buffon writes that a bee should not take up more space in the mind of a naturalist than it takes in nature itself.[9]

Indeed, the reader quickly enough manages to overcome the risk posed by this presumed humiliation of human beings. In the volumes of the *Histoire Naturelle* published between 1749 and 1753, we find at least two important texts in which we see a strong distinction drawn between humans and animals. In the four volumes published in 1749, in addition to the "Initial Discourse," we have some texts from a more general point of view, such as the "Natural History of Animals," in which Buffon distinguishes animals from plants and describes their nutrition, generation, and development, the "Formation of Planets," and, finally, the "Natural History of Man," this being the first text specifically focused on a particular species. In the latter text, Buffon argues that the human being has an "entirely different nature," distinguished from and superior to animals, and that "of himself he forms a distinct class."[10]

It is easy to see traces of Cartesian dualism in this text, something that becomes even more evident in "Of the Nature of Animals" (1753), where Buffon develops a theory that seems, at first glance, to be a new version of René Descartes's notion of the animal-machine. In general terms, the distance between human and animal is seen as infinite, because while humans are "duplex" (Buffon employs the term *homo duplex*)—both spiritual and material—animals are strictly material.[11] As in Descartes, the spiritual principle is associated with the capacity for thinking and language.[12] From this perspective, the behavior of animals is understood as the immediate result of their physical organization; they are natural automatons or machines.

With this in mind, scholars of Buffon have rightly pointed out that, in his *Histoire Naturelle*, language and thought are the two elements that distinguish human beings from animals. For example, whereas François Dagognet, José Martinez-Contreras and Francine Markovitz refer to the Cartesian traits in Buffon's thought, Julia Douthwaite attributes to him the "Aristotelian premise that the essence of man resides in his rational mind and not in such 'accidental' properties as the forms of his body."[13] Furthermore, Hoquet explains how all of the virtues, passions, and understandings of animals in Buffon's *Histoire Naturelle* are strictly material, in the sense that they result from physiological processes. As Hoquet puts it: "natural history moves away from the didactic functions of the bestiary to become a physical theory of the functions of organized beings" (Avi Lifschitz opposes this idea, at least as far as concerns the elephant).[14]

I would like to shed light on a specific aspect of the ways in which language and thought express the human–animal difference that has not yet received its due attention. Considering Buffon's works within a general framework of natural history, rather than metaphysics, I would like to highlight the link between the above-mentioned difference and a phenomenon that he observes as a naturalist: the historical subjugation of animals by human beings. Although our focus will be on domestication, Buffon's writings on wild animals can help us understand that subjugation: as we will see, wild animals, just like the domestic, are victims of the same human ascendency. Recasting the terms under discussion (previously considered to fall within the realms of philosophy and theology), Buffon establishes the difference between humans and animals from the perspective of natural history: one species rises by dominating others, or rather at the expense of others. This seems to be the real sense of what Buffon refers to as the primacy of thought over matter.

> It is by the *right of conquest*, however, that he [i.e., a human being] reigns, for he rather enjoys than possesses, and it is by constant and perpetual activity and vigilance that he preserves his advantage, for if those are neglected everything languishes, changes, and returns to the absolute dominion of Nature. She resumes her power, destroys the operations of man, envelops with moss and dust his most pompous monuments, and in the progress of time entirely effaces them, leaving man to regret having lost by his negligence what his ancestors had acquired by their industry.[15]

Such considerations allow us to situate Buffon's thinking in relation to his contemporaries. By defining this separation between humans and animals, Buffon attempts to refute other views that equate human beings and animals, such as in the most influential empiricist doctrines, especially those of David Hume and Etienne Bonnot de Condillac. However, this does not mean that Buffon takes the opposite stance of affirming the traditional view of the animal-machine. The ascension of human beings in the *Histoire Naturelle* is not based on a refutation of animal rationality, but rather on the superiority of human rationality compared to animal rationality (a superiority that is not just a matter of degree, as the aforementioned empiricist doctrines claim).

The so-called French materialists, such as Julien Offray de La Mettrie or Denis Diderot, do not hesitate to endow animals with thought; indeed, it would seem rather necessary for them to do so, since their aim is to affirm the unity of both substances in opposition to Cartesian dualism. Matter and spirit, then, are conceived to be of one and the same nature in such a way that thought cannot be conceived independently of the body; on the contrary, it is rooted in the organic configuration. Not even the fiercest opponent to the proximity of or analogy between human and animal denied their bodily resemblances; hence, for the materialists, since thought is rooted in the body, there is no reason to refuse it to animals—they too have a body—or to deny the evidence of experience. La Mettrie, for example, in his *L'Homme machine* (1747), treats human–animal difference regarding thought as a matter of their respective complexity, much like the higher or lower level of complexity we supposedly find in animal bodies.[16] From this perspective, the human condition no longer rests on a difference in kind, but rather in degree. This change in perspective can also be seen in Diderot, who at points treats the human condition as the result of a particular organization of the senses: in humans, there is an equality of the senses (touch, smell, vision, etc.) in such a way that any of them may prevail over the others, and, as a result, understanding (the "organ of reason") may prevail.[17] Whether we consider Diderot's vitalist and cosmological perspective, or La Mettrie's mechanical and medical view, the habit of separating humans from animals via a Cartesian perspective was deeply questioned in the mid-eighteenth century.[18]

There was no need to be committed to the materialist thesis in order to accord thought to animals. Philosophers such as Hume and Condillac engaged in promoting what we could call a positive psychology devoted to investigating the operations of ideas and passions do not hesitate to affirm that there is a strong analogy between humans and animals. According to them, the analogy must be extended from their resemblances of body to their resemblances of mind. In his *Treatise of Human Nature* (1739–40), Hume includes sections on the reason and passions of animals. Here we find passages about dogs, horses, swans, and turkeys, among others. For example, Hume considers an old greyhound that draws inferences of cause and effect and a peacock that entertains a high idea of himself—and contempt for all others—since he is conscious of his uncommon beauty.[19] In 1755, Condillac wrote his *Traité des animaux* to reject Buffon's automatism as developed in "Of the Nature of Animals." Condillac, like Hume, thinks that animal behavior must be explained through the same principles as human behavior; both are based on experimental reasoning—knowledge acquired from experience through habit—taken as a fundamental principle of the mind. Another prominent eighteenth-century figure who addressed the animal problem is Jean-Jacques Rousseau, who shifts the uniqueness of humans from their capacity for thought to their capacity for perfectibility and liberty.[20]

In order to understand the importance of Buffon's intervention in eighteenth-century thinking about human–animal difference, the Cartesian aspects of his thought—notably the spirit–matter duality—must be set in their proper place, and that is where domestication comes in. The metaphysical and theological perspectives in Buffon must be approached through their association with another, *naturalistic* perspective, one that is more suitable to the *Histoire Naturelle*'s empiricism. That is where Buffon's contribution to the debate about human–animal difference resides.

Here is a brief overview of our next steps: first, we will consider domestication in order to see how it is related to an idea of the human conquest of nature, referring not only to domestic animals but also to wild ones. Second, we will examine some of Buffon's thoughts regarding animal intelligence in order to develop an account of the human-animal difference that emerges from his perspective on domestication.

Animal Domestication and the Conquest of Nature

In Buffon's view, few phenomena express the separation between human and animal as clearly as domestication. Through domestication, the animal itself becomes a product of human thought. Similar to the human species' use of fire and clothing, a domestic animal is a new "thing" that is manufactured and enhanced by human rationality. Its nature is altered; it is forced away from what is natural to its species in order to conform to its master's way of life. In this regard, Hoquet notes that "man is everywhere a monster to himself, while domestic animals are others of man's monsters, produced by him, ... showing the power of man as the principal catalyst of change."[21] According to Buffon,

> Man can, therefore, not only make every individual in the universe useful to his wants, but, with the aid of time, change, modify, and improve their species; and this is the greatest power he has over Nature. To have transformed a barren herb into wheat is a kind of creation, on which, however, he has no reason to pride himself, since it is only by the sweat of his brow, and reiterated culture, that he is enabled to obtain from the bosom of the earth this, and sometimes bitter, subsistence.[22]

There are species that are by nature more prone than others to this type of alteration. The cat, for example, is *demie domestique*: although cats live in our homes, we "cannot say that they are ... entirely domestic animals."[23] Resistance to domestication can be seen as the absence of a certain type of intelligence on the part of domestic animals. Whereas Buffon finds in wild animals an intelligence that is characteristic of the animal in nature—and that operates in balance with nature—he finds that domestic animals have an intelligence that favors their ability to communicate with their master, molding their behavior according to what their master expects from them.

In Buffon's texts, domestication is at once a degeneration and an ennoblement of the animal. From a human perspective, the dog, for example, elevates himself over other animals through an uncommon capacity for learning and developing under our standards—his genius is "borrowed," writes Buffon.[24] No wonder dogs are our most valuable ally in nature: without them, he states, we would never have dominated other animals as we did.[25] However, from the perspective of nature, this perfectibility is rather a degeneration and this too is an important element of Buffon's conception of animal nature.[26] Concerning the domestic pigeon, he writes, this bird's "slave races" are "all the more perfect to us as they are more degenerated, more flawed to Nature."[27]

Human influence seems to be found where least expected. Buffon observes, for instance, that dogs' barking is for the most part the fruit of perfectibility, given that it is less frequent in wild dogs.[28] And, like barking, Buffon considers that even sexual desire, "that appetite which Nature has ... most deeply implanted in the animal frame," has been changed because of domesticity: "domestic quadrupeds and birds are almost constantly in season, while those which roam in perfect freedom are only at certain stated times stimulated by the ardour of passion."[29] The natural thus gives way to qualities that are acquired through an animal's relationship with humans, and these qualities are rarely devoid of the domination intrinsic to this relationship. It is from this perspective that we may think of the dog's outstanding fidelity towards its master and his close relations:

> More docile and tractable than any other animal, the dog is not only instructed in a very short time, but he even conforms himself to the manners, motions, and habits, of those who command him. He assumes all the modes of the family in which he lives. … When the care of a house is committed to him during the night he becomes more bold, and sometimes perfectly ferocious; he watches, goes his rounds, scents strangers at a distance, and if they stop, or attempt to break in, he flies to oppose them, and by reiterated barking, and other efforts of passion, he gives the alarm to the family. He is equally furious against thieves as rapacious animals; he attacks, wounds, and forces from them what they were endeavouring to take away; but contented with having conquered, he will lie down upon the spoil, nor even touch it to satisfy his appetite; giving at once an example of courage, temperance, and fidelity.[30]

The dog behaves exactly as it must in order to attend to the needs of the family. Like a little soldier, he is in charge of the house, knowing quite clearly who to attack and to whom to give passage. His disposition to conform himself to human habits unfolds as a disposition to acquire qualities that better allow him to serve humans. Buffon is far from ignoring, however, the advantages that dogs themselves draw from their submission: "faithful to man, [the dog] will always preserve a portion of his empire, and a degree of superiority over other animals; he reigns at the head of a flock, and makes himself better understood than the voice of the shepherd."[31]

In the matter of fidelity and servility, horses are not left behind. They are very favorably placed in Buffon's "grading of dignity," coming first in his chapter on domestic animals as the noblest conquest of human creatures.[32] With humans, for example, they share the exhaustion and pleasures of war, while their disposition to servility seems equivalent to or even stronger than that in dogs: "The horse is a creature which renounces his very being for the service of man, whose will he even knows how to anticipate, and execute by the promptitude of his movements: he gives himself up without reserve, refuses nothing, exerts himself beyond his strength, and often dies sooner than disobey."[33] The metaphysical distinction between human and animal is here transposed into a naturalistic version. There is a capacity for using the other to serve yourself that, in Buffon's work, is considered peculiar to humans. Yes, he writes, stronger animals "devour the weaker, but this action implies no more than an urgent necessity, or a rage of appetite; qualities very different from that which produces a series of actions, all tending to the same end."[34] Only humans were capable of subjugating [*prendre empire sur*] others and obliging "them to furnish their food, to watch over them, and to attend them when sick or wounded."[35]

As we have seen, Buffon does not hesitate to use the term *empire* to describe human superiority over animals. The human being appears as the conqueror in a war against nature: while domestic animals are akin to the spoils of victory, wild ones are scattered among remote, small portions of land. The extreme precarity of wild animals was already a subject of Natural History in this period. Buffon considers it to be humanity's fault: because of humanity, wild animals are much wilder than they would be if we weren't here.[36] We are dangerous to them in that the more we increase our dominion on the surface of Earth, the less peace they have and, consequently, the less developed become their faculties, talents, and intelligence:

> In countries, on the contrary, over which man is diffused, all society is lost among animals, all industry ceases, and every art is suppressed; they relinquish the occupation of building, and neglect every accommodation; always pressed by fear and necessity, their only study is to live, and their only employment flight and concealment; and if, as may reasonably be supposed, the whole surface of the earth should, in process of time, be equally inhabited by the human species, in a few centuries the history of a beaver would be considered as a fable.[37]

From this passage, we are led to think that our views on wild animals must take into account human domination just as much as our ideas regarding domestic animals do. Once again, human influence over animals is found where least expected. The weight of this influence seems to be felt in every aspect of wild life, which is reduced to the satisfaction of the most basic needs, such as providing food and keeping safe from danger. From this perspective, the renowned works of beavers appear as the last ruins of an ancient animal intelligence—doomed to disappear—dating from a time when humans were not omnipresent and destroying every other species' society, industry, art, etc.[38]

In the beginning of the chapter "Of Carnivorous Animals" (1758), Buffon makes a statement that today we would find hard to deny: that humans are, of all species, the most destructive. There is no other species that kills more living beings than us, says Buffon—writing in a period that we would see as a green paradise in comparison to today. Perhaps, besides the augmentation of the human population, he had in mind hunting, a structural practice of the aristocracy that could kill hundreds of animals in one single day.[39] One must not, however, conclude that Buffon proposed a general critique of hunting. In his article on "The Stag" (1756), Buffon praises the *vénérie*, probably the most important hunting tradition of the time in France. He was not opposed to the practice—unlike others such as Friedrich Melchior, Frieherr von Grimm, who condemned every hunt that did not have, as its end, the "feeding of man or even the pleasures of the table," asserting that otherwise hunting would be, "under the wise man's eyes," no more than "the shameful and reprehensible occupation of a fool, a hundred times more savage than the animal he chases."[40] To make hunting possible, an effective system of animal management was enacted between different estates (*domaines*), avoiding the eradication of animals where hunting was practiced; as a result, nature could seem endless.[41] In this sense, Buffon's conclusion about humanity's destructive power seems less pertinent to our own era: according to him, we are so destructive that "we should exhaust Nature if she were not exhaustless, and by a fertility superior to our depredations, renovate the destruction we continually make":

> The faculties and talents of animals, therefore, instead of increasing are constantly diminishing, for time may be said to oppose them. The more the human species are multiplied and improved the more the wild animals become subjected to the dominion of an absolute tyrant, who will hardly permit their individual existence, deprives them of liberty, of every avenue to society, and destroys the very root of their intelligence. What they are become, or what they may become, is an inadequate indication of what they may have been or might be. Who can say, if the human species were annihilated, to which of the animals would the sceptre of the earth belong?[42]

Repressed, sterilized, almost completely destroyed, animal intelligence is thus pushed to the brink of automatism. If there truly is automatism in Buffon, one cannot fail to distinguish it from that of the traditional notion. In Buffon, the separation is radical, but it is also contingent, since there is no obstacle preventing things from having happened otherwise. For instance, another animal could have developed a capacity to stand up and overcome humans, which would put us in a very uncomfortable position—perhaps we too would be reduced to a quasi-mechanical life. This is to say that, ultimately, neither human progress nor animal sterility can be taken as ontological attributes.

This point has important consequences for how we understand the limits of animal intelligence in Buffon's writings: if there were no oppression on the part of humans, what would become of these limits?

Together with the radical separation between human and animal, Buffon also identifies a form of rationality in animals. This encourages us to understand his account of the separation from the perspective of his views about the struggle for sovereignty in nature, rather than any metaphysical-theological premises. In other words, for Buffon, the deprecation of animal intelligence is not to be explained in terms of animals' exclusion from a metaphysical and spiritual principle, but rather by their defeat and their consequent inability to evolve, due to being terrorized by the human empire. This, therefore, is how one can understand the subordination of matter to thought: due to the harsh circumstances in which animals are forced to exist, their intelligence is reduced to the mere satisfaction of needs, to the point that their movements can be explained as mere mechanical adjustments.

However, even in these harsh circumstances, several signs of their (repressed) intelligence may be recognized. Looking at these signs should help us better understand what Buffon is claiming through his account of human–animal difference as being brought about by domestication.

Animal Intelligence

Buffon recognizes the intelligence behind animal behavior, both domesticated and wild. His article on "The Elephant" (1764), for instance, is remarkable: after considering several narratives from different sources, such as ancient philosophers and modern travelers, and putting aside those that he could not trust, he praises this animal's intelligence above all other animals.[43] In contrast to the Cartesian strands of his thought, Buffon writes that the elephant "seems to reflect, to think, and to deliberate, and never acts till he has examined and observed several times, without passion or precipitation, the signs which he is to obey."[44] Buffon relates the elephant's extraordinary intelligence to the existence of its trunk, which he considers to be probably the most complete and most admirable production of nature. Having "the hand in his nose," the elephant unites different senses such as feeling and smelling, as well as the facility of movement and the power to move heavy objects, with the power of the suction of his lungs.[45]

"The Beaver" (1760) is another article worth reading for those interested in Buffon's views on animal intelligence. He insists that individual beavers come together in society by means of "a kind of a choice" and not mere necessity, which is also true for the formation of a beaver couple.[46] Given that their union is not a forced one, Buffon considers that it supposes "at least a general concurrence and common views" among different members of the species.[47] Nor must we forget the complexity of their works, in which we see an effective division of labor.[48] The extraordinary behavior observed in this animal leads Buffon to reflect, in the extract quoted earlier, that if "the whole surface of the earth should, in the process of time, be equally inhabited by the human species, in a few centuries the history of a beaver would be considered as a fable."[49]

Some would take Buffon's work to be a precursor of ethology.[50] Although most of his own observations are restricted to domestic animals, whether at the *Jardin des Plantes* in Paris or on his own property in Montbard, Buffon's accounts of wild animals are well done and based upon a rigorous systematization of the knowledge available to him. We can see the correspondence between Buffon and contemporary ethology, for example, in some of Georges Canguilhem's writings, such as "Le vivant et son milieu."[51] R. W. Burkhardt, Jr. for his part, relates Buffon to the contemporary ethologists Konrad Lorenz and Charles Otis Whitman under the perspective of their writings on domestication (remarking, for instance, on the supposed promiscuity of domesticated quadrupeds and birds).[52]

Throughout the *Histoire Naturelle,* we see the unfolding of a vast investigation that connects intelligence, the structure of the senses, and the natural environment of each species. We can find affinities with French materialists such as Diderot and La Mettrie, as well as with the sensualism of Condillac. From this perspective, his *Histoire Naturelle* contributes to the central epistemological problems of its century. For example, Buffon relates the exquisite sense of sight in birds to the organic structure of their eyes, which is also related to the acquisition of extraordinarily accurate ideas concerning movement.

> The idea of motion and all the other ideas which accompany or flow from it, such as those of relative velocities, of the extent of country, of the proportional height of eminences, and of the various inequalities that prevail on the surface, are, therefore, more precise in birds, and occupy a larger share of their conceptions than in quadrupeds. Nature would seem to have pointed out this superiority of vision by the more conspicuous and more elaborate structure of its organ; for in birds the eye is larger in proportion to the bulk of the head than in quadrupeds; it is also more delicate and more finely fashioned, and the impressions which it receives must excite more vivid ideas.[53]

Buffon thinks that only birds, among all of the animals, move in such a way that movement seems more natural to them than repose.[54] Without their excellent vision, they would never be able to move with the speed, the continuity, and the duration we observe: "Indeed, we may consider the celerity with which an animal moves, as the just indication of the perfection of its vision."[55] According to him, all the speed they achieve—thanks to their agility and vast muscular strength—would be absolutely useless if they were born short-sighted: "the danger of dashing against every intervening obstacle would have repressed or extinguished their ardour."[56]

Humans, too, are frequently divested of their metaphysical greatness in Buffon's work in order to be examined through the frame of their organic conformation. Within a sensualist perspective, knowledge is related to the sensorial configuration, which emerges as a key feature for defining human–animal difference.

> The predominating sensations will also follow the same order: man will be most affected by touch; the quadruped by smell; and the birds by sight. These will likewise give a cast to the general character, since certain motives of action will acquire peculiar force, and gain the ascendency. Thus, man will be more thoughtful and profound, as the sense of touch would appear to be more calm and intimate; the quadrupeds will have more vehement appetites; and the birds will have emotions as extensive and volatile as is the glance of sight.[57]

In this passage, although humans differ from animals in terms of the relation of knowledge to sentiment, the difference is not absolute, since it is not associated with a metaphysical attribute presumed to be exclusive to humankind. Rather, the distinction turns on the predominance of specific senses: touch for humans, and smell for animals. But humans are also provided with a sense of smell, and animals with a sense of touch—making the distinction one of degree, not kind. This may explain why Buffon affirms, in the extract, that animals have *less* judgment than sentiment, thereby avoiding a complete denial of judgment to animals.

Yet despite Buffon's sensualist affinities, we can also discern a persisting separation between humans and animals that seems to be just as strong as his Cartesian dualism itself.[58] Although, as the *Histoire Naturelle* goes on, the philosophical and metaphysical perspectives give way to the naturalistic, and the reader is constantly reminded of the separation established in the first volumes of the series. Here animals do not have memory, but only a species of memory; they do not have choice, but only a species of choice; not intelligence, but glimpses of intelligence; not imagination, but another form of imagination, and so on.[59] By this perspective, the analogy between human and animal perhaps "seems well founded"—but it is not.[60] Even if their actions are very similar, we cannot ignore the fact that the principles that cause those actions are different. Animal actions are determined by sentiment (a mechanist perspective), while human actions are determined by sentiment and spirit.[61] There are several suggestions that this distinction never disappears entirely, even with the prevalence of the naturalistic perspective: one of these concerns the intelligence of the elephant, whose extraordinary capacity is explained to be the result of a "material" combination of the information derived from the senses, here seen as equivalent to the combination that in humans is effected by reflection.

> They [elephants], therefore, with the same member, and by one simultaneous act, feel, perceive, and judge of diverse things at once. His multiplied sensations are equivalent to reflection; and though this animal is, like others, incapable of thinking, as his sensations are combined in the same organ, are coeval and undivided, it is not surprising that he has ideas of his own, and that he acquires in a little time those we inculcate to him.[62]

Sentiment *versus* idea: the human–animal difference thus persists, despite the connection between intelligence and the senses. One must note, though, that the borders seem less fixed. In the following extract, we see the distinction between sentiment and knowledge associated with the notion of "prevailing" sensations, which may suggest a difference of degree and not kind: "In man, where everything should be judgement and reason, the sense of touch is more exquisite than in animal, where there is less judgment than sentiment; in these, on the contrary, smell is more perfect than in man: for touch is the foundation of knowledge, and smell is only the source of sentiment."[63]

Since the uniqueness of human nature is located in the capacity of thinking, every perspective that endows animals with thought or intelligence could threaten that uniqueness. No wonder Descartes is constrained to argue against animal thought. Under this perspective, the *homo duplex* and the animal-machine emerge as two sides of the same coin, as Paul-Laurent Assoun points out in his introduction to La Mettrie's *L'homme machine*.[64] Descartes considers "the belief in animal thought" to be "the strongest of all our infantile prejudices."[65] This mistake takes place, according to Descartes, because the resemblance in external figure and movement leads us to believe that they have a soul similar to ours. This "prejudice" makes us lose sight of the fact that their movements derive from an exclusively material principle, that is, the animal spirits.[66] We should instead understand that this infantile habit must be dissolved and replaced by the cultivation of a different habit: that of conceiving of animals as analogous to automata.[67] If the human spiritual principle existed in animals, Descartes thought, we would be forced to endow even oysters or sponges with a soul, which would be absurd.[68]

It has been suggested that the traces of Cartesianism in the *Histoire Naturelle*, as well as the theological aspects to be found in that work, should be considered as evidence of Buffon's caution with regards to the censors at the Faculty of Theology of the Sorbonne.[69] Holding an eminent place in the royal court, that of director of the *Jardin du Roi* (today, the *Jardin des Plantes*), which carried considerable scientific status with it, Buffon had a lot to lose from persecution like that suffered by several of the so-called *philosophes*, such as Diderot, Rousseau, and, later, Helvétius. The condemnation of Helvétius's *De L'Esprit* in 1758 resulted in the deposition of the royal censor, Jean Pierre Tercier, and the demand for a retraction from Helvétius himself. Buffon was also obliged to make a retraction on more than one occasion, the first with his "Of the Nature of Animals" in 1753. We must remember, however, that not all specialists on Buffon agree with this explanation.[70]

Irrespective of the reason for the Cartesian traces, the fact remains that the naturalistic perspective itself offers a radical separation between human and animal and, precisely because of this, may still be in harmony with the Cartesian perspective. Buffon engages in a deep exploration of animal intelligence, and his resistance to extending the human–animal analogy from the body to the mind cannot be considered a mere façade. In view of this, we should perhaps ask ourselves how independent these two perspectives on the definition of humanity really are—i.e., the one based on the acknowledgment of domination, and the other founded in metaphysics. Might we think, in a certain Nietzschean vein, that these two dimensions are in fact intimately related to one another? In this perspective, if animality arises as the necessary other of humanity, then metaphysical superiority would arise as the necessary other in a relation of power. Thus we should not be surprised to find metaphysical terms mixed in with the naturalistic point of view: concerning the human empire, Buffon writes that it is an empire of spirit over matter.[71] Where classifications or the establishment of borders are concerned, science looks less impartial and more political than one might initially think.

Notes

I would like to thank São Paulo Research Foundation (FAPESP) for support in researching and drafting this paper (grant #2018/03829-0). I am also grateful to the editors and anonymous reviewers at *Studies in Eighteenth-Century Culture* for their careful reading and thoughtful suggestions. A shorter version of this paper was presented to the Animal History Group (King's College London) in 2020, which contributed to the development of some of the ideas here presented.

1. Buffon, "Initial Discourse: On the Manner of Studying and Writing about Natural History," in John Lyon, "The 'Initial Discourse' to Buffon's *Histoire Naturelle*," *Journal of the History of Biology* 9, no. 1 (1976): 133–81, 150; Buffon, *Histoire Naturelle, générale et particulière*, 36 vols. (Paris: Imprimerie royale, 1749–89), 1:12, hereafter cited as *HN*. The "Initial Discourse" was not included in the first English translations of Buffon's *Histoire Naturelle*. Phillip Sloan suggested to Lyon that the exclusion was due to Buffon's attack on Carl von Linné (Lyon, "The 'Initial Discourse,'" 134).

2. Buffon, "Initial Discourse," 150; *HN*, 1:12.

3. See Jacques Roger, *Buffon, un philosophe au Jardin du Roi* (Paris: Fayard, 1989), 106; Jean Ehrard, *L'idée de nature en France dans la première moitié du XVIIIᵉ siècle* (Paris: Albin Michel, 1994), 190; and Phillip R. Sloan, "The Buffon-Linnaeus Controversy," *Isis* 67, no. 3 (1976): 356–75.

4. See Jorge Martinez-Contreras, "Des mœurs des singes: Buffon et ses contemporains," in *Buffon 88: Actes du Colloque international pour le bicentenaire de la mort de Buffon* (Paris: J. Vrin, 1992), 557–68.

5. See Sloan, "Buffon-Linnaeus Controversy"; Thierry Hoquet, "La comparaison des espèces: ordre et méthode dans l'*Histoire Naturelle* de Buffon," *Corpus. Revue de philosophie* no. 43 (2003): 355–416; and Franck Dougherty, *La métaphysique des sciences. Les origines de la pensée scientifique et philosophique de Buffon en 1749* (Ph.D. thesis, Université Paris 1, 1980). Cf. Paolo Casini, "Buffon et Newton," in *Buffon 88,* 299–308.

6. In Roger's words, there is a "decreasing order of dignity." See his *Les sciences de la vie dans la pensée française aux XVIIIᵉ siècle* (Paris: Albin Michel, 1993), 531. Cf. Michèle Duchet, *Anthropologie et histoire au siècle des Lumières* (Paris: Albin Michel, 1995), 230.

7. Roger, *Les sciences de la vie*, 531.

8. Hoquet, "La comparaison des espèces," 393.

9. Buffon, "Of the Nature of Animals" (1753), in *Buffon's Natural History. Containing a Theory of the Earth, a General History of Man, of the Brute Creation, and of Vegetables, Minerals, &c. &c.,* trans. J. S. Barr, 10 vols. (London, 1797), 5:77, hereafter cited as *Natural History*; *HN*, 4:92. On the quarrel with Réaumur, see the notice concerning it in the Pleiade edition of Buffon's *Histoire Naturelle* (Paris: Éditions Gallimard, 2007), 1501.

10. Buffon, "Of the Nature of Man," *Natural History*, 3:333; *HN*, 2:443.

11. For the history of this term, see François Azouvi, "Homo duplex," *Gesnerus* no. 42 (1985): 229–44.

12. See Descartes, *Discours de la méthode* (1637), Part V. Concerning the animal-machine theory, see the chapter about Descartes's "La fable des machines," in Élisabeth de Fontenay, *Le silence des bêtes: la philosophie à l'épreuve de l'animalité* (Paris: Fayard, 1998). For a detailed examination of Descartes's views on animals

and their relations to medieval and ancient thought, see Thierry Gontier, *De l'homme à l'animal. Montaigne et Descartes ou les paradoxes sur la nature des animaux* (Paris: Vrin, 1998); and *La question animale. Les origines du débat moderne* (Paris: Hermann, 2011).

13. Julia Douthwaite, *The Wild Girl, Natural Man, and the Monster: Dangerous Experiments in the Age of Enlightenment* (London: University of Chicago Press, 2002), 17. See Dagognet, *L'animal selon Condillac* (Paris: Vrin, 2004), 68; Contreras, "Des mœurs des singes"; and Markovitz, "Remarques sur l'histoire du problème de l'âme des bêtes," *Corpus: Revue de philosophie* no. 16 (1991): 79–92.

14. Hoquet, *Buffon: Histoire Naturelle et philosophie* (Paris: Honoré Champion, 2005), 495; Lifschitz, "The Book of Job and the Sex Life of Elephants: The Limits of Evidential Credibility in Eighteenth-Century Natural History and Biblical Criticism," *Journal of Modern History* no. 91 (2019): 739–75, 758.

15. Buffon, "General Views of Nature. First View," *Natural History*, 10:340 (emphasis added); *HN,* 12:14. Cf. Titus Lucretius Carus, *De Rerum Natura*, 5:206–18.

16. See La Mettrie, *L'Homme-machine* (Paris: Éditions Denoël/Gonthier, 1981), 157.

17. Diderot, *Réfutation suivie de l'ouvrage d'Helvétius intitulé L'Homme*, in *Œuvres completes*, 20 vols. (Paris, 1875–77), 2:323.

18. For the French materialists and the problem of animality, see Jean-Luc Guichet, "Âme des bêtes et matérialisme au XVIIIᵉ siècle," in *De L'Animal-machine à l'âme des machines. Querelles biomécaniques de l'âme (xviie-xxie siècle),* ed. Jean-Luc Guichet (Paris: Publication de la Sorbonne, 2010), 135–51.

19. See the sections "Of the reason of animals" (Book 1), "Of the pride and humility in animals" (Book 2), and "Of the love and hatred of animals" (Book 2), in Hume's *Treatise of Human Nature.*

20. For Rousseau's thinking about animals, see Jean-Luc Guichet, *Rousseau, l'animal et l'homme. L'animalité dans l'horizon anthropologique des Lumières* (Paris: Les Éditions du Cerf, 2006).

21. Hoquet, "La comparaison des espèces," 397.

22. Buffon, "The Dog," *Natural History*, 5:313; *HN*, 5:195.

23. Buffon, "The Cat," *Natural History*, 6:6; *HN*, 6:7.

24. Buffon, "The Elephant," *Natural History*, 7:257; *HN*, 11:4.

25. Buffon, "The Dog," *Natural History*, 5:305; *HN*, 187. See also the following text dedicated exclusively to the essay on the dog: Buffon, *Le chien,* ed. Bruno Vincent (Paris: Arléa, 1994).

26. The notion of degeneration is central to understanding Buffon's place in the history of transformism. See Buffon, "On the Degeneration of Animals," in *Natural History*, vol. 10; *HN*, vol. 14.

27. Buffon, "The Pigeon" (1771), *Histoire Naturelle des oiseaux* (Paris: Imprimerie Royale, 1770–83), 2:496 (my translation), henceforth cited as *HNO.* N.B. this passage is not in the 1792–93 translation cited in note 29. According to Buffon, besides human beings, the climate is another important cause of change in animal forms (see *HN,* 9:126).

28. Buffon, "The Dog," *Natural History*, 5:340; *HN*, 5:225.

29. Buffon, "On the Nature of Birds," *The Natural History of Birds,* 9 vols. (London, 1792–93), 1:17; *HNO,* 1:40.

30. Buffon, "The Dog," *Natural History,* 5:304; *HN,* 5:186.

31. Buffon, "The Dog," *Natural History,* 5:306; *HN,* 5:18.

32. With Louis-Jean-Marie Daubenton's writings in mind, Hoquet observes that the horse is the animal that is the most familiar to the anatomists of the period—after, of course, the human being ("La comparaison des espèces," 402).

33. Buffon, "The Horse," *Natural History,* 5:94; *HN,* 4:174.

34. Buffon, "Of the Nature of Man," *Natural History,* 3:327; *HN,* 2:438.

35. Buffon, "Of the Nature of Man," *Natural History,* 3:328; *HN,* 2:438.

36. Buffon, "Of Wild Animals," *Natural History,* 6:25; *HN,* 6:61.

37. Buffon, "Of Wild Animals," *Natural History,* 6:26; *HN,* 6:62. Cf. the introduction of "The Beaver," *Natural History,* 6:287; *HN,* 8:282.

38. See Buffon, "The Beaver," *Natural History,* 6:288; *HN,* 8:283.

39. "Yesterday, the King went to the park of Versailles and killed around 280 pieces. The Duke and the Prince of Conty were with the King, as well as several courtiers. The Duke used muskets and killed 120 pieces. The King authorised Mr. Courtenvaux and Mr. Souvise to use pistols: one killed 26 or 27 and the other about 15" ["Le Roi fut hier tirer dans le parc de Versailles et y tua environ 280 pièces. M. le duc et M. le prince de Conty avoient suivi le Roi à la chasse, et grand nombre de courtisans. M. le Duc avait fait porter des fusils, et tua 120 pièces. Le Roi avait permis à M. de Courtenvaux et M. de Souvise de tirer à coups de pistolet. Ils tuèrent, l'un 26 ou 27 pièces, et l'autre une quinzaine"]; Grégory Quenet, *Versailles, une histoire Naturelle* (Paris: La Découverte, 2015), 239.

40. Grimm, *Correspondance littéraire, philosophique et critique,* 16 vols. (Paris: Garnier frères, 1877–82), 3:303. Cf. Renan Larue, *Le Végétarisme des Lumières. L'abstinence de viande dans la France du xviiiᵉ siècle* (Paris: Classiques Garnier, 2019).

41. Concerning the management of the *gibier,* see Quenet, *Versailles,* 114.

42. Buffon, "Of Carnivorous Animals," *Natural History,* 7:116; *HN,* 7:4; "Of Wild Animals," *Natural History,* 6:26; *HN,* 6:62. Buffon's understanding of humankind's destructive powers exists side-by-side with his views on the elevated place reserved for human beings. Thus, if one seeks a critique of mankind in Buffon, one must take into account the complexity of his position.

43. For instance, Buffon discounts the belief in India that elephants are the reincarnations of great men or ancient kings, which supposedly explains why they are treated with such respect and bestowed with luxurious ornaments. Buffon quips that since all this respect and luxury does not corrupt the elephants' souls, they "consequently" do not have "a human soul, and this circumstance should be sufficient to prove it to the Indians" ("The Elephant," *Natural History,* 7:261; *HN,* 11:9).

44. Buffon, "The Elephant," *Natural History,* 7:285–86; *HN,* 11:50.

45. Buffon, "The Elephant," *Natural History,* 7:286; *HN,* 11:52.

46. Buffon, "The Beaver," *Natural History,* 6:289, 301; *HN,* 8:285, 296.

47. Buffon, "The Beaver," *Natural History*, 6:289; *HN*, 8:285. For the limits of animal society in comparison with that of humans, see "The Beaver," *Natural History*, 6:287; *HN*, 8:283.

48. Buffon, "The Beaver," *Natural History*, 6:295; *HN*, 8:291.

49. Buffon, "Of Wild Animals," *Natural History*, 6:26; *HN*, 6:62.

50. See, for example, Martinez-Contreras, "Des mœurs des singes."

51. Canguilhem, *La connaissance de la vie* (Paris: Vrin, 1965). See also Jacques Roger, *Buffon,* 376.

52. Burkhardt, "Le comportement animal et l'idéologie de domestication chez Buffon et chez les éthologues modernes," in *Buffon 88,* 569–82.

53. Buffon, "On the Nature of Birds," *The Natural History of Birds*, 1:5; *HNO*, 1:11.

54. Buffon, "On the Nature of Birds," *The Natural History of Birds*, 1:17; *HNO*, 1:40.

55. Buffon, "On the Nature of Birds," *The Natural History of Birds*, 1:5; *HNO*, 1:10.

56. Buffon, "On the Nature of Birds," *The Natural History of Birds*, 1:19, 1:5; *HNO*, 1:45, 1:10. I have slightly modified the translation.

57. Buffon, "On the Nature of Birds," *The Natural History of Birds*, 1:28; *HNO*, 1:67.

58. We reserve for another occasion a careful examination concerning these affinities. For the moment, we refer to Roger, *Les sciences de la vie*, 536; and, for the complexity of Buffon's writings on this topic, Dougherty, *La métaphysique des sciences.*

59. See Buffon, "Of the Nature of Animals," *Natural History*, 5:42 (memory), 5:78 (choice and intelligence), 5:54 (imagination); *HN*, 4:55, 4:95, 4:68. Regarding choice and intelligence, see also "Of Wild Animals," *Natural History*, 6:25; *HN*, 6:61.

60. Buffon, "Of the Nature of Animals," *Natural History*, 5:28; *HN*, 4:38.

61. In his *Traité des animaux* (1755), Condillac rejects Buffon's conception of sentiment independent of the production of ideas. This is probably the central point of his criticism of Buffon's automatism.

62. Buffon, "The Elephant," *Natural History*, 7:289; *HN*, 11:54.

63. Buffon, "On the Nature of Birds," *The Natural History of Birds*, 1:2; *HNO*, 1:5. I have slightly modified the translation.

64. Assoun, "Lire La Mettrie," in La Mettrie, *L'Homme-machine*, 54.

65. Descartes, letter to Henry More, 5 February 1649, in *Œuvres Philosophiques*, ed. Ferdinand Alquié, 3 vols. (Paris: Éditions Classiques Garnier, 2010), 3:884.

66. The soul of animals is directly related to the blood; it is "a fluid body which moves very fast, of which the most subtle part is called spirit" ("un corps fluide qui se meut très vite, duquel la partie la plus subtile s'appelle esprit"); Descartes, letter to Van Buitendijck, 1643, in *Œuvres Philosophiques*, 3:59). Concerning this, see Fontenay, *Le Silence des bêtes*, 382.

67. See Descartes, letter to Marin Mersenne, 30 July 1640, in *Œuvres Philosophiques,* 2:249.

68. See Descartes, letter to William Cavendish, Marquis of Newcastle, 23 November 1646, in *Œuvres Philosophiques,* 3:696.
69. Roger, *Buffon,* 221. At the time, Cartesian dualism was the orthodox doctrine of the Church.
70. See Roger, *Buffon,* 221; and Dagognet, *L'animal selon Condillac*, 66.
71. Buffon, "Of Domestic Animals," *Natural History*, 5:89; *HN*, 4:170.

Marvelous Maples: Visions of Maple Sugar in New France, 1691–1761

NATHAN D. BROWN

This is the study of a breakfast topping. At first glance, this would seem far afield from eighteenth-century studies. Yet, the dark, thick, boiled down tree sap known as maple syrup, which twenty-first century North Americans frequently pour on top of their morning pancakes and waffles, has a surprising connection to the eighteenth-century colonial project in North America, particularly New France.[1] In this article I contend that this natural sweetener, which remains an important economic engine and cultural touchstone in modern day Québec, troubled eighteenth-century French beliefs about their own mastery of knowledge, the environment, technology, and the Indigenous Peoples of the Great Lakes.[2] Toward this end, I analyze and assess descriptions of maple sugar in both French texts, such as those by Sieur de Dièreville, Baron de Lahontan, Joseph-François de Lafitau, and Pierre-Xavier de Charlevoix, and in texts associated with different Native Peoples.

Recent scholarship on the French colonial project in North America has focused heavily on contact between the French and the Indigenous Peoples of the region. Apart from missionaries sent to evangelize, interactions between the communities in eighteenth-century Canada were predicated on material and commercial exchange, typically of manufactured goods for beaver skins and other pelts. In these exchanges, scholars have drawn out colonial discourses that had been neglected by traditional research methods.[3]

Likewise, the ecocritical turn in the humanities shows the importance of better understanding what Christopher M. Parsons has recently called "colonial political ecology."[4] Together these two scholarly paradigms reveal the importance of taking seriously the discursive potentiality of a seemingly quotidian product like maple sugar. After all, it was through interaction with the Natives that the French learned about the sugar maples of New France and the sweet sap that flows from the trees in the spring. As such, maple sugar lies at the intersection of the ecocritical and cross-cultural discourses and economics that have become the focus of many scholars in contemporary eighteenth-century studies.

Although contemporary North Americans are most acquainted with maple sugar as a syrup or as maple candy, in the eighteenth century it took a variety of forms. As such, "maple sugar" is an admittedly vague term that stands in for a plurality of products from eighteenth-century New France. French writers from the period could be frustratingly imprecise about what they mean by "maple sugar." For André Thevet, Dièreville, and Lahontan, maple was a beverage, compared favorably to a fine wine or lemonade. Pehr Kalm and Charlevoix at times describe a liquid with a cough-syrup-like viscosity (and similar medicinal properties). At other times, those writers compare it to a spread or even a loaf comprised of compressed grains of sugar. These various products all fell under the umbrella of "maple sugar," although terms like "juice" (*suc*) and "maple water" (*eau d'érable*) were sometimes used as well. Despite this conflation, the prevalence of the term "sugar" in regards to maple in these texts underlines the material connection to its cane cousin in the minds of French writers. In short, they were building an epistemology of sweetness that foregrounded maple as a substitute for sugar cane. This imprecision also had economic implications as it reveals that maple sugar had no clear uniformity at the time. Throughout the period, maple products remained largely an artisanal, small-batch phenomenon that the French and Indigenous Peoples produced for their own private consumption. What is clear is that maple sugar was a multivalent product that captured both the philosophical and economic imagination of the writers of New France.

At the same time, maple sugar was a quotidian product in eighteenth-century Canada. By all accounts, it had already become a staple in the French colonial diet by the mid-eighteenth century. As the Swedish botanist Pehr Kalm writes in *En resa til Norra America* (1753–61): "practically every soldier in the French forts manufactures a year's supply of this necessity for himself in the spring. If you visit the French you will see no other sugar used."[5] Since cane sugar from the islands was expensive to import to Canada, maple sugar was a sweetener for the masses: "the common people eat sugar with the bread or spread it on the bread thick."[6] But, maple sugar was no mere substitute and was considered by most to be superior to its cane counterpart.

Under Kalm's pen, maple sugar is practically a health food with medicinal properties by comparison: "it is more healthful than ordinary sugar and is unusually good for the chest and its diseases."[7] With such ubiquity and praise, maple sugar was a product that greatly affected the lived experience of French settlers, as well as the Native People from whom they learned the process. Yet, maple sugar has received little scholarly attention.

The reasons for this are rather straightforward. Outside of eighteenth-century Canada, maple sugar never achieved the same status as other products from the New World. Cane sugar from the islands, tobacco, and cotton were traded on an international scale; maple sugar was not. Why did maple sugar fail to enter international trade systems? Lack of proper storage methods left maple sugar prone to spoilage, and the short intensive season made sustained agricultural interest difficult. Maple trees are unpredictable and the weather's vagaries make forecasting maple sap output difficult. Efforts at large-scale maple production were, as eco-scholars have noted, "frequently met with forces of cultural and environmental resistance."[8] The abundance of maple trees also made the development of a market difficult. As Kalm's account suggests, supply met localized demand as the French colonists and Native Peoples in Canada produced and consumed their entire stock themselves.

Despite the tantalizing possibility of turning the fledgling colony along the Saint Lawrence into a veritable sugar colony, interest in maple sugar as a possible large-scale substitute for cane sugar was slow to take form.[9] It took the upheavals in the Caribbean sugar colonies of the 1790s, which disturbed the cane market and fueled abolitionist opposition to cane sugar among Europeans and settler communities, to spark a reassessment of maple sugar within the larger Atlantic world.[10] As a result, maple sugar remained a geographically limited product throughout the eighteenth century.

Nonetheless, maple sugar represented a natural marvel and an early cultural touchstone for French colonists. It also represented a potential source of profits. We will remember that New France, not having the mines of Spanish South America or a navigable Northwest passage to India, somewhat lacked a clear *raison d'être*. Accordingly, the search for viable raw goods was a perennial preoccupation for both colonial and metropolitan administrators. For writers like Charlevoix, maple sugar held the possibility of diversifying the colony's economy. Along with ginseng, Charlevoix saw in maple a possible commercial product that could reinforce the importance of the colony to a mercantilist metropole. Maple sugar must be contextualized within the logic of this system. While ginseng harvesting held promise and had some success as an export, New France largely remained a subsistence farming economy with an additional monoculture focused on buying and selling beaver and other animal pelts.[11]

Beyond the intriguing—but ultimately unrealized—economic possibilities, maple sugar also fueled utopian visions of New France and shaped colonial discourses about Native Americans in ways we have yet to fully appreciate. For example, what were French travelers to make of Indigenous women who crafted the various forms of this marvelous sugar? As a natural marvel tied to indigenous *savoir-faire*, and as a potential alternative to its cane cousin, maple sugar played an unexpectedly important role in the formation of early modern discourses of civilizational contact and the colonial project in the North American French empire, at least among certain writers of New France.

To date, the few scholarly articles on maple sugar in the eighteenth-century world have focused almost exclusively on the United States. Mark Sturges's 2018 article, "'Bleed on, Blest Tree!': Maple Sugar Georgics in the Early American Republic," exemplifies this approach. Sturges highlights the ways in which the American boosters of maple sugar blended abolitionist rhetoric with a georgic yearning for rustic, small-scale farm life in the new American republic of the 1790s.[12] As Sturges notes, the other extant scholarly works implicating maple sugar tend to focus on nationalist or proto-capitalist topics in the early United States, particularly the so-called maple bubble of the 1820s.[13] However, the Anglo-American leaders of the fledgling republic, such as Thomas Jefferson, William Cooper, and Benjamin Rush, seem to have only "discovered" maple's potential late in the eighteenth century. Lucien Campeau, for example, notes in his 1990 essay, "Les origines du sucre d'érable," that the word "maple" is nowhere to be found in the early archives of New York State, although it was one of the British colonies closest to New France.[14] As such, current research on maple, while provocative and insightful, does not fully attend to French and Native American contributions. This is unfortunate because the discourses around maple sugar, like those around cane sugar, transcended national and imperial boundaries and were instrumentalized for different ends in the Atlantic World.[15] Furthermore, French visions of maple sugar were particularly well established and developed long before those in English.

Indeed, French colonists in Canada had an extensive history with maple sugar. For example, in his 1567 work, *Les Singularitez de la France antarctique*, André Thevet, who documented Jacques Cartier's voyages, gives an account of maple consumption by the Cartier expedition:

> [Canada] has several trees and fruits, which we don't have any knowledge about. Among these is a tree the size and shape of a large walnut from one side to another, which remained useless for a long time, and unknown, until someone wanting to cut it down brought forth a juice, which was found to be as good tasting and delicate as a fine wine from Orleans or Beaune: our people who

were able to experience it judged it similarly: that is to say, the
Captain, and other gentlemen in his entourage, and they gathered
in an hour four or five large pots of this juice. I'll let you think,
if from then on these Canadians attached to this liqueur did not
keep this tree dearly for their drinks since it was so excellent.
This tree, in their language, is called *Couton*.[16]

This short passage highlights many of the themes and rhetoric around maple
in the French New World that will continue into the eighteenth century. The
lexicographic field clearly depicts maple sugaring as a *native* knowledge,
something "we don't have any knowledge about." It was also supposedly
discovered serendipitously, and its products are compared favorably to ones
from other colonies or the metropole—in this case, wine. Finally, maple
sap is described as abundant, thereby rendering the tree itself valuable.
Despite Thevet's rather commendatory description of maple's properties, the
archives provide little indication that maple consumption was widespread
in the decades following this initial discovery. In his review of the *Jesuit
Relations,* for example, Campeau finds few references to maple sugar among
the missionaries and not a single description of the sugaring process by
the religious order.[17] We must wait for the late seventeenth and eighteenth
centuries to find more consistent references to maple production and use.
By 1691, Chréstien Le Clerq, a missionary to the Mi'kmaq nation of the
Gaspesian peninsula, gives a brief, but thorough description of maple
sugaring in his work, *Nouvelle relation de la Gaspésie*. He claims, "As for
maple water … it is equally delicious for the French and the Savages."[18]
French use in the colony seems common, although the product was little
known in the metropole: "little loaves are formed from it, which are
rarely sent to France, and which in everyday use replaces French sugar."[19]
Despite the relative absence of a transatlantic trade in maple sugar, by
the late eighteenth century, knowledge of it had crossed the Atlantic, and
Denis Diderot and Jean Le Rond d'Alembert included an entry on it in the
Encyclopédie.[20] At minimum, this suggests that cane's maple cousin was
known among the learned populations of Europe by 1780. The entry, which
predates widespread consumption or familiarity with the maple products in
the metropole, was drawn from travelers' accounts. Therefore, the texts about
and from New France in the late seventeenth and early to mid-eighteenth
centuries are of significant value in understanding the rise of the discourses
around maple in the French empire.

Visions of maple sugar did not arise in a vacuum and must be
contextualized within a larger ecological and discursive framework that
shaped visions of New France. Foremost among the contexts to consider
is the role of the woods in the colonial imagination. European travelers to

Canada often commented on what they presumed were two interconnected aspects of the physical world of Canada: it was extremely wooded and extremely cold. The dense forests of New France supposedly represented both the cause of and the cure for its unfortunate climate. Charlevoix, a Catholic priest and traveler to New France, gives voice to this tension in *Histoire et description générale de la Nouvelle France* (1744). As he writes, "there is indeed no Want of Wood to provide against the Cold, which soon becomes excessive."[21] Thus, the trees provide all the fuel needed to keep warm in the winter. Moreover, colonists were free to cut down the trees in New France, a privilege not afforded to French peasants in the metropole. At the same time, the trees were also (wrongly) supposed to be the source of the cold climate. As Charlevoix explains, "the greatest Part of the Authors, who have treated on this Matter, have satisfied themselves with saying, that this long and severe Cold proceeds from the Snow's lying so long on the Ground, that it is impossible that the Ground should be well warmed again" (133–34). The sheer number of trees, it seems, were preventing the snow from melting, thereby keeping the weather cool. Charlevoix remains somewhat dubious of such simplistic links:

> there is no Doubt but that, generally speaking, the Mountains, Woods, and Lakes, contribute much to it; but. … [w]e cannot allow that we should attribute the Cold, of which we seek the Cause, to any of the Causes I have just mentioned … for there is nothing to answer against Experience, which makes us sensible of the Abatement of the Cold, in Proportion as the Country is cleared of the Woods, altho' it is not in so great a Proportion as it ought to be, if the Thickness of the Woods was the principal Cause of it. (134)

Charlevoix presents an empirical and holistic vision of the possible causes of the cold weather of New France, which lies after all, at a similar latitude as France. In so doing, he gives voice to the ecological mystery that was the New World environment.[22] In order to solve such a befuddling environment, he suggests a sort of human-made global warming brought on by cutting down the trees, settling the land, and planting crops: "if Canada was as free from Woods, and as well peopled as France, the Winters would not be so long and so severe" (137). His belief in the power of humans to change the ecological conditions of their world is clear; the French have come to change nature itself to suit their needs.

Clearing forests and trying to cultivate land when winter lasts six months is, of course, not the most attractive of options. Colonists had little interest in doing so, a fact that did not escape notice by both Charlevoix and colonial administrators. Instead, settlers preferred to trade beaver skins and other pelts with the Indigenous Peoples of the region. While the metropole profited from this activity, they also viewed this type of commerce with suspicion. Interactions with Natives and the very environment of Canada supposedly made colonists lazy and independent. Charlevoix insists that "the Air which they breathe in this vast Continent contributes to" the "flaws" ["défauts"] of "Canadiens français": "our Adventurers, whom they call here *Coureurs de Bois, (Forest Rangers)* ... who taking a Liking to Independency, and a wandering Life ... from whence it proceeds, that Arts have been a long Time neglected, that much good Land lies still uncultivated, and that the Country is not peopled" (47–48). In fact, the French became like the Indigenous Peoples, whom Charlevoix terms the *"Sauvages."* Indeed, the *"Coureurs de Bois"* "remained among the Savages; from whom they could not be distinguished, but by their Vices" (47). The forest, and the lifestyle of Indigenous populations, supposedly promised a life of "vicious" independence, as opposed to the joys of settled agrarian life.

There is, in fact, an etymological link between *"sauvage"* and *"coureur des bois."* Both terms refer to the forest: the Latin root of "savage" is, after all, *silvia* [wood] or *silvaticus* [of the woods]. The term *"coureur des bois"*—literally, "wood runner"—also references the woods, underlining the extent to which this subset of the French settler community was defined by its relationship with the forest. In short, a *"coureur de bois"* is a "savage" by another name. As this terminology reveals, writing about New France was a deeply ecocritical endeavor for Charlevoix, as he draws the link between nature and the culture of the French in North America. The French had come to reshape North America, but it was North America that reshaped them.[23]

Within this context, it would be easy enough to assume the woods were a *locus terribilis* —a horrible place of danger—to be avoided. Yet, even as Charlevoix associates the forests with the undesirable effects of French wandering and fraternizing with the Natives, he also views the trees favorably. Charlevoix calls the woods, "the Finest Forests in the World" (71). He is wonderstruck by their expansiveness: "nothing is more magnificent to the Sight; the Trees lose themselves in the Clouds" (71). The economic potential is clear: "as there is not perhaps a Country in the World that has more Variety of Wood, nor a better Sort: Judge what Riches this may one Day produce" (49). Moreover, for Charlevoix, the woods are gifts from God: "In all Appearance they are as old as the World itself, and were not planted by the Hands of Men" (125). Representations of forests as a godsend continue in Charlevoix's treatment of the game in the forests and the abundant fish of Canada's rivers. He draws on religious imagery to describe the forests and rivers that "furnish the Inhabitants with two Sorts of Manna" (137). The use of the term "manna," of course, draws a clear comparison between the products of Canada's forests and the miraculous food given to the Jewish people by God in the book of Exodus. In contrast to the dangerous independence the forest provided for the "*coureurs de bois*," here the woods are a *locus amoenus*—a source of sustenance amid the bitter cold of New France.

It is within this tension around the forests of New France that maple sugar discourses emerge. Charlevoix describes maple sugar as a miraculous food for the people of New France. For example, in his passage on maple sugaring, Charlevoix concludes his otherwise dry description of the practice of maple sugar harvesting by asking Mme de Lesdiguières, his hypothetical reader, rhetorically: "Could you have believed, Madam, that we should find in *Canada*, what *Virgil* says in foretelling the Renewal of the golden Age, that Honey should flow from the Trees?" (84). Charlevoix here references Virgil's fourth eclogue in which the Roman poet predicts the arrival of a new age when "a golden race [will] spring up throughout the world!" and "the stubborn oak [will] distill dewy honey."[24] Seen in this context, Charlevoix's allusion to Virgil's Golden Age illustrates the potential he saw in New France and his hope for the settler community. The discovery of this sugar promises a "Renewal" and a return to the glory of antiquity. As the use of the past conditional ("Could you have believed …") and subjunctive mood ("should find") suggest, this is quite contrary to expectations. Yet, these references to antiquity typify French colonial rhetoric that scholars have drawn out in other research.[25] By linking the French empire to the Romans, the French are employing a discourse of *translatio imperii* as they portray themselves as the rightful torchbearers of Western civilization. As Charlevoix brags, "the *French* Empire in America, [is] of greater Extent than was ever that of the Romans" (31). By depicting Canada as the land of honey and in favorable contrast to the Roman Empire, he recasts the French colonial project in Canada. Under his pen, it becomes a reflection of French grandeur and an example of heavenly favor bestowed upon the French empire. Maple sugar was the supposed physical manifestation of this favor.

Beyond the forest and ancient prophecies, maple sugar also fared well in contrast with cane sugar. Sieur de Dièreville's passage about maple sugar from his 1708 *Relation du voyage du Port Royal de l'Acadie, ou de la Nouvelle France*, is representative of the frequent comparisons made between the two sugars. In his passage about maple sugaring, Dièreville inserts a poem into his narrative in which he lauds maple sugar:

> In place of cane whose pores
> Make white sugar that comes from afar,
> For the Acadians, nature took care
> To place some in the sycamores.
> At the beginning of spring,
> From their bark comes a sweet liqueur,
> Which the inhabitants with great care
> Gather in each land.
> This drink seemed good to me,
> I drank it in gulps;
> It only needed some lemon
> To make a lemonade.[26]

Dièreville's poem lends itself to several observations about the rhetorical strategies around maple at the time. First, he draws a clear link between the cane sugar of the islands and the maple sugar of New France. They become foils for one another, accentuated by the rhyme that couples cane sugar's "pores" and maple sugar's "sycamores." Second, he draws our attention to the ubiquity of the sugar maples. Third, their harvesting would appear to require little work. Although the Acadians may need to take "great care" to acquire the liquid sugar of the maples—by tapping the trees correctly, for example—they are relatively passive in the sugar's creation, simply "gathering" it. Unlike the intense production needed to render cane sugar consumable, this sweet beverage only lacks a bit of lemon to be perfect.

The advantages of maple sugar over cane sugar were frequently touted and made explicit by travel writers. On this point, the Baron de Lahontan and Charlevoix—who, at times, are antagonistic regarding other issues— are in agreement. Lahontan praises maple in superlative terms in his 1703 *Mémoire*: "there is no lemonade nor cherry water with such a nice taste, nor any drink in the world that is healthier."[27] Charlevoix echoes Lahontan, but contextualizes maple sugar within the larger colonial project and mercantilist impulses of France. Charlevoix writes: "this Sugar made with Care, and it requires much less than ours, is natural, pectoral, and does not burn the Stomach ... it is certain, that as it comes out of the Hands of the Savages, it is purer and much better than the Sugar of the Islands" (84). This Native technology, improved by the French, becomes better than cane sugar. While acknowledging, backhandedly, the debt owed to Native People, Charlevoix also subtly highlights maple sugar as a product borne of hybrid technology. If the Natives taught the French about the marvelous maples, it was French refinement and purification that made it a suitable potential substitute for cane sugar.

Furthermore, its advantages reinforced the Virgilian prophecy discussed above. Joseph-François Lafitau, author of the proto-ethnographic *Moeurs des Sauvages ameriquains* (1724), was arguably even more emphatic about maple sugar's superiority to cane than Dièreville, Lahontan, and Charlevoix. As he wrote in a particularly illustrative passage: "for the sugar we use today is an artificial sugar. The cane from which we draw it, is a knotty stalk, spongy, with a very thin peel, and full of a very sweet honey-like material. Canes are broken by Mills; where the juice is expressed by presses. ... It is a method of making sugar and refining it that the Ancients did not know."[28] The vocabulary is revelatory of his disdain of cane sugar; it is "factice": fake or imitation. It must be refined and purified, requiring mills, presses, and slave labor, which he elides. Cane sugar is a new product and thus innately inferior to maple, the "natural" sugar, according to the battle lines drawn in the longstanding quarrel between the ancients and the moderns. Moreover, Lafitau shares with Charlevoix a belief that maple sugar represents a regeneration of the world according to Virgilian prophecy. As he suggests: "The Poets in their descriptions of the Golden Age, or the Centuries that are compared to it, tell us that among other miracles, the hardest oaks distilled or will distill honey ... our Savages show that they know more than them, having learned to draw from maple ... a natural juice that is just as, or more, pleasing, than Bees' honey."[29] Canada, in this description, becomes the land of honey and its Native Peoples the new Romans. In fact, by suggesting that the Natives "know more than them," Lafitau implies that their maple technology places Indigeneous People in some ways above the Romans. The discovery of maple sugar represents a return to a golden age, a replication of the glory of Rome. The passage also gestures toward New France as a new Eden, a persistent motif that scholars have noted elsewhere in the study of North American colonization.[30] While we cannot discount the propagandist nature of the accounts of Lafitau and Charlevoix, the internal logic of these passages challenges their facile notions of European supremacy and Indigenous backwardness or degeneration, judgments that they express elsewhere in their texts.

At the same time, French accounts gender Indigenous knowledge, placing maple sugaring squarely within the traditional feminine domain of Native women. In Lafitau's comments on the sugaring process, for example, we learn that "the French work it better than the Savage women from whom they learned to make it."[31] In this way, Lafitau creates what Louis Montrose calls "a powerful conjunction of the savage and the feminine."[32] If we put aside the Eurocentrism of Lafitau's comments, what remains clear is the debt that Europeans owed to Indigenous women for their knowledge of maple sugar. This is clearly a Native female technology; supposedly perfected by the French, of course. This is important because while maple sugar has been appropriated by the Europeans, the Indigenous communities have not yet been erased from the narrative.[33] Thus, in his acknowledgment of the Indigenous roots and subsequent refinement of maple sugar by the French, Lafitau already points to a process of hybridization of cultures and technology.

This emphasis on hybridization helps explain the pictorial representation of maple sugaring in Lafitau's *Moeurs des Sauvages* (see Figure 1). At first glance, the image seems to be a straightforward depiction of the tapping of maples by Indigenous People. It shows various steps of maple production: drawing forth the sap, boiling it down, and creating maple loaves for consumption. Yet, in its depiction of Native People in various agricultural activities, the print actually offers an idyllic vision of colonial progress, as imagined by French officials. For example, copper pots and roaring fires, as depicted in the bottom left corner of the image, were not the traditional method of reducing maple sap.[34] Although European copper kettles were traded among the Mi'kmaq in the Arcadian peninsula from the late sixteenth century, these, as Laurier Turgeon points out, "were reserved for ceremonial and ritual use … copper kettles did not replace traditional earthenware pots."[35] Moreover, Sue Denholm has noted that "no firm archeological evidence" suggests that flat bottom copper pots, like those shown in the engraving, were used by Native Peoples in eastern North America before the nineteenth century.[36] The depiction in *Moeurs des Sauvages*, therefore, is most likely anachronistic in its suggestion that Indigenous communities had incorporated European technology in the sugaring process. As the eye moves up the engraving beyond the maple sugaring, the viewer sees a more agrarian use of land. Natives clear the forest and till the soil using what appear to be European, rather than Native, hoes. The crop they are sowing is decidedly New World and Indigenous, according to Lafitau's description of the plate: "The fields, as they are at the end of winter; it shows women busy giving them their first toiling, and planting their maize in their fashion."[37] In this way, corn harvesting and maple sugaring become examples of Natives blending their practices with European technology. This is an idealized colonial vision of Indigenous People making their first steps towards acculturation and hybridization under the auspices of the imperial project.

Several aspects of the image drive home the notion that this is a piece of colonial imagination rather than an earnest depiction of the maple sugaring process. First, the image depicts the climate of the sugaring season quite improbably. We see little evidence of snow, for example. In addition, the Indigenous People are dressed only in skirts with their torsos exposed. Maple sugaring season, of course, takes place in the spring between February and

Figure 1. An idealized depiction of Indigenous agriculture from Joseph-François Lafitau, *Moeurs des sauvages amériquains, comparées aux moeurs des premiers temps* (Paris: Chez Saugrain l'aîné, 1724). Courtesy of The Rare Books and Manuscripts Library, The Ohio State University.

April when temperatures remain chilly and the ground is still too hard to till in eastern Canada. Native women would not be planting corn at the same time as others tapped the maple trees. Lafitau was aware of this and admitted as much, since he indicates that March was the sugaring season and explains that in order for the maple to produce sap, "it is necessary for there to be a certain quantity of snow at the foot" of the tree.[38] Rather than verisimilitude, the juxtaposition of the two moments in the agricultural year suggests a certain "settledness," which, in turn, gestures toward a use of the land that aligns with colonial desires. In this way, both maple sugaring and corn harvesting represent an imagined ideal of agrarian "progress," in which Indigenous Peoples demonstrated that they were willing participants in the imperial ambitions of France by settling and clearing the land.

The apparent clemency of the climate depicted in the illustration from *Moeurs des Sauvages*, more akin to a vision of the tropics, helps create an amalgam of various French colonial projects. The image blends North and South and attempts to tie into a cohesive whole the colonial projects of the French Caribbean sugar islands with the frigid terrain of Canada. This juxtaposition, or rather confusion, in the image under consideration is an example of what Michel de Certeau refers to in his analysis of Lafitau as "the comparatist technique of the 'connection.'"[39] In other words, the image suggests an erroneous temporal link between maple sugaring and corn harvesting. As such, it invites the viewer to locate what Certeau calls a "'space between' ... where we are to situate the springboard that lets the work function as a 'system.' A ruse is the condition of possibility of this science. This ruse is an art of *playing on two places*."[40] In the print we are considering, the artist has created "a ruse" of space and time. He is playing on two temporal moments and two climates from different colonial endeavors, uniting them in the same physical space for propagandist ends.

The illustration also plays on erotic tropes of non-European women, common in eighteenth-century Europe.[41] In the image's figures, we can see what Certeau refers to as "an *eroticism of the origin*. They offer *that which one can still see* of the 'first times.'"[42] Not only is Lafitau depicting "primitive" times, but he is also endowing the central figure in the image with a certain nobility, as her pose recalls statues from classical antiquity. This blending of Native eroticism, suggested by the central figure's nudity, with certain elements of Greco-Roman artistic positioning presents the figure as an Indigenous Venus. With her knees slightly bent and a tunic-like dress covering her lower torso, she recalls the Venus d'Arles, to cite just one possible example, a statue displayed in the Hall of Mirrors at Versailles from 1681 until the French Revolution (see Figure 2). Similarly, her outstretched arms and distant gaze share many of the hallmarks of classical

Figure 2. The Venus d'Arles. First century BCE. Marble, 194 cm, Musée du Louvre. Courtesy of Rama, Cc-by-sa-2.0-fr.

depictions of goddesses. Given the comparative thesis announced in the title of Lafitau's work, which the Champlain Society renders as *Customs of the American Indians Compared with the Customs of Primitive Times* in its 1974 translation, it is unsurprising that the artist draws this comparison between the Native Peoples of the Great Lakes and the ancient Greeks and Romans. Lafitau puts forward, after all, a vision of history that scholars have summarized as "universal," "unitary[,] and progressive."[43] Lafitau understands Indigenous Peoples as progressing along the same singular historical trajectory as Europeans. Yet his discussion of maple sugar presents a seeming contradiction to this vision of European cultural and technological superiority. The Natives taught the Europeans how to produce this miraculous sugar, not the other way around. Although Lafitau claims the French had improved on the process, in this image the Indigenous People are the ones who have married European tools and Native *savoir faire*.

We can also notice in the image the tension inherent in depictions of the woods as both a *locus amoenus* and a *locus terribilis*. In the foreground, we see Indigenous People busy tapping the trees and cooking down the sap. The figures are mostly upright and posed in positions reminiscent of neoclassical art. In the background we see quite the opposite as Native People are hunched over their tools as they work the land, clearing away the forest, removing this element (*silvia*) that was considered by the Europeans as the essential element of their "savageness" (*silvestre*, or wood-dwelling). This juxtaposition gestures to a related question: do depictions of maple sugar belong to the pastoral or georgic mode? If, as Timothy Sweet has suggested, the pastoral "understands the natural world primarily as a site of leisure" and the georgic "primarily as a site of labor," then here we have both.[44] While not quite free of labor, and therefore wholly pastoral, the figures boiling down the sap in the foreground are certainly going about their work more leisurely than those in the background. This tension, in turn, heightens the discursive contradictions surrounding forests. The forest is both a natural good, providing the miracle of maple sugar, *and* a hindrance to the spread of "civilization," as defined by Europeans, who saw clearing and settling the land as integral to the civilizing process. The image seems to gesture toward an impossibility: a desire both to clear the forest and to keep on getting maple sugar from the destroyed forest.

French accounts of maple sugar harvesting elide the friction created by the European co-option of maple sugar and Native-derived knowledge. Unfortunately, vanishingly few Native accounts of the European adoption of maple sugar remain from the period. It is difficult to know with much specificity, for example, what different Indigenous Peoples knew about the maple sugaring process, beyond broad generalities. Indeed, Denholm suggests that forced migration, brought on by the expansion of English (and French) colonists into the Great Lakes region clouds the archeological record.[45] Moreover, French travel narratives often collapse the differences between disparate Native Peoples, depriving us of specific details about what the French thought the Indigenous Peoples knew. Therefore, a methodical recovery of Indigenous knowledge about maple sugaring is beyond the reach of this current project. However, in the few Native texts from the late eighteenth and early nineteenth century that remain, it is clear that European appropriation of the sugar maple caused consternation among certain Indigenous nations. The Native Peoples of the St. Lawrence river valley and the Great Lakes had developed a deep connection to the maple that was not easily relinquished to the French.

For certain Native populations, maple sugar was more than a natural product with certain economic implications; it was tied to religious beliefs and seasonal traditions. The Anishinaabe, Ojibwe, and Algonquin, for example, all celebrated the maple sugaring season with festivals of the "maple moon" or the "time of melting snow."[46] The Cree used the word *Sisbaskwat* ("maple sugar"); the Ojibwe referred to *Ninutik* ("our own tree"); and the Algonquin used the term *Sinzibuckwud* ("drawn from wood") to speak of maple sugaring.[47] Accordingly, Native alarm about the European co-option of maple is best contextualized within a socio-religious framework. The Odawa nation, for example, tell the story of the trickster god Nanabozho who made sugar production more difficult in order to help his people appreciate the natural gift:

> The most remarkable, wonderful, and supernatural being that ever trod upon the earth. ... [t]his mischievous Ne-naw-bo-zhoo spoiled the sugar trees by diluting their sap with water. The legends say, that once upon a time the sugar trees did produce sap at [a] certain season of the year which was almost like a pure syrup; but when this mischievous Ne-naw-bo-zhoo had tasted it, he said to himself, "Ah, that is too cheap. It will not do. My nephews will obtain this sugar too easily in the future time and the sugar will be worthless." And therefore he diluted the sap until he could not taste any sweetness therein. Then he said, "Now my nephews will have to labor hard to make the sugar out of this sap, and the sugar will be much more valuable to them in the future time."[48]

The legend thus highlights labor as an essential element in the production of maple sugar for Native People. Through the effort they put into the process, the community returns the sap to its "natural" state—before it was "spoiled" by the trickster god. It is a process that connects the tribe to the land and links effort, value, and the metaphysical. The trees are not only a divine gift; the labor associated with their sugaring is a quasi-religious duty.

Economics and religion often overlapped in Native Peoples' understanding of maple sugaring. While the French writers imagined maple sugar to be essentially "free" and boundless, the Shawnee nation, for example, had a clear sense of the limits of maple exploitation. Consequently, they feared the loss to their community that would come from increased settler consumption. In 1807, a Captain Dunham recorded an admonishment given by the prophet Tenskwatawa of the Shawnee to the Native Peoples of the Great Lakes regarding selling maple sugar to newly arrived Anglo-American settlers, whose expansion threatened Native sovereignty. Although the context differs from the earlier French colonial project, the admonition reveals a late eighteenth- and early nineteenth-century conception of maple's stakes on the part of the Shawnee and may hint at the perceptions of other nations and earlier periods. In fact, the implied audience of the speech suggests a large-scale inter-nation apprehension concerning European maple sugar consumption. Referring to European exploitation of sugar maples, Tenskwatawa called for his people to protect the trees from the settlers. Tenskwatawa is recorded by Dunham to have said: "The Great Spirit bids me address you in his own words, which are these. ... My Children ... I made all the Trees of the forest for your use, but the maple I love best, because it yields sugar for your little ones. You must make it only for them; but sell none to the *whites*. They have another sugar, which was made expressly for them."[49] As we see in this passage, Tenskwatawa considered the maples a godsend, a sentiment shared, moreover, by the more religiously minded writers of New France, such as Charlevoix. The reference to Native children plays on the auditors' emotional sensibilities—the White settlers are stealing candy from babes! The passage also casts maple as a heritage to be passed from generation to generation; sale of its sugar to White settlers jeopardizes this legacy. At the same time, this passage also sets up maple sugar as "Native sugar" and depicts cane sugar as the "White man's" sugar. Like their European counterparts, the Indigenous communities of the Great Lakes clearly recognize the competition between sugars in the early modern Atlantic world. But, while the French view maple sugar as a universal product available to all who are willing to tap the trees, Natives are being instructed to claim it as uniquely theirs. Although Tenskwatawa's admonition comes after the large-scale adoption of maple sugaring by French settlers, these reflections on the stakes of sugaring by Europeans highlight the ecocritical and zero-sum terms of the debate. If Europeans are allowed access to maple sugar, Native children will suffer.

In this way, maple sugar can be added to the long list of Native cultural material appropriated by Europeans and exploited for their own ends. While we have only scratched the surface of Indigenous Peoples' relationship to maple, what I have sketched out should suffice to demonstrate that maple sugar was not an innocent sugar, as later English-speaking abolitionists would claim. Indigenous People appear to have viewed maple sugaring by Europeans as a theft and an affront to their culture and religious mores.

In the immediate aftermath of the Seven Years War and the loss of New France in the Treaty of Paris, more pressing concerns occupied the remaining settler population of Canada than the question of maple sugar exploitation. Yet, maple sugar's potential would again awake the fantasies of future-anticipating capitalists before the end of the century. In 1792, Samuel Nielson, a Scottish-born transplant to Lower Canada and publisher of the influential bilingual newspaper, *The Quebec Gazette / La Gazette de Québec*, saw the chance to make Canada a (maple) sugar colony. In an editorial from 1 March 1792 he wrote,

> Notice to maple owners. Whereas the troubles that rule currently in the sugar colonies will make this product expensive in the future, it is fortunate that Canada produces one that can supplement it. What a shame that the maples are notched, instead of being pierced, to withdraw the sap ... it is hoped that all who become interested by the New Concessions will be convinced of the extraordinary value of the sugar-producing trees, and of the almost certain growth in their value by the discontinuation of the African Slave Trade.[50]

Nearly fifty years after Charlevoix mused about the economic potential of maple sugar and more than 200 years after André Thevet first directed European attention to the marvelous maple, Nielson calls for the development of a maple sugar industry in Canada. Despite his observation that drilling, or piercing, the tree might be a more efficient way to extract the sap, his remarks are largely theoretical. The growth of the maple sugar market would remain limited in the period by the economic and social realities of maple production.

Nielson's rhetoric parts company with that employed by the previous Francophone boosters of maple sugar and instead closely mirrors that of Benjamin Rush and Thomas Jefferson to the south. Specifically, he links the fortunes of the North Atlantic with those of the sugar islands of the Caribbean. He positions maple sugar as an alternative to cane and links its future to the end of the slave trade, if not slavery itself. Nielson marks, then, the end of the earlier French colonial understanding of maples, marked by Virgilian fantasies and illusions of imperial grandeur. Here his comments align more with Anglophone abolitionist thought emanating from the United States.

Beyond the sense of wonder and the references to antiquity in earlier French texts, one of the major differences between the maple discourses of the Anglo tradition and those of the French tradition lies in their respective elisions. The evils of slavery in the Caribbean are always a subtext in, or impetus for, U.S. propaganda in favor of maple sugar as a cane substitute. Native Peoples' contribution to maple sugaring, conversely, is largely absent in English texts. In *An Account of the Sugar Maple*, for example, Benjamin Rush makes a single passing reference to Native consumption of maple sugar: "it is preferred by the Indians in their excursions from home."[51] But, how did the Natives acquire this sugar? Where did their knowledge of these marvels of nature come from? These are questions Rush shows little interest in exploring.[52]

On the French side of things, the writers almost uniformly point to the importance of Native technology, combined with French *savoir-faire,* as a means of creating a viable maple alternative to cane sugar. The various writers, however, make no explicit reference to the enslavement of Black people in the Caribbean as a reason to prefer maple to cane sugar; they are not abolitionists. While the English set the "innocent maple" as a foil to the "immoral" cane, French writers speak of maple simply as one more missed opportunity in New France. As Charlevoix writes wistfully, "It will be objected, that if it was of such a good Quality, it would have become an Object of Trade, but there is not enough made for this Purpose; but perhaps they are in the wrong in not trying what may be done. There are many other Things besides this, that are neglected in this Country" (84). Charlevoix seems acutely aware of the challenges of creating a market for maple sugar and places it within the context of a mercantilist search for exploitable North American products beyond the beaver pelt. In short, for Charlevoix, a (maple) sugar colony in Canada to rival the Caribbean sugar islands was just an unrealized dream.

The importance of studying texts about maple sugar, then, is not for insight into the economic or strategic importance of the sugar itself. Only in the nineteenth century, with the advent of new technology, would maple producers be able to ramp up production to an exportable quantity. Rather, these texts shed light on French colonial discourses around grandeur, Native Peoples, and technology. French accounts of maple sugar depict it as a miraculous, Indigenous product and a godsend. The various descriptions of maple sugar help recast New France as a Virgilian land of honey. In turn, these texts challenge some received historiographical ideas about the early French colonial project in North America. In the passages about maple sugar, New France becomes a place of wondrous possibilities, rather than a frozen wasteland—"several acres of snow," as Voltaire famously put it in *Candide.*[53] As we have seen, the snow and the trees could represent wealth and opportunity, rather than poverty and desolation.

As an underexplored part of sugar foodways, maple sugar serves as a missing link in the story of sweetness. Each group—French visitors and settlers, Indigenous Peoples, and boosters of the new United States— employed different rhetorical strategies around maple sugar and articulated their own relationship to this natural product. By neglecting the French colonial period's impact on the development of this discourse, scholars have failed to understand some of the texture of this story. The rise of the abolitionist discourses of the late eighteenth and early nineteenth centuries have eclipsed these earlier French visions of maple. By bringing these earlier discourses to the fore, this article points to the complex story of sugar beyond the cane plantations. While we have only just begun to draw out the rhetorical differences around maple sugar among the various actors in the New World, what is clear is that all the inhabitants of the North Atlantic would come to see in sugar maples the stuff of sweet dreams.

Notes

1. Although today we are most familiar with maple sugar as a viscous syrup, in the eighteenth century maple sap was boiled down to varying degrees. From here on, I will be referring to "maple sugar" as a general term, regardless of the specific liquid or solid form it took.

2. The economics of maple syrup are considerable. According to statistics from the Federation of Québec Maple Syrup Producers, in 2019 Québec produced 71 percent of the worldwide supply of maple syrup, which represented 91 percent of all Canadian production, with $465 million (CAN) dollars in sales. See Fédération des producteurs acéricoles du Québec. *Statistiques acéricoles, 2019, https://ppaq. ca/app/uploads/2020/10/Dossier_economique-Statistiques_2019.pdf.*

3. See, for example, Gordon M. Sayre, *Les Sauvages Américains: Representations of Native Americans in French and English Colonial Literature* (Chapel Hill: University of North Carolina Press, 1997); Gilles Havard and Cécile Vidal, *Histoire de l'Amérique française* (Paris: Flammarion, 2003); and Sophie White, *Wild Frenchmen and Frenchified Indians: Material Culture and Race in Colonial Louisiana* (Philadelphia: University of Pennsylvania Press, 2012).

4. Parsons, *A Not-So-New World: Empire and Environment in French Colonial North America* (Philadelphia: University of Pennsylvania Press, 2018), 10.

5. Kalm, *The America of 1750: Peter Kalm's Travels in North America. The English Version of 1770,* ed. Adolph B. Benson (New York: Dover Publications, 1966), 154.

6. Kalm, *America of 1750,* 155.

7. Kalm, *America of 1750,* 154.

8. Mark Sturges, "'Bleed on, Blest Tree!': Maple Sugar Georgics in the Early American Republic," *Early American Studies* 16, no. 2 (2018): 379.

9. For more on the possibility of the Saint Lawrence river valley as a sugar colony, see Mathieu Peron, "Visions d'avenir, sucre d'érable et progress," *Histoire d'utopie* no. 136 (Winter 2019): 12.

10. Sturges, "'Bleed on, Blest Tree!,'" 354.

11. For more on ginseng in New France, see Parsons, *A Not-So-New World,* 178.

12. Sturges, "'Bleed on Blest Tree!,'" 355.

13. Sturges, "'Bleed on Blest Tree!,'" 354.

14. Campeau, "Les Origines du sucre d'érable," *Les Cahiers des dix* 45 (1990): 53.

15. Unlike maple sugar, cane sugar has been the subject of several full-length studies. See, for example, Sidney W. Mintz, *Sweetness and Power: The Place of Sugar in Modern History* (New York: Viking, 1985), and Marc Aronson and Marina Tamar Budhos, *Sugar Changed the World: A Story of Magic, Spice, Slavery, Freedom, and Science* (Boston: Clarion Books, 2010).

16. "[Canada] porte plusieurs arbres et fruits, dont nous n'avons la congnoissance par deça. Entre lesquels y a un arbre de la grosseur et forme d'un gros noyer de deça, lequel a demeuré long temps inutile, et sans estre congnu, iusjques à tant que quelcun le voulant coupper en saillit un suc, lequel fut trouvé d'autant bon goust, et delicat, que le bon vin d'Orleans, ou de Beaune: mesmes fut ainsi iugé par noz gens, qui lors en firent l'experience: c'est à sçavoir le Capitaine, et autres gentilshommes de sa compagnie, et recueillirent de ce ius sur l'heure de quatre à cinq grand pots. Ie vous laisse à penser, si depuis ces Canadiens afriandez à ceste liqueur, ne gardent pas cest arbre cherement, pour leur bruvages, puis qu'il est ainsi excellent. Cest arbre, en leur langue, est appelé *Couton*." André Thevet, *Singvlaritez de la France Antarctiqve* (Paris: Chez les héritiers de Maurice de la Porte, 1558), 158. Translations are my own, unless otherwise indicated.

17. Campeau, "Les Origines du sucre d'érable," 55.

18. "Quant à l'éau d'érable … elle est également délicieuse pour les Français et les Sauvages." Le Clercq, *Nouvelle Relation de la Gaspésie,* ed. Réal Ouellet (Montréal: Presses de l'Université de Montréal, 1999), 125.

19. "On en forme des petits pains, qu'on envoie en France par rareté, et qui dans l'usage sert bien souvent au défaut du sucre François." Le Clerq, *Nouvelle Relation,* 125.

20. See Paul Thiry, Baron d'Holbach, "Sucre d'érable," in *Encyclopédie, ou dictionnaire raisonné des sciences, des arts et des métiers, etc.*, ARTFL Encyclopédie Project, ed. Robert Morrissey and Glenn Roe, *https://artflsrv03.uchicago.edu/philologic4/encyclopedie1117/navigate/15/3003/.*

21. Charlevoix, *A Voyage to North-America* (Dublin, 1766), 131. Subsequent citations will be made parenthetically.

22. Karen Ordahl Kupperman, "The Puzzle of the American Climate in the Early Colonial Period, *American Historical Review* 87, no. 5 (1982): 1262–89.

23. See also Leslie Choquette, *Frenchmen into Peasants: Modernity and Tradition in the Peopling of French Canada* (Cambridge: Harvard University Press, 1997).

24. Virgil. *Eclogue* 4, v. 9, v. 30.

25. I am thinking specifically of colonial discourses of "la plus grande France," which we associate with the later colonial projects in Africa and Asia. See, for example, Raoul Girardet, *L'idée coloniale en France de 1871 à 1962* (Paris: La Table Ronde, 1972).

26.   Au lieu des cannes dont les pores
      Rendent le sucre blanc qui nous vient de plus loin,
      Pour les Acadiens, la nature a pris soin
      D'en mettre dans les sycomores.
      Au commencement du printemps,
      De leur écorce il sort une liqueur sucrée,

> Qu'avec grand soin les habitants
> Recueillent dans chaque contrée.
> Ce breuvage me semblait bon,
> Et je le buvais en rasade;
> Il ne fallait que du citron
> Pour faire de la limonade.

—Sieur de Dièreville, *Voyage du Sieur de Diéreville en Acadie* (Québec: Imprimerie A. Côté et Cie, 1885), 61.

27. "Il n'y a point de limonade, ni d'eau de cerise qui ait si bon goût, ni de breuvage au monde qui soit plus salutaire." Louis Armand de Lom d'Arce Lahontan, *Oeuvres Complètes,* ed Réal Ouellet, 2 vols. (Les Presses de l'Université de Montréal, 1990), 1:599.

28. "Or le sucre dont on use aujourd'huy, est un sucre factice. La canne dont on le tire, est une tige noüeuse, spongieuse, d'une écorce fort mince, et pleine d'une matiere miellée d'une très-grande douceur. On brise les cannes dans des Moulins; ou en exprime tout le suc dans des pressoirs. … C'est cette maniere de faire le sucre et de le raffiner que les Anciens n'ont pas connuë." Lafitau, *Moeurs des sauvages ameriquains, comparées aux moeurs des premiers temps* (Paris: Chez Saugrain l'aîné, 1724), 146.

29. "Les Poëtes, dans les descriptions qu'ils font de l'Age d'or, ou des Siècles qui lui être compares, nous dissent entr'autres merveilles, que les chênes les plus durs distilloient du miel ou qu'ils en distilleront … nos Sauvages font voir qu'ils en sçavent plus qu'eux, ayant sçu tirer des érables … un suc naturel, lequel a autant, ou plus d'agrément, que le miel que font les Abeilles." Lafitau, *Moeurs des sauvages ameriquains*, 155.

30. Zachary McLeod Hutchins, *Inventing Eden: Primitivism, Millennialism, and the Making of New England* (Oxford University Press, 2014), 3.

31. "Les François le travaillent mieux que les *Sauvagesses* de qui ils ont appris à le faire." Lafitau, *Moeurs des sauvages ameriquains*, 150.

32. Montrose, "The Work of Gender in the Discourse of Discovery," *Representations* no. 33 (1991): 5.

33. This is in contrast to the contemporary discourse around maple syrup that has largely erased Indigenous knowledge and recast syrup as a Québécois national product. See *Goût d'un pays,* dir. Francis Legault (2016; Montréal: Zone 3).

34. One traditional method was to heat up stones and place them in hollowed out logs filled with maple sap. For a more detailed description of Native maple sugaring techniques and tools, see Alan Corbiere and Kate Higginson, "Ninaatigwaaboo (Maple Tree Water): An Anishinaabe History of Maple Sugaring," *https://grasac.artsci.utoronto.ca/?p=136.*

35. Turgeon, "The Tale of the Kettle: Odyssey of an Intercultural Object." *Ethnohistory* 44, no. 1 (1997): 10.

36. Denholm, "The History of Maple Syruping in Wisconsin," *University Place.* PBS-WI, 18 September 2018, *https://www.pbs.org/video/the-history-of-maple-syruping-in-wisconsin-8baw7u/,* 14:40–15:05.

37. "Les champs, tels qu'ils sont à l'issüe de l'hyver; on y voit les femmes occupées à leur donner la premiere façon, et à y semer leur bled d'inde de [leur] maniere." Lafitau, *Moeurs des sauvages ameriquains*, sig. a4r.

38. "Il faut qu'il y ait au pied une certaine quantité de neige." Lafitau, *Moeurs des sauvages ameriquains*, 254.

39. Certeau, "Writing vs. Time: History and Anthropology in the Works of Lafitau," trans. James Hovde, *Yale French Studies* no. 59 (1980): 60.

40. Certeau, "Writing vs. Time," 60.

41. Scholars have noted a link between sugar in the Caribbean and the erotic gaze. See Omise'eke Natasha Tinsley, *Thiefing Sugar: Eroticism Between Women in Caribbean Literature* (Durham: Duke University Press, 2010). Maple sugar also appears to have been associated with femininity and sexual objectification of Indigenous women.

42. Certeau, "Writing vs. Time," 42.

43. David Allen Harvey, "Living Antiquity: Lafitau's *Moeurs des sauvages amériquains* and the Religious Roots of the Enlightenment Science of Man," *Journal of the Western Society for French History* 36 (2008): 91.

44. Sweet, *American Georgics: Economy and Environment in American Literature, 1580–1864* (Philadelphia: University of Pennsylvania Press, 2013), 3.

45. "Here I see the influence of trade starting. So you start talking about the 1800s ... [it's] very confusing because which group of people was here making sugar or making sap into sugar in the 1400s, 1500s, 1600s ... changed as Native Americans were being pushed farther and farther west, so the mixing of tribes that would have been here when early Europeans came here would not have been the same as if you'd come, say, a hundred years earlier" (Denholm, "History of Maple Syruping in Wisconsin," 19:10–19:54).

46. Denholm, "History of Maple Syruping in Wisconsin," 15:15–15:30.

47. Rosemary Chambers, "'Sugaring-off': A Brief History of Maple Syrup," *The Voice of Pelham,* 8 March 2017: 3.

48. Andrew J. Blackbird, *History of the Ottawa and Chippewa Indians of Michigan: A Grammar of their Language, and Personal and Family History of the Author* (Ypsilanti: The Ypsilantian Job Printing House, 1887), 62.

49. Letter from Dunham to William Hull, May 1807, quoted in R. E. Banta, *The Ohio* (Lexington: University Press of Kentucky, 1998), 210–11.

50. "Avis aux propriétaire d'érablières. Comme les troubles qui règnent actuellement dans les Colonies à sucre doivent rendre cet article cher à l'avenir, il est heureux que le Canada en produise un qui peut y suppléer. Quel dommage que l'on entaille des érables au lieu de les percer pour en tirer la sève ... il est à souhaiter que tous ceux qui deviennent intéressés dans les Nouvelles Concessions fussent convaincus de la valeur inappréciable des arbres qui produisent le sucre, et de l'accroissement presque certain de cette valeur par la discontinuation du Trafic d'Esclaves d'Afrique." Cited in Peron, "Visions d'avenir," 15.

51. Rush, *An Account of the Sugar Maple* (Philadelphia, 1792), 12.

52. For Jefferson's maple ambitions, see Lucia C. Stanton, "Sugar Maple," *Thomas Jefferson Encyclopedia, https://www.monticello.org/site/research-and-collections/sugar-maple.*

53. "Quelques arpents de neige." Voltaire, *Candide: ou L'optimisme, traduit de l'allemand de Mr. le docteur Ralph* (Netherlands: Lambert, 1759), 170.

"Pirate Vices, Public Benefits": The Social Ethics of Piracy in the 1720s

NOEL CHEVALIER

The end of the Golden Age of Piracy, that period in the early decades of the eighteenth century that forms the core narratives of Charles Johnson's *A General History of the Pyrates*, can perhaps be dated specifically to 12 July 1726, the date of the execution of the pirate William Fly. Fly's story is chronologically the latest in the *General History*. In Johnson's version, he appears very much as the last of a dying breed, stubbornly trying to operate within a culture that had largely been eradicated, thanks to Woodes Rogers's aggressive war on piracy. Fly himself, although defiant and rebellious to the end, is hard to romanticize as a swashbuckling, freedom-loving adventurer; exceptionally violent, short-tempered, and foul-mouthed (even for a sailor), Fly's pirate career was brief and mostly undistinguished. What makes him noteworthy is his appearance in a remarkable 1726 pamphlet by Cotton Mather, *The Vial Poured Out upon the Sea*. In the pamphlet, Mather, already well-known as a minister to convicted pirates, engages in a series of conversations with the condemned Fly and his crew. Mather hopes to bring them to true repentance before their sentences are carried out. His concern for the pirates' salvation is genuine—following his religious principles, Mather believes that the pirates, even at the point of immanent death, can still acknowledge the wrongs they have done and hope for God's grace to be merciful to them. The pirates' submission to a temporal authority that has justly and fairly determined death to be the proper punishment for their wrongdoings is to be the first step in their proving themselves worthy to receive God's mercy.

The trick, of course, is getting the pirates to believe in a just and fair authority. To that end, Mather engages Fly in a fascinating debate over the place of forgiveness as a preparation to receive justice. Fly has acknowledged his own failings, though he will not admit to murder, but at the same time he insists that there are people who have wronged him whom he cannot forgive. Mather reminds him, "Our Lord has taught us to pray, *Forgive us as we forgive*. I hope you *pray*, according to that *Prayer*." Fly replies, "*Yes, I do!—But for all that, I cannot Forgive that Man.—GOD Almighty Revenge me on him!—'Tis a Vain thing.—I won't dy with a Lye in my Mouth*."[1] A few days later, Mather again urged Fly to forgive, arguing that a truly repentant soul forgives all wrongs and has made peace with all of his enemies. However, Fly argues that for him simply to pretend to forgiveness would make him guilty of lying, an even greater sin. Then, he challenges Mather's whole notion of justice: "*I can't Charge myself,—I shan't own myself Guilty of any Murder,—our Captain and his Mate used us Barbarously. We poor Men can't have Justice done us. There is nothing said to our Commanders, let them never so much abuse us, and use us like Dogs*."[2] Fly openly declares that the game is rigged, thereby suggesting that Mather's efforts to get him to confess are, in effect, simply attempts to get him to acknowledge that the status quo is right and that neither he, nor any of the other condemned pirates, had any justification for their actions.

Fly accurately notes the double standard that existed on ships. He was hardly unique in making that complaint. Part of the motivation for turning pirate, as Marcus Rediker has noted, involved rejecting a social order that was so manifestly unjust and that offered little hope or comfort beyond that of resigned forbearance. Captains, answerable only to the ships' owners, could indulge in sometimes horrific abuses, especially in the name of discipline. Fly's conversation with Mather, then, became a debate about the ethical boundaries of life aboard ship: are the victims of such abuse expected to submit unquestioningly? Between sadistic captains and bloodthirsty pirates, who, in fact, is guilty of the greater moral wrong? Intentionally or not, then, Mather's pamphlet highlights the complex relationship between crime, vice, and morality revealed by piracy in the 1720s.

The whole debate over the true nature of forgiveness, penitence, and even justice, takes us a long way from the central, defining feature of pirates: namely, that they were sailors who attacked and plundered other ships for personal gain. At the same time, in both popular and legal culture, pirates were almost never regarded simply as sailors who steal: as the "enemies of all humanity," pirates somehow struck at the very heart of commerce and challenged the fabric of civilization itself. There is no question that Fly and his crew were criminals, but Mather's discourse focuses less on the moral wrong of theft and more on the entire character of pirates. Mather's moral sparring with Fly at least suggests a man who possesses a distinct ethical framework, even if Mather disagrees with that framework.

A shift in emphasis away from the purely economic value of what pirates stole to the moral affront posed by their stealing reflects a shift in the view of pirates themselves after 1713. Margarette Lincoln has noted that, prior to the War of the Spanish Succession, pirates—usually acting as legally sanctioned privateers—enjoyed not only the sanction of the law to plunder as they saw fit, but also the sanction of aristocratic society, some of whom even supported their expeditions.[3] In colonial settlements, too, pirates were generally welcomed as eager supporters of local economies. Mark Hanna has noted that the influx of cheap commodities to British colonies after the Treaty of Utrecht and the general improvement of colonial economies that resulted from the expansion of the slave trade made the pirates' support of maritime communities "unnecessary" and even a threat to this newfound economic stability.[4] At the same time, the early 1720s in Britain were marked by the destabilizing effects of the South Sea Bubble, which raised pertinent questions about the right uses of money, credit, and financial speculation. Within this economic context, the pirate figure could not be normalized as a necessary part of colonial commerce, nor even simply regarded as an occasional nuisance to transatlantic trade. In pirate narratives of the 1720s, the pirate is recast as a monstrous outsider, the *hostis humani generis*, the universal enemy of all humanity. We can see this recasting at work dramatically in *A General History of the Pyrates*, that compendium of pirate stories assembled under the name of one "Captain Charles Johnson."

In this essay, I want to focus specifically on how Johnson's *General History* engages with the social ethics of the 1720s—a period in which the very idea of the public good was being re-evaluated after the collapse of the South Sea Bubble—and in the process helps construct a figure of the pirate still well known to us: not simply a maritime criminal, but a monstrous embodiment of the spirit of an ethically troublesome age.

Pirates and Morality I

By the second decade of the eighteenth century, Britain had come to regard the health of its commercial interests as a barometer of the overall health of the nation. Colonial trade, especially, provided an influx of luxury goods, as well as considerable profits for the merchants who undertook overseas trade. Margarette Lincoln quotes William King's *The British Merchant*, published in 1721, as proof that merchants of the day "like[d] to flatter themselves" as being "as essential ... to the state as blood to the body."[5] Lincoln notes that, in official discourse, piracy was almost always considered a particular evil, one damaging to the national interest. Yet, at the same time, to the London merchants, the pirate was an especially abstract figure, often discussed, certainly feared, but rarely if ever seen. As *hostis humani generis*—the enemy of all humanity—the pirate was bestowed with the qualities of a monster: always lurking in the margins of civilization, cut off from respectable human society, forever elusive and shadowy, the repository of all fears, perpetually terrifying.[6] Pirates were a new breed of "masterless men" whose refusal to submit to any authority but their own seemed to threaten the very foundations of society.[7] Peter Linebaugh and Marcus Rediker have explored the connection between the growth of maritime trade between 1670 and 1730 and the preservation of the political challenge posed by the mid-seventeenth-century masterless men. They note, for instance, that "the ship became both an engine of capitalism in the wake of the bourgeois revolution in England *and* a setting of resistance, a place to which and in which the ideas and practices of revolutionaries defeated and repressed by Cromwell and then by King Charles escaped, reformed, circulated, and persisted."[8] While the crimes that pirates committed certainly resembled those of land robbers or murderers, the pirate was a unique category of felon in that their primary victim was supposedly not the individual sailor or merchant ship owner, but rather Commerce itself.

Given the early eighteenth-century change in the perception of pirates, it is perhaps unsurprising that an overview of contemporary piracy should emerge that would attempt to define and articulate a distinct pirate culture. Johnson's *General History* made pirates knowable to its urban, largely middle-class readership, even to the point where its biases and errors became incorporated into the general iconography of piracy. Johnson's treatment of pirates, more than anything, is what led to the pirates of the 1713–26 period's becoming the archetype for all pirates in popular culture. The book is largely an attempt to understand the pirates of the Golden Age as a political, economic, and social phenomenon, one that stands in opposition to, but also grows directly out of, the society that produced them. Charles Johnson, whoever he may have been, repeatedly shows his awareness of the intellectual conversations in print surrounding vice, luxury, criminality, and the proper use of money and credit, especially in the aftermath of the South Sea Bubble (to which Johnson specifically refers at one point). The pirate, as the monstrous *hostis humani generis*, the perpetual margin-walker, is the quintessential anti-hero, the *doublûre* of the Great Man that exposes all the vice, rapacity, and squalor that lies behind that elevated figure. Since the pirate-monster exists mainly in relation to the state, it is the pirate's assault on the state—a form of petty treason—that occupies the moral focus of arguments against piracy. Part of the issue here is how the law contributes to the formation of virtue. This is not an insignificant question, since the law is the State's exercise of moral authority—especially if the Church's exercise of moral authority (namely, encouraging the hope of Heaven and the fear of Hell) didn't seem to hold much sway with pirates. A sailor who refused to be terrified by the threat of hellfire could be cowed by the promise of the gallows. Except, of course, often they couldn't.

Johnson frequently acknowledges in his narratives that pirates are complex, even paradoxical figures. Not all pirate captains, he understands, are created equal: some, such as Blackbeard, swagger onto the page as larger-than-life figures, meriting (in the original editions) full-page engravings; others, such as John Gow, are barely the main actors in their own chapters and reveal how easy it is for otherwise unremarkable sailors to become caught up in the drama of piracy. Richard Frohock suggests that the "*General History* enacts a double satire, upholding the pirates' view that mainstream society is structured to privilege the rich and powerful at the expense of the weak and disadvantaged while simultaneously mocking pirates who cannot—and often intend not—to live up to their principled claims."[9] Johnson's challenge in the *General History* is how to acknowledge that, despite their monstrosity, pirates have much in common with the so-called great men of the age. Even the fact that the *General History* enshrines the public lives—and, sometimes, the public deaths—of common pirates, suggests an unusual importance in the acts of men and women who would otherwise be considered mere members of the mob. Johnson himself addresses the issue in his preface: "*I presume we need make no Apology for giving the Name of a History to the following Sheets, though they contain nothing but the Actions of a Parcel of Robbers. It is Bravery and Stratagem in War which make Actions worthy of Record; in which Sense the Adventures here related will be thought deserving that Name*" (*1724a*, sigs. A4ʳ–A4ᵛ [6]).[10] Bestowing the title of "history" on his pirate tales allows Johnson to treat his subjects as something nobler than a "Parcel of Robbers," even if at times he seems to treat the "Bravery and Stratagem" of pirates ironically. One reason that Fly appears as such a shabby and uninspiring figure in Johnson is that readers have already seen much more successful—even admirable—examples of pirates, such as Henry Every, Edward "Blackbeard" Teach, and Bartholomew Roberts. While Johnson does not go out of his way to romanticize his pirate subjects, he does acknowledge that pirates can and do display some aspects of "greatness," however perverted it may be.

Johnson's suggestion that pirates may exhibit greatness coincidentally echoes Mather's deep engagement with Fly and his crew. Mather embraces the somewhat radical idea that the so-called lower orders are even worth encouraging to reform. After all, why bother wasting time and energy trying to coerce an eleventh-hour repentance out of a hardened criminal who expects no mercy either in this world or the next? If pirates are, truly, the "enemies of all humanity," then does their monstrous nature preclude them from genuinely seeking God's grace? Mather, of course, wishes to use Fly and his crew as rhetorical devices and hopes that his readers will see in their example a warning against considering piracy at all. And yet, Mather's allowing Fly a voice and a rational perspective elevates him from simply being a disposable member of the mob into someone whose ultimate destiny actually matters.

Piracy and the "Publick Good": Johnson, Defoe, and Mandeville

It is assumed in the moral literature against pirates that merchant ships and merchant sailors act out of a sense of public benevolence; indeed, commerce itself is said to be undertaken for the general health of the nation. Pirates, on the other hand, act *only* out of self-interest, since their aim is not to carry on legitimate trade, but rather to take what they want for themselves and to dispose of it as they see fit. Pirates' predation on merchant ships, therefore, is a crime against the public good; everyone suffers from acts of piracy. Johnson's *General History* acknowledges this view, but also shows it to be problematic, since the idea of what actually constitutes a public benefit is itself problematic. The *General History*'s perspective on social ethics clearly has little in common with Cotton Mather's Puritan piety or with the admonitions to sailors to submit to authority, however harsh, that can be found in *The Seaman's Monitor*, a standard *vade-mecum* issued to sailors that even included, in its 1723 edition, a special section warning sailors against considering a life of piracy.

Piracy's relationship to the rest of society, as Johnson demonstrates, is complex and multi-faceted. Pirates themselves are not easily branded as just deviants, in part because, as he takes great pains to show, pirates themselves both mimic conventional society and yet also deconstruct it. Johnson is fascinated with the codes of conduct that existed on pirate ships, reprinting several lists of rules that were to be followed. He is also fascinated by the collective nature of piracy, that pirates operated within networks and associations, even as those associations were often unstable. The solidarity implied by the buccaneer term "Brethren of the Coast" is not really applicable to Johnson's pirates—there is too much distrust and self-interest for these associations to last indefinitely—and yet, there was a high degree of cooperation among the Caribbean pirates. Pirate society, then, was primarily utilitarian, with all pirates understanding that friendship was based on convenience and mutual benefit. This utilitarian model that accepts that self-interest and avarice form the backbone of society is fully articulated in Bernard Mandeville's *Fable of the Bees,* which, perhaps not insignificantly, became a *cause célèbre* after it was reprinted in 1723.

In the *Fable of the Bees,* Mandeville argues for a holistic model of society, as in his famous analogy in "Remark K" comparing society to a bowl of punch, whose individual elements may seem unpalatable, but come together to make a pleasing taste. In this analogy, "Avarice" is "a griping Acid that sets our Teeth on edge, and is unpleasant to every Palate that is not debauch'd," while "Prodigality," which Mandeville calls a "Noble Sin," is "a pleasing Balsam that heals and makes amends for the smart."[11] Mandeville's remarks are clearly based on a radically different conception of "virtue" than the religious moralists. The *Fable of the Bees* is important not only as an iteration of the philosophical debates around the very features of commerce and luxury that also occupied pirates, but also as a critique of the social and political forces that, in part, explain the prominence of pirates in the 1720s. There is a shared feeling in the *General History* and the *Fable of the Bees* that criminal behavior is endemic to society: the love of gold and material wealth is far too ingrained in us to be driven out easily, and Johnson's remarks about "Bravery and Stratagem" align the pirate with the celebrated military hero. Moreover—and this is where both texts ask to be read politically—when the same behavior is being exhibited by the so-called betters of the lower orders, then we can hardly expect pirates or land criminals to behave any differently. If Mandeville, as F. B. Kaye contends, is working out a utilitarian view of morality and suggesting that morality is not an absolute concept, then it would stand to reason that the moral arguments against piracy are null and void.[12] In fact, Mandeville suggests that highwaymen (and, by extension, pirates) participate in the public good—something Hanna also argues in terms of colonial ports that benefited from pirate plunder.

So what is the solution for pirates? One option is to enact their own laws, as with Bartholomew Roberts's famous set of rules that Johnson reproduces. Alternately, they might take issue with the practice of law, the unfairness with which laws are applied, or the corruptions of those given authority to uphold the law, all of which Johnson underlines in the text of a remarkable—but very likely fictional—satirical sketch said to have been performed by Thomas Anstis's men when they were marooned.[13] Piracy is unsettling because, for Johnson at least, it moved beyond simply living outside the law—Roberts's rules in effect recognized the pirate ship as an autonomous state, to which an alternative moral and legal code could then apply. The *General History* reveals the limitations of law in much the same way that Mandeville reveals the limitations of morality.

Johnson's engagement with Mandeville's ideas of self-interest also resonate with two critics of Mandeville who, perhaps not surprisingly, have also been closely associated with the *General History*: Daniel Defoe and Nathaniel Mist. It's easy to understand why John Robert Moore was so eager to ascribe the *General History* to Defoe. It's too important a text to be mere hack work, although parts of it show evidence of haphazard revision and hurried printing. Yet, there is not a shred of solid evidence that Defoe had anything to do with it. Moore may well have been overzealous in seeing Defoe's hand everywhere (his methods for determining attribution are certainly questionable), but he was not wrong in seeing the connections between Defoe, the *General History*, and texts that concern them both: texts that share a similar perspective on the social, political, and economic questions of the time.[14]

In "Mandeville and Defoe," Moore considers Defoe's remarks on the *Fable of the Bees*. Moore argues that, far from joining in the near universal condemnation of Mandeville's defense of vice in the *Fable*, Defoe actually shared a good deal of Mandeville's sentiments.[15] Defoe engages with Mandeville's central thesis that what can be called "the public good" depends on encouraging private vices. While Defoe is very much a keen moralist, he appreciates that Mandeville, in the *Fable*, is actively working out a definition of the public good that tries to encompass the full complexity of that term. Defoe himself works out his own definition of the public good both in his pamphlets on the South Sea Trade and in his curious handbook for merchants, *The Complete English Tradesman*, with the latter composed and published at the same time as the most intense period of the *Fable of the Bees* controversy and the first two editions of the *General History*.

Defoe, Mandeville, and Johnson all, in various ways, specifically engage the question of how much public benefit depends on private vice. Common to all three writers is the tricky distinction between treating criminal behavior in a way that is not simply a reaction to its moral repugnance, while at the same time not appearing to encourage vice. Johnson, in particular, remarks on the viciousness of some individual pirates, while passing up many opportunities to condemn piracy itself. All three writers share the notion that crime is an inevitable part of modern society, which is itself an outward and visible sign of the inherently degraded nature of that society. What we find in Defoe and Mandeville, and also in Mist and Johnson, is a particular focus on criminality and the public good, on understanding crime not merely as a marker of human depravity, but also as a distinct and complex social phenomenon, and especially on the ways in which crime and criminal activity affect the public benefits of trade and commerce.

In number 107 of the *Review* (18 October 1707), Defoe uses the stories of Henry Avery's Madagascar pirates as a way of introducing the subject of business ethics that he will return to in more detail in *The Compleat English Tradesman*. Defoe notes that these pirates have petitioned for a pardon, vowing to "return to their own Country, live quietly at home, and ceasing their old Trade, become honest Freeholders," rather in the same way that "others of our *West-India* Pyrates, *Merchants I should have said,* have done before them."[16] Defoe then comes to his main point: that in terms of ethics, there is little to distinguish between the "Litteral" pirates who have established themselves on Madagascar and the "Allegorical" pirates whom Defoe sees as unethical colonial tradesmen:

> the Clandestine Trade Pyrates, who pyrate upon fair Trade at home; the Custom-stealing Pyrates, who pyrate upon the Government; the Owling Pyrates, who rob the Manufactures; the privateering Pyrates, who rob by Law; and because *A* the *French* Man of St. *Maloes* rob'd them, rob *B* of *Marsellies*, that never did them any Hurt; whether we mean the cheating Pyrate, that robs at home, or the Factor Pyrate, that robs abroad, of all Sorts, from the *Madagascar* Man to the *Buchaneer*—If all these should be taken off of the *Exchang*, and rendezvous'd, might we not say of them, as once of the Coward Captains of the Fleet, *Bless Us, what Crowding there'd be when they meet!*[17]

Clearly, Defoe is less interested in pirates as such than in using the term "pirate" to cover a wide range of dishonest business practices among supposedly honest tradesmen. Yet that in itself is noteworthy, since Defoe raises the question of why some criminals, who at least honestly identify themselves as criminals, should be punished for committing the same crimes as those who flock to Exchange-Alley daily. Defoe even draws the parallel of colonial merchants who build up great estates in Jamaica, just as the Madagascar pirates have supposedly done, and then bring their wealth home to retire in England.

Defoe's real point in the essay—ostensibly a continuation of the previous number—is the power of money to obliterate all wrongs. The Madagascar pirates' offer to purchase a pardon, though morally outrageous at first sight, is actually the best of all possible options, argues Defoe. The government can set its own price on the pirates' freedom and use the money they have stolen and return it back to the public purse: a clear case of a private vice yielding a public benefit. None of this, of course, condones piracy itself; nor does Defoe much concern himself with the lives of the actual pirates. But he does see piracy as an intrinsic and perhaps even necessary part of global commerce, and, as such, he sees a direct connection between pirates and merchants—especially colonial merchants who enter into trade primarily to make money, regardless of ethics: "Who would not be a Thief ... that could live in all manner of Luxury and Wealth for a Time, and then having gotten Money enough to buy his Pardon, turn honest Fellow again."[18] Defoe's point will, with some expansion, form the basis of much of Mandeville's arguments in the *Fable of the Bees* and will lie behind much of the *General History*'s perspective on pirates.

Defoe picks up the threads of the argument in his *Essay on the South Sea Trade* (1712). While the focus of the essay is undoubtedly the economic viability of the South Sea Company, Defoe is well aware that trade is not an isolated phenomenon, and he is unwilling to separate considerations of trade from their social effects. Indeed, although Defoe wrote extensively and passionately about trade his entire life, although economics and commerce are never far from his thoughts, even in his fiction, his entire outlook is driven by his sense of their effects upon society as a whole; or, to put it another way, he is always aware that discussions of human activity—whether politics, economics, or religion—must always place real humans at their center.[19] Therefore, there can be no study of trade without considering its effect upon the public good, since all activity within the public sphere must be directed towards that end.

We can see Defoe's focus on the human factor in trade most succinctly in a short work published on 2 April 1724, a month before the first edition of the *General History*: *The Great Law of Subordination Consider'd*. An essay on the proper behavior of servants (and a surprisingly conservative document for anyone who might have considered Defoe a proto-egalitarian), it is also a meditation on the power of law to reaffirm what Defoe sees as a natural social hierarchy. Central to Defoe's argument is a particular definition of "liberty" that qualifies the notion of the rights of the free-born Englishman with the restrictions on that freedom demanded by one's place within the social hierarchy. Specifically, Defoe points out the danger of subordinates acting rashly or uncivilly: he relates the case of a servant who desired to take a gentleman to court for public swearing (an offense punishable by paying a fine for each instance noted). The master points out that, while the servant is free under the law to pursue his legal action, the master is also free to terminate his servant's employment should he do so. Just because one is free to take an action, Defoe suggests, does not mean that such actions may not have consequences. The implication here is that servants who assume a level of moral or legal superiority over their masters must not assume that they themselves can escape legal scrutiny. This, he asserts, is one of the problems an unqualified focus on "liberty" might engender.

Having reworked the notion of liberty, Defoe next considers the place of wages. What Defoe says of the corrupting influence of money on servants may just as easily be applied to pirates: *"The Error is in their Morals*; the Money prompts their Vice, and their Vice depraves their Manners; so that every Advantage which shou'd encourage them to Diligence, and an humble Behaviour, is the ruin both of their Diligence, and Behaviour."[20] For Defoe, everything proceeds from the basic principle of lax morals: the existing hierarchy is unsustainable in a social structure that admits the possibility of a meritocracy.

Does Defoe believe in a meritocracy?

On 8 August 1724, just a few weeks before the publication of the second edition of the *General History*, Nathaniel Mist published an essay in the *Weekly Journal; or, Saturday's Post* attacking Mandeville's defense of vice. There is a considerable body of circumstantial evidence linking Mist with Johnson, and at the very least, *Mist's Weekly Journal* heavily promoted the book from 1724 onward, and Mist even advertised himself as a vendor of copies. It is entirely possible, perhaps even likely, that Mist was the originator of the *General History* project, even if he was not actually the author. It would not be out of character, then, for Mist to direct readers' attentions toward the revision and reissue of what was clearly for him a major title.

In his attack on Mandeville, Mist echoes the sentiments of publications such as the *Seasonable Admonition Against Mutiny and Piracy* (a 1723 addendum to Josiah Woodward's well-known *Seaman's Monitor*, a standard conduct book for sailors), warning "young people" against reading such publications as *The Fable of the Bees*: "the loose Ideas they raise, are Temptations to loose Actions, and a strong Provocation to Lewdness is within a Degree of the Thing it self.—I shall not take upon me to dictate to my Superiors, what Course to take with those who draw their Pens against good Manners and Modesty; but tis I know, that Vertue never flourishes more than when Vice is removed out of Sight."[21]

Mist continues his argument in the following week's issue, which is essentially a defense of the clergy:

> What makes Men despise Government, rob, defraud, oppress, or malign each other, but this want of Veneration to Religion, the Conclusion is right with the Profligate and Irreligious. *Let us eat and drink, for to Morrow we dye.* For why should any Man who is perswaded he has no Interest in another Life, sit down, despair, and starve, while others of the same earthly Original live in Power, Affluence, and Plenty? No, when under no such

> Restraint, every Man of Spirit only watches more carefully
> against the Penalty of human Laws. ... To hazard the Punishment
> than want always: Hence proceeds our Land and Sea Robbers
> more numerous amongst us (to the Disgrace of our Nation be it
> spoken) than in all the other European kingdoms put together,
> and hence, with those who have more Fear and less Courage,
> ensue Prisons, Starvings, Suicides.[22]

Taken as a whole, Mist's essays of August 1724 constitute an extended attack on Mandeville. Significantly, however, they also include a curious puff piece for the *General History*. That Mist should refer to the *General History* on 29 August is hardly surprising: it was obviously written to coincide with the publication of the second edition. But it is the nature of that piece that is most remarkable. The essay suggests a political reading of the *General History* that, in fact, ties in with the argument against anti-clericalism that Mist had been developing. It includes an imaginary letter from a member of a club of gentlemen in some unnamed country location. The letter describes another club member, a Justice of the Peace, who was formerly a "Fanatick and a Tradesman" in London. This Justice, clearly both a dissenting Protestant and a Whig (and so the very sort of person whom Mist had blamed the previous week for promoting vice and for attacking the Anglican clergy), overhears some of the other club members reading Mist's essays from May and June aloud. He immediately assumes that Mist is talking about pirates only metaphorically, since "this shim-sham Story of Pyrates is an impudent Libel upon great Men."[23] Mist thus cleverly directs his readers' attention to a particular way of approaching the *General History*—as a commentary upon the present government—and yet, at the same time, suggests that the ardent Whig supporters of the government would find such a reading disgusting. Mist, moreover, does not deny the validity of such a reading, only notes that it was not apparent to the other club members.

Pirates and Morality II

The monster-pirate embodied in Johnson's *General History* stands as an incarnation of the anxieties of colonial trade. That pirates could openly flout both civil and moral law, that they could construct proto-societies of their own, organized along radically different lines, all suggested a moral crisis at the heart of the society of the 1720s that events such as the South Sea Bubble only seemed to verify. That pirates could also be successful at what they did, that relatively few of Johnson's narratives end with capture and execution, only serves to highlight the ways in which the pirate is offered up here as an apt image of the moral bankruptcy of the age.[24]

Lest it seem, though, that pirates were entirely without any ethical dimension, we may return to the hapless William Fly and examine more closely his reason for refusing to forgive William Atkinson. As the *General History* records, Fly had pressed Atkinson into navigational service, in effect relying on him to bring the pirates out of danger of being captured. Fly, of course, threatened Atkinson with execution if he refused to comply, but he presents Atkinson's compliance as a moral obligation, rather than a coerced action:

> *Now, Capt. Atkinson, you may do as you please, you may be a Son of a Whore and pilot us wrong, which, G—d d—n ye, would be a rascally Trick by G—d, because you would betray Men who trust in you; but, by the eternal J—s, you shan't live to see us hang'd. I don't love many Words, G—d d—n ye, if you have a Mind to be well used you shall, G—d's B—d; but if you will be a Villain and betray your Trust, may G—d strike me dead, and may I drink a Bowl of Brimstone and Fire with the D—l, if I don't send you head-long to H—ll, G—d d—n me; and so there needs no more Arguments by G—d, for I've told you my Mind, and here's all the Ships Crew for Witnesses, that if I do blow your Brains out, you may blame no Body but your self, G—d d—n ye.* (*1728.2*, 234 [611]).

Fly's refusal to forgive Atkinson, therefore, stemmed from Atkinson's betrayal of trust, from his "rascally Trick" of pretending to navigate them to safety. Fly's moral sense is consistent with other pirate codes: that, though self-interest is a major part of the pirate ethos, one may also appeal to the larger "public good" of the ship itself. Fly is not without a social ethic, even if that ethic would satisfy neither the authorities who hanged him, nor the Puritan minister who attempted to redeem him.

By incorporating pirates into discussions of the public good, Johnson, Defoe, and Mist all reaffirm the anxieties about piracy that permeate discussions of commercial activity—especially colonial commercial activity—and attempt to assuage those anxieties. The pirates of Johnson's *General History* already exist within a morally ambiguous universe. And, it is clear, that universe dominated discussions of public and private good throughout the decade. The ideas that a criminal may also be a "great man," or that "greatness" may be a mask for criminality, and that the wealthy and powerful exhibit the same vices as common sailors, only to escape without punishment, permeate Johnson's accounts of pirate activity, especially since Johnson avoids the kind of overt moralizing against piracy that normally accompanies such narratives. This discussion of the relationship between greatness and vice, the acknowledgement of a double standard under the law for crimes against property, would find its best-known expression in 1728—the same year as Volume II of the *General History* was published—in John Gay's *The Beggar's Opera*.

Notes

1. *"That Man"* refers to William Atkinson, first mate aboard the sloop *John and Hannah*, which Fly and his men attacked in June 1726. Fly released the ship and its captain but pressed Atkinson into service as a pilot. Atkinson pretended to comply with the pirates but ultimately betrayed Fly and his crew and was directly responsible for their capture. The *General History* features a remarkably oath-strewn speech by Fly denouncing Atkinson's initial resistance to piloting the pirates' ship. Mather, *The Vial Poured Out upon the Sea: A Remarkable Relation of Certain Pirates Brought unto a Tragical and Untimely End* (Boston, 1726), 16.

2. Mather, *Vial Poured Out*, 21.

3. Lincoln, *British Pirates and Society, 1680–1730* (Farnham: Ashgate Press, 2014), 115–25.

4. Hanna, *Pirate Nests and the Rise of the British Empire, 1570–1740* (University of North Carolina Press, 2015), 327.

5. Lincoln, *British Pirates and Society*, 82.

6. See Jeffrey Jerome Cohen's "Monster Culture: Seven Theses," in *Monster Theory: Reading Culture*, ed. Cohen (Minneapolis: University of Minnesota Press, 1996), 3–25, for an anatomy of features that comprise the literary monster. Although Cohen focuses on traditional monsters, such as vampires, werewolves, and aberrations of nature, many of the attributes of these more familiar monsters also apply quite neatly to pirates.

7. See Christopher Hill, *The World Turned Upside Down: Radical Ideas during the English Revolution* (New York: Viking Press, 1972), for a fuller discussion of the anxiety generated by masterless men.

8. Linebaugh and Rediker, *The Many-Headed Hydra: Sailors, Slaves, Commoners, and the Hidden History of the Revolutionary Atlantic* (Boston: Beacon Press, 2000), 144–45.

9. Frohock, "Satire and Civil Governance in *A General History of the Pyrates*." *The Eighteenth Century* 56, no. 4 (2015): 467–83, 468.

10. The publication history of the *General History* is complex, with textual variants between editions generally unrecorded in the standard scholarly text, edited by Manuel Schonhorn (London: Dent, 1972; rev. ed., Mineola: Dover Publications, 1999). I have chosen to cite the original editions, using the following shorthand:

> *1724a*: first edition (C. Rivington, J. Lacy, J. Stone), May 1724
> *1724b*: second edition (T. Warner), August 1724
> *1725*: "third edition" (T. Warner), June 1725
> *1728.1* and *1728.2*: fourth edition, 2 vols. (T. Woodward), July 1728

Thus, *1724a* A4ʳ–A4ᵛ refers to the unpaginated preface in the first edition, in which this passage originally appeared. I hope that, by citing the original editions, readers may discern the additions and revisions to the *General History*. For ease of reference, however, I have also cited in brackets the page numbers in Schonhorn's revised edition. For a demonstration of why distinguishing between the various editions of the *General History* matters, see my article, "Creative Accounting: Alternative Facts in the History of the Pirate, John Gow" (*Humanities* 9, no. 43 [2020]), which explains in detail the circumstances of the publication of the so-called third edition of the *General History*.

11. Mandeville, *The Fable of the Bees*, ed. Philip Harth (London: Penguin Books, 1989), 136.

12. For a discussion of Mandeville's moral thought, including an explanation of what Kaye means by "utilitarian," see Mandeville, *The Fable of the Bees*, with commentary by F. B. Kaye, 2 vols. (Oxford: Clarendon Press, 1924), 1:xlv–lii.

13. See Johnson, *General History*, *1724b*, 336–38 [292–94].

14. The story of Moore's attribution of the *General History* to Defoe—and its subsequent de-attribution by P. N. Furbank and W. R. Owens—is too lengthy to go into here, but see Furbank and Owens, *The Canonisation of Daniel Defoe* (Yale University Press, 1988) for a lengthy critique of Moore's attribution methodology, specifically related to his work on the *General History*. Even if Defoe had nothing to do with the volume as such, his influence is still significant, as I will shortly examine. Nathaniel Mist has been proposed as the man behind Johnson by Arne Bialuschewski, "Daniel Defoe, Nathaniel Mist, and the *General History of the Pyrates*," *Papers of the Bibliographical Society of America* 98, no. 1 (2004): 21–38. For a critique of Bialuschewski's arguments, see Pat Rogers, "Nathaniel Mist, Daniel Defoe, and the Perils of Publishing," *The Library*, 7ᵗʰ ser, 10, no. 3 (2009): 298–313. While there are considerable connections between Mist and Johnson, Mist more likely acted as a general editor of the *General History* than as its sole author. Nevertheless, his remarks on Mandeville and on the public good offer some useful ways of reading Johnson's view of social ethics.

15. Moore, "Defoe and Mandeville," in *Mandeville Studies: New Explorations in the Art and Thought of Dr Bernard Mandeville*, ed. Irwin Primer (The Hague: Nijhoff, 1975), 119–25.

16. Defoe, *Defoe's Review, Reproduced from the Original Editions*, 9 vols. in 22 (New York: Columbia University Press for the Facsimile Text Society, 1938), 4:425.

17. Defoe, *Review*, 4:425–26.

18. Defoe, *Review*, 4:426.

19. While this principle is abundantly evident in his fiction, we may also observe it clearly at work in his *Family Instructor* series, in which Defoe takes what could

be a series of dry, prescriptive principles for private religious observance and sets them within a surprisingly fascinating and realistic family drama.

20. Defoe, *The Great Law of Subordination Consider'd* (London, 1724), 115.

21. *Weekly Journal; or, Saturday's Post*, 8 August 1724.

22. *Weekly Journal; or, Saturday's Post*, 15 August 1724.

23. *Weekly Journal; or, Saturday's Post*, 29 August 1724.

24. Margarette Lincoln, drawing on the work of Erin Mackie, notes that the few portraits included in the *General History* underscore the splendor of some pirate captains, especially Bartholomew Roberts, who was the most successful pirate of his day. Lincoln muddies the waters somewhat by including illustrations from other versions of the *General History* (for example, the portrait of Stede Bonnet is taken from an unauthorized abridgement of Johnson: *The History and Lives of all the Most Notorious Pyrates* [1725]), but her larger point is clear: successful pirates often displayed their success with flamboyant and expensive clothing, a trope that has shaped the subsequent image of the pirate-dandy through Captain Hook, the paintings of N. C. Wyeth, and even Johnny Depp's Captain Jack Sparrow.

Defoe's "Mobbish" Utopias

MAXIMILLIAN E. NOVAK

At the beginning of Daniel Defoe's *Captain Singleton*, Captain Bob, acting as if he is being interviewed for a biographical dictionary recording the deeds of great men such as he, notes that he cannot give much information about his "Pedigree" other than knowing that he was stolen away from his parents, sold to a woman, and used as a sales prop, much as Daniel Day Lewis does with an orphan in *There Will Be Blood*.[1] Some irony may implicate the wealthy pirate who perhaps half-believes he is indeed a great figure, but most of it points to the concept of noble birth as nonsensical. As Defoe was to argue in the conclusion to his poem, *The True-Born Englishman*, such concepts are a "Cheat": it is only what we achieve—"*Personal Virtue*"—that makes us "*great*."[2] And why not after all a great, famous pirate? At the base of Defoe's conception of society, spread through his journalism, poetry, and novels, is a radical egalitarian ethic—no more radical perhaps than that which informed the English Jacobins at the end of the century, but radical enough for a time when Henry Gandy could proclaim, in 1707, that the people had no power, no rights, and no access to the sword.[3] All power came from God and was lodged in the monarch. Despite John Locke's derision, Sir Robert Filmer, that enthusiastic advocate of patriarchalism, still had his followers.[4]

In describing Defoe's politics, Ned Ward rhymed "Mobbish" with "Hobbish."[5] He regarded everything that Defoe had to say about politics as completely wrongheaded. The talk of natural rights (particularly the right to self-preservation), a seeming indifference to the monarchy, an antipathy toward the Church of England—to Ward, all of this was radical. And to his mind Defoe had taken Thomas Hobbes's arguments about a right to self-defense and made them popular through his poetry and journalism.[6] Indeed Defoe turned this part of Hobbes's ideas into an indisputable fact of existence and politics:

> No man was ever yet so void of Sense,
> As to debate the Right of Self-Defence;
> A Principle so grafted in the Mind,
> With Nature born, and does like Nature bind:
> Twisted with Reason, and with Nature too:
> As neither one nor t'other can undo.[7]

Ward considered such beliefs to be a return to 1642 and 1649: the revolt against Charles I, his beheading, and the power of the army under Henry Ireton.[8]

Ward, of course, was a High Church Tory and continued to attack Defoe throughout the reign of Queen Anne. And he was hardly alone in viewing Defoe as an *agent provocateur*. One writer said, on noticing Defoe at a celebration, that one could see the "downfall of Parliaments in his very Countenance."[9] Others saw him as an opponent of both the monarchy and of Parliament, and still others, like Ward, accused him of trying to bring back "Commonwealth-Principles."[10] John Dunton called him "Bold."[11] The author of *The Reformer Reform'd* accused him of advocating "King Killing."[12] Like Ward, Mary Astell argued that Defoe was a follower of Hobbes in that he placed the law above the monarchy. Indeed Defoe's assumed persona, the "Poor Man," has no reluctance about referring to himself as part of the "Mob" in protesting the unfair treatment of the poor by the Law.[13] At the very least, his writings were unsettling.

Everything that Defoe had to say about the "Rights" of the citizenry infuriated his enemies. It was not only *The True Born Englishman*, the *Hymn to the Pillory*, and *The Original Rights of the People of England* that seemed to irritate his opponents, it was a seeming tolerance of mob behavior. As Defoe put it in the latter:

> The Government's ungirt when Justice dies,
> And Constitutions are non Entities:
> The Nation's all a Mob; there's no such thing
> As Lords and Commons, Parliament or King,
> A great promiscuous Croud the Hydra lies,
> Till Laws revive, and mutual Contract ties.
> A Chaos free to chuse for their own share
> What Case of Government they please to wear.[14]

In the fight over the Kentish Petitioners and the Legion Papers, Defoe showed a contempt for Parliament or what was supposed to be the people as represented in Parliament. The true voice of the people was not to be found there, he contended. And in signing the protest as Legion ("our name is Legion for we are many"), he was evoking the image of the "unclean spirits" whom Jesus encountered and overcame.[15] The biblical allusion gave to this protest a Satanic political force—a seeming revolt of the masses. These years mark a time when Defoe was an activist radical. The story of his assuming the disguise of a woman when delivering the petition to Robert Harley, the then leader of Parliament, may be apocryphal, but the delivering itself was daring enough.[16] There is no doubt that at this point in his life, Defoe was in the midst of the political action and enjoying every minute.

Defoe interpreted the Act of Settlement (1701) to mean that there was no real hereditary right to the throne. He may have been scornful of Parliament when it failed to carry out the beliefs of the people, but there was no question in Defoe's mind that Parliament had the right to choose what monarch would rule over England. He regarded any argument about royal blood as nonsense—the equivalent of "Tyranny."[17] And his lengthy poem, *Jure Divino*, set out to show that attaching the concept of divinity to monarchs was ridiculous. Rehearsing the early history of monarchy in England, Defoe dismissed any divine claim to the throne:

> The strongest King, the *Weaker's Crown possest*,
> Conquest was always Law, *Descent's a Jest*.[18]

He argued that the concept of divine right was an absurd idea that had been introduced relatively recently by James I. The established laws of the nation—the English "Constitution"—were always superior to those that any monarch might want to impose.[19]

Sections of Defoe's writings putting forward these notions were read aloud during the Sacheverell Trial (1710), shocking some members of the audience. His comment in the *Review* attacking the notion of the divine right of monarchs argued, with some hyperbole, that Queen Anne "had no more title to the crown than my Lord Mayor's Horse."[20] This horrified Abigail Harley, who was present at the trial and who felt it proved that both the Church and the State were in danger.[21] It is hardly surprising then that the 1711 engraving of *The Whig's Medley* by George Bickham, which had Defoe as its central figure, surrounded by the Pope and the Devil, also included a portrait of Oliver Cromwell, thereby associating the writer with the radicalism of the Interregnum (see Figure 1). Bickham's insinuation that Defoe was somehow an agent of the Vatican was unusual; less so was the notion that he was somehow in the pay of the Devil. But that his ideas represented a continuation of the radical politics of the Interregnum, along with the execution of Charles I, was a common theme in many pamphlets

Figure 1. George Bickham, *The Whig's Medly: The Three False Brethren* (1711).
© The Trustees of the British Museum.

of the time. After the rioting of 1715, Defoe wrote his *Hymn to the Mob*. He exhorted the mob to recognize the advantages of having George I as King, but in the process he put forward the viewpoint that, although the mob might occasionally be led astray, it was usually right.

> Nor is thy Judgment *often wrong,*
> Thou seldom are mistaken, *never long;*
> However *wrong* in Means thou may'st appear,
> Thou gener'ly art in *thy Designs* sincere;
> *Just Government* and *Liberty*
> Often's upheld, always *belov'd* by thee.[22]

All of this amounts to a career in which Defoe was perceived as radical and subversive. Admittedly some of this resulted from his desire to scandalize his contemporaries. When the first issue of the *Review* appeared, dedicated to accurately describing France's status in Europe at a time when England was at war with that nation, Sidney Godolphin wrote a letter suggesting that Defoe should be tried for treason. In fact, Defoe was hardly supporting the French; he was mainly recounting the history of French power in Europe to a largely uninformed audience. But putting aside this inclination to shock his audience, he also held a radical Whig view of political power.

When it came to writing fiction, Defoe finds its expression in the stories of successful criminals—pirates, thieves, prostitutes, and courtesans—that he wrote. And he made his readers like them. As previously mentioned, Captain Singleton wants his narrative to be equivalent to a genre not yet invented: the biographies of successful businessmen. Defoe often enough compared stock jobbers to thieves.[23] If they were permitted to keep their ill-gotten gains, buy an estate, and pass as gentlemen, why should not a retired pirate? Moll Flanders ends up returning to England after her transportation to Virginia (and subsequent sojourn in Maryland) and living off her earnings as a thief, with the husband she always wanted, along with a loving son.[24] Only on rare occasions do we laugh at her as we might at the traditional picaresque heroine. Instead, we sympathize with her sufferings and how she was driven by necessity. When she is imprisoned, we feel her sorrow, we want her to escape somehow, and we enjoy her final success.

In some ways, Colonel Jack embodies Defoe's idealization of how a man born into poverty might advance himself in the world. His foster mother told him that his father was a gentleman, and this motivates him despite a variety of setbacks. After being advised about securing the money he makes as a thief, he strives to educate himself, teaching himself to read and write. Jack eventually becomes a wealthy plantation owner in the North American colonies. He further educates himself with the help of a tutor and, at least in his own mind, achieves the status of a gentleman. A true gentleman, in Defoe's view, was not necessarily someone born to an estate, but rather a person who had educated himself and had a certain degree of wealth.[25] By the dominant standards of his time, though, a person who had actually worked could not claim to be a gentleman no matter how wealthy he might be. However, that wealth might enable his children to claim that they had wiped away the stain of actual labor. After achieving the status of a wealthy plantation owner in the North American colonies, Jack goes abroad and becomes a Lieutenant Colonel in the French army at a time when a military officer could claim gentility.[26] There are problems with Jack's pursuit of gentility. He gets implicated in the Jacobite cause, and toward the end he becomes involved in an illicit trade with various people in the Spanish colonies. But at the conclusion Jack is back on his plantation, a true gentleman in Defoe's eyes.[27] It was a radical concept of gentility.

It seems to me that some recent critics have failed to see this radical aspect of Defoe. It was apparent enough to a number of critics of the twentieth century—especially the Marxist critic Arnold Kettle, whose two-volume *Introduction to the English Novel* first appeared between 1951 and 1953. He admired Defoe's treatment of members of the lower classes and of their insistence on struggling to survive.[28] After all, Defoe had been willing to support workers against what Kettle's generation termed the "bosses."[29] Ian Watt, of course, admitted to being a Marxist of a sort and credited Defoe with starting the novel, even if his training in a Cambridge dominated by Q. D. and F. R. Leavis brought him to deny Defoe the status of a true artist.[30] The exaltation of realism as the essence of the novel may have been a passing phase, but Defoe's interest in extreme states of being—solitude and sickness along with sympathy for the poor—will surely always attract readers and scholars of fiction.

Perhaps the most interesting example of this sympathy occurs in *A Journal of the Plague Year*. I am not pointing to the wonderfully sympathetic conversation with the Waterman, whose family has become sick from the plague. I have dealt with this almost Wordsworthian encounter elsewhere.[31] What I want to look at more closely are the travels of the three artisans through London to Epping Forest and the society that they construct along with other Londoners fleeing from the plague. I want to approach it from the standpoint of its radical view of social and political origins: how societies get built.

The reader of *A Journal of the Plague Year* needs to respond to a situation in which government is temporarily dissolved. H. F., who carries the burden of the narrative, may applaud the methods used by the Lord Mayor of London to provide food for the poor as a means of keeping order. He also has a Malthusian appreciation of the swiftness of the plague itself in carrying off so many of those who might have revolted against all order. But the narrative of the three artisans tells another story—that of government reduced to the relationship of a few friends. Perhaps Ward was not so far off in seeing Defoe as a follower of Hobbes. Defoe did believe that the right of self-defense took priority over any other aspect of existence. The three artisans reject any attempt by legal authorities to prevent them from crossing through the city to safety. Although they never have to use physical force to overcome their opponents, they are certainly determined to prevail against the obstacles placed in their way, particularly the attempts of officials to restrict the movement of persons wishing to leave London.

[margin handwriting: Who was against the right of self defense?]

The aim of the three artisans is survival for themselves, but they are not unwilling to take up with people they meet along the way. When they finally manage to settle in Epping Forest, they restart society more or less from the beginning. They get their own food and find people to manufacture what they need. We don't learn in any detail what happens to their community after the plague is over, except for being told that the severe cold made life difficult and that the three artisans eventually returned to the city. The narrative shifts back to H. F. and to the pronouncement of both his and London's survival. But this notion of founding society anew without titles of nobility, with "no one there to tell us / What to do," as the Beatles would have it, was always at the back of Defoe's mind, whether he was contemplating London mobs or Crusoe on his island.

What can be said about this small utopian grouping, and what does it tell us about Defoe's way of looking at society—a viewpoint that, through his fictions, managed to be in some ways more influential than any of the more clearly organized utopias written during this period? To begin with, we might recognize its essentially egalitarian elements. Defoe had, after all, experimented with this in his Crusoe volumes. Crusoe was supposed to illustrate the essential sameness of all human beings: the idea that each of us contains within him- or herself the seeds of invention that Crusoe draws upon in his varied degrees of success as a hunter and gatherer, pastoralist, farmer, manufacturer of pots, and weaver of baskets. His semi-ironic notions of himself as monarch of his island ruling over his pets, then, gradually, compelling allegiance through gratitude, and finally governing through real and implicit contracts should not disguise the essential egalitarian quality of this island utopia. There is no aristocratic class. When Crusoe boasts of the toleration that prevails among the later inhabitants of his island as including Catholics, Protestants, and Friday's Father, a pagan, Crusoe does not distinguish among them on the basis of class. And if he upbraids himself for failing to act as a kind of governor for them, for not providing some

[margin handwriting: Is Friday's Father a pagan?]

kind of control over those whom he considers his subjects, he nevertheless refuses to assume that role or to establish some kind of order. If the colony seems doomed to failure at the end, it is unclear what lesson the reader was to draw, but the more or less anarchic colony that he discovers on returning to his island seems to be functioning well enough.

Defoe enjoyed playing with the paradoxical extremes of anarchic life. Hence his interest in the liberty that governed the pirate life in which the boatswain, rather than the captain, was the real leader—in which the potential excesses of the captain were always kept under control. Thus his version of the real (though mostly mythical) Captain Avery and the fictional Captain Singleton lead a very independent and dangerous band of pirates. In both cases, they eventually flee from pirate society, preferring instead to live a dangerous life of disguise in England. Defoe seems to be saying that anarchy is fun but that some form of government is necessary. He was an advocate of high wages for workers at a time when mercantilist economics demanded paying as little as possible.[32] And at times he flirted with the ideas of the Levellers during an era when the very notion of doing so was anathema from the standpoint of both economics and politics. In other words, the radical political experiments of the Interregnum, more or less unmentionable during the decades following the Restoration, caught the attention of at least one interested journalist during the early eighteenth century.

This brings us back to 1722 and *A Journal of the Plague Year.* In the seemingly heroic artisans, functioning in a world in which all true government had apparently broken down, Defoe once more confronts the reader with a society formed under extreme conditions. In some ways, the situation resembled that of his proposal for a self-sustaining colony for the Palatine refugees in New Forest in 1707.[33] Defoe was to replay that scheme in his *Tour thro' the Whole Island of Great Britain* in 1724 where he supplied a diagram of the imaginary community with straight streets and a square in the middle.[34] Such schemes are typical enough of Defoe the projector, but it is significant that such imagined communities are set away from the world of commerce with which he is so often associated. Thus it is not entirely surprising that in the same *Tour* in which he appears to revel in the magnificence of London, he also informs the reader that it may one day collapse entirely. If Defoe enjoyed the spectacle of the growth of a commercial society, there was a part of him that fantasized about starting over again with a more or less egalitarian social structure and a primitive economy.

The view of Defoe's positions that I have been outlining contrasts oddly with the many recent laments that appeared on the occasion of the 300th anniversary of the publication of *The Life and Strange Surprizing Adventures of Robinson Crusoe,* most of which presented Defoe as a firm monarchist and a reactionary.[35] Let me end this essay with a few replies to these objections, along with some admissions of what, from a modern standpoint, may be regarded as Defoe's faults. As I have shown, Defoe was not a strong believer in hereditary monarchy. He was certainly in favor of colonial expansion. But he was not in any sense a believer in the racial superiority of Europeans.[36] Of course, the thoughts and actions of Defoe's fictional characters are not to be confused with what we know, with some certainty, to be the settled principles of their creator. And there may be a lesson in that: although Crusoe dreams of acquiring slaves, in Friday he finds someone equivalent to a student and a companion. Similarly, Lincoln Faller notes that Defoe's advocacy of treating slaves well through the character of Colonel Jack is hardly a satisfying position.[37] As an economist, Defoe defended slavery; as a moralist, he condemned it.[38] Defoe believed that the existence of society depended upon a hierarchy based on property, but, unlike many his contemporaries, he believed in a society open to individual initiative. And he acknowledged the legitimacy of the attempts of those without property to correct violations of the law by engaging in violent protest and rebellion as they had in 1688. He did not believe in suppressing the poor.[39] Gratitude is the motivation that binds Friday to Crusoe, and to a great extent Defoe followed Seneca's view of a society based on such a system.[40] Other ways in which a society might function in Defoe's system were through contract and through power. Although Crusoe insists on a contract of obedience from the Spanish sailors he brings to his island, it is never enforced. The invention of guns gave Western forces an advantage over societies without firearms, and Defoe seemed to believe that where such power existed it would be used, that, as he wrote in *Jure Divino,* "all Men wou'd be Tyrants *if they durst.*"[41] And as he argued throughout that poem, it was up to each individual to assert his own liberty and equality when encountering the will of those trying to infringe upon his natural rights.

Notes

1. Daniel Defoe, *The Adventures of Captain Singleton*, Shakespeare Head Edition of Daniel Defoe, 14 vols. (Oxford: Blackwell, 1927), 1:1.
2. Daniel Defoe, *The True-Born Englishman*, in *Poems on Affairs of State*, ed. George de F. Lord, et al., 7 vols. (New Haven: Yale University Press, 1963–75), 6:309.

3. Gandy, *Jure Divino: or An Answer to All That Hath or Shall Be Written by Republicans. Against the Old English Constitution* (London, 1707).

4. John Locke, *Two Treatises of Government*, ed. Peter Laslett (Cambridge: Cambridge University Press, 1967), 159–281. Locke devoted the entire "First Treatise" to attacking Filmer's concept of patriarchy.

5. Edward Ward, *The Dissenting Hypocrite; or, Occasional Conformist* (London, 1704), 12.

6. See Thomas Hobbes, *Leviathan*, ed. A. R. Waller (Cambridge: Cambridge University Press, 1935), 89, 217.

7. Daniel Defoe, *True-Born Englishman*, in *Poems on Affairs of State*, 6:293; see also Defoe, *Jure Divino* (London, 1706), Book 3, 10.

8. Ward, *Dissenting Hypocrite*, 24.

9. *An Account of Some Late Designs to Create a Misunderstanding betwixt the King and His People* (London, 1702), 18.

10. Ward, *Dissenting Hypocrite*, 24,

11. Dunton, *The Life and Errors of John Dunton* (London, 1705), 240.

12. *The Reformer Reform'd* (London, 1703), 4.

13. Defoe, *The Poor Man's Plea*, in *The Shortest Way with Dissenters and Other Pamphlets* (Oxford: Blackwell, 1927), 91.

14. Daniel Defoe, *The Original Right of the People of England Examin'd and Asserted*, in *A True Collection of the Writings of the Author of the True Born Englishman*, 2 vols. (London, 1703–5), 1:155.

15. See Mark 5:9 and Luke 8:30.

16. Defoe, *The History of the Kentish Petition*, in *The Shortest Way*, 91.

17. Defoe, *Defoe's Review, Reproduced from the Original Editions*, 9 vols. in 22 (New York: Columbia University Press for the Facsimile Text Society, 1938), 2:326–30; 2:459–60.

18. Defoe, *Jure Divino*, Book 9, 24.

19. See Defoe, *Jure Divino*, Book 11, 3–4.

20. Defoe, *Review*, 2:319.

21. See Geoffrey Holmes, *The Trial of Doctor Sacheverell* (London: Eyre Methuen, 1973), 195.

22. Daniel Defoe, *Hymn to the Mob* (London, 1715), 11. Defoe denied what was his clearly established belief about the mob as a force for change in a *Review* of 3 November 1709 (*Defoe's Review*, 6:362), but anyone who had followed his writings would have known this was far from the truth.

23. See, for example, Daniel Defoe, *The Villany of Stock-Jobbers Detected* (London, 1701) and Defoe, *The Anatomy of Exchange-Alley* (London, 1719), especially his description in the latter of stock-jobbing as "a Branch of Highway Robbing" (8).

24. Moll eventually inherits an estate from her mother worth £60–150 and receives money and gifts from her son. But she manages to establish herself and her Lancashire husband through the wealth she had accumulated as a thief. See Defoe, *Moll Flanders*, ed. G. A. Starr (London: Oxford University Press, 1971), 312, 336.

25. Defoe's fullest treatise on education and gentility was *The Compleat English Gentleman*, ed. Karl Bülbring (London: David Nutt, 1890). It remained in manuscript until Bülbring's edition.

26. Jack undergoes an education in the kind of courage not demanded of him before. For a discussion of this particular education, see Maximillian Novak, *Defoe and the Nature of Man* (Oxford: Oxford University Press, 1963), 142–44.

27. Defoe put forward his theory concerning education and gentility in two issues of his journal, *The Commentator* no. 54 (8 July 1720) and no. 55 (11 July 1720). For Defoe, a "Compleat Gentleman" is a person with a full grasp of history, geography, and the sciences. An ignorant person, no matter how wealthy or possessed of a noble pedigree he may be, does not deserve to be classified as gentle.

28. Arnold Kettle later defended *Moll Flanders* against Ian Watt's contention that it lacked artistry. See his "In Defence of *Moll Flanders*," in *Imagined Worlds: Essays on Some English Novelists in Honour of John Butt*, ed. Maynard Mack and Ian Gregor (London: Methuen, 1968).

29. In the *Review,* Defoe supported the Keelmen of Newcastle in what was the eighteenth-century equivalent of a strike, and his journal, *The Manufacturer* (1719–20), supported the weavers against the importers of calicoes.

30. See Ian Watt, *The Rise of the Novel: Studies in Defoe, Richardson, and Fielding* (Berkeley: University of California Press, 1957), 93–130; and F. R. Leavis, *The Great Tradition: George Eliot, Henry James, Joseph Conrad* (London: Chatto and Windus, 1950), 2. See also Watt, "Flat-Footed and Fly-Blown: The Realities of Realism," *Stanford Review* 8 (2000): 68.

31. See Maximillian Novak, "Defoe and the Disordered City," in Defoe, *A Journal of the Plague Year* ed. Paula Backscheider (New York: Norton, 1992), 315.

32. See Eli Heckscher, *Mercantilism*, trans. Mendel Shapiro, 2 vols. (London: George Allen, 1925), 2:171.

33. Defoe, *Review*, 6:154, 6:157–58, 6:207–8.

34. Defoe, *Tour thro' the Whole Island of Great Britain*, ed., G. D. H. Cole, 2 vols. (London: Peter Davies, 1927), 1:201–6.

35. See, for example, Charles Boyle, "Robinson Crusoe at 300: Why it's Time to Let Go of this Colonial Fairytale," *The Guardian*, 19 April 2019.

36. See *Atlas Maritimus* (London, 1728), 160–61, for his criticism of the refusal of the Spaniards to intermarry with Indigenous peoples.

37. See Lincoln Faller, *Crime and Defoe* (Cambridge: Cambridge University Press, 1993), 190. See also Dennis Todd, *Defoe's America* (Cambridge: Cambridge University Press, 2010), 96–98.

38. In *Atlas Maritimus*, 237, Defoe quoted a line from his poem *More Reformation* critical of those engaged in the slave trade:

They barter Baubles for the Souls of Men.

It may be rightly said that unlike contemporary abolitionists such as Thomas Tryon, Defoe did participate in the general guilt of British society.

39. Sir William Petty (whose writings Defoe knew) and later Bernard Mandeville argued that it was in the interest of society to keep the poor in their place. They regarded idleness among the poor as threatening the social status quo. Petty wanted

them forced to work for low wages at tasks that had no useful purpose beyond keeping them occupied. Mandeville wanted them drunk and ignorant. In contrast, Defoe advocated high wages and education. See William Petty, *Economic Writings*, ed. Charles Hull (Cambridge: Cambridge University Press, 1899), 31, 274–75, and Bernard Mandeville, *The Fable of the Bees*, 2 vols. (Oxford: Clarendon Press, 1924), 192–94, 313–17.

40.   William Godwin was to argue against gratitude as a component in social life, seeing behind what was usually considered a virtue the system of patronage that he rightly considered a corrupting force in British society. See Godwin, *Enquiry Concerning Political Justice* (Harmondsworth: Penguin Books, 1976), 170–78.

41.   Defoe, *Jure Divino*, Book 4, 4.

Fragile Communities in the Crusoe Trilogy

LI QI PEH

That Robinson Crusoe is the quintessential model of *homo economicus* is now a critical commonplace. Such an interpretation became increasingly widespread in the wake of the 1762 publication of Jean-Jacques Rousseau's *Émile*, in which Rousseau praises Crusoe for his ability to independently carry out a variety of tasks ranging from building furniture to baking bread. For Rousseau, the fact that Crusoe does not have to cooperate with another to complete each task means that he is less likely to be transformed into an automaton, a fate that tends to await those who participate in an economic system founded on specialization and the division of labor.[1] As Rousseau suggests, then, Crusoe's self-reliance guarantees his economic freedom. Karl Marx's presentation, in *Das Kapital* (1867), of Crusoe as one who works for himself and owns the products of his labor only served to cement Crusoe's status as an emblem of economic individualism, and ninety years later, most did not blink when Ian Watt declared that the notion "that Robinson Crusoe ... is the embodiment of economic individualism hardly needs demonstration."[2]

Since Watt's sweeping declaration, several scholars have worked to complicate such a characterization of Crusoe. Soon after the publication of Watt's *The Rise of the Novel*, Maximillian E. Novak, George A. Starr, and J. Paul Hunter each made the point that, contrary to what Watt argues, Crusoe is shaped as much by religious concerns as he is by economic ones.

In recent years, such critics as Dennis Todd and Ramesh Mallipeddi have also located Crusoe's economic individualism within the context of empire.[3] Todd, for one, persuasively demonstrates that the sudden influxes of money and property Crusoe receives for no rhyme or reason—all of which enable him to establish his plantation in Brazil— speaks to the lie of economic self-sufficiency and, more importantly, Daniel Defoe's awareness of this lie.[4] The current consensus, then, seems to be that Defoe's Crusoe is not quite the Crusoe of neoclassical economics.

Yet, just because the Crusoe of twentieth-century economics textbooks appears to lack nuance does not mean that it is no longer productive to regard Defoe's Crusoe as the model of an economic man. Indeed, economists like Matthew Watson have increasingly worked to expand the definition of *homo economicus* so that it does not merely symbolize the rational, self-interested, solitary individual who remains unaffected by all communal ties. In a recent article, for instance, Watson connects Crusoe's maximization of individual gain to his enslavement of Friday to make the point that the abstract, self-determining economic man theorized by mainstream economics is always already plugged into raced market institutions that yoke their participants to one another in unequal relations of power.[5] In a similar vein, an essay collection edited by Ulla Grapard and Gillian Hewitson traces the myriad ways by which the invisible labor of women and the enslaved allows Crusoe to work "seemingly unencumbered by physicality and social ties."[6] Like these scholars, this essay complicates commonplace understandings of the *homo economicus* by attending to Defoe's complex portrayal of Crusoe and, in doing so, seeks to demonstrate that characterizations of Crusoe as a free-wheeling, independent economic agent are flawed not only because they fail to take into account Crusoe's implicit reliance on others, both on and off the island, but also because they neglect his explicit efforts to seek out community in order to survive. Contrary to Watt's claims that emotional ties and personal relationships "play a very minor part in *Robinson Crusoe,* except where they are focused on economic matters" and that "friendship is accorded only to those who can be safely entrusted with Crusoe's economic interests," the economic man as exemplified by Defoe's actual Crusoe is one who is constantly aware that he cannot carry out the economic activities of production, consumption, and trade without forming filiative as well as affiliative associations.[7] Put another way, Crusoe is invested in forming close, tight-knit communities with those he meets and ensuring the continuity of these communities *precisely because* economic matters are at the forefront of his mind. It is not only money, then, that is "the proper cause of deep feeling" for Crusoe: the various social relations that allow for the accumulation of wealth by making possible his physical survival also prompt intense emotion.[8] That is why his behavior in the second and third books of the trilogy differs so radically from his conduct in the first. In the uncertain world of the Crusoe trilogy, the production and exchange of goods and the destruction of life and property all count as rational, economic decisions, for these decisions are all made in a bid to ensure the survival of the groups to which Crusoe belongs.

Guilds of Empire

During the early modern period, Greater London was in a state of constant flux. From the sixteenth to the eighteenth century, its population, which included that of the City and its surrounding areas, increased approximately five-fold due to massive immigration, and by 1700, it was the largest metropolis in Europe.[9] This rapid, ongoing change in the make-up and culture of the area meant that those who lived there, particularly the Londoners, were constantly reassessing their values and allegiances to the communities to which they belonged. They were not only uncertain whether the governors of London would safeguard their interests over those they considered newcomers, but also worried that the trade guilds that many of them were part of and on which they counted to amplify their voices would be fractured by the diverse interests of an expanding membership.[10] Defoe was cognizant of these swirling anxieties. His father, James Foe, was a high-ranking member within the Worshipful Company of Butchers, and Defoe himself was inducted into the guild in 1687.[11] Like many of his contemporaries, Defoe experienced the difficult negotiation of guild identity first-hand.

For Defoe, managing his membership in the guild was a fraught affair not only because of general population changes, but also because of his own political affiliations. In the wake of the 1685 Monmouth Rebellion, which saw Defoe and his fellow Dissenters attempt to overthrow the crown, James II issued a charter declaring that all officers of the Butchers' Company had to take an oath of allegiance and that all members had to be part of the Church of England and of "approved loyalty."[12] Despite these stipulations, Defoe—who was still writing Dissenting pamphlets on the side—was allowed to be a member of the guild, but it is safe to say that the ties he had with the Butchers' Company were ambivalent and that he was deeply aware of the fact that his goals and values were not necessarily shared by his fellow guild members.

This ever-present awareness of the tenuousness of communal ties inflects the Crusoe trilogy. Defoe's fraught guild membership and his close friendships with men such as John Russell who were highly ranked members of guilds in Edinburgh would have meant that he seriously considered questions about how individuals with diverse commitments could stay together in the long term.[13] Such questions were only made more pressing by contemporary perceptions of the speed with which communities broke up across the Atlantic, communities that Defoe was deeply aware of and invested in, given his strong involvement in the shipping business and foreign trade.

In *The Reaper's Garden*, Vincent Brown remarks that the Caribbean in the eighteenth century was widely looked upon by both Europeans and enslaved peoples as a site of violence and disease. Beliefs about the odds of survival mediated how group and property relations in the New World were understood, especially given the overwhelming rate at which young, white planters in the Caribbean succumbed to diseases like malaria and yellow fever.[14] As Richard Dunn argues, the ever-present "specter of death contributed to the frenetic tempo and the mirage-like quality of West Indian life," ensuring that those who participated in it—however remotely—brooded constantly on how communities there could perpetuate and regenerate themselves given the incessant loss of life.[15] Defoe, who owned stock in the South Sea Company, a British enterprise granted the exclusive right to trade with Spanish colonies in South America and the West Indies, was no exception.[16] He not only wrote numerous pamphlets on the likelihood of the company—and by connection the territories it traded with—thriving, but also advocated for a colony to be set up in the Americas that would serve as a base for goods to be distributed without having to be taxed by Spain.[17] These writings, together with his experiences involving the guilds of London, suggest that concerns about how fragile groups can survive were constantly on Defoe's mind and indeed shape his representations of Crusoe and his companions. To read the Crusoe trilogy in light of Defoe's anxiety about the longevity of communities, then, is to read Crusoe's contradictory behaviors as unique strategies undertaken to enable the communities he builds to survive.

To better understand the eclectic actions of Crusoe, I study how he behaves within collectives and how the members of his collectives respond in turn. In particular, I read his mundane actions of sharing food and cultivating land alongside his wanton violence, mapping out how these seemingly disparate deeds all express the same anxiety and fear. In her study of indigeneity and the U.S. empire, Jodi Byrd contends that to place "seemingly disparate histories, temporalities, and geographies into conversation" is "to connect the violences and genocides of colonization to cultural productions and political movements in order to disrupt the elisions of multicultural liberal democracy that seek to rationalize the originary historical traumas that birthed settler colonialism through inclusion."[18] Analogously, placing violent and non-violent actions into conversation connects the violences and genocides of colonization to benign or neutral acts of community-building and, in doing so, destabilizes accounts of cross-cultural contact that distinguish between friendly relationships and hostile ones and consequently downplay the concrete harms seemingly innocuous interactions cause.

This move of connecting the violent and the non-violent is warranted given the historical backdrop against which the Crusoe trilogy is set. The complicated group dynamics that characterized Britain's fragile guilds and colonies, after all, were symptomatic of a larger mercantilist worldview that saw the English state working to maximize its wealth and power by whatever means necessary. As Aida Ramos notes, the English government in the seventeenth and eighteenth centuries regarded the resources of the world as finite and every interaction as a zero-sum game.[19] They therefore strove to "impose conditions that would ensure they were the winners" and made use of economic policy, trade law, and their military might to establish unequal trading relationships with rival nations.[20] Ramos, building on the work of Paul Farmer, reads such expressions of mercantilism as forms of structural violence, arguing that the English used both formal institutions like the law and informal institutions like attitudes, customs, and beliefs to "limit others' agency" and "force people to make choices consistent with English goals."[21] Such subtle expressions of violence allowed England to expand its empire without always having to engage in military conquest.

Viewed through a mercantilist lens, then, it becomes clear that the bloodless exploitation of Indigeneous peoples and the unleashing of violence against them go hand in hand in the Crusoe trilogy. It is not simply that an expression of friendship and the massacre of an entire town both concern the exercise of power, although that is certainly true. Rather, it is also that the maintenance of communal bonds in the death-ridden Caribbean depended upon colonists being kind and violent in turn. In a world in which colonists were both eager to accumulate resources to bolster their chances of survival and fearful of losing the resources they had, kindness in the form of the sharing of resources was used to encourage or coerce new members of a community into contributing their labor, while violence against non-members was used to warn existing members away from leaving. The Crusoe trilogy provides a literary example of how such a relationship might play out in the case of individual groups.[22]

Calculated Kindnesses

The first step to understanding Crusoe's actions as expressive of his paranoia about surviving alone in a dangerous place entails reading his treatment of Friday anew. That Crusoe offers Friday food and shelter after slaughtering his enemies is common knowledge and is often read as an attempt to buy Friday's loyalty. In his illuminating examination of the figure of the grateful slave in eighteenth-century writing, for instance, George Boulukos demonstrates that such novels as Defoe's *Colonel Jack* (1722) and Sarah Scott's *History of Sir George Ellison* (1766) justified slavery by depicting the kind treatment of enslaved people and the intense gratitude such treatment inspired.[23] Portrayals of the grateful slave, as Boulukos argues, were not simply aimed at working to prevent the abuse of enslaved people as is commonly assumed. They were also used to model a way of ensuring the continued dependence of enslaved peoples and to make an insidious case for prolonging the institution of slavery.

Such a dynamic is certainly at work in the interactions between Crusoe and Friday, but I want to suggest that Crusoe is also working to induct Friday into a new way of life. He is attempting, that is, to make living with him so desirable that Friday does not wish to leave. Such a notion can be observed in how Crusoe steps up his hospitality from the moment Friday awakens from his nap. He gives Friday clothes, a sword, a gun, a bow and arrows, as well as a tent. Even the quality of the food he feeds Friday increases. Friday is first fed bread, then boiled meat and broth, and finally roast goat. Granted, these actions are designed to inspire Friday's gratitude, but such statements as "I was resolv'd to feast him the next day with roasting a piece of the kid" and "I began to consider where I should lodge him, and that I might do well for him, and yet be perfectly easy myself" suggest that they are also designed to demonstrate that Crusoe cares for Friday's well-being.[24] Crusoe, in other words, is eager to make Friday feel like part of a community where everyone works together so everyone can gain. This explains why he does not simply shower Friday with gifts, but also makes sure that Friday recognizes these gifts as the products of his labor. He takes care to alter the linen drawers he gives to Friday, for instance, to ensure that they "fitted him very well," makes sure that Friday sees him killing the goat they later eat, and even attempts to impress Friday with his mode of cooking (*RC,* 211). His spit-roasting of a piece of goat, for instance, is done in a manner that "Friday admir'd very much" (*RC,* 214). As Crusoe seems eager for Friday to learn, being part of a community entails offering up one's time and labor for the other members of that community. Self-sacrifice, in other words, is necessary.

In his study of how the members of communes behave, Laurence R. Iannoccone argues that the most successful of these groups often demand huge sacrifices of time and energy because the satisfaction of each individual depends upon the enthusiastic participation of all the other group members. Demanding a significant amount of sacrifice allows such groups to ensure a high level of group participation in two ways. First, it ensures that those who are not inclined to contribute enthusiastically are deterred from joining the group, and second, it ensures that existing members have no choice but to participate in group activities, because the time and energy they put in makes them inevitably forego alternative activities that have nothing to do with the group. This isolates them from individuals who are not part of the commune and in turn guarantees their participation in future group activities. According to Iannoccone, sacrifice for these collectives not only takes the form of time and energy spent engaging in group activities, but also the forgoing of alternative ways of living or spending one's time.[25]

Iannoccone's theory describes a more extreme form of how the guilds of London sought to guarantee the long-term involvement of their members by extracting their time and energy. New guild members whose fathers were not part of the guild had to pay expensive premiums or serve seven-year apprenticeships before being inducted, while low-ranking members who had gained the right to political participation—or what was called the "Freedom of the City"—often had to assume political offices that came with onerous duties and obligations.[26] Time spent on guild activities hence formed a significant part of their members' social lives.

Considered in the light of Iannaccone's theory, then, Crusoe's contrived acts of kindness appear more insidious than they already are, for Crusoe's gifts are not merely transactional in the sense that they oblige Friday to repay him in some way, but also limiting in how they make it difficult for Friday to leave. Crusoe's spit-roasting of the goat serves as an example of this, for it works to distance Friday from his previous ways of life. Before roasting the goat, Crusoe speaks of wishing to "let [Friday] taste other flesh" in order to turn him away "from his horrid way of feeding, and from the relish of a cannibal's stomach" (*RC,* 213). These efforts succeed. When Friday "came to taste the flesh" of the goat, Crusoe writes, "he took so many ways to tell me how well he lik'd it, that I could not but understand him; and at last he told me he would never eat man's flesh any more" (*RC,* 214). In providing Friday with goat meat, then, Crusoe limits Friday's food choices to the ones he provides, making it such that Friday becomes more inclined to remain part of the community if he wishes to continue eating the food he so loves. Because Friday cannot see himself going back to his old ways of eating human flesh and Crusoe is the only one who can support his newly acquired habits, staying with Crusoe and sacrificing his old way of life becomes his obvious choice. By replacing Friday's old needs with new ones, Crusoe persuades him to adhere to the norms of the community he leads.

At first glance, reading the Crusoe trilogy through the lens of Iannoccone's theory may seem like an aggravatingly anachronistic move, but it is also a productive one, given how it frames the trilogy as a realistic case study

[margin annotations: Crusoe is threatened by strong bond of members of idol worship of community]

of group relations instead of a self-contradictory manifestation of Defoe's colonial fantasies. To be sure, Iannoccone's ideas are born out of his study of modern-day religious cults, but I refer to them as well as to those of his colleague, Eli Berman, because they foreground some of the key concerns communities working with limited resources face and the strategies these communities systematically undertake to address these concerns, many of which transcend both space and time. Communities in general, as Samuel Bowles and Herbert Gintis have influentially argued, tend to encourage frequent interactions between their members and discourage migration to and from other communities regardless of when or where they are set up.[27] The observations of Iannoccone and Berman on group dynamics and how commune leaders maintain and grow their membership can hence be put to transhistorical and transgeographical use.

Considering *The Life and Strange Surprizing Adventures* anachronistically, I find, uncovers the various practical concerns of the *homo economicus*, the ones that exist even if the economic man is assumed to be operating within an ideal world. Defoe's Caribbean is often regarded as a utopia, but the overwhelming sense that one can die without the company of friends or kin still remains, given the ease with which one can fall prey to illness or disease. Crusoe himself succumbs to a violent ague. His sheer anxiety when he observes Friday's "extraordinary sense of pleasure" upon catching sight of his country is therefore no surprise (*RC*, 222). He notes: "This observation of mine, put a great many thoughts into me, which made me at first not so easy about my new man *Friday* as I was before; and I made no doubt, but that if *Friday* could get back to his own nation again, he would not only forget all his religion, but all his obligation to me" (*RC*, 222). Here, Crusoe's fear of Friday leaving and his obsession with whether Friday is a true Christian gesture towards his belief that the community he has set up is too fragile to survive. Friday may, as Crusoe believes, recognize the benefits of being part of a community where resources are shared and may be perfectly willing to contribute to such a community. After all, as Defoe writes, Friday "appear'd very sensible" of the fact that Crusoe now had to "provide more Ground for [his] Harvest, and plant a Larger Quantity of Corn" given that there were now two of them and even expresses his willingness to do the work (*RC*, 214). Yet, as Crusoe's interrogations of Friday about his intention to leave suggest, Crusoe is also aware that Friday's gratitude does not guarantee that he will stay. Indeed, when Crusoe repeatedly asks Friday if he would "turn Wild again, eat Mens flesh again, and be a Savage" if he returned to his nation, what he is trying to ascertain is the extent to which Friday is attached to Crusoe and the community they have formed together (*RC*, 222). Put a different way, Crusoe is trying to suss out whether Friday has a compelling reason to stay with him, be it moral, religious, dietary, or otherwise. As evidenced by his worried observation that Friday demonstrates "an extraordinary Sense of Pleasure" and "a strange Eagerness" when he speaks of returning home, Crusoe is extremely conscious of the fact that a successful community, in addition to being able to produce and accumulate resources, must maintain a strong emotional hold over its members in order to thrive (*RC*, 222). Crusoe's conversion of Friday, then, can be read as an attempt to strengthen the hold he has over his community's most newly acquired member and, more importantly, as an act of desperation.

At the end of the day, the fact that Crusoe's actions are constantly undertaken with the longevity of his community in mind is brought home by his selective conversion of those he meets. As his treatment of Friday's father and the Spaniard suggests, Crusoe only attempts to convert those he meets when they have more incentive to leave rather than to stay. He declares: "I had but three Subjects, and they were of three different Religions. My Man *Friday* was a Protestant, his Father was a *Pagan* and a *Cannibal*, and the Spaniard was a Papist. However, I allow'd Liberty of Conscience throughout my Dominions" (*RC*, 235). That Crusoe treats Friday and the other individuals he meets so differently suggests that religion for him is a concern only when the individuals he recruits have a high risk of leaving. In this case, attempting to convert Friday's father and the Spaniard proves unnecessary because they have little reason to go: the former proves more eager to stay with his son than to return home, and the latter has no viable community to turn to on the island. As he informs Crusoe, his sixteen other countrymen might live "at Peace indeed with the Savages," but because they lived "at the Mercy and Discretion of the *Savages*," their condition was "miserable," and they were "under the greatest Distress imaginable" (*RC*, 237). Staying with Crusoe is therefore his best option.

The Violence of Community Building

Thus far, I have shown how Crusoe's behavior towards the individuals he meets in the first volume of the trilogy is exemplary of one who is attempting to set up and maintain a fragile community. I want to move on now to consider how we can read his violent behavior in the second volume as an extension of his initial efforts to ensure that the members he has recruited do not leave. Tracing this lineage, I argue, allows us to see how doubt about the sustainability of a community can realize itself in the extreme form of violence.

One finds glimmers of this in how the guilds of London worked to maintain power towards the end of the seventeenth century, a time when guild regulation was becoming increasingly difficult due to the growth of densely populated urban areas that fell outside of guild purview. In order to police their members and intimidate non-members who had no right to trade openly within the City's limits into joining the guild, guilds conducted regular "searches," inspections of stalls and workshops by guild officials to ensure that the raw materials members used and the products they crafted were up to par.[28] While quality control and fraud prevention were the purported goals of these inspections, which took place from four to twelve times a year, they also served the purpose of coercion. Guild officials had "the right to seize faulty goods, to levy fines, to inflict punishments of imprisonment and to destroy the seized products," and these penalties were often imposed in a deliberately public way.[29] Before huge assemblies, supposedly defective baskets were burnt, and sub-standard spectacles were broken.[30] Such brutal rituals suggest that guild leaders saw intimidation and the destruction of property as viable methods for maintaining social control.

The second book of the Crusoe trilogy takes this insidious model of group regulation one step further by implying that it is not subtle coercion that best ensures a group's longevity, but wanton violence. In the first half of *The Farther Adventures*, a narrative depicting Crusoe's return to his island colony and his subsequent travels through Central Asia, Defoe makes the point that attempting to keep a community going through religious conversion and the sharing of resources alone simply does not work. This can be observed in the beginning of the novel, where Defoe charts the unwillingness of three Englishmen to abide by the norms of the colony that Crusoe has founded. "The *English* Men," Defoe writes, "did nothing but ramble about the Island, shoot Parrots, and ketch Tortoises, and when they came home at Night, the Spaniards provided their Suppers for them."[31] This antisociality only intensifies as time progresses, and the Englishmen move from turning "two New-Comers out of Doors to shift for themselves" to pulling up the newly planted crops of these newcomers and attempting to burn their houses down (*FA,* 32).

Notably, what ultimately fuels the Englishmen's integration into the island community is witnessing and participating in acts of violence against native people. Before coming together to launch attacks on Indigenous inhabitants of the region, the community was split into three towns that had nothing to do with one another. It is only after two settlers kill and wound a group of natives that all three towns begin to work as one. Upon receiving news of the skirmish, for instance, even the three Englishmen "who were not yet noted for having the least Inclination to do any Good … came and offer'd their Help and Assistance" to rebuild the infrastructure that the Indigenous people had destroyed (*FA,* 64). Previously, even the discovery of captives some cannibals had been planning to eat did not change their behavior. In this case, however, the news of blood being shed spurs them into action, implying that, for Defoe, it is the infliction of violence and not the threat of it that inspires camaraderie. Put another way, the possibility of being attacked by cannibals does not move the three Englishmen to contribute to the causes the colony holds dear, but the opportunity to attack others certainly does.

What this suggests about Defoe's understanding of communal dynamics is that a communal sense of purpose is difficult to sustain. For all of Crusoe's investment in growing his colony, he ultimately leaves, and despite the fact that their fellow settlers are their only companions, the Englishmen refuse to labor for the common good. Read as an oblique representation of the Caribbean, Crusoe's island colony also stands as a testament to the limits of the British imperial imagination. Such writers as Defoe simply could not conceive of a world in which overseas colonies could succeed and thrive with the labor of settlers alone. As *The Farther Adventures* implies, even in a utopian world where crops seem to grow without much cultivation and Indigenous people seem eager to labor alongside white settlers, colonies lack the shared convictions necessary for them to stay together in the long term, and it is only violence that can fill the void.

As the clashes against the native inhabitants of the region become increasingly intense, one of the most antisocial Englishmen, Will Atkins, even takes on a leadership role in an attack the colony launches and continues fighting, despite being severely wounded. Atkins's willingness to go above and beyond, when he has never done so before, demonstrates how violence can inspire a sense of *esprit de corps* when other means fail, and, as the novel progresses, it becomes clear that, for Defoe, the constant pursuit of violence is often the only means by which a fragile community can stay together in a hostile world. Because the infliction of violence almost always invites retaliation, members, from the moment an attack is launched, either fully commit to continuing the violent behavior begun by their peers or suffer the violence those outside the community undertake in revenge. The uncooperative Englishmen might be able to avoid partaking in the mundane activities required to keep a community going and still remain part of it, but in the ongoing battle between the natives and the settlers, they have to pick a side. In the presence of violence, that is, they have no choice but to face up to their responsibilities as members of the community.

After winning the battle against the Indigenous inhabitants of the region, the colony is said to enjoy two years of "perfect Tranquility" (*FA,* 73). This tranquillity, however, does not last. A few years later, Crusoe receives a letter noting that those on the island "went on but poorly" and that the Spaniards, for all their previous enthusiasm about settling on the island, wished for him "to fetch them away, that they might see their own Country again before they dy'd" (*FA*, 126). This is, I would argue, no accident. If the initially divided colony was united by everyone partaking in violence together, it collapses because Crusoe subsequently discouraged the planters from taking part in this shared activity. Before he leaves the island to journey onward, he decides not to leave the colony a boat or weapons that would have allowed them to launch offensive attacks against the natives, declaring that "for many Reasons I did not think fit to let them know any Thing of the Sloop I had fram'd ... nor did I leave the two Pieces of Brass Cannon that I had on board, or the two Quarter-Deck Guns ... I thought ... not to ... encourage them to go Abroad to attack others, which in the End would only bring Ruin and Destruction upon themselves and all their Undertaking" (*FA*, 119). Left bereft of the means of periodically inflicting violence upon others, the colony is no longer able to generate compelling reminders for its members to stay together for the sake of mutual protection and aid, and a vulnerable community that depends upon everybody's full participation falls apart.

Deterrence and the Turn to Massacre

In the world that Defoe has designed, then, the willingness to inflict violence upon others serves as the ultimate litmus test for and guarantor of loyalty. This is a lesson that is repeatedly foisted upon Crusoe, even after he has left the island. While sailing aboard his nephew's ship, for instance, Crusoe learns that the crew wishes to abandon him midway because of his refusal to partake in "the Massacre of Madagascar," which sees the crew setting fire to an entire town (*FA*, 140). A boatswain informs Crusoe that "he had used the Men very ill on that Account" and that the crew suspected "he might have some ill Design in [his] Head, and perhaps to call them to Account for it, when they came to *England*" (*FA*, 141). The boatswain thus "did not think it was safe to sail with [Crusoe] among them" (*FA*, 141).

As I see it, the crew's declaration that they do not feel safe with Crusoe is not simply a rhetorical move and also does not merely entail them feeling concerned that they will be reported to the authorities for massacring an entire village. The crew is also fearful that Crusoe will defect at any moment and, in so doing, compromise their future expeditions. *The Farther Adventures*, after all, makes clear that the crew is operating within a hostile world. They are constantly outnumbered, and crew members are always at risk of injury or death. That Crusoe is unwilling to participate when their plans involve violence suggests that he is not committed enough to be dependable.

Eli Berman's analysis of how such religious organizations as the Taliban morph from being charitable and conflict-averse to disturbingly violent lends credence to such a counterintuitive claim. Berman argues that terrorist groups often start out benign, and tend to sprout in places where the government is weak. By providing essential social services to local populations, they gain political power as new members join them in order to access healthcare, education, and physical infrastructure that would otherwise be unavailable. As their numbers increase and their ability to control defection decreases, however, they turn to violence to ensure that their members remain obedient and docile. By undertaking such acts as the attacking of civilians or the destruction of sacred sites not their own, these religious organizations warn their members of the consequences of defection by inspiring fear among them, and, in so doing, they maintain their numbers and their political and economic might.[32]

Considered in this light, the crew's paranoid reaction to Crusoe's refusal to participate in the massacre begins to make disturbing sense. After all, by choosing to adhere to external norms instead of the norms of the group to which he belongs, Crusoe reveals his unwillingness to sacrifice an alternative way of life that is fundamentally at odds with the life of murder and plunder that the crew leads. He is part of a community where manpower is scarce and members depend upon one another for protection and to accumulate resources by force, but as the crew sees it, he cannot be trusted to pull his own weight. That is why he is ultimately expelled and also why he is expelled with the bizarre chant of "One and ALL, One and ALL" (*FA,* 142). For the crew, after all, the concept of teamwork is one that Crusoe, who refuses to engage in violence, clearly does not get.

This is a mistake that Crusoe does not make again. Towards the end of *The Farther Adventures,* Crusoe joins a caravan of over a hundred people to travel to Muscovy, and from then on, belonging to a community and fighting on behalf of it for him go hand in hand. He defends the caravan against robbers, and later on, even burns down an entire village with four of his fellow travellers, despite his clear abhorrence of violence before. The implication, then, is that the Crusoe of the second half of *The Farther Adventures* is a desperate man, one willing to resort to anything to keep the new community he has found going.

After being abandoned by his nephew's crew, Crusoe is left in the exact same situation he was in before he met Friday: bereft of a community. His actions are thus representative of someone who is working at rebuilding a community from scratch and ensuring it survives. As in *The Life and Strange Surprizing Adventures,* Crusoe quickly acquires new members for his community, but most of them come and go: only his manservant, an English merchant, whom he terms his partner, and the partner's servant stay. It is against such a precarious backdrop that Crusoe proposes his murderous expedition, an expedition that is consciously modeled after the massacre of Madagascar. Recounting a conversation he had with a Scots merchant, Crusoe notes that "I related the Story of our Men at Madagascar, and how they burnt and sack'd the Village there, and kill'd Man, Woman and Child, for their murdering one of our Men ... and when I had done, I added, that I thought we ought to do so to this Village" (*FA,* 194). No one from this village has injured Crusoe's companions, but Crusoe is nonetheless eager to perform the actions he had so strongly condemned before. This deliberate repetition of history, I argue, gestures towards Crusoe's desire to become part of a close-knit group that is reminiscent of his nephew's crew. By committing to violence, Crusoe is effectively declaring his loyalty to the new community he has claimed.

Unlike the crew members, of course, no one in the caravan is asking him to demonstrate his loyalty by participating in acts of violence. Crusoe himself also says nothing about wishing to inspire or pledge allegiance, declaring instead that his bloodthirst is due to his hatred of idolatry alone. Nevertheless, however, his violent actions have a charismatic effect: they draw the people around him closer. The Scots merchant who mocks Crusoe's zeal initially, for instance, ultimately decides to join his enterprise and even declares to him that "I abhor the Idol and the Idolatry as much as you can do" (*FA,* 194). Upon hearing of Crusoe's plans, another Scotsman informs Crusoe that "he would go with [him] if it cost him his Life" (*FA,* 195). Crusoe's partner is loath to join in, but even he claims to be "ready to assist [Crusoe] to the utmost, and upon all Occasions for [his] Defence" (*FA,* 195). That these individuals rally around Crusoe without requiring much persuasion is proof of the binding power of violence, but it is worth noting that in *The Farther Adventures,* violence binds, as Berman argues, not only by assuming the form of a compelling shared experience, but also by making it impossible for group members to leave.

I discussed such a concept briefly earlier in this essay, where I showed how violent acts undertaken by a few members of a community can deter other members from defecting by turning the rest of the world against them, as in the case of Will Atkins and his companions. Crusoe's secretive massacre of the Muscovite village ("no Body knew any Thing of the Matter") takes this one step further by leaving his companions unsure about why they are being attacked in the first place (*FA,* 198). For the members of Crusoe's caravan, both isolation and hostility are mere facts, rather than the products of human action. On the day after Crusoe and three other men sacked and burned the village, the caravan is confronted by "one hundred thousand" people and followed for three days (*FA,* 199). They are also attacked by "a cloud of Arrows," but even after their journey together ends, only Crusoe and his three comrades know that the violence the caravan experienced was a form of vengeance, provoked by their own actions (*FA,* 199). Notably, as a result of these attacks, members of the caravan come to rely more heavily upon one another for defense and support, and the entire caravan stays together for more than seven months.

I do not wish to overstate the role that Crusoe's violent massacre plays in the caravan staying together for so long, but it does seem glaring that his act of violence changes the situation enough that "a great Caravan of Muscovite and Polish Merchants" faces significant trouble traveling through a land that is home for many of them (*FA,* 178). Because of Crusoe's actions, the merchants lose the option of leaving the caravan along the way in order to market their goods to a people with whom they are likely to be familiar. This serves Crusoe's purposes: the fewer options his caravan members have to leave, the more likely his goods will be transported safely across Muscovite lands. This is, of course, a speculation, but reading a canonical text speculatively allows us to glimpse the unexpected connections that exist between forms of benevolence and forms of violence. As I hope I have shown, these connections have deep historical roots and shaped the way power was exercised in small collectives during the long eighteenth century.

Notes

1. Mary Bellhouse, "On Understanding Rousseau's Praise of Robinson Crusoe," *Canadian Journal of Social and Political Theory* 6, no. 3 (1982): 120–37.

2. Watt, *The Rise of the Novel: Studies in Defoe, Richardson, and Fielding* (Berkeley: University of California Press, 1957), 63.

3. For the intertwining of religion and economics in *Robinson Crusoe,* see Novak, "Robinson Crusoe's 'Original Sin,'" *Studies in English Literature, 1500–1900* 1, no. 3 (Summer 1961): 19–29; Starr, *Defoe and Spiritual Autobiography* (Princeton: Princeton University Press, 1965); and Hunter, *The Reluctant Pilgrim: Defoe's Emblematic Method and Quest for Form in Robinson Crusoe* (Baltimore: Johns Hopkins University Press, 1966). For interpretations of Defoe's work within the context of empire, see Todd, *Defoe's America* (New York: Cambridge University Press, 2010) and Mallipeddi, *Spectacular Suffering: Witnessing Slavery in the Eighteenth-Century British Atlantic* (Charlottesville: University of Virginia Press, 2016).

4. Todd, *Defoe's America,* 29.

5. Watson, "Crusoe, Friday, and the Raced Market Frame of Orthodox Economics Textbooks," *New Political Economy* 23, no. 5 (2018): 544–59.

6. Grapard, "Robinson Crusoe: the quintessential economic man?" in *Robinson Crusoe's Economic Man: A Construction and Deconstruction*, ed. Grapard and Hewitson (New York: Routledge, 2011), 105.

7. Watt, *The Rise of the Novel*, 70.

8. Watt, *The Rise of the Novel*, 70.

9. Joseph Ward, *Metropolitan Communities: Trade Guilds, Identity, and Change in Early Modern London* (Stanford: Stanford University Press, 1997), 2.

10. Ward, *Metropolitan Communities*, 7–26.

11. Paula Backscheider, *Daniel Defoe: His Life* (Baltimore: Johns Hopkins University Press, 1989), 41.

12. Arthur Pearce, *The History of the Butchers' Company* (London: Meat Trades' Journal Co., 1929), 104.

13. For an account of Defoe's interactions with Russell and the merchants of Edinburgh, see Backscheider, *Daniel Defoe*, 226–52.

14. Brown, *The Reaper's Garden: Death and Power in the World of Atlantic Slavery* (Cambridge: Harvard University Press, 2010).

15. Dunn, *Sugar and Slaves: The Rise of the Planter Class in the English West-Indies, 1624–1713* (Chapel Hill: University of North Carolina Press for the Omohundro Institute of Early American History and Culture, 2000), 334.

16. For Defoe's thoughts on the South Sea trade, see Carl Fisher, "The Project and the People: Defoe on the South Sea Bubble and the Public Good," in *Defoe's Footprints: Essays in Honour of Maximillian E. Novak*, ed. Robert M. Maniquis and Carl Fisher (Toronto: University of Toronto Press in association with the UCLA Center for Seventeenth- and Eighteenth-Century Studies and the William Andrews Clark Memorial Library, 2009): 170–88.

17. Maximillian Novak, *Master of Fictions* (New York: Oxford University Press, 2001), 402.

18. Byrd, *The Transit of Empire: Indigenous Critiques of Colonialism* (Minneapolis: University of Minnesota Press, 2011), xii. For another influential mode of reading that takes decolonization as its goal, see Tiffany King, *The Black Shoals: Offshore Formations of Black and Native Studies* (Durham: Duke University Press, 2019).

19. Ramos, *Shifting Capital: Mercantilism and the Economics of the Act of Union of 1707* (Cham: Palgrave Macmillan, 2018).

20. Ramos, *Shifting Capital*, 10.

21. Ramos, *Shifting Capital*, 13.

22. In this essay, I read Crusoe's behavior in the second and third volumes of the trilogy as an extension of his actions in the first volume, instead of as departures from it. In doing so, I am inspired by the readings of such scholars as Leah Thomas and Anne Thell, who do the same thing in order to foreground Crusoe's complex motivations. Thomas, for instance, argues that the seeming disconnect between the Crusoe who allows for "Liberty of Conscience throughout [his] dominions" and the Crusoe who advocates for massacre and Christian world domination reveals how his religious beliefs have changed over time, while Thell demonstrates how Crusoe's unconquerable wanderlust throughout the trilogy gestures towards an inherent

insanity that is gradually revealed as the story progresses. See Thomas, "Providence and Religion in the Crusoe Trilogy," *Eighteenth Century Life* 38, no. 2 (2014): 1–27; and Thell, "The Aesthetics of Mental Illness in Defoe's Crusoe Trilogy," *Review of English Studies* 71, no. 301 (2019): 1–20. See also Kevin Seidel, *"Robinson Crusoe* as Defoe's Theory of Fiction," *NOVEL: A Forum on Fiction* 44, no. 2 (2011): 165–85, which models how the trilogy should be read as a self-contained whole by attending to Defoe's use of irony and literary form.

23.   Boulukos, *The Grateful Slave: The Emergence of Race in Eighteenth-Century British and American Culture* (Cambridge: Cambridge University Press, 2008).

24.   Defoe, *The Life and Strange Surprizing Adventures of Robinson Crusoe*, ed. W. R. Owens (London: Pickering & Chatto, 2008), 214, 211. Subsequent citations will be made parenthetically as *RC*.

25.   These ideas are fleshed out more fully in Iannaccone, "Sacrifice and Stigma: Reducing Free-riding in Cults, Communes, and Other Collectives," *Journal of Political Economy* 100, no. 2 (1992): 271–91.

26.   Valerie Pearl, "Change and Stability in Seventeenth-Century London," in *The Tudor and Stuart Town, 1530–1688*, ed. Jonathan Barry (New York: Routledge, 2014), 139.

27.   Bowles and Gintis, "The Moral Economy of Communities," *Evolution and Human Behavior* 19, no. 1 (1998): 3–25.

28.   Michael Berlin, "'Broken in all Pieces': Artisans and the Regulation of Workmanship in Early Modern London," in *The Artisan and the European Town, 1500–1900* (New York: Routledge, 2016): 79.

29.   Berlin, "'Broken in all Pieces,'" 79.

30.   Berlin, "'Broken in all Pieces,'" 87.

31.   Defoe, *The Farther Adventures of Robinson Crusoe*, ed. W. R. Owens (London: Pickering & Chatto, 2008), 32. Subsequent citations will be made parenthetically as *FA*.

32.   Berman, *Radical, Religious, and Violent: The New Economics of Terrorism* (Cambridge: MIT Press, 2009), 75–78.

Family Instruction in
The Farther Adventures of Robinson Crusoe: Consider the Children

JUDITH STUCHINER

In his *Present State of the Parties* (1712), Daniel Defoe allows himself a brief but unreservedly nostalgic journey into the glorious "Last Age of *Dissenters*":

> Their *Ministers* were Men known over the Whole World; their general Character was own'd even by their Enemies; generally speaking they were Men of liberal Education; had a vast Stock of Learning; were Exemplar in Piety. ... As were the Ministers, so in a Proportion were the People ... their Families were little Churches, where the Worship of God was constantly kept up; Their Children and Families were duly Instructed.[1]

After a few pages of wallowing, however, Defoe turns to the present and informs his fellow Dissenters of the more pressing issue at hand—the current crisis in religious education. A proud graduate of Newington Green, a school acknowledged to be part of a superior, but dying breed of Dissenting academies, Defoe deplores the quality of education in their contemporary equivalent: "'Tis evident, the great Imperfection of our Academies is want of Conversation; this the Publick Universities enjoy; ours cannot: If a Man pores upon his Book, and despises the Advantage of Conversation, he always comes out a Pedant, a meer Scholar, rough and unfit for anything out of the Walls of his College."[2] Needless to say, the quality of men produced by these newfangled dissenting schools also falls short: "Here and there one, a Youth bless'd with an extraordinary Genius, strong Parts and great Application, may Out-strip Others; and these, under all the Discouragements and Difficulties above, may rise to a Pitch beyond the common Rate: But, like *David's* Second Rate Worthies, they may be great; howbeit they do not come up to the Fate of the First?"[3]

Defoe's dissatisfaction with the decline in the quality of Dissenting academies merely compounded his longstanding frustration with the political environment. The failure of Parliament to exempt Dissenters from the requirement of the Test Act—"as if the Test-Act had been made entirely and singly against the Dissenters, and not against Papists"—was the first of a long list of disappointments that followed the Revolution of 1688.[4] The death of King William III, on whose leadership Defoe had relied; the division of the Tory and Whig parties into factions that were not supportive of Dissenter interests; the refusal of the Low-Church party to view Dissenters "as a Religious Party, *there they all give us up*, but as Members of their Politick Party"—all of these things contributed to a bleak political landscape for Dissenters.[5] But just as much as the political setbacks, the way in which Dissenters conducted themselves on the political scene was a source of vexation for Defoe. From the beginning of William's reign, Defoe insists, Dissenters had not protected their own interests. They had shown "Weakness."[6] They had not used "Prudence."[7] "They had not entered into Particulars."[8] They had viewed the future through rose-tinted glasses and naively believed in the Church of England's goodwill: "that having Granted them a Tolleration by Parliament, [the Church] could never pretend to restrain them from Educating their Youth and breeding up Ministers to Preach to them; they left all these things to the Generosity and Gratitude of the Church."[9]

The passage of the Schism Act (1714) merely added to Defoe's growing anxiety about the plight of education for the children of Dissenters. With characteristic alacrity, he responded in print with his *The Schism Act Explain'd* (1714).[10] In a departure from his previous emphasis on education in the schools, in *The Present State of The Parties,* Defoe here turns his attention to education in the home. Certainly *The Schism Act Explain'd* registers Defoe's horror at the Schism Act's injunction to curtail instruction by Dissenting schoolmasters: "If the design of the Law is that our Children shall not be Educated as Dissenters, this, as before, we cannot comply with, and must chuse to Suffer rather than to Sin; such Dissenting Schools as can be found must have our Children, and where the Teachers are content to hazard their

Safety and Liberty, they will very well deserve the Encouragement."[11] But even more tellingly, *The Schism Act Explain'd* is a passionate plea to those Dissenting parents who have fallen down on the job and become lax in the day-to-day religious education of their children: "I conclude with a serious Exhortation to the Dissenters, and especially to those among them who are Masters of Families and Fathers of Children, that they would consider their immediate Duty, and to which they have a particular call from Heaven by this remarkable Providence, and this is, That they would revive That lost practice of Family Instruction."[12] Defoe's suggestion that the Schism Act is a "remarkable Providence" is consistent with his message of urgency. Perhaps it was an attempt to reassure himself that the Act would pressure those families who had neglected "that lost practice of Family Instruction" to do their duty and finally practice family instruction—before it died out.

I would like to use this important shift in Defoe's thought from Dissenting education as a public good to something that could only happen inside the home to recast our understanding of *The Farther Adventures of Robinson Crusoe*. We cannot understand how key family instruction is to *The Farther Adventures*, and indeed to the entire Crusoe trilogy, without first attending to Defoe's "story-fication" of religious instruction in *The Family Instructor*.[13] In the verdant forest of Crusoe's island, we see a kind of transplantation of some of the dialogues that were initially presented in the domestic space of *The Family Instructor*. This essay draws attention to the permeability, for Defoe, of the line between didactic literature and fiction. The novel, with its space for deep exploration of family dynamics, was the perfect instrument for Defoe to put forth an argument for warm and passionate religious instruction in the home, as opposed to the lukewarm and formulaic teaching offered by the Church and the schools—even the Dissenting academies.

I join other scholars in drawing a connection between *The Family Instructor* and *Robinson Crusoe*. Richard Barney argues that "in all three stories related in [*The Family Instructor*], Defoe's concern is the pedagogical situation that stands *after* the most opportune season of educating children has already passed—when parents are confronted by the results of their negligence in providing their children with rigorous religious instruction. … This scenario … has ready application to *Robinson Crusoe* … and [to] Crusoe's development in the novel."[14] Christopher Flint also compares the conversations between Atkins and his wife in *The Farther Adventures* to the dialogues between the father and son in *The Family Instructor*: "Crusoe maintains a supererogatory role in its 'Government,' but for all intents and purposes he withdraws, having himself become the obsolete father."[15] Finally, in his "Narratives of Amelioration," Alpen Razi finds parallels between Defoe's "treatment of slave amelioration" in *The Family Instructor* and *Farther Adventures*.[16]

A cursory examination of *The Family Instructor* conveys two crucial points. First, parents who do not provide religious instruction to their children fail to perform their duty. Second, parents who do not instruct their children in religion do not deserve the love of their children: "Such Parents are certainly the most unnatural and may justly be reproach'd by their Children, not with neglect of their Duty only, but with their being without Natural Affections, and consequently can by no means expect suitable returns of Affection from their Children when they come to be made sensible of the Treatment they have receiv'd from them" (*FI*, 56). While Defoe's message that religious instruction is an act of love may be familiar, the method he uses is "*entirely New*" (*FI*, 2). In a series of dialogues between family members, in the course of which many sighs are exhaled and many tears are shed, he conveys religious doctrine with feeling. It is the emotive quality of these dialogues that perhaps accounts for the enormous popularity of *The Family Instructor* amongst Protestant worshipers who had been subsisting on a steady diet of cold catechism.[17]

Five years later, in *The Farther Adventures*, Defoe has Crusoe do the very thing that he inveighed against so forcefully in *The Schism Act Explain'd* and *The Family Instructor*. Like the negligent Dissenting parents who, Defoe implies, deserved to be punished with the passage of the Schism Act, the widowed Crusoe is guilty of squandering his opportunity to fulfill the most important tenet of his religion: the molding of his own children into good Protestants. *The Farther Adventures* begins with a short recap of how Crusoe has spent the years since the close of the first volume. Eager for adventure, Crusoe, who has since married, fathered two children, and become a widower, admits to passing on his parental duties to his "ancient good Friend the Widow, who earnestly struggled with me to consider my Years, my easy Circumstances, and the needless Hazards of a long Voyage; and *above all my young Children*" (emphasis mine).[18] In the context of the impassioned *Schism Act Explain'd*, which insists that the education of the child is the sole responsibility of the parent—"the Teaching of one Parent, is more than that of Ten School masters, not only as it is before them, and takes the young Mind when it is tender, easy to bend to Instruction, and like Wax takes any Impression, and when taken hardens and retains it, but also because there is the Affections in the Child to join with the Authority of a Parent"—Crusoe's rambling takes on a more sinister tinge.[19] What does Defoe gain by beginning his story with a hero who, before he has even set out on his journey, chooses "to Sin" rather than "to Suffer?"[20] Perhaps Crusoe's "Distemper of Wandering" is not mere wanderlust, but negligence at the expense of innocent children (*FA*, 10).

Farther Adventures

The Farther Adventures can be viewed as a series of squandered opportunities for Crusoe. The first such squandering is Crusoe's failure to provide "Family Instruction" to his children; by handing them over to the care of the widow, he gives up his chance to furnish his offspring with a solid foundation in the principles of Christianity. Just as Defoe argues in his didactic writing that the family unit must be the locus for religious instruction, he makes a similar claim in the Crusoe novels. While Crusoe never expresses remorse for his abandonment of his children, the complete absence of any further mention of his children hangs over both *The Farther Adventures* and *Serious Reflections during the Life and Surprising Adventures of Robinson Crusoe*.[21]

Furthermore, Defoe appears to make the argument in the Crusoe trilogy that religious ignorance is passed down in families, from one generation to the next. Though Crusoe's father is authoritative and seemingly involved with respect to his son's future, and Crusoe leaves his children to the care of a friend and divests himself of responsibility for them, in certain respects the parenting style of the two men is not that different. At least so far as we know, Crusoe's father, like Crusoe himself, does not instruct his children regarding faith or their souls. His guidance is limited to practical matters, such as "where [Crusoe] might be well introduced, and had a Prospect of raising [his] Fortune by Application and Industry."[22] Crusoe allows that "my Father, who was very ancient, had given me a competent Share of Learning, as far as House-Education, and a Country Free-School generally goes, and design'd me for the Law," but he does not mention any instances in which he received religious instruction from either of his parents (*RC,* 57). Similarly, Crusoe's absence ensures that any meaningful discussion between him and his children is unlikely. His willingness to deprive his own children of "Family Instruction" and thereby subject them to the same deprivation from which he has suffered demonstrates his unwitting participation in a repetitive cycle of parental neglect.

As we see in *The Family Instructor*, family instruction covers more than religious doctrine. It includes issues that Defoe thought important to children, such as one's origins and one's purpose—not just in the social and economic sense, but also in a more basic and essential sense.[23] These are some of the crucial questions that come up in family instruction: "Who made me? What was I made for? What am I?" (*FI,* 57). It gives children a forum in which to reflect "seriously about themselves and the Original of their being" (*FI,* 58). Additionally, family instruction provides time for the lost art of conversation—something that we know was important to Defoe.[24]

The second opportunity that Crusoe chooses not to seize is the chance to learn from the example of Will Atkins. While it is true that Atkins, a convicted criminal, has more for which to repent than Crusoe, Defoe draws a clear parallel between their pasts. In the contrast that Defoe sketches between Will Atkins, a reformed "prodigal son," and Crusoe, a "prodigal son" who has failed to reform, we see the outline of Defoe's argument for "Family Instruction."

Crusoe's third missed opportunity is his refusal of the French priest's offer to assist him with the conversion of the Indigenous local inhabitants. Crusoe is not only willing to risk the possibility that his own children will not be saved, but he is also willing to imperil the souls of the inhabitants of his colony. The French priest is bewildered by Crusoe's attitude: "Now, Sir, you have such an Opportunity here, to have six or seven and thirty poor Savages brought over from Idolatry to the Knowledge of God their Maker and Redeemer, that I wonder how you can pass such an Occasion of doing Good, which is really worth the Expence of a Man's whole Life." Yet, in contrast to the priest, who is concerned with the souls of the native people, Crusoe is preoccupied with the productivity of his "Subjects": "I look'd upon these Savages as Slaves, and People, who, had we had any Work for them to do, we would ha' used as such, or would ha' been glad to have transported them to any other Part of the World" (*FA*, 90). True, Crusoe, unlike the priest, does not have saving souls as his profession; nevertheless, it is difficult to ignore Crusoe's presumption that the "Savage" is a "Slave."

Defoe and the Religious Metaphor of Slavery

Razi argues that a preoccupation with the "unfinished history of the Protestant reformation" pervades Defoe's works. Like other Protestants, Defoe "lived in dread of not just a possible, but indeed a probable, reversal of England's collective emergence from the nonage of 'Catholick' slavery."[25] Defoe believed the Reformation needed to be an ongoing process—"a continual protest against the forces that threatened to re-enslave the Protestant nation state, forces that sought to enervate and corrupt the critical and mental faculties of its subjects, plunge them into mental torpor and incite them toward vice."[26] Do the Protestants to whom Defoe directs his rhetoric in *The Schism Act Explain'd* need another Reformation? If they allow others to take over the education of their children, do they risk the mental enslavement, both of themselves and of their children? What's more, is Crusoe's abandonment of his children to the care of the "ancient ... Widow" evidence of his own need of ongoing Reformation? Is Crusoe himself a kind of slave?[27]

In *Defoe's America*, Dennis Todd helpfully contextualizes Crusoe's wandering within the larger context of Christianity. "'Christian Liberty,' Todd writes, "conventionally was defined as the 'Freedom from the Bondage of Sin and Satan, and from the Dominion of Men's Lusts and passions and inordinate Desires.'"[28] This idea is endorsed by the father in *The Family Instructor*: "Liberty to do Evil is an abandon'd *Slavery*, the worst of *Bondage*; and Confinement *from doing Evil* is the only *true Liberty*" (*FI*, 135). Todd argues that Defoe applies this notion of liberty to Robinson Crusoe's "Propensity to rambling" (*FA*, 5) and concludes that Crusoe's wandering, was not evidence of freedom, but of enslavement. Todd points to Crusoe's admission—"the same Day that I broke away from my Father ... the same Day afterwards I was taken by the Sally Man of War, and made a Slave" (*RC*, 155).

Paradoxically, it is through submission that Crusoe achieves self-mastery: "I liv'd mighty comfortably, my Mind being entirely composed by resigning to the Will of God, and throwing my self wholly upon the Disposal of his Providence" (*RC*, 157). Thus, it is not until he is a servant (of God) that Crusoe becomes master of himself. My focus here is on Crusoe's self-described enslavement to and possession by a "Wandering Spirit" (*FA*, 125), rather than his actual servitude, since this kind of "enslavement" to the passions is what Defoe addresses in *The Family Instructor*. I want to stress, however, that this essay is primarily about metaphorical, rather than actual, slavery in *The Farther Adventures*; I do not want, in any way, to create the impression that I am equating metaphorical and actual chattel slavery.

In *The Farther Adventures* Defoe changes the way he applies the religious metaphor of slavery to his characterization of Crusoe. In the first volume of the trilogy, Crusoe accomplishes a great deal in his quest for spirituality. He not only converts himself to Protestant Christianity, he also converts his servant, Friday. But his self-conversion is not complete. In *The Farther Adventures*, Crusoe suffers a "crisis of faith" and does not exhibit self-mastery, but self-enslavement (in the metaphorical, religious sense we've been discussing).[29] After he has abandoned his children, he is presented with another opportunity to reform once he is on the island—by learning from the French priest and from the example of Atkins's reform. Instead he "chooses" the life of a wanderer.

Family Instruction in *The Farther Adventures*

Despite the spiritual rebirth and enlightenment that Crusoe convincingly claims to achieve in the first volume of the trilogy, a spiritual malaise descends upon him in *The Farther Adventures*. Indeed, Defoe seems to suggest that Crusoe never really embraced the principles of Protestantism. In this section, I will examine certain student-instructor pairs that Defoe devises—Will Atkins and his wife, the French priest and Atkins, and Crusoe and Friday—and situate them within his overarching juxtaposition of the two prodigal sons, Crusoe and Atkins, in order to demonstrate how family instruction gets novelized in the *Crusoe* novels. Like Crusoe, Atkins was unreceptive to the guidance of his father. Like Crusoe, Atkins rebelled against and metaphorically "Murthered" his father. Like Crusoe, Atkins was enslaved by his passions. Recently, however, in the timeline of *The Farther Adventures*, Atkins has, unlike Crusoe, shown improvement, particularly in his marriage to his "tawny Savage Wife" (*FA*, 98).

Atkins and his wife

Defoe goes to considerable lengths to convince us that, in contrast to Crusoe, Atkins's marriage is of vital and central importance to him. Crusoe's description of his wife, to which Defoe allots a single paragraph, has a false ring to it. It is an "Elegy," Crusoe himself concedes, with the "Flattery of a Funeral Sermon": "the Stay of all my Affairs, the Centre of all my Enterprizes, the Engine, ... [she] reduc'd me to that happy Compass I was in, from the most extravagant and ruinous Project that flutter'd in my Head" (*FA*, 9). The word "reduc'd" inadvertently conveys Crusoe's feeling that his wife diminished him, lessened him, shrank him. Crusoe's "rambling Genius," we might conclude, was constrained by the institution of marriage (*FA*, 9). Although Atkins's marriage can only be conceived in terms of colonial domination (i.e., Atkins's Caribbean wife can't bind Atkins in a "Compass" in the same way as an English wife supposedly bound Crusoe), we are nonetheless presented, almost voyeuristically, with their unfolding love story: "sitting under the Shade of a Bush, very eager in Discourse," Atkins and his wife are completely absorbed in one another. Though it is "far harder to *see in* than to *see out*," Crusoe and the French priest can still see plenty from their hiding place at the "Edge of the Wood" (*FA*, 98).

In this scene, Defoe injects his human drama with both a religious and a secular perspective. Building upon his method in *The Family Instructor*, in which he uses "Notes" to reinforce the instruction in the dialogues, Defoe here presents the dialogue between Atkins and his wife through the double perspective of a Catholic priest, who is married to God, and a layperson, who is "married" to rambling, to convey the values of Christian marriage. While neither the priest nor Crusoe can hear the conversation between Atkins and his wife, each infers, according to his own bias, the content of the conversation.

Defoe's use of the French priest as an enthusiastic spokesperson for the spiritual aspect of love is a brilliantly humorous touch. As the priest observes Atkins pointing up at the sky, then at the ground, then at himself, then at his wife, he elatedly explains to Crusoe the pious meaning of Atkins's gestures: "the Man preaches to her. ... Our God has made him, and her, the Heavens, the Earth, the Sea, the Woods, the Trees" (*FA,* 98). Indeed, the sight of Will Atkins on his knees, praying, moves the French priest to tears: "while the poor fellow was upon his Knees, I could see the Tears run plentifully down my Clergy-man's Cheeks" (*FA,* 99). When Atkins and his wife kneel down together, Crusoe notes, "My Friend could bear it no longer, but cries out aloud, "St. PAUL St. PAUL! *behold he prayeth*" (*FA,* 99). The French priest's euphoria apparently knows no bounds: "well, he strove with himself and contain'd himself for a while, but was in such Raptures of Joy, to think that the poor Heathen Woman was become a Christian, that he was not able to contain himself; he wept several times, then throwing up his hands and crossing his Breast, said over several Things ... some in Latin, some in French; then two or three times the Tears would interrupt him" (*FA,* 99). Rather than something that needs to be contained or controlled, the French priest, it would appear, believes that effusive passion is something to be celebrated.

While the French priest is excited by Atkins's growing piety, Crusoe is captivated by Atkins's earthly passion for his wife. The choice of words he uses to convey Atkins's devotion—"two or three times we could see him embrace her most passionately"—and his tenderness—"another time we saw him take out his Handkerchief and wipe her Eyes"—is different from the tone he uses to describe his own marriage (*FA,* 99). Rather than a source of passion, marriage, for Crusoe, is the thing that stands between himself and his passion for wandering. He dreams of escape almost from the moment he is saddled with a wife and family. His emphasis on the all-consuming way in which Atkins and his wife relate—"He stood talking still eagerly to her; and we observ'd by her Motion that she was greatly affected with what he said"—reveals the vicarious wish of the eavesdropper to participate in what he observes (*FA,* 99). While Atkins's marriage is notable for its all-consuming nature, Crusoe's marriage could not compete with his desire to return to his island and to the colony that he left there—"I dream'd of it all Night, and my Imagination run upon it all Day; ... my Fancy work'd so steadily and strongly upon it, that I talk'd of it in my Sleep"—a desire that his wife not only does not share, but considers to be "a most preposterous Thing" (*FA,* 7). Is it any wonder that Crusoe envies Atkins's marriage?

Using Crusoe and the priest as both observers and narrators of the interactions between Atkins and his wife, Defoe implies a kind of symbiosis in their joint "narrative." What is fascinating about the separate ways in which Crusoe and the priest observe the scene is the way in which Defoe merges their different preconceptions of passion into a robust notion of passion that embodies the physical and the spiritual. In his choice of words, "we saw him … kiss her again with a kind of Transport, very unusual," Crusoe describes an act of physical intimacy that is able to "transport" Atkins and his wife to an otherworldly realm. A "kiss," Defoe implies, exemplifies both corporeal and spiritual passions.

As the following dialogue shows, Atkins, a former "Reprobate," exhibits a laudable receptivity to religious instruction (*FA,* 57). Initially the rational quality in his Caribbean wife's questions about a Christian God activates in Atkins a desire to answer her questions. In other words, Atkins's wife brings out the teacher in Atkins. Furthermore, after a certain point, she brings out the learner in Atkins, whose desire to learn has lain dormant since he "murthered" his father.

> *Wife.* But you say me, [God] is Great, much Great, have much great Power … why he no make kill when you no serve him? No say O to him? No be good Mans.
>
> *W.A.* That is true; he might strike me Dead … but God is merciful. …
>
> *Wife.* But then, do not you tell God Tankee for that too?
>
> *W.A.* No, indeed, I have not thank'd God for his Mercy, any more than I have fear'd God for his Power.
>
> *Wife.* Then you God no God; me no think believe, he be such one, great much Power, Strong; no makee kill you tho' you make him much Angry.
>
> *W.A.* What? Will my wicked Life hinder you from believing in God! What a dreadful Creature am I; and what a sad Truth is it, that the horrid Lives of Christians hinders the Conversion of Heathens?" (*FA,* 105)

Although the power of the dialogue is lessened by the patriarchal and racial biases that are built into it, it demonstrates a genuine reciprocity and a mode of interaction in which the roles of student and teacher are interchangeable. The logic of Atkins's wife is irrefutable: either God has "much great Power" and will eventually "strike [Atkins] dead" or God is powerless and Atkins can continue to "make him much Angry" with no ill consequences. Her questions are as much for Atkins's as for her own understanding. As the

French priest says, "Attempting to teach others, is sometimes the best way of teaching ourselves" (*FA*, 98).

However, although the institution of Christian marriage may participate in the abatement of Will Atkins's spiritual crisis, it also participates in the erasure of Atkins's nameless wife. Indeed, we never learn anything about Atkins's wife, including her original name. Once the priest baptizes her, her name is "MARY" and her Caribbean name, along with all the other aspects of her indigeneity, is subsumed within her Christian identity (*FA*, 109). The romance of Atkins and his wife plays right into the conversion project of the French priest, which utilizes and perpetuates the racial and gendered dominance accorded white men. The French priest is able to accomplish the ruthless replacement of the Caribbean wife's belief in "the great old *Benamuckee* God" (*FA*, 104) with the Christian God by taking advantage of Atkins and his wife's romance in which the male and female reenact the familiar roles of dominance and submission. While the conversion of Atkins's wife has a twist in which the student becomes a teacher, as is demonstrated by the powerful "Sermon" she delivers, the dominance inherent in the conversion process benefits from Defoe's cloaking it within a familiar, western-style romance in which a white man occupies the figure of authority. Thus, although Atkins is a "Brute" and a "Murtherer," his whiteness, maleness, and Christianity allow him to refer to his possibly more logical and moral wife as "Child" and to perpetuate his domination in the conversion of his "Heathen" wife.

The French Priest and Atkins

For the most part, passion is depicted as a bad thing in the first volume of the trilogy; right from the start, it is presented as something that needs to be avoided or governed. Crusoe's father warns Crusoe against "the Passion of Envy," and Crusoe's mother receives his news that he will travel with anger—"this put my Mother into a great Passion" (*RC*, 58, 60). As Todd has pointed out, Crusoe describes cannibals as people who are at the mercy of "their own abominable and vitiated Passions" (*RC*, 182).[30]

In *The Farther Adventures*, however, we see passion painted in a more complex way. Crusoe presents the French priest as the personification of passion and religious zeal—"I had here a Spirit of True Christian Zeal for God and Religion before me" (*FA*, 90). Though Crusoe frequently describes the physical evidence of the French priest's zeal—"I discovered a kind of Rapture in his Face, while he spoke this to me; his Eyes sparkl'd like Fire, his Face glow'd, and his Colour came and went, as if he had been falling into Fits" (91)—he also points out that the priest's passion is deep and genuine.

For despite his protectiveness of his own autonomy and his right to wander, Crusoe cannot help but be impressed by the French priest's willingness "to be lock'd up in an unplanted Island for, perhaps, his Life" simply for the chance to convert the thirty-seven men (*FA*, 91). The sharpness of the priest's response to Crusoe's callous characterization of his work as a "Venture" is notable: "Do you think, if I can convert these seven and thirty Men to the Faith of Christ, it is not worth my time, tho' I should never be fetch'd off the Island again; nay, is it not infinitely of more worth to save so many Souls, than my Life is, or the Life of 20 more of the same Profession?" (*FA*, 91–92).

In his reassurance to the passionate Will Atkins who fears it is too late for him to mend his sinful ways, the French priest himself describes how passion fits into his philosophy of religion. Through Crusoe, who acts as Atkins's emissary, the priest gives Atkins the following message: "You may assure him it is not too late; Christ will give him Repentance: But as no Man is sav'd but by Christ and the Merit of his Passion, procuring divine Mercy for him, how can it be too late for any Man to receive Mercy?" (*FA*, 97). Defoe's use of the phrase "the Merit of his Passion" was controversial to say the least. Raised on the Calvinist view that we are fallen sinners and justified solely by our faith, Defoe's mere use of the term "merit"—what's more by a Catholic priest— may have raised Protestant eyebrows. Furthermore, the French priest's use of "merit" in conjunction with "Passion," or "justification by faith," was problematic. Traditionally used to describe "justification by works," the word "merit" was an unlikely word to be applied to passion or faith. Actually, the phrase "the Merit of his Passion" had received considerable attention ever since the Council of Trent's publication of the *Index Expurgatorius* in 1584, which ordered the following question and answer sequence to be expunged from the official writings of the Catholic Church.

> Quest: Dost thou believe that thou shalt come to Heaven not by thine own merits, but by the virtue and merits of Christ's passion?
>
> Answ: I do believe it.
>
> Quest: Dost thou believe that Christ died for our salvation, and that none can be saved by their own merits?
>
> Answ: I do believe it.

The expunged question and answer sequence gets at the heart of the faith versus works controversy. The Catholic belief in justification by works is contradicted by the affirmation—"that none can be saved by their own merits"—which explains the suppression of the text. In contrast, a sermon written by Defoe's contemporary John Newman (a Protestant) approves of the text's affirmation that salvation is not due to human merit, but to the "virtue and merits of Christ's passion" and disapproves of the Catholic authorities who put the conversation on the Index: "How could these men, who pretend to believe the scriptures, without shame and blushing reject such questions and answers, as favoring of heretical pravity?," he asks. "No wonder," he answers, "they contend for another rule of faith beside the scripture, by which to judge of heresy."[31]

Considering the resonance of the phrase, Defoe's decision to have it emanate from the Catholic priest is significant. The priest's statement—"no Man is sav'd but by Christ and the Merit of his Passion"—is slightly ambiguous. Of course, we know that theological passion is not human passion and that the French priest refers to the merit of Christ's passion. Still in employing the Catholic priest as a mouthpiece for the statement, I suggest that Defoe uses the French priest both as an example of, and as a spokesperson for, a meritorious kind of passion. Rather than selfish passion that enslaves, such as cannibalism or rambling, the French priest models selfless passion. When the priest sees Atkins and his wife kneeling on the ground, he passionately exclaims "Behold he prayeth!" because he is so excited that a fellow human being will be saved. In other words, his faith is not just about his own salvation; it is about the salvation of others. In the same vein, the priest's "Raptures of Joy" and copious "Tears" do not stem from his own fortunes but from the fortunes of another. "In a word," as Crusoe comments, "He was fir'd with the Joy of being embark'd in such a Work" (*FA,* 91). In the language of the faith versus works controversy, the French priest exemplifies a merging of faith and works in which faith is supported by good works and good works are fueled by the passion of faith.

Although ultimately it is the French priest's aim to convert the entire population of Crusoe's island, he begins with Crusoe's "English Subjects" and the native women with whom they have been cohabitating for the past seven years (*FA,* 89). "If you will give me Leave, and God his Blessing," he confides to Crusoe, "I do not doubt the poor ignorant Souls shall be brought home into the great Circle of Christianity" (*FA,* 90). The French priest's "circle of Christianity" seems like a blue print for the family circle, and the spiritual love that he preaches is something he wishes to instill in the families on the island. Certainly, Defoe strives to create the impression that Atkins and his wife's familial love replicates the French priest's example of spiritual love.

The French priest gives Atkins the tools to persevere in his spiritual journey. When Atkins voices, "with a great deal of Passion," his doubts about his chance of being saved—"he believ'd he should one Time or other cut his Throat to put an End to the Terror of it"—it is the priest who helps Atkins. It is crucial that Atkins's spiritual journey is not solitary, but familial; what motivates Atkins is not just his own salvation but the salvation of his wife. The possibility that he could be what stands between the salvation and destruction of his wife pains Atkins so much that even Crusoe finds it excruciating: "I cannot bear it" (*FA,* 102).

What is striking about Atkins's conversation, as filtered through Crusoe, who "interpreted every Word as he spoke it," is its raw emotive quality (*FA,* 102). As Atkins tells Crusoe, "Sir, you have set me about a Work that has struck a Dart thro my very Soul; I have been talking about God and Religion to my Wife, in order as you directed me to make a Christian of her, and she has preach'd such a Sermon to me, as I shall never forget while I live" (*FA,* 103). Atkins, Crusoe observes, has a "Conscience" (*FA,* 103). Like a "Dart," his wife's "Sermon" forces him to acknowledge his own "brutish" behavior (*FA,* 52). Although the pain of unworthiness that Atkins feels is almost palpable—"I am an unthankful, ungrateful Dog, that's true"—he nonetheless subjects himself to the pain of family instruction (*FA,* 106). And, as Crusoe diligently informs us, Atkins's attempt to comply with his wife's request to "makee God know me" almost does him in: "*Here* Will. Atkins *said his Heart sunk within him, to hear a poor untaught Creature desire to be taught to know God and he such a wicked Wretch that he could not say one word to her about God*" (*FA,* 106). As in the previous scene that Crusoe had viewed, but not heard, Crusoe is moved as much by Atkins's body language as by his words. For Atkins does not merely talk to his wife; he gets down on his knees and prays:

> *The poor fellow was in such an Agony at her desiring him to make her know God ... that, he said, he fell down on his Knees before her and pray'd to God to enlighten her Mind with the saving Knowledge of Jesus Christ and to pardon his Sins, and accept of his being the unworthy Instrument of instructing her in the Principles of Religion. ... He was at a great Loss to make her understand, that God has reveal'd himself to us by his Word, and what his Word was:* ... Here the poor Man could forbear no longer; but raising her up, made her kneel by him, and he pray'd to God aloud to instruct her in the Knowledge of himself by his Spirit. (*FA,* 106–7)

In short, Atkins teaches his wife how to pray. It is the act of praying— and the passion that Atkins brings to it— that resonates, even with Crusoe. Indeed, Crusoe makes sure to mention the physical act of praying at several points in his description. Consider, for example, Crusoe's specification that "N.B. This was the Time when we saw him kneel down, and hold up his Hands" and "This was the Time that we saw him lift her up by the Hand, and saw him kneel down by her, as above" (*FA,* 107, 108).

In a similar manner, the dialogues in *The Family Instructor* discuss the actual act of prayer. In many of the dialogues Defoe emphasizes the way in which family members who worship in the home, within the family circle, rather than in public at a church, connect both with God and with each other on a deeper level. Defoe recounts the story of a daughter who experiences family prayer for the first time at the home of her devout aunt, later telling her mother:

> I believe it is the pleasantest thing in the World. I thought I was in Heaven. ... They all agree to be a sober, pious *Family* ...; they all love one another *so entirely.* ... *My Uncle* every Night and Morning calls them all together to Prayers: *My Aunt* takes all her Daughters together *once a Day*, and makes one of them read a Chapter, and then she says anything she finds occasion to say to them, by way of *Reproof* or *Direction*; and I observ'd when I went up Stairs at *Night*, not one of my Cousins would go to Bed, till they had retir'd into their Closets to their prayers by *themselves.* (*FI*, 112–13)

In contrast, Defoe clearly sympathizes with the young boy whose parents do not practice family instruction and whose mother carries him to church simply to "show [his] new Coat, and [his] *fine Hat*" (*FI,* 32). The boy scolds his father who has not set an example regarding how to practice religion: "I liv'd just as I *saw you live* Father! I never pray'd to God in all my Life Father." The boy has given up on his mother, who did "teach" him to pray, but whose instruction was inadequate: "I said the Prayers over, but I never thought a word what they meant; I only said them by rote, sure God does not take notice of that, *does he*, Father! If he does, *our Parrot can pray* as well as I" (*FI*, 13). Here we are reminded of Crusoe's parrot and, in some respects, of Crusoe's spirituality.

The parents of children are not the only ones whom Defoe urges to institute the practice of family prayer. The masters of servants, also, cannot escape the penetrating glare of his moral gaze. Defoe includes a dialogue between a successful alderman and his wife:

> Ald's Wife. It tempts my curiosity. ... If he puts his Body under our care and, not his Soul, pray what must become of the youth?
>
> Ald.   I'd rather have no apprentices
>
> Ald's Wife: Indeed my Dear you had better take none, for tis but murthering youth. (*FI,* 270, 274–75)

In the end it is the alderman's overhearing his servants' conversation that causes him to include his servants in family instruction. He hears the journeymen ask the other apprentices, "Do you believe if my Master should come now and say to us all ... that he resolves to go to Prayer every Night and Morning, and we may come ... that we would not all say we would come with all our Hearts?" To which one of the apprentices says, "I am sure I'd down on my knees and thank him for it," and Thomas, the youngest apprentice, says, "I am sure I'd ... think it the best Day that I ever saw in my Life." He also hears the third apprentice, who had formerly ridiculed the idea of praying, say, "I wish my Master would begin with us and try" (*FI*, 290–91). "Anyone may judge," Defoe writes,

> how the Master, who heard all this Discourse, was moved with it. ... Wherefore, coming hastily out of his Closet into the Place, and the Young Men rising up to be gone, he bids them all stay and sit still: I will not be wanting to you nor wanting to my self in performing my Duty any longer, but according to my Duty, and your Desire, call you all up together, with the rest of my Family to worship God, and pray to him for his Blessing, I hope you will convince me you are in earnest, by your Attendance at that Time. (*FI*, 291–92)

The journeyman and the three apprentices enthusiastically agree to the plan. And "Poor *Thomas*['s] ... Heart was so full he cried for joy and could not speak a Word" (*FI*, 292).

The Containment of Crusoe: Crusoe and Friday

Defoe juxtaposes Crusoe's containment of passion with both the French priest's and Will Atkins's emotive effusiveness. Crusoe's and the priest's witnessing of the lovers is punctuated by Crusoe's entreaties that the French priest "would compose himself." True, Crusoe is worried that the lovers will hear them—"I was afraid *Atkins* would hear [the French priest], therefore I entreated him to withhold himself awhile, that we might see an End of the Scene," but his quieting of the priest seems to involve more than a desire to remain unheard (*FA*, 99). Atkins's outbursts of emotion also prompt Crusoe to plead with Atkins to restrain himself: "You talk too feelingly and sensibly for me *Atkins*" (*FA*, 102). Crusoe concedes that Atkins's remorse and anguish reminds him of his own: "Yes, Atkins, every Shore, every Hill, nay, I may say every Tree in this Island, is witness to the Anguish of my Soul, for my Ingratitude and base Usage of a good tender Father; ... and I murther'd my Father as well as you, *Will. Atkins*; but I think, for all that my Repentance is short of yours too* by a great deal." In a footnote, Crusoe elaborates on his state of mind: "**I would have said more, if I could have restrain'd my Passions; but I thought this poor Man's Repentance was so much sincerer than mine, that I was going to leave off the Discourse and retire*" (*FA*, 102). It is not that Crusoe lacks emotion—he hugs the French priest with an "Excess of Passion" (*FA*, 89)—but that he has too much. Crusoe however is afraid that his passion is excessive and so, as a result, he curtails his repentance.

Todd and others have drawn attention to the focus Crusoe places on "composure": "a state in which one is possessed with a 'steady Calm of Mind, a clear Head, and serene Thoughts always acting the Mastership upon him.'"[32] Todd argues that it is through the writing down, or composing, of his thoughts that Crusoe achieves mastery over them: "by subduing the appetites and passions and shaping the self in accordance with the higher powers of reason, Crusoe becomes 'his *own* Man.'"[33] In short Crusoe achieves self-mastery. But is self-mastery an obstacle to true penitence? And is true penitence and the consequent real—as opposed to manufactured—"serenity" that follows true penitence, what eludes Crusoe? I suggest that Defoe's focus on Atkins's tortured repentance is a purposeful juxtaposition to Crusoe's lack of repentance.

In marked contrast to the instruction of the French priest and Will Atkins, Crusoe's religious instruction of Friday is surprisingly free of emotive content. "Without Passions, Sullenness or Designs," Friday is the perfect pupil, and Crusoe answers all of Friday's questions with the kind of logic that is expected of a teacher of religion (*RC*, 211). But there is something that is perfunctory in Crusoe's mode of instruction. He does not allow himself to get drawn into the inner searching that Friday's questions should provoke. In response to the question, "*Why God no kill the devil, so make him no more do wicked?*," Crusoe composes an unsatisfactory answer: "You may as well ask me, said I, Why God does not kill you and I, when we do wicked Things here that offend him? We are preserv'd to repent and be pardon'd." To this, Friday cleverly replies: "*well, well*, says he, mighty affectionately, *that well; so you, I, Devil, all wicked, all preserve, repent, God pardon all*" (*RC*, 218–19). Unlike Atkins, Crusoe does not go to great lengths to acknowledge his own need for repentance and then show Friday *how* to repent. Rather, he recites religious doctrine and rather pathetically seeks solace in the assertion that Friday may have "knowledge of God," but lacks "Knowledge of Jesus Christ."[34] He then "divert[s] the present Discourse … rising up hastily, as upon some sudden Occasion of going out; then sending [Friday] for something a good way off. … When he came again to me, I entered into a long Discourse with him upon the subject of the Redemption of Man" (*RC*, 219).

At least in Crusoe's view, however, the education of Friday was an astounding success: "The Savage was now a good Christian, a much better than I; though I have reason to hope, and bless God for it, that we were equally penitent" (*RC,* 220) And in fairness to Crusoe, he does expend considerable effort to the project and devotes many hours to study of the bible with his pupil: "I always apply'd my self in Reading the Scripture, to let him know, as well as I could, the Meaning of what I read; and he again, by his serious Enquiries and Questionings, made me, *as I said before*, a much better Scholar in the Scripture Knowledge, than I should ever have been by my own private meer Reading" (*RC,* 220). As in Atkins's discussions with his wife, Crusoe does engage in some form of reciprocity in his question and answer sessions with Friday. But unlike Atkins, Crusoe is a composed teacher, rather than a passionate penitent. Thus, while Crusoe does attend to Friday's questions, and even concedes that he learns from his student, at no point does he allow himself to let go of his carefully acquired composure.

In *The Family Instructor*, Defoe asserts that it is the responsibility of parents "to direct young Persons in their first Reflections, guiding them to enquire about themselves, their Original, their State, their Progress in this World" (*FI*, 5). True, Defoe does leave open the possibility of such reflections later on, even for those children who did not receive family instruction in their early years: "The meanest Capacity, and the youngest Child may supply the Defect of Education, if they think but a little seriously of themselves, and the Original of their Being" (*FI,* 58). For the most part, however, Defoe conveys the message that the un-taught child is at a spiritual disadvantage. His description of Will Atkins's experience corroborates the view that above all he believed in the value of parental involvement:

> [Will Atkins] is a standing Rule to us all, for the well instructing
> Children, (*viz.*) that Parents should never give over to teach and
> instruct, or ever despair of the Success of their Endeavors, let
> the Children be ever so obstinate, refractory, or to Appearance,
> insensible of Instruction; for if ever God in his Providence,
> touches the Consciences of such, the Force of their Education
> returns upon them, and the early Instruction of Parents is not lost;
> tho' it may have been many Years Laid asleep; but some Time or
> other, they may find the Benefit of it. (*FA*, 115)

Even though Atkins's early education was not ideal, it was better than nothing. It gave Atkins a foundation for the religious instruction he would receive in the future.

Crusoe's lack of early education deprives him of such a foundation. As a consequence, his educational technique is based on an ineffective method of lecture and indoctrination. Acting as a kind of human sponge that absorbs information and then squeezes it out again, he scuttles back and forth between the French priest and Atkins. "*Lord! SIR, says Will. Atkins,*" in response to one of Crusoe's deliveries, "How should we teach them Religion? Why we know nothing our selves. ... Folks must have some Religion themselves, before they pretend to teach other People" (*FA,* 95). To which, Crusoe glibly responds, "Can you not tell your Wife, that she is in the wrong? That there is a God and a Religion better than her own?" (*FA,* 96). Unlike Atkins, who sees the inherent contradiction in a "Wicked Creature," such as himself, pontificating on the value of Christianity, Crusoe insulates himself from the painful process of introspection.

The French Priest's Circle of Christianity

In the language of Defoean Protestantism, Crusoe's spiritual crisis mirrors the "unfinished reformation" at home.[35] In Defoe's view, the Schism Act was a "fortunate fall"; it reminded Protestant heads of households of their duty to instruct their families in religion.[36] Just as the Schism Act gave Dissenters the opportunity to reaffirm their devotion to God, acceptance of the French priest's offer provides Crusoe with the opportunity to instruct his metaphorical family in religion and to help create a community founded on devotion to God. The French priest states the situation plainly: "I wonder how you can pass such an Occasion of doing Good" (*FA,* 90). But despite his acknowledgment of the sincerity of the French priest's request, Crusoe instead goes off on a "*Wild Goose Chase*" (*FA,* 126).

On three occasions, Crusoe interferes with the French priest's conversion project. The first involves Crusoe himself. Crusoe is unwilling to participate in the French priest's proposal "of doing Good" and instead focuses on fabricating an excuse—"I am bound to the East-Indies in a Ship freighted by Merchants ... it would be an unsufferable Piece of Injustice to detain their Ship here" (*FA,* 90). The French priest, however, is not so easily diverted: "How can you think, but that let the Time past lie on who it will, all the Guilt for the future, will lie entirely upon you?" (*FA,* 88). The topic of "Guilt" prompts Crusoe's natural talent for rhetoric and, at least temporarily, puts an end to the French priest's demands: "Why Sir it is a valuable Thing indeed to be an Instrument in God's Hand," Crusoe replies, "but as you are an Ecclesiastic and are given over to the Work, how is it that you do not rather offer your self to undertake it, than press me to it?" (*FA,* 91).

The second occasion involves the priest's wish for the services of his servant Friday. Once again, Crusoe nimbly meets the priest's request with an array of excuses: "As I had bred Friday up to be a Protestant, it would quite confound him to embrace another Profession" and "[Friday] would never leave me, unless I put him away" (*FA*, 92). The resourceful priest comes up with an alternative plan: could Crusoe let the French priest have Friday's father serve as an interpreter in his conversations with the thirty-seven Indigenous men? However, Crusoe's obvious lack of enthusiasm for the priest's conversion project once again becomes apparent. Though the priest, "bound never to finish any Voyage he began," is entirely willing to stay on the island, Crusoe has no interest in making available to the inhabitants the obvious passion the priest would bring to his work with them (*FA*, 127). Accordingly, with only a cursory explanation, and overriding the priest's objections, he interferes for the third time and puts in place a watered-down conversion plan: "It now came into my Thoughts, that I had hinted to my Friend the Clergy-man, that the Work of converting the Savages, might perhaps be set on foot in his Absence, to his Satisfaction; and I told him, that now I thought it was put in a fair Way; for the Savages being thus divided among the Christians, if they would but every one of them do their Part, with those which came under their Hands" (*FA*. 113). In other words, Crusoe prevents a viable father-figure (the French priest) from molding his children with his own "Hands."

I do not mean to suggest that we should regard the French priest as a hero. Though neither British nor Protestant, the French priest and his "circle of Christianity" is certainly part of Defoe's agenda to champion the place of Christianity in the colonization of the Caribbean. As Todd notes, "the role that conversion plays in colonial ideology in justifying the English venture in the New World helps explain its pervasiveness in the *Crusoe* books."[37] Inherent in the French priest's conversion project, characterized by Crusoe as a plan that embodies the essence of Christianity—"to love the Interest of the Christian Church, and the good of other Mens Souls"—is the imposition of Western culture and values on a way of life and religion that he does not try to understand (*FA*, 89).

Still, Crusoe's strange, almost perverse, attempt to keep the French priest from achieving a regenerate Christian community is odd. Why would he leave the conversion of the thirty-seven Indigenous men to a motley crew of Protestant and Catholic inhabitants who show neither the zeal nor the experience of the French priest? It is one thing for Crusoe himself to decline to participate in the French priest's vision of a Christian family; for, as Crusoe rightly points out, he is not an "Ecclesiastic." However, it is quite another thing for Crusoe to actively prevent the French priest from achieving his dream of creating a "circle of Christianity" that unites foreigners of different (prior) creeds, ethnicities, and nations. In Crusoe's recommendation to the priest to "divide" the thirty-seven men amongst the Christians, there is a quality of dilution. Rather than nurturing the French priest's utopian dream of a Christian colony, Crusoe waters it down. Crusoe, Defoe seems to argue, is simply unable to envision the French priest's "circle of Christianity."

In light of Crusoe's plan to evangelize the "uncivilized" parts of the world in the *Serious Reflections during the Life and Surprizing Adventures of Robinson Crusoe*, it is natural to wonder why Defoe would have Crusoe change his mind about converting, rather than ignoring, non-Christians. In *The Farther Adventures*, Crusoe is, at best, an uninvolved observer of the French Priest's plans for conversion and, at worst, a willful and destructive saboteur of those plans. Neither of these roles is consistent with the ambitious project he lays out in the final section of the *Serious Reflections*: "A VISION of the Angelick World." Still, as Nicholas Seager points out, it is inadequate to read "Crusoe's Crusade" either as a "psychedelic flight of fantasy" or as "full-blown irony."[38] Rather, we need to look at Crusoe's scheme within the context of Defoe's effort "to understand the religious predicament of the world at large."[39] As Seager notes, "Defoe often occupies 'contrarian' positions: ... with the aim of defying simple solutions and compelling readerly reflection, all in order to achieve a fuller, spiritual apprehension of reality."[40]

Consider the Children

The contradictions of Crusoe's expostulations on childhood education, however, are another matter. For, both in light of Defoe's consistency on the topic of parenting in his didactic literature and in light of Crusoe's irresponsible behavior in the first volume of the trilogy, what are we to make of Crusoe's numerous sermons on the responsibility of parents to educate their children in the *Serious Reflections*? In the second chapter of that volume, entitled "*An Essay upon Honesty*," Crusoe insists that:

> A wife and children are creditors to the father of the family and he cannot be an honest man that does not discharge his debt to them. ... By this I mean, not only putting children to school, which some parents think is all they have to do ... but several other additional cares, as: 1) Directing what School, what Parts of Learning, is proper for them, what Improvements they are to be taught. (2) Studying the Genius and Capacities of their Children, in what they teach them: Some Children will voluntarily learn one Thing, and can never be forced to learn another; and for Want of which observing the Genius of Children, we have so many learned Blockheads in the World. ... (3) But the main Part of this Debt, which Relative Honesty calls upon us to pay to our Children is the Debt of Instruction, the Debt of Government, the Debt of Example. (*SR,* 98)

This quotation is both an accurate summary of Defoe's philosophy of education and a list of the many things that Crusoe neglects to do in his role as a parent. What does Defoe accomplish by adding lack of self-awareness, at best, or psychopathic lying, at worst, to Crusoe's crime of negligence? On the topic of early childhood education, Crusoe's sermonizing in *Serious Reflections* seems to be outright hypocrisy.

At the end of the first volume of the trilogy, Crusoe acquires, and then dispenses with, a nuclear family in the space of a few sentences: "in the meantime ... I marry'd, and that not to my Disadvantage or Dissatisfaction, and had three Children, two Sons and one Daughter: But my Wife dying, and my Nephew coming Home with good Success from a Voyage to *Spain*, my Inclination to go Abroad, and his Importunity prevailed and engaged me to go in his Ship as a private Trader to the *East Indies*" (*RC*, 284). At the beginning of *The Farther Adventures*, he takes a little longer to acquire, and then discharge himself of his obligations to his second family before he goes off on his adventure, but, as Flint notes, his narrative treatment of his wife's death is expeditious, to say the least, dispatching her with a single sentence: "this Blow was the Loss of my Wife" (*FA*, 9).[41] In *The Farther Adventures*, Crusoe does not acknowledge his abandonment of his family, nor does he express any remorse about leaving the education of his children to a friend of the family. But he is more self-aware than he is in the *Serious Reflections*. He admits to Will Atkins that his penitence falls short of Atkins's: "*I thought that this Man's Repentance was so much sincerer than mine, that I was going to leave off the Discourse and retire*" (*FA*, 103). Furthermore, although he lacks Atkins's capacity for introspection, he admits his shortcomings. Statements like "You talk too feelingly" or "I would have said more but I had to restrain my passion" seem to be a conscious admission of a lack of emotional stamina. Certainly the French priest's fervor—"I wonder how you can pass such an Occasion of doing Good"—shakes up Crusoe's carefully constructed composure—"I was now struck dumb indeed"— and demonstrates that, at least occasionally, the normally chatty Crusoe is at a loss for answers (*FA*, 90). Perhaps in creating a clear opposition between Crusoe's actual history in the first volume, and his philosophy in the *Serious Reflections*, Defoe means to demonstrate that novels are, after all, the best truth-tellers.

Crusoe's shortcomings in the *Serious Reflections* are hard to deny. He is less able to express blatant falsehoods in the narrative first volume of the trilogy than he is in the putatively reflective *Serious Reflections*. Put more positively, Crusoe is better able to strive for truth in his purely fictional adventure novel than he is in his semi-fictional memoir. On numerous occasions, in the trilogy, Crusoe obsessively confesses his guilt for all to see. As Crusoe himself admits, his rambling not only brought harm to himself, it ensured the demise of his entire colony:

> I ... left it as I found it, belonging to no Body; and the People ... had I stayed there, would have done well enough; but as I rambl'd from them, and came there no more, the last Letters I had from any of them, was by my Partner's means; ... that they went on but poorly, were Male content with their long stay there: That *Will. Atkins* was dead; that five of the *Spaniards* were come away ...; and that they begg'd of [my Partner] to write to me, to think of the Promise I had made. ... But I was gone a *Wild Goose Chase* indeed. (*FA*, 125–26)

The Farther Adventures is a novelized argument for family instruction in which some of the bitter taste of Crusoe's regret at abandoning his family, not once but twice, comes across. Crusoe's statements on the importance of childhood education in the *Serious Reflections*, therefore, need to be assessed for what they are: the hypocritical sermonizing of a self-confessed rambler.

Notes

For assistance with this article, I am grateful for the generosity and thoughtfulness of Jenny Davidson. I also wish to thank both of my readers for their invaluable suggestions and advice, and Susan Greenfield and Karen Pittelman for their stalwart support.

1. Defoe, *The Present State of the Parties in Great Britain: Particularly an Enquiry into the State of the Dissenters in England, and the Presbyterians in Scotland* (London, 1712), 288–89.

2. Defoe, *Present State*, 316.

3. Defoe, *Present State*, 296.

4. Defoe, *The Weakest go to the Wall, or the Dissenters Sacrific'd by all Parties* (London, 1714), 25.

5. Defoe, *Weakest*, 40.

6. Defoe, *Weakest*, 31.

7. Defoe, *Weakest*, 40.

8. Defoe, *Weakest*, 20.

9. Defoe, *Weakest*, 21.

10. [Defoe?], *The Schism Act Explain'd* (London, 1714). This text does not appear in P. N. Furbank and W. R. Owens's *A Critical Bibliography of Daniel Defoe* (London: Pickering and Chatto, 1998). However, I would argue that the continuity between Defoe's focus on family instruction in *The Schism Act Explain'd* and in *The Family Instructor*, written one year later, supports the argument that Defoe did indeed write *The Schism Act Explain'd*. For a discussion of the authorship of the pamphlet, see B. G. Ivanyi, "Defoe's Prelude to the Family Instructor" (*TLS* 7 [April

1966], 312), and Andreas K. E. Mueller, "Daniel Defoe's *The Family Instructor, The Schism Act, and Jacobite Unrest: The Conduct Book as a Political Act,*" in *Positioning Daniel Defoe's Non-Fiction: Form, Function, Genre,* ed. Aino Mäkikalli and Andreas K. E. Mueller (Cambridge: Cambridge Scholars Publishing, 2011), 125–47.

11. [Defoe?], *Schism Act*, 15.

12. [Defoe?], *Schism Act*, 36.

13. Defoe, *The Family Instructor*, ed. Paula R. Backscheider (Delmar: Scholars Facsimiles & Reprints, 1989), 58. Subsequent citations will be made parenthetically as *FI*.

14. Barney, *Plots of Enlightenment: Education and the Novel in Eighteenth-Century England* (Stanford: Stanford University Press,1999), 207.

15. Flint, *Family Fictions: Narrative and Domestic Relations in Britain, 1688–1798* (Stanford, California: Stanford University Press, 1998), 152–53.

16. Razi, "Narratives of Amelioration," (Ph.D. dissertation, University of Toronto, 2016), 13.

17. For the popularity of *The Family Instructor*, see Backscheider's introduction to her facsimile—"until the twentieth century only *Robinson Crusoe* … could compete with *The Family Instructor* … as Defoe's most popular book" (1)—and Irving N. Rothman: "the book had been read to tatters" (Rothman, "Defoe's *The Family Instructor*: A Response to the Schism Act," *Papers of the Bibliographical Society of America* 74, no. 3 [1980]: 201).

18. Defoe, *The Farther Adventures of Robinson Crusoe*, ed. W. R. Owens and P. N. Furbank (London: Pickering & Chatto, 2008), 11. Subsequent citations will be made parenthetically as *FA*.

19. [Defoe?], *Schism Act*, 39.

20. [Defoe?], *Schism Act*, 15.

21. Defoe, *Serious Reflections during the Life and Surprising Adventures of Robinson Crusoe,* ed. G. A. Starr (London: Pickering & Chatto, 2008). Subsequent citations will be made parenthetically as *SR*.

22. Defoe, *The Life and Strange Surprizing Adventures of Robinson Crusoe,* ed. W. R. Owens (London: Pickering & Chatto, 2008), 58. Subsequent citations will be made parenthetically as *RC*.

23. See Flint, *Family Fictions*, 125.

24. See D. P. Leinster-McKay's discussion of Defoe's *The Compleat English Gentleman* (*The Educational World of Daniel Defoe* [Victoria: English Literary Studies, University of Victoria, 1981], 81–82).

25. Razi, "Narratives of Amelioration," 7.

26. Razi, "Narratives of Amelioration," 7.

27. Scholars have long recognized the centrality of the episodes of liberation and enslavement to the first installment of the *Crusoe* story, and in recent years many critics have devoted close scrutiny to Crusoe's role as both a slave and a master, someone whose experience of the brutality of slavery does not stop him from owning and selling slaves. For influential discussions of Crusoe and slavery, see Peter Hulme, *Colonial Encounters: Europe and the Native Caribbean, 1492–1797* (New York:

Routledge, 1986), 175–222; George Boulukos, *The Grateful Slave: The Emergence of Race in British and American Culture* (Cambridge: Cambridge University Press, 2008), 75–94; Daniel Carey, "Reading Contrapuntally: *Robinson Crusoe*, Slavery, and Postcolonial Theory," in *Postcolonial Enlightenment: Eighteenth-Century Colonialism and Postcolonial Theory*, ed. Daniel Carey and Lynn Festa (New York: Oxford University Press, 2009), 105–36; Dennis Todd, *Defoe's America* (Cambridge: Cambridge University Press, 2010); and Christopher F. Loar, *Political Magic: British Fictions of Savagery and Sovereignty, 1650–1750* (New York: Fordham University Press, 2014), 104–41. Both Todd and Carey point out that Friday is technically a servant, not a slave.

28. Todd, *Defoe's America*, 74.

29. Flint, *Family Fictions*, 150.

30. Todd, *Defoe's America*, 38

31. Newman, *The Popish Doctrine of Merit and Justification Considered. A Sermon Preached at Salters-Hall, March 20, 1734–35* (London, 1735), 15–16.

32. Todd, *Defoe's America*, 68–69. The phrase quoted comes from Defoe (*SR*, 102). For another consideration of "composure," see Hulme, *Colonial Encounters*, 197–201.

33. Todd, *Defoe's America*, 70.

34. See Barney, *Plots of Enlightenment*, 247.

35. Razi, "Narratives of Amelioration," iii.

36. Razi, "Narratives of Amelioration," 23.

37. Todd, *Defoe's America*, 48.

38. Seager, "Crusoe's Crusade: Defoe, Genocide, and Imperialism," *Etudes Anglaises* 72, no. 2 (2019): 197–98.

39. Seager, "Crusoe's Crusade," 196.

40. Seager, "Crusoe's Crusade," 199.

41. Flint, *Family Fictions*, 147.

Friendship, Not Freedom: Dependent Friends in the Late Eighteenth-Century Novel

RENEE BRYZIK

The topic of friendship has in recent years gained much attention from scholars aiming to consider anew canonical eighteenth-century novels. Two book-length studies on friendship in the eighteenth-century British novel were published in 2017 alone. Katrin Berndt, whose study connects Enlightenment-era conceptions of friendship to late eighteenth-century British novels, usefully observes that the language of friendship sits on a continuum of social reform that, at its most radical, turns into the language of revolution. She emphasizes this point with a epigraph from the Swiss thinker Ernst Halter: "There is no friendship without equality."[1] Bryan Mangano likewise considers how eighteenth-century novelists use the "dear friend" trope to establish relationships between readers and writers situated in the morality of ideal friendship. Mangano argues that this relationship allows the novel to function as a space where virtues like loyalty and benevolence are tested and upheld.[2] Together, the studies provide an overview of the many persuasive, evocative, and creative functions of friendship in the early novel. By focusing on friendship as an ideal, however, neither study accounts for the fact that many novels, including those central to Berndt's and Mangano's arguments, present friendship as a way for their protagonists to navigate relationships of inequality.

Berndt's work usefully explains how the emphasis that Francis Hutcheson, David Hume, and Adam Smith placed on friendship strongly influenced developments in the early novel. Hutcheson's conception of friendship provides a "double significance … it is understood both as nourished by an innate virtue and as a form of relationship that allows people to put into practice this inherent beneficence."[3] Thus, novelists are able to develop the psychological complexity of their characters by providing conflicts between innate benevolence and real-life scenarios. Smith likewise emphasizes the importance of friendship to the modern reader when he explains that sympathy allows people to "encounter strangers as potential friends."[4] Neither of these theorists require friends to be social equals. In fact, Daniel M. Gross's *The Secret History of Emotion* reminds us that moral sense theory invited the commercial class to understand their moral responsibility as integral to their self-interest and that it also worked towards codifying hierarchies of gender by assigning selfhood to masculine emotions. David Hume's theory of the self was also influential for novelists because of its emphasis on the imbalance of emotion between women and men. Hume contends in *An Enquiry Concerning Human Understanding* that the self is established through passions both supportive and constitutive: humility and pride. Women were expected to provide supportive roles through humility while men were given the full reign of emotional expression. Gross observes that an imbalance of emotion seems to be the most appealing aspect of friendship in the novel, as symmetrical emotions provide little conflict.[5]

Janet Todd's seminal work on female friendship in the eighteenth-century novel demonstrates that asymmetrical emotional expression exists in hierarchical female friendships as well, but suggests in the end that these friendship plots are generally "less realized than the patriarchal" marriage plot.[6] Gross and Todd acknowledge, however, that asymmetrical friendships provide narrative opportunities for socially dependent friends, especially women. Gross, for example, observes that female characters do not always suppress their emotions in friendship to male characters and, as Todd notes, although friendship plots often serve a secondary function to marriage plots, they provide an imaginative space of possibility parallel to marriage. Implicit in Todd's study is the idea that the friendship plot allows the reader to see inequalities of gender in the marriage plot. Many female protagonists use the terms of friendship to navigate courtships between characters whose unions may be controversial, while others, perhaps even more controversially, favor friendship over courtship altogether. As I show in this article, these observations on friendship in relation to gender and social hierarchy can also be applied to late eighteenth-century novels that take on issues of racial inequality.

The challenge that all studies of friendship in literature face is that the term "friend" lacks definition. Unlike family relations, friendship bears no distinct obligations. Naomi Tadmor's work on the language of friendship among the mid-eighteenth-century British merchant class shows how this ubiquity also allowed its users a greater sense of agency over the mandatory relationships in their lives. She notes that the term "friend" was used in life writing and novels to describe a wide range of relations: parents, spouses and other family members, neighbors and business acquaintances, as well as those above and below an individual's social position. Rather than denoting economic equality, Tadmor's work indicates that the label enabled a freedom of choice within the domestic and occupational exchanges in limited social spheres. The term "friend" links kinship to the consumer economy, classical ideals to practical transactions.[7] While friendships across vastly different social strata do not capture the literary imagination until the Victorian era, late eighteenth-century female protagonists are able to navigate situations where they experience practical limitations of class, rank, gender, and race because of their positions as "friend."

This article focuses on the dependent friend, rather than on asymmetrical or hierarchical friendship more generally, because of the early novel's emphasis on the individual. The concept of the protagonist-as-friend, however, insists that we always view these characters in connection to the social obligations that shape and define them. In an article defending the place of the eighteenth-century novel in the twenty-first-century college classroom, Terry Castle explains: "The absence of the parent, the frightening yet galvanizing solitude of the child—may be the defining fixation of the novel as a genre." She suggests that novels like *Pamela* or *Robinson Crusoe* are helpful to students living in an age of extended adolescence.[8] Castle's emphasis on solitude and self-reliance assumes that both the protagonist and the present-day reader are privileged enough to consider severed ties in terms of opportunity. Wolfram Schmidgen helpfully observes that many of the characters we have come to regard as orphans were actually bastards trapped between the "complicating social ranks" of eighteenth-century Britain on one hand, and the "persistence of a hierarchical organization" on the other.[9] These characters must actively create all of their relationships, even family ones, often revealing economic, gender, and even racial discrimination in the process. Ruth Perry's *Novel Relations* acknowledges that women in the eighteenth century found themselves in a liminal space where fewer family obligations correlated with less freedom, not more. Perry explains that a gradual shift to more lineage-based inheritance over the course of the seventeenth and eighteenth centuries stripped England's daughters of their influence in the family. This shift can be seen in novels with women who describe themselves as being "without friends," a loss that originates with their consanguineal relations, but that expresses a desperation for intimate relations outside of the family.[10] Dependent friend status affords the female protagonists discussed below opportunities to showcase virtues like loyalty and benevolence. Friendships of advantage (friendships that disproportionately benefit one individual in the relationship socially and/or economically) allow these women to escape ridicule as outsiders because they supplement or substitute lost or insufficient family relations.

In this article, I show how female protagonists acting as socially dependent friends use the mitigating language of friendship to broach topics of racial prejudice and misogyny without alarming an audience for whom "freedom" corresponds to foreign revolution. This article will consider examples from two late eighteenth-century society novels that focus on asymmetrical female-female and male-female friendships where inequalities of race and gender are discussed: Maria Edgeworth's *Belinda* (1801) and the anonymously published *The Woman of Colour* (1808). These novels are unique examples of how late eighteenth-century authors and readers were working to extend the dynamics of friendship because they make inequalities of gender and race the primary challenge to friendship in each novel. The protagonists of these novels voice thoughts and experiences that are distinct from their patrons but, because of their subordinate positions, do not pose direct threats to traditional hierarchies. Their feelings and desires—whether they be love, pride, gratitude, or disgust—are only ever presented in relation to, and usually in support of, their social superiors, and thus these characters participate in sentimental or rational discourse only to the extent that their social surroundings allow them to. Their dependence thus limits our ability to view the protagonist-as-friend in the traditional terms of affective individualism because their thoughts and feelings seem inextricably yoked to their benefactors.

Maria Edgeworth's first novel *Belinda* consists of interconnected conflicts regarding how to be a good friend. The central relationship is the friendship between Belinda and Lady Delacour, her mentor. As the novel progresses, the relationship that begins as one of reluctant companionship develops into a model asymmetrical domestic friendship against which to compare the many false friendships of the novel. Salon scenes throughout the novel encourage a comparative, intertextual approach to social reform through friendship. These scenes present chauvinistic opinions on race and gender from a cross-section of upper-class English society alongside staged readings of texts from the English literary canon that represent the domestic sphere as a place of luxury and false female friendship. As Mitzi Myers points out, *Belinda* is a place of "emancipatory recycling, challenging, and reinvention of patriarchal narrative."[11] As a dependent friend, Belinda encourages Lady Delacour to use her position as salon director to revise pieces from the English literary canon so that they better represent the experiences of women and people of color, thereby transforming the sentiments of the English readership. This early work by Edgeworth celebrates and encourages women writers who, despite political pressure to remain in their private-sphere roles as wives and mothers or to conform to socially accepted, and enervated, sentimental modes, instead work as editors, compilers, and translators with intersectional feminist aims.

Cross-references begin with Belinda's name, which Lady Delacour connects to Alexander Pope's *The Rape of the Lock* (1712) and that poem's characterization of women as incapable of friendship. Early in the novel, Lady Delacour claims her request to use the horses of an eligible young suitor, Clarence Hervey, was in fact made by Belinda. When the suitor appears at Lady Delacour's drawing room to receive Belinda's gratitude and finds instead her reserve, Lady Delacour attempts to diffuse Hervey by calling the situation a "tempest in a teapot" and requesting "a second rape of the lock" as payment for the horses.[12] Lady Delacour's allusion to Pope's text is meant to infantilize Belinda and disregard her refusal to feed Hervey's pride. Lady Delacour is still playing the role of the false female friend Clarissa who attempts to gain the Baron's approval through stolen hair. But in refusing to react, Belinda illustrates her awareness of the chauvinistic characterization of women as well as her social dependence: she cannot betray Lady Delacour, but she is not required to cater to Hervey. Unlike Pope's mock heroic, which suggests that little sprites prompt Belinda's emotions, Edgeworth describes the social pressures that inhibit the friendship of these two women. We know from the start that Belinda is angered by Lady Delacour's deception, and learn soon after that Lady Delacour's attempts to degrade Belinda and borrow horses from Hervey come from her frustration over her disempowered position as a wife.[13] Belinda responds to Lady Delacour's reference to *The Rape of the Lock* by emphasizing to her would-be suitor and benefactor that she is not a commodity. She states that while her arrival to town has been advertised by others "as well ... as Packwood's razor strops," she feels no need to advertise herself in such a way (73). Furthermore, Belinda redirects the frivolity of Pope's scene from the lady's dressing room to the man's, thus providing Lady Delacour with an opportunity to forge a friendship through wit, rather than consider Belinda a competitor for male attention, as she does with her other female acquaintances. In this scene, Lady Delacour shows her new understanding of Belinda. Instead of attempting to humiliate her further, Lady Delacour demonstrates that she understands Belinda's point by challenging Hervey to wear a hoop skirt so that he will understand how women suffer under the imperatives of fashion. The scene ends with Hervey wearing the skirt "with skill and dexterity"—a performance that signals early on his ability to respect feminine social custom and female friendship, which eventually earns him Belinda's hand (75). This early scene also establishes the drawing room as a site of social criticism based in feminine sociability.

Throughout the novel, Lady Delacour emphasizes how competition and jealousy inhibit female friendship with her peers and expresses instead her own reliance on Belinda with statements like, "Not a female friend in the world but yourself, my dear Belinda!" (168). Berndt claims that, with the exception of Wollstonecraft, philosophers substituted talk of freedom for their previous talk of friendship in intellectual discussions of the late eighteenth and early nineteenth centuries.[14] Berndt's passing acknowledgment of Wollstonecraft as an exception signals an opportunity for considering friendships where inequalities are brought on by gender and racial difference. The principal threat to Lady Delacour and Belinda throughout the novel, Harriet Freke, appears as a shape-shifting post-revolutionary false friend representative of upper-class feminist privilege: she woos like a rake, pontificates like a romantic philosopher, and conjures like an obeah woman in order to gain control over every character in the novel. Her movements ultimately alienate her from patriarchal literary traditions and the new social discourse of the post-revolutionary salon that Belinda's friendship with Lady Delacour achieves.

Nowhere are Freke's dangers as a false friend more evident than in the chapter titled "Rights of Woman," wherein Belinda repeatedly rejects Freke's invitation to a ball in the presence of Freke's peers and Belinda's benefactors. The chapter opens with a tête-à-tête between the two women that shows Freke's intention to use her drag performance in men's attire merely as an assertion of upper-class feminism. However, the scene reveals instead how she has adopted male chauvinism along with its accoutrements. Freke finds Belinda reading Smith's *Theory of Moral Sentiments* and declares, "I did not know you were a reading girl. ... Books only spoil the originality of genius ... [of] minds of a certain class" (227). The first half of this response is standard rake dialogue, but because her masculine performance is enabled by upper-class feminism, instead of justifying this denial of female education with the claim that reading ruins a woman's natural sensibility, a decidedly anti-feminist stance, she declares that reading is vocational, while intellect is divine. Freke attempts to use Belinda's economic insecurity to persuade her to attend the ball as her companion—Belinda has just been cast out of Lady Delacour's house under accusations that Belinda has, in anticipation of her benefactor's death, tried to seduce Lord Delacour (201). Harriet Freke represents how failed female friendship interrupts post-revolutionary salon dialogue over issues of empire fueled by domestic consumption. When Belinda rejects the invitation by admitting that she cannot afford a dress, Freke argues that Belinda cannot afford not to attend by emphasizing her class otherness in connection with her physical beauty in racialized terms: Freke has "a bet of twenty guineas on your head—on your face, I mean" that only her beautiful presence at the ball could settle among the other gentlemen (224). Freke's slip, referring to Belinda's "head" instead of her "face," is one of many parallels drawn in the novel between the marriage market and the auction block from which enslaved persons were sold. Belinda's retorts are simple: "I read that I may think for myself," "[I am] neither a prisoner nor a distressed damsel," and, to the appeal that Belinda betray her friendship with Lady Delacour, she shines as an exemplary friend, stating, "People are apt to suffer more by their friends than their enemies" and "I hope that will never be the case with Lady Delacour" (225–226). Belinda's effortless retorts understate the real threat Freke poses to women who depend on friendship for domestic security, especially young women; Freke's enemies are the qualities that empower young heroines of this post-revolutionary domestic era: self-education and beauty borne from attentiveness and reserve. Her aggression shows the danger that Enlightenment texts on understanding the emotions pose to the personae she inhabits, all of which rely on manipulating fear and jealousy in women who have no other means of expression. Hitherto, unlike Lady Delacour, whose literary allusion to Pope's courtship scene gives both women and men an opportunity to make conscious revisions to gendered expectations, Freke's unselfconscious use of privilege—masculine, class, race—leaves no room for discussion, only complicity.

Lisa Moore identifies Freke as a representation of the dangerous man-woman, warned against by Wollstonecraft in *Rights of Women,* who attempts to use her masculinity to oppress her female friends. With Freke, Moore sees a clear moral: "Women who attempt to usurp the position of men are not just inappropriate, but dangerous friends for young ladies hoping to marry well."[15] While Moore rightfully identifies Freke's normalizing function— she is not, indeed, the appropriate suitor for Belinda—Moore's search for same-sex equivalency to the romance plot overlooks Freke's function within the friendship plot. In the realm of friendship, Freke acts as a foil for Lady Delacour—a friend who, because of her social position as a rich married woman, could help Belinda, but instead uses her privilege to adopt masculine modes of oppression. Freke's threat as a rakish false friend is not that she woos Belinda, but that she works against friendships that empower dependent friends.

Deborah Weiss yokes Freke with Belinda to describe how the novel represents the comprehensive reception of Enlightenment feminism in the post-revolutionary decade. She notes that both women belong to the female philosopher trope that appears in novels following the death of Mary Wollstonecraft, but she persuasively argues that critics have read this trope using a "shorthand version of the *Rights of Woman*" and have focused on satirical representations, such as Freke, without also acknowledging their non-parodic appearances as well, such as Belinda. She cites several feminist critics who read the parodic-female philosopher as a distraction that enables post-revolutionary women writers to integrate "subversive secret [feminist] sympathies" into the main plotlines of their novels. Weiss argues that Freke is a "caricature of a caricature," a "false female philosopher" who represents the "idea of Wollstonecraft that circulated in the culture"—an argument that follows Mitzi Myers's intuition that most of *Belinda* functions at the metatextual level.[16] Belinda, on the other hand, takes a pragmatic feminist approach by foregrounding the importance of self-awareness in her social context as a dependent friend at the Delacour and Percival homes and in her potential future role as a wife and mother in the households of Hervey and Augustus Vincent. Freke's empty sloganeering requires that she interact with others only through combat or forced compliance, while Belinda's engagement with philosophical dialogue carries the pragmatic utility of helping her understand her own position as a friend in relation to the expectations of others.

Freke makes illogical references to slavery throughout the "Rights of Woman" chapter that draw attention to the enervation of abolitionist rhetoric by upper-class feminists as well. For example, Freke's crude analogy between Belinda and an enslaved person on an auction block might be considered a friendly warning to beware of suitors who will view her as less than human. But Freke apparently does this in the hope of convincing Belinda that she has no choice but to be mortified in public for the economic gains of the upper class. Later in that scene, Freke again employs the language of slavery, but this time in purported defense of women, declaring, "Delicacy enslaves the pretty delicate dears." Mr. Vincent, the slave owner, enervates the language even more by announcing that masculine social custom also "enslaves us." Freke responds, "I hate slavery! Vive la liberté! … I'm a champion for the Rights of Women" (227). The exchange shows that the affective excitement that sloganeering produces is most effective among those least supportive of social dependents—both characters are protesting against inequalities of gender and implied inequalities of race that they depend on for their own influence.

Belinda and Harriet Freke, false and true friend, are already placed in opposition in the chapter preceding "Rights of Women" through each one's interaction with Juba, Mr. Vincent's Black servant. Freke terrorizes Juba by causing a chemical reaction that burns a figure of a woman without apparent human contact because Juba refuses to give Freke the spot in the stable at Oakley-Park that he had secured for Vincent's horses. Suvendrini Perera reads Freke's performance as the obeah woman in this scene as offering a parallel between radical feminism and the insurrection of enslaved people.[17] The scene certainly condemns Freke's attempt to scare Juba out of his loyalty for his master, but Juba's offense is slightly more complicated than that—he treats Freke according to the gender that she performs, rather than acknowledging the performance as an assertion of her social privilege as an upper-class married woman. Belinda, on the other hand, remedies the situation by first working to understand the source of Juba's fears, and then by using her knowledge to improve Juba's situation. Later in the novel, when Lady Delacour overdoses on opium and Methodist literature in preparation for her breast wound surgery, she sees Freke outside of her window and imagines that Freke is the ghost of Lawless (301–13). Sharon Smith cites the similarly irrational reactions of Juba and Lady Delacour to Freke-as-obeah woman to underscore the novel's association between radical feminism and the rebellion of enslaved people and argues that this is evidence of the anxiety feminism arouses in the domestic realm.[18] But while Freke serves an agitating purpose in both, her intention for each is distinct and in accordance with a classist feminist perspective; Freke seeks revenge for Juba's insolence, but she is unaware of Lady Delacour's terror in response to her later appearance as a ghost—in Lady Delacour's situation, she is merely acting as a false female friend, looking for evidence of Lady Delacour's infidelity. The parallel between Lady Delacour and Juba distinguishes between the effects of upper-class feminism on social dependents, which is active oppression, and its effects on social equals, which are the internalized stereotypes of false female friendship, jealousy, and envy.

Edgeworth's allusions to Pope and later references to Mary Wollstonecraft in terms of female friendship create a continuity between the false female friend in Augustan poetry and the false feminist in post-revolutionary discourse. In a scene late in the novel, after the two women's friendship has been tested by Freke, the women again return to drawing room-style literary sociability, and Lady Delacour is now able to provide the protection from bad suitors that Belinda's loyalty and benevolence deserves. Lady Delacour again uses masculine English poetry to emphasize the faults of courtship and marriage, again foregrounding the white male chauvinism in Belinda's suitors. Lady Delacour assigns each man a poem by sentimental poet Thomas Day, an abolitionist with a complex personal history of misogynistic behavior that includes impeding Edgeworth's own writing career on the grounds of her gender. Each poem alludes to faults expounded upon in the body of the novel. Hervey reads "To the authoress of 'verses to be inscribed on Delia's tomb,'" which admonishes a young female poet for her expressions of female friendship and suggests that she should instead "seek a virtuous love" in a man (349). The poem's chauvinism corresponds with Hervey's decision, prior to meeting Belinda, to isolate an orphaned country girl from civilization, educate her exclusively in sentimental literature under the guise of charity, and even rename her with the hopes of one day making her his wife. The extreme lack of concern over the girl's own thoughts and desires corresponds with Hervey's expectations for Belinda's gratitude over the horses that he shows at the start of the novel.[19] The attempt to understand perspectives that are not his own that he demonstrates in this scene, coupled with his remorse for his treatment of the orphan girl, shows that, while he is inclined towards male chauvinism, he is also open to critique and revision and a suitable match for Belinda.

The faults highlighted by the poem that Lady Delacour selects for Mr. Vincent are less related to gender bias, but more disturbing in their implications for domestic felicity. Vincent is a West Indian plantation owner who bears the stereotypes of a Creole: he is irrational and overemotional, drinking and gambling to excess. Belinda's courtship by Vincent closely involves his Black servant Juba, for whom he expresses an affection appropriate for a pet, but not a human. Belinda must point out to Vincent that Juba's loyalty in the face of prejudice against Creoles deserves Vincent's gratitude, but, even after she explains this, Vincent struggles to understand that Juba deserves his protection from kidnapping and re-enslavement. Lady Delacour assigns Vincent an abolitionist poem, "The Dying Negro," which was published in 1773 after the landmark Somerset case in 1772 that ruled that a free Black person could not legally be returned to slavery if they resided in England or Wales. The sympathetic tone of the poem reminds the reader that it is not legislation, but rather friendship that will create lasting resistance to the slave trade. The speaker of the poem is a free Black man who is kidnapped and taken aboard a slave ship on the Thames while on his way to his baptism in preparation for marriage. The poem's circumstances, which are based on actual events, emphasize that the slave trade is fueled by false friendship—first among Europeans in Africa and now in the British Isles among those who would kidnap and return free Blacks like Juba to slavery. The speaker describes his freedom in terms of friendship, rather than as a single moment of emancipation: he finds "friendship" in Gambia and with his intended English bride and describes himself, after his enslavement, as "the friendless victim of despair!"[20] Juba relies on Vincent's friendship and consequent protection in order to remain in England and free. The poem does not sensitize Vincent to the precariousness of Juba's position in England, however, but rather merely provides him with the idea of co-opting the position of "the dying negro" to bolster sympathy for his own unsuccessful attempts at courtship. After Belinda rejects his marriage proposal, Vincent claims that he has "no friend" and thus believes suicide his only recourse (432). Vincent's emotional overindulgence shows his complete disregard for his responsibility as benefactor and protector to Juba in their own domestic hierarchical relationship and serves as proof that Belinda's rejection is the right decision.

Juba, the only Black character in the novel, plays a key role in the discovery of the main threat of the novel, Harriet Freke, and he is christened and marries a white servant as his reward. At the same time, Vincent struggles to integrate into British domestic society, failing to win Belinda's hand because of his poor money management skills and extreme emotions. Despite these narrative decisions, several critics argue that Edgeworth's engagement with race and gender in this novel is paternalist and gradualist.[21] In 1809, prior to the novel's inclusion in Anna Barbauld's series *The British Novelists*, Edgeworth revised out Juba and Vincent in order to accommodate male readers who criticized these plot points, her own father among them. Critics also accuse her of paternalism for this edit.[22] But the novel's focus on asymmetrical friendship as a means of saving domestic relations from patriarchal tyranny suggests that these accusations are shortsighted.

Published the year after the abolition of the British slave trade, *The Woman of Colour* also uses a dependent friend as its protagonist to foreground inequalities of race and gender and to address the perceived threat of miscegenation in Britain at the turn of the nineteenth century. While Edgeworth's title gives support to the prevailing notion that the eighteenth-century novel focuses on the independence of its characters, *The Woman of Colour* emphasizes from the start that the protagonist's identity is constrained by categories of race and gender. Olivia Fairfield is a sympathetic biracial character who highlights throughout the redemptive potential that the term "friend" bears for those who find themselves to be extreme outsiders in England. She is the recognized illegitimate daughter of an enslaved woman and a white plantation owner who is the second son to an English aristocrat. The novel describes Olivia's experiences as she travels from her father's plantation in Jamaica to her uncle's estate in England in order to marry her cousin, the heir to the family estate. Olivia possesses knowledge, confidence, sensitivity, and piety, as well as a dowry of sixty thousand pounds. Her father tries to ensure that her race does not disqualify her from becoming the ideal English aristocratic wife by stipulating in his will that she will only inherit this sum, and the Merton family will only benefit from Fairfield's estate, if she is wed to Fairfield's nephew. While racism presents insurmountable barriers to Olivia's future as a wife, friendship provides her with enough financial and emotional sustenance to live comfortably in England. We see Olivia's reliance on friendship through her relationships with her former governess (the recipient of her letters to the West Indies), her Black servant and companion Dido, the Honeywoods (a mother and son whom Olivia meets aboard ship while sailing to England), and, later, the elderly Mr. Bellfield and her expected husband, Augustus Merton. Each friendship helps provide Olivia with enough support to continue, despite the injustice and humiliation that she is subject to throughout the novel, ultimately allowing her to settle in relative comfort in England as an unwed woman.

The Woman of Colour consists almost exclusively of letters addressed by Olivia to her former governess and friend in Jamaica, Mrs. Milbanke, establishing from the start a narrative based in friendship. The letters reveal a complicated asymmetrical friendship: Olivia is an heiress of considerable wealth, but Mrs. Milbanke is Olivia's teacher, initially her only friend, and a married woman who, unlike Olivia, is free to stay in Jamaica. We learn in the first letter that Mrs. Milbanke is also Black, but darker than Olivia; Olivia explains through her description of her own treatment by the English that, while Mrs. Milbanke would have been viewed in Jamaica as inferior to Olivia due to her skin color, in England both would be considered equally inferior to the "white planters."[23] Olivia emphasizes the point with italics—"*We* are considered, my dear Mrs. Milbanke, as an inferior race"—and again reminds us that she has lighter skin than her governess: "I say *our* for though the jet has been faded to the olive in my own ..." (53). This explanation of complexion is an useful preface to the many letters that Olivia sends to Mrs. Milbanke dutifully chronicling her mortifying and tragic experiences in England because it emphasizes that the values placed on racial categories are culturally determined; in Jamaica, Olivia's skin is "olive," but in England, it is Black.

The epistolary form of the novel allows first-person narration that places the reader in the sympathetic position of Mrs. Milbanke and provides Olivia with a much-needed emotional outlet and alternative to the extraordinary reserve she exhibits throughout the novel to her English family and their friends. This unwavering outward restraint and humility shows Olivia trying, and failing, to use attributes of eighteenth-century femininity to also navigate racial inequality. For example, when she overhears her sister-in-law observe to another, "she is not near so *dark* as I expected to find her, and for one of *that* sort of people, she is very well looking!," and she hears her betrothed defend her, she writes: "I wonder I did not get up to clasp his hand in mine; and *you* will wonder, Mrs. Milbanke, how I can overhear this conversation without standing confessed a curious listener" (117). With the support of Mrs. Milbanke, Olivia is able to explain the difficulty with which she maintains her reserve. A more shocking example is when she describes her discovery that the man she believes to be her husband is actually already married; in this case, she describes herself to Mrs. Milbanke as "stabbed to the heart at such an irrefragable proof of mercenary selfishness," even as she addresses him as "my good friend" and tells him that "if I cannot be happy myself, I will not retard the happiness of others" (147). The letters thus provide us with examples of Olivia's outward feminine reserve as well as her full range of inward emotions, making the dependent friend a sympathetic, dynamic protagonist.

In addition to establishing Olivia's sympathetic position as a dependent friend to Mrs. Milbanke, the epistolary form uses friendships between Olivia and the other characters to illustrate the tension between the stability that friendship potentially offers and the volatility of family duty where its members act according to personal prejudice and self-interest. The opening letters situate the conflict of the novel in the systems of entail and slavery. Written aboard the ship that carries Olivia from Jamaica to England, Olivia compares her own migration with her mother's passage from Africa to Jamaica. Olivia describes her mother torn from her family and its regal lineage, while she describes herself and her departure from Jamaica as an orphan in terms of nostalgia and friendship. She laments in her opening letter, "What can have power to console me for leaving the scenes of my infancy, and the friend of my youth?," and then concludes: "nothing but the consciousness of acting in obedience to the commands of my departed father" (53). Olivia's letters are replete with sometimes nauseating conviction about her duty to a family that finds her repellent, but they also express her sense of loss, exile, and affection for her former governess. Olivia describes her parentage without judgement: her father seduced a young enslaved person and then, out of guilt, educated and converted her to Christianity. Olivia's mother then convinced her master that slavery was a sin for which he must repent, but she was unable to convince him to emancipate his enslaved people. Thus, although Olivia expresses a desire at the outset to have remained in Jamaica to help improve the living conditions of enslaved people, her position as the recognized, biracial daughter of an owner of enslaved people makes her an outsider, to some extent, even in Jamaican society. The dissonance between friendship and family duty that she expresses in this first letter follows her throughout her voyage. When Mrs. Honeywood dies, for example, Olivia, out of obligation to her father and the Merton family, must discontinue her correspondence with Mr. Honeywood. This suspended friendship is particularly distressing to Olivia because of the kindness that the Honeywoods have offered, despite her color. They are the only people she encounters who were compassionate enough to warn her, early on, about the racial prejudices she would experience.

Olivia's situation in England shows how the challenges of abolition and the complexities of race relations add to the preexisting conflicts in a family whose lineage links it to English aristocracy, but whose wealth and life experiences are partially situated in the West Indies. As the younger son of an aristocratic English family, Olivia's father left England to make his fortune on a West Indian slave plantation while his elder brother inherited the family estate in England. Olivia attributes her father's decision to first recognize his illegitimate biracial daughter, and then bequeath her an enormous sum of money, to her mother's interpretation of the Bible, but his decision not to emancipate his own enslaved people makes this theory seem less persuasive. The marriage requirement in Fairfield's will suggests that Olivia's father was well aware of the turmoil that his decisions regarding his daughter would produce among his brother's family. Olivia represents Fairfield's hostility towards a system of entail that claims to consolidate family wealth, but that actually relies on understated incomes from abroad to exist. Fairfield's decision to place his biracial daughter as wife to the heir of the estate is a form of reparation aimed at forcing his family to face their own racism and recognize that they are forever altered by the plantation money that props up their aristocratic livelihoods. The novel's focus on Olivia's friendships, however, insists that the early nineteenth-century reader also consider the personal cost of this sort of reparation on virtuous social dependents like Olivia.

Olivia's almost-friendless position at the outset illustrates Perry's observation regarding the deterioration of a family role beyond that of "wife" for young women in the final decades of the eighteenth century, which Olivia's skin color makes only more apparent. As Perry notes: "shifts in the social and economic purposes of kinship over the previous half-century resulted in a reconception of the daughter's place in the family as temporary, partial, and burdensome."[24] The will assumes that Olivia will only receive sufficient protection from her English relatives if she becomes a wife in that family, not merely a niece and daughter. While her father appears naïve regarding the barrier that Olivia's race poses to these plans, Olivia unflinchingly accepts the racist comments and treatment she receives from the Fairfield family, even as she demonstrates friendship to the few individuals that show her the respect she deserves.

The conflict between familial duty and friendship forces the reader to confront racism head on, from the benevolent cousin who must work through his physical aversion to Olivia's skin color in order to wed her to the social sabotage of family and neighbors who hate her because she is rich, Black, and married to a white man. In order to overcome his aversion, the cousin tells himself, "it is I alone who must rescue her from a state of miserable dependence. It is on me that her future happiness depends"—a statement that, in the context of the overt racism of most of the other characters, looks like kindness, or at least an attempt at it (103). In return for this compassion, Olivia bestows upon the young Augustus not only her enormous fortune, but also complete, selfless loyalty to him, even after their marriage is nullified because he has already entered into a clandestine marriage with his lover. She willingly gives up her inheritance and her protection as his wife with the declaration, "I shall always consider you as a friend" (152), an expression of loyalty that may seem too virtuous, but gains her the ultimate reward: a means of living comfortably in England on her own. At this moment, Olivia is again faced with the prospect of marriage, this time to Charles Honeywood, the man from the ship who expressed his unbounded love for her at the start of the novel. It is here, after Olivia's many experiences of friendlessness, that the reader receives the greatest shock: Olivia turns down the proposal and instead accepts the more modest request he makes for her to "allow me your friendship" (165). In this moment of extreme reserve, Olivia relies on the language of friendship not only to maintain a relationship with Honeywood, which is beneficial to her, but also to keep her would-be lover at arm's length so as to continue in her relative affluence and avoid, whenever possible, interactions with her hateful and prejudiced family members and neighbors.

It is also in this opposition between friendship and marriage that the language of friendship comes up for some scrutiny. Olivia makes enough abolitionist statements in her letters to make it clear that this is most certainly an abolitionist text. But her final refusal to marry can be read several ways. As a woman, this refusal seems empowering; she is no longer reliant on the pity of others. She is not a dependent friend and can forge friendships in equality. As a Black woman, her refusal to marry, to follow what we have taken to be her desires, can also be read as her internalizing the racism that she has experienced in England. A decision against interracial marriage is also a decision not to have biracial children, who will also find themselves in compromised social situations. The ending is uncomfortably incomplete, with the prospect of an honored friendship of equality as Olivia's sole connection with society, a freedom that seems, at best, a partial solution to the racism and sexism rampant throughout the novel. The novel uses the language of friendship as a nonthreatening alternative to the imperatives of courtship and marriage without directly representing the fear and anxiety that a Black woman inspires for many when considering a biracial English aristocracy. The challenge is still relevant to the British royal family today.

The two novels discussed here are not revolutionary—both have been read as conservative pieces that in no way rock the boat. *Belinda* ends with Lady Delacour's suggestion that Belinda will marry, and in its publication history, the interracial marriage between Black and white servants is removed. Similarly, Olivia resigns herself to a life of celibacy—an uncomfortable conclusion that suggests that a happy ending is one that neuters the threat of biracial offspring. Yet in each case, the dependent friend-protagonist gains some traction in her world through her ability to create and maintain relationships of intimacy and obligation, which is to say, friendship, beyond the duties of family. The intersection between these characters and issues of race in the final decades of the long eighteenth century suggests that friendship should be viewed as more than just a fashionable catch-all for social frivolities, but as a viable means through which individuals on the margins of society were able to express their own thoughts and experiences in conversation with those of their patrons and benefactors.

Notes

1. Berndt, *Narrating Friendship and the British Novel, 1760–1830* (New York: Routledge, 2017), 1. Berndt is translating and quoting from Halter's "Freundschaft: Perspektiven eines Begriffes," in *Ars et Amicitia: Bieträge zum Thema Freundschaft in Geschichte, Kunst und Literatur*, ed. Ferdinand van Ingen et al. (Amsterdam: Rodopi, 1998), 23.

2. Mangano, *Fictions of Friendship in the Eighteenth-Century Novel* (New York: Palgrave, 2017), 27–35.

3. Berndt, *Narrating Friendship*, 24.

4. Berndt, *Narrating Friendship*, 25–27.

5. Gross, *The Secret History of Emotion: From Aristotle's Rhetoric to Modern Brain Science* (Chicago: University of Chicago Press, 2006), 113–56; Hume, *An Enquiry concerning Human Understanding*, ed. Tom L. Beaucham (Oxford: Oxford University Press, 1999), 277–79.

6. Janet Todd, *Women's Friendship in Literature* (New York: Columbia University Press, 1980) remains the most comprehensive monograph to address the topic of friendships in literature of this period.

7. Tadmor, *Family and Friends in Eighteenth-Century England: Household, Kinship, and Patronage* (New York: Cambridge University Press, 2001).

8. Castle, "Don't Pick Up: Why Kids Need to Separate from Their Parents," *Chronicle of Higher Education,* 6 May 2012.

9. Schmidgen, "Illegitimacy and Social Observation: The Bastard in the Eighteenth-Century Novel," *ELH* 69, no. 1 (2002): 133–66, and *Exquisite Mixture: The Virtues of Impurity in Early Modern England* (Philadelphia: University of Pennsylvania Press, 2012).

10. Perry, *Novel Relations: The Transformation of Kinship in English Literature and Culture, 1748–1818* (Cambridge: Cambridge University Press, 2006), 40–42.

11. Myers largely focuses on how Edgeworth revises misogynist relationships from her own life in the novel, especially her problems with Thomas Day. Myers, "My Art Belongs to Daddy? Thomas Day, Maria Edgeworth, and the Pre-Texts of *Belinda*: Women Writers and Patriarchal Authority," in *Revising Women: Eighteenth-Century Women's Fiction and Social Engagement,* ed. Paula R. Backscheider (Baltimore: Johns Hopkins University Press, 2000), 104–46.

12. Edgeworth, *Belinda,* ed. Kathryn Kirkpatrick (New York: Oxford University Press, 1994), 76. Subsequent citations will be made parenthetically.

13. Betty Rizzo discusses the phenomenon of the "toady" in *Companions Without Vows: Relationships Among Eighteenth-Century British Women* (Athens: University of Georgia Press, 1994). This fate befell genteel women whose economic situations limited their marriageability; these women acted as friends to married women who, according to Rizzo, often vented their frustrations over disempowering marriages on these unlucky women (41–60).

14. Berndt, *Narrating Friendship,* 18.

15. Moore, "'Something More Tender Still than Friendship': Romantic Friendship in Early Nineteenth-Century England," *Feminist Studies* 18, no. 4. (1992), 505.

16. Weiss cites Claudia Johnson, Mary Poovey, Marilyn Butler, Adriana Cracuin, and Barbara Taylor as all relying on "female philosopher" figures in their analyses of novels published after Wollstonecraft's death in 1797. Weiss, "The Extraordinary Ordinary Belinda: Maria Edgeworth's Female Philosopher." *Eighteenth-Century Fiction* 19, no. 4 (2007): 445–46.

17. Perera, *Reaches of Empire: The English Novel from Edgeworth to Dickens* (New York: Columbia University Press, 1991), 15–34.

18. Smith, "Juba's 'Black face' / Lady Delacour's 'Mask': Plotting Domesticity in Maria Edgeworth's *Belinda,*" *The Eighteenth Century: Theory and Interpretation* 54, no. 1 (2013): 71–90.

19. Myers shows that this story of Hervey's plans for the orphan girl closely resemble Thomas Day's own project to educate a country girl and then marry her. See Myers, "My Art Belongs to Daddy?," 27.

20. [Thomas Day and John Bicknell], *The Dying Negro, A Poetical Epistle, Supposed to be Written by a Black, (Who Lately Shot Himself on Board a Vessel in the River Thames;) to his Intended Wife* (London, 1773), 12, 15, 4.

21. For one version of the charge that Edgeworth was a colonizer, see Elizabeth S. Kim, "Maria Edgeworth's *The Grateful Negro*: A Site for Rewriting Rebellion," *Eighteenth-Century Fiction* 16, no. 1 (2003): 103–26. Kim argues that Edgeworth "relies on understatement, masking, and containment" to promote the interest of

the colonial ruling class in Ireland via analogy with pro-slavery sentiments in the British West Indies (104).

22. See Elizabeth Kowaleski-Wallace, *Their Fathers' Daughters: Hannah More, Maria Edgeworth, and Patriarchal Complicity* (New York: Oxford University Press, 1991), 110.

23. *The Woman of Colour: A Tale*, ed. Lyndon J. Dominique (Peterborough: Broadview Press, 2008), 53. Subsequent citations will be made parenthetically.

24. Perry, *Novel Relations*, 41.

THE ART OF INTERCULTURAL ENGAGEMENT

A Cluster on Daniel O'Quinn's *Engaging the Ottoman Empire:*
Vexed Mediations, 1690–1815

Introduction: Daniel O'Quinn's Melancholy Cosmopolitanism

ASHLEY L. COHEN

An English bluestocking traveling with her ambassador husband is detained in Belgrade for a month thanks to the military rule of a corrupt pasha. Trapped inside, she takes solace in the good company of her host, an accomplished scribe who long ago eschewed the dangers of a political career in favor of a retired life of cultivated ease. Treated to the comforts of fine wine, her host's good table, and excellent conversation on everything from the woman question to poetry, she is quite comfortably entertained. In this "scene of hospitality" she finds "a kind of sanctuary from" the world outside, which is a nightmarish "historical zone of violence, irrationality, and death." The bluestocking in question is, of course, Lady Mary Wortley Montagu, and this rarely discussed episode from her *Turkish Embassy Letters* epitomizes the casual, quotidian scenes of "cosmopolitan interculturalism" that are often overlooked in scholarship on the global eighteenth century, but which take central stage in Daniel O'Quinn's *Engaging the Ottoman Empire*.[1]

O'Quinn's book does not give us what Virginia Woolf, in *A Room of One's Own*, calls "the historian's view of the past."[2] Of course, Woolf is writing prior to the inception of women's history and social history, let alone what we now call cultural history. One hundred years ago, History was still the stomping grounds of Great Men and the Wars they started. Such men are not absent from *Engaging the Ottoman Empire*—the subject of the book might very well be described as their wars. But both appear askew, as if we are viewing them from an unaccustomed angle. And we are. The remarkable gift O'Quinn gives readers of his new book is a glimpse of war stolen through what William Cowper famously termed "the loopholes of retreat," which afford a view of the outside world from a safe and sheltered remove.[3] It is through these loopholes that we experience, along with Lady Mary, the siege of Belgrade. With her, we take refuge in the hospitality of Achmet Beg and take delight in the "intimate enlightened conversation" that unfolds at his dinner table and in his library (194). Her host's mistaken belief that Lady Mary understands Persian may be no more than a polite feint—a willingness to believe that his extraordinary guest must be cultured to a degree that exceeds Europe's narrow bounds—but linguistic hurdles prove no serious obstacle to lively conversation about "Arabian poetry" and "Persian tales," as well as a few friendly "disputes" about the difference between European and Ottoman "customs, particularly the confinements of Women" (193). This is what geopolitical horrors look like when viewed from inside the intimate bunkers that privileged people build to survive them.

Fantasy and domination are the usual poles of scholarly engagement with non-European "Others" in eighteenth-century studies. Neither of these keywords is fully absent from *Engaging the Ottoman Empire*. Indeed, fantasies of domination proliferate in the book's second half, "Besides War," which focuses on the post-Seven Years' War era, when European imperial ambitions intensified. But, to a remarkable extent, this book gives us something different than what we have come to expect from studies of empire. In place of exotic projections and outright oppression, we find quotidian intimacies, unexpected friendships, and artistic collaborations. In part, this focal shift is a product of O'Quinn's subject: the Ottoman Empire was a rival to European imperialism, not a victim of it. The benefits of studying this powerful non-European empire have already been well established for the early modern period by scholars like Nabil Matar and Gerald MacLean, who have shown us the extent to which England's geopolitical ambitions were alternately tempered and kindled by "imperial envy" of Europe's nearest neighbor to the East. O'Quinn brings these insights to the field of eighteenth-century studies, where they are not yet mainstream, and builds on them using one of the field's most distinctive preoccupations: sociability. *Engaging the Ottoman Empire* shows us sociability as we have rarely seen it before. Far from London, far from England, far from the capital (or even provincial) cities of Europe, we enter the sociable world of the expats who gather around English, French, and Dutch ambassadors to the Sublime Porte. In this book, ambassadors are the closest thing we get to agents of imperialism, and while O'Quinn certainly attends to their political maneuvers, the center of gravity in his account lies elsewhere. Ambassadors are of interest primarily for the retinues they accumulate—of friends, artists, informants, assistants, translators, lovers, wives—and the visual and textual archives they generate. These archives tell a story about what O'Quinn calls "intercultural sociability" and what we might also call melancholy cosmopolitanism (19).

Of late, cosmopolitanism has arguably lost its vogue as a keyword: its utopian naïveté seems hopelessly out of step in scholarship far more concerned with histories of enslavement, dispossession, and genocide than with the Enlightenment's self-proclaimed virtues. O'Quinn's cosmopolitanism *redux* makes the term useful again by folding its utopian strain into a history of loss: "'Cosmopolitanism' is a term so imbued with hope," he writes, "that we need to ask what it means for it to be inextricably tied to mutilation, loss, and the tangible relics of slaughter" (194). The specific context for this provocation is the death of Lady Mary's convivial host, Achmet Beg, when Belgrade is captured and burned during the Austro-Turkish War shortly after her stay. But this sentiment is equally applicable to the book as a whole, which repeatedly reveals cosmopolitanism to be what happens in the interstices of geopolitics. Cosmopolitanism is the normal magic of sociality that occurs when people from different sides of a cultural divide work and play together; and it is always melancholy because the interstices that sustain it are always fleeting. These evanescent interstices are what O'Quinn calls "peace." When peace ends—as it does at regular intervals throughout the century and a quarter covered here—we are left with "the sadness that attends the momentary contemplation and ensuing foreclosure of an unrealized future" (332). The sadness, in other words, of seeing the world as it might have been.

Inevitably, *Engaging the Ottoman Empire* tells the story of Europe's march towards global domination. But it also tells a different story: the Europe that conquered the world, O'Quinn reveals, was not an autochthonous ~~indigenous~~ marvel of self-creation. Instead, we find that Europe's art and media, its invented classical past and its imagined imperial future were all, in important ways, shaped by its engagements with the Ottoman empire. For me, as a scholar of British imperialism, the most refreshing and the most subtly revolutionary aspect of O'Quinn's book is its decentering of Britain, its refusal to re-inscribe Britain's imperial hegemony. This is what it looks like to truly "provincialize Europe": the British empire becomes one of many empires overlapping in space and time. Without getting sucked into the centripetal orbit of the British empire, O'Quinn nonetheless manages to make a contribution to the study of British imperialism. To name just one example, his account of how European diplomats tried (often unsuccessfully) to negotiate the rituals of Ottoman state ceremonies, public processions, and court audiences designed to visualize and perform Ottoman state power has profoundly enriched my own understanding of the strategic use and abuse of Mughal ritual by the colonial state in nineteenth-century India. It now seems clear to me that the trials and tribulations of European ambassadors like Sir Robert Ainslie in the Sublime Porte represent the prehistory to British colonial manipulations of Mughal vocabularies and repertoires of state power a century later in India. When O'Quinn's chapters on Ainslie and the choreographed spectacles surrounding the mediation of the Treaty of Karlowitz are read alongside Bernard S. Cohn's classic essay on "Representing Authority in Victorian India," the only logical conclusion is that the road to British imperial supremacy in South Asia was paved in Asia Minor with centuries of humiliation by a non-European adversary who almost always had the upper hand.[4]

The short essays that follow testify to the importance of *Engaging the Ottoman Empire* across an unusually broad range of disciplines and field formations. Many of the responses focus on method, with the implication that the book's use value is portable beyond its particular subject matter. Angelina Del Balzo contextualizes this book's *modus operandi* with reference to O'Quinn's two previous monographs on the London theater: "paradoxically, by moving away from conversations around the representation of the Ottoman Empire onstage," Del Balzo explains, "O'Quinn has made a compelling argument for the importance of theater scholarship to literary study beyond questions of representation." The complexities of the eighteenth-century "media environment" are taken up by Douglas Fordham. An art historian, Fordham fleshes out the importance of an aspect of the book easily overlooked by literary scholars: its "integration of paint on canvas into a larger world of printed images and documents." This is merely one example of how O'Quinn's interdisciplinary, mixed-media approach might challenge or even upend critical narratives whose stability requires the controlled environment of hermetically sealed disciplines.

In a related vein, Lynn Festa throws into relief the book's profound critique of the conventional "chronologies that organize our histories." If O'Quinn uses "formal disturbance" in media as a kind of blue dye test to reveal the presence of intercultural influence, then Festa locates the success of *Engaging the Ottoman Empire* as a truly intercultural study in the book's chronological disturbance: a "temporal hiatus at the heart of O'Quinn's book" that works to rupture "the smooth chronologies that underwrite periodization" and "remind us of the partiality of our own perspectives, the violence implicit in the imposition of contemporaneity, and the ways in which the periodizations we invoke stabilize the totality of our own point of view." Katherine Calvin locates the book's capacity to upend conventional critical narratives in O'Quinn's blended method. While O'Quinn's microscopic attention to detail—what literary scholars call "close reading"—is certainly indebted to the "reduction of scale" associated with microhistory, O'Quinn innovates, Calvin argues, by "positioning ... multiple microhistorical studies in a dynamic, constellatory field." O'Quinn's exquisitely minute close readings add up to a magisterial big picture—much as the tiny threads in an Ottoman carpet combine into a single fabulous design.

Perhaps the most surprising payoffs of *Engaging the Ottoman Empire* pertain to its profound engagement with the classics, as well as the European reinvention of the classical past. Zirwat Chowdhury suggests that O'Quinn's attention to the usually overlooked "Ottoman interlocuters" who assisted—and thereby made possible—European antiquarian expeditions offers "necessary alternatives to more conventional histories of Enlightenment antiquarianism and archaeology, according to which white British men like Pars, Revett, and Chandler step into the arcs of progress that we call modernity by rescuing ancient patrimony from the hands of purportedly declining cultures ... histories [that] continue to underpin the forms of custodianship that institutions such as the British Museum (controversially) still claim for themselves." Finally, Charlotte Sussman sifts out the book's subtle, but profound challenge to the conventional wisdom that, by "the eighteenth century ... the epic was a genre both *about* the past and *of* the past"—that is, "distressed, or residual," in short, played out. Contrary to this assumption, Sussman explains, O'Quinn unearths a stunning use value for classical allusion: in a virtuosic reading of the *Turkish Embassy Letters*, he reveals how Montagu used classical allusion as a vital "practice through which to articulate intercultural exchange." In a remarkable reversal of the kind of Eurocentrism Johannes Fabian censured in *Time and the Other*, O'Quinn reveals how Montagu used epic, in Sussman's words, "to confront not temporal inaccessibility, but geographical accessibility: she relies on classical epic as a site of translation, a basis for allegory, and a source of allusion to describe and engage the world through which she travels."

My first encounter with *Engaging the Ottoman Empire* was an exercise in humility: it is disconcerting to discover that a subject you know very little about is so crucially important to the subjects you hold most dear. Rarely have I learned so much from a single book. *Engaging the Ottoman Empire* has the potential to upend so much of what we thought we already knew—about art history, the classics, periodization, media history, European imperialism, and so much more. Its ripple effects will be felt in scholarship on all of these topics for years to come.

Notes

1. O'Quinn, *Engaging the Ottoman Empire: Vexed Mediations, 1690–1815* (Philadelphia: University of Pennsylvania Press, 2019), 193–94. Subsequent citations will be made parenthetically.

2. Woolf, *A Room of One's Own and Three Guineas,* ed. Anna Snaith (Oxford: Oxford University Press, 2015), 34.

3. Cowper, *The Poems of William Cowper*, ed. John D. Baird and Charles Ryskamp, 3 vols. (Oxford: Clarendon Press, 1996), 2:189.

4. Cohn, "Representing Authority in Victorian India," in *The Invention of Tradition*, ed. Eric Hobsbawm and Terence Ranger (Cambridge: Cambridge University Press, 1983).

The Archive and the Repertoire of the Treaty of Karlowitz

ANGELINA DEL BALZO

At first glance, Daniel O'Quinn's new monograph, *Engaging the Ottoman Empire: Vexed Mediations, 1690–1815,* seems like a departure from his previous monumental work in eighteenth-century theater history. O'Quinn here eschews discussion of any of the myriad of plays set in the Ottoman Empire from the Restoration and eighteenth century, such as William Davenant's *The Siege of Rhodes* and Voltaire's *Mahomet*. Much scholarship looking at English-Ottoman relations focuses on the representation of the Turks, and nowhere was this transcultural fascination more prominent than on the stage.[1] As O'Quinn states in the introduction to *Engaging the Ottoman Empire*, eighteenth-century imperial thought was comparative, and the empires in question were both European and non-European.[2] As both Bridget Orr and O'Quinn's previous work has shown, the theater of the period was central to that comparative analysis.[3] Plays dramatized empires from around the world, including Rome, the Americas, and China. Europeans did have extended, real-life interactions with the Ottomans, unlike some of these other empires, and *Engaging the Ottoman Empire* focuses on materials that mediated these interchanges, such as paintings, maps, architectural plans, costume books, letters, and antiquarian illustrations. But despite the lack of theatrical texts as objects of study, O'Quinn's methodology owes as much to performance studies as it does to cultural studies. Paradoxically, by moving away from conversations around the representation of the Ottoman Empire onstage, O'Quinn has made a compelling argument for the importance of theater scholarship to literary study beyond questions of representation. *Engaging the Ottoman Empire* applies performance theories of embodiment to printed media.

This analytical move is especially evident in the book's first chapter, "*Theatrum Pacis:* Mediating the Treating of Karlowitz," in which O'Quinn's performance approach leads to more nuanced readings of often familiar tropes. O'Quinn's intention is "to use this informational archive, especially the interaction of text and image, to understand a repertoire of particularly auspicious intercultural performances—performances that quite literally changed the world" (40). Here, he specifically evokes the language of Diana Taylor's field-defining *The Archive and the Repertoire*, which moved the critical conversation away from the written/oral dichotomy in order to deprioritize cultural studies' emphasis on the textual and reframe the modalities of analysis as "the archive of supposedly enduring materials (i.e., texts, documents, buildings, bones) and the so-called ephemeral repertoire of embodied practice/knowledge (i.e., spoken language, dance, sports, ritual)."[4] In order to do this, Taylor substitutes for the text, as the site of analysis, the scenario, which adds new concerns, like gestures and other corporeal communicative systems, to traditional objects of literary analysis, such as narrative and setting. As O'Quinn does here, Taylor uses the scenario to interpret the performance of a major geopolitical point of contact: the initial conquest of the Americas by Spain, in which "performing the act of possession makes the claim; the witnessing and writing down legitimates it."[5]

Engaging the Ottoman Empire contextualizes Karlowitz within the familiar corpus of Ottoman/Oriental texts from the period through its reading of the Ottoman procession, a state performance described in Madeleine de Scudéry's romances, Paul Rycaut's *History of the Turkish Empire*, Antoine Galland's *Les mille et une nuits*, and Lady Mary Wortley Montagu's *Turkish Embassy Letters*. The procession is often interpreted as an occasion for the European reader's scopophilia, but O'Quinn argues that it is a "spatialization of power relations" (66) that not only required measured viewing, but also relied on the spectators' familiarity with previous performances in order to be correctly interpreted. The power of the procession lay not just in Ottoman exoticism or the material promise of empire, but in recognizing repeated visual signifiers. For Rycaut, this new state of international relations is celebrated through the British Embassy's own procession, in which "rather than cavalry and sword bearers—the appropriate props of the sultan—we have the dragomans, secretaries, and *giovane di lingua* (interpreters) employed by the British embassy—the very embodiments of mediation in both senses of the word" (69). The Ottomans may be mediated through European writing, but the British are equally mediated in their use of a visual language perfected by the sultans in order to communicate their own position. Developing that language was important for both the historical actors and later scholars, conveying meaning in a way that could be understood across cultures and time. Given the language barriers often hindering truly global scholarship, reading the procession as a performance genre introduces an object of analysis without having to rely on text or speech.[6]

The procession is the most recognizable performance discussed in the chapter, but O'Quinn uses the "repertoire" to reframe one of the most important moments in the history of Ottoman-European relations. *Engaging the Ottoman Empire* begins with the 1699 treaty as the end of the Ottomans' western expansion, which "set the terms for phantasmal oppositions between 'Europe' and 'the East'" (13), a juxtaposition that would be at the foundation of late eighteenth-century Orientalism. The English and Dutch ambassadors to the Ottoman Empire, Lord William Paget and Jacobus Colyer respectively, served as mediators between the Holy Roman Empire and the Ottomans. As the first treaty negotiated by civil servants, Karlowitz arguably marks the beginning of modern diplomacy. There are thus two mediations under discussion in this chapter: this new form of negotiation itself and the ways in which it was broadcast and communicated, as Karlowitz was quite literally a performance of diplomacy.

Central to O'Quinn's exploration is an anonymous engraving, *Theatre de la paix entre les Chrestiens et les Turcs* (c. 1704), depicting the exterior and interior of the "maison des conferences." The *Theatre* is not only a metaphor for the process of peacemaking, but also an actual theater where a performance took place. O'Quinn supplements his analysis of the *Theatre de la paix* with the written archives of Paget and the Venetian delegation.

Through his use of Taylor, O'Quinn's analysis moves beyond the standard two poles of literary discussions of performance: representation, which uses the play text as the primary (and too often sole) source of analysis, and performance or the performative as metaphor. O'Quinn instead considers performance as a site of embodied enactment. This is fundamental to the field of performance studies, but O'Quinn shows how crucial this methodology should also be for the study of material culture, travel writing, and military history. The *Theatre de la paix* shows how the site was consciously designed as a venue for performance: it was purposely built on neutral ground with extra doors to avoid conflict over precedence. The relatively plain adornment of the tents and *maison* reinforces how these structures were hosting an embodied performance; they are not the primary locus of meaning. Included in the engraving are smaller inserts showing the Austrians, Ottomans, and mediators at various moments in the discussions, seated together on cushions and chairs. The treaty is enacted through the "small gestures and words only discernible through intimate contact" (65), and the print shows writing implements on display, but untouched, so as to de-emphasize the role of writing in the actual negotiations.

At the same time as he reads Karlowitz as a performance, O'Quinn also makes a formalist argument for the ways in which theatrical conventions shape the written archive. In the assistants' notes on the negotiations, the Austrian and Ottoman delegates are represented by dialogue written in direct speech, as in a script, while the mediators' contributions are narratively described, giving the English greater agency in the process: "Put bluntly, the various delegates make proposals and counterproposals, but Lord Paget makes things happen" (76). By staying attuned to the scenario, we can see where the archive deviates into alternative, more literary forms, and what the implications are for that change. Here, the Englishmen give themselves the privilege of narrative agency in an event in which they are not the primary actors.

Reading Karlowitz as a scenario also allows O'Quinn to move away from an ahistorical reading of the treaty as the "beginning of the end" for the Ottomans, given that they remained in power for more than two centuries afterwards. The Ottomans arrive on equal footing to the negotiations (often from a position of strength, despite their defeat in battle). The pictorial representation of the *Theatre de la paix* privileges the oral negotiations in the moment over their written communications after the fact. Indeed, O'Quinn argues that the contemporary culture of conversation was integral to imagining a peaceful and cosmopolitan world order "where two Ottomans, an Englishman and a Dutchman, and two Austrians and their multilingual secretaries communicate orally at table" (65). And this is at the crux of Karlowitz: both the event and the treaty are indicative of the commonalities between the Ottomans and the Austrians, bordering empires that would later become exemplars of drastically opposed "Western/Christian" and "Eastern/Islamic" worlds. Despite their geographic proximity, they were estranged by language and religion, and this ideological divide would only widen as the imperial balance of power shifted over time. *Engaging the Ottoman Empire* shows how performance studies does not just offer a way of supplementing the written record with the repertoire, but also provides a mode of analysis that reframes and nuances our understanding of that archive.

Notes

1. See, for example, Esin Akalin, *Staging the Ottoman Turk: British Drama, 1656–1792* (Stuttgart: Ibidem Press, 2016); Emily M. N. Kugler, *The Sway of the Ottoman Empire on English Identity in the Long Eighteenth Century* (Leiden: Brill, 2012); and Daniel Viktus, *Turning Turk: English Theater and the Multicultural Mediterranean, 1570–1630* (New York: Palgrave Macmillan, 2003).

2. O'Quinn, *Engaging the Ottoman Empire: Vexed Mediations, 1690–1815* (Philadelphia: University of Pennsylvania Press, 2019), 5. Subsequent citations will be made parenthetically.

3. Orr, *Empire on the English Stage, 1660–1714* (Cambridge: Cambridge University Press, 2001); O'Quinn, *Staging Governance: Theatrical Imperialism in London, 1770–1800* (Baltimore: Johns Hopkins University Press, 2005) and *Entertaining Crisis in the Atlantic Imperium, 1770–1790* (Baltimore: Johns Hopkins University Press, 2011).

4. Taylor, *The Archive and the Repertoire: Performing Cultural Memory in the Americas* (Durham: Duke University Press, 2003), 19.

5. Taylor, *Archive and the Repertoire,* 62.

6. Ottoman history offers additional challenges to comparative analysis by nonspecialists. The replacement of the Ottoman Turkish alphabet with the Latin-based modern alphabet in 1928 has required additional training for even Turkish scholars to read untranslated primary documents.

Empire and Modern Media: Vanmour or Less

DOUGLAS FORDHAM

The opening *mise en scène* in Daniel O'Quinn's *Engaging the Ottoman Empire* is sure to capture the attention of art historians. Gaining permission to visit the Rijksmuseum's storerooms, while the museum was closed for renovation, O'Quinn makes his way to the museum director's office where he encounters Jean-Baptiste Vanmour's monumental painting, *View of Istanbul from the Dutch Embassy at Pera*. "It is a labored, confused painting. Time passes. In so many words, the director indicates that he will be happy not to look at this painting when he moves into his new office."[1] I chuckled when I read this, because I've had similar moments in my own quest for the "art of empire": creative works that occupy an uneasy place in fine art museums grappling with the legacies of empire as well as the questionable artistic status of its representation. Not so long ago, art relating to the British empire was buried deep in the stores of the Yale Center for British Art, Tate Britain, and a great many English provincial museums. Like those institutions, the Rijksmuseum is now moving many works "from the periphery" up into its public galleries. Sixty-three paintings of Ottoman subjects by Vanmour and his workshop now hold pride of place in gallery thirteen of the Rijksmuseum, including the *View of Istanbul* mentioned above. The painting's shortcomings remain, however, and O'Quinn is particularly good at engaging with flawed paintings. Indeed, his book offers a sustained inquiry into the kinds of pressures that Ottoman culture and difference placed on Western European artistic forms.

The Ottoman paintings of Vanmour provide foundational evidence for part one of O'Quinn's book, receiving sustained visual analysis in the introduction, chapter 2 on costume, and chapter 3 on Vanmour's multi-figure subject pictures. On the one hand, Vanmour's prominence is unsurprising. Vanmour was the most accomplished European artist working in Constantinople in the first third of the eighteenth century. Working for a variety of European ambassadors in Constantinople, Vanmour created paintings that circulated throughout Europe, and his "costume" paintings gained even wider circulation in print. On the other hand, O'Quinn's careful reading of individual paintings reveals how little we really know about the artist and his work. Despite a number of recent exhibitions and a bevy of scholarly articles, Vanmour's paintings rarely attract sustained visual analysis. Like much of the "art of empire," Vanmour's paintings are frequently dismissed as either straightforward descriptions or as Orientalist projections. Cultural historians (including art historians) fall all too easily for this Jekyll and Hyde response, viewing the work as either too benign to merit serious attention or too suspect to welcome inside. O'Quinn makes a more interesting and productive move, considering Vanmour within the wider world of European media: "as I work through a very mixed archive of drawings, maps, letters, dispatches, memoirs, travel narratives, engraved books, paintings, poems, and architecture, I argue that the repository of European representations of Ottoman culture constitutes a valuable resource not only for Ottoman cultural history but also for media archaeology in the eighteenth century" (3). Vanmour offers a challenging test case for this approach, not least because oil painting on canvas carries a powerful ideological charge in the West. As O'Quinn inadvertently demonstrates in his visit to the Rijksmuseum, paintings carry with them a preservation and curation history very different from that of other modern media. Even so, I find O'Quinn's approach promising and productive, and I want to point out a few of the highlights and possible shortcomings that caught my attention.

There is a vacillation in *Engaging the Ottoman Empire* between Vanmour the courtly client and Vanmour the modern entrepreneur. This tension runs particularly high in O'Quinn's discussion of the "costume paintings" that Vanmour produced for his first patron, Marquis Charles de Ferriol, the French ambassador to the Ottoman Empire. Completed in 1707 and 1708, these paintings "were transformed into engravings and published in 1714 under the title *Recueil de cent estampes representant différentes nations du Levant* ... immediately after Ferriol's return to Paris" (93). To the extent that Vanmour belongs to a larger media environment, then, basic questions about how these paintings "were transformed" into print become pressing ones. To begin, why did either Vanmour or Ferriol wish to create the series in oil on canvas? One possibility is that a unique set of painted proto-ethnographic studies constituted a diplomatic showpiece. Rulers from the Ottoman world to Qing China commissioned painted costume series such as this, documenting the variety of their subjects within either their real or their hoped-for jurisdictions. O'Quinn notes that Vanmour and his studio assistants painted copies of these costume studies over an extended period of time. This edges the painted series into the realm of tourist art that could be found "within the local market in Constantinople and within a larger circuit of exchange" (94). Not long after the first painted set was completed, it was engraved and published as what became commonly known as the *Recueil Ferriol*. As a publication, it expanded into an even larger commercial world, in which it influenced European art, dress, theater, and more. At one point O'Quinn notes that "the commission for Ferriol is mired in an obsolete genre" (118), and I would suggest that this claim should be qualified with respect to its medium: that is, unique sets of painted costumes created for or at the behest of rulers were perhaps becoming obsolete (a point that could still be challenged). Certainly, painted copies for tourists and printed illustrations for costume books only gained in popularity as the century progressed. Indeed, a more strenuous case could be made about the significance and priority of the *Recueil Ferriol* in the world of European book illustration.[2]

I'm drawing attention to a kind of fragmentation within the media environment that scholars could use to tease out artistic motivation, patronage decisions, and public reception. There are advantages, of course, to keeping the media environment as large and homogenous as possible. In chapter 2, O'Quinn reads the Vanmour costume prints against the letters of Lady Mary Wortley Montagu to great effect: "she supplements the painter's practice by rendering costume from the inside out, and thus her description condenses multiple images in Vanmour's series. ... By augmenting Vanmour's necessarily external scopophilic catalog, Montagu effectively argues that costume albums offer ethnography without people because they are fundamentally disconnected from the experience of wearing these items" (114). A century later, a British artist named Mary Adelaide Walker combined Vanmour's talents with Lady Mary's access to the world of female sociability in Istanbul. Unfortunately, as Mary Roberts documents, much of that work was lost, leaving behind a suggestive, but incomplete paper trail.[3]

I find O'Quinn's visual analysis particularly effective when he plays one painting genre off another. For example, at the end of chapter 2, he describes Vanmour's portrait of Lady Mary and her son as "an uneasy blend of costume album and portraiture," noting the female musician on her left and the Ottoman letter bearer on her right: "this uneasy blending of genres is perhaps most forcefully felt in the rather noncommittal transitional spaces between each figure" (120). Lady Mary's liminal status between private and public spaces, and between male and female worlds, leaves literal gaps in the portrait, to which O'Quinn expertly draws our attention.

The last three plates of the *Recueil Ferriol* break with the single-figure mold of most of its predecessors with double-sized foldout engravings of a Turkish marriage, a Turkish funeral, and the dervishes at Pera. With an examination of these works, O'Quinn pivots to the complex, multi-figure compositions in Vanmour's oeuvre. Here again, O'Quinn emphasizes the rhetoric of space in which these figures operate and highlights their allegorical qualities. He contrasts these multi-figure compositions with "Vanmour's costume images [that] attempt to supplant and thus contain the threat posed by the narrative structure of Ottoman processional theater" (92). O'Quinn notes that many of the paintings move right to left, whereas the Turkish wedding print moved left to right across the page (131). Might this shift in direction be in anticipation of a possible engraving, since intaglio prints are conveniently reversed in the reproduction process? While *Engaging the Ottoman Empire* includes excellent color illustrations in the center of the book, I often wished for a better sense of scale; how large are these works and does their relative size offer clues to their meaning, purpose, or ambition?

Chapter 2 culminates with Vanmour's portrait of Lady Mary Wortley Montagu and her son, thereby bringing costume into direct dialogue with questions of gender and privacy, questions also raised by Lady Mary's letters. Chapter 3 concludes with a curious pair of paintings referring to the Patrona Halil rebellion in 1730, which brings Vanmour's subject paintings into direct dialogue with Ottoman politics. Like Vanmour's paintings of the harem, these rebellion pictures "render information secondhand," and so O'Quinn proposes that it is "useful to think about the pictures first in terms of mediation" (149). As with Vanmour's paintings of costume and processions, the rebellion pictures reveal in their formal structure the kinds of constraints and controls that the artist sought to impose on an unruly body of information.

O'Quinn does not entirely manage to bring Vanmour's paintings into a media archaeology of the eighteenth century. That would require extensive legwork on the production and reception ends of the equation, and there are substantial ideological forces (both then and now) working against the integration of paint on canvas into a larger world of printed images and documents. What O'Quinn does give us is a finely textured, closely observed social history of art, one that is attentive to various registers of visual meaning and the slipperiness of evidentiary claims. I find this all the more remarkable coming from a scholar trained in literary and theater studies. *Engaging the Ottoman Empire* is interdisciplinary in the very best sense, for it demonstrates a command of the methods and techniques of art history while considering a wide array of cultural products and forms.

Notes

1. Daniel O'Quinn, *Engaging the Ottoman Empire: Vexed Mediations, 1690–1815* (Philadelphia: University of Pennsylvania Press, 2019), 1. Subsequent citations will be made parenthetically.

2. I've gestured in this direction in *Aquatint Worlds: Travel, Print, and Empire* (New Haven: Yale University Press, 2019), 122.

3. Mary Roberts, *Intimate Outsiders: The Harem in Ottoman and Orientalist Art and Travel Literature* (Durham: Duke University Press, 2007), 109–27.

author?

Wrinkles in Imperial Time

LYNN FESTA

Exposing the intricate connections between global geopolitical machinations and local intimate bonds, between classical inheritances and Enlightened modernity, Daniel O'Quinn's magisterial *Engaging the Ottoman Empire: Vexed Mediations, 1690–1815* illuminates how aesthetic forms and knowledge practices mediate affective, cultural, erotic, and political relations across competing spatial and temporal scales. The book summons a dazzling array of materials— paintings, travel narratives, memoirs, letters, maps, poems, buildings, antiquarian collections— to testify to the complexity of European relations with the Ottoman Empire during the long eighteenth century. The sheer abundance and variety of objects thrust the reader into multifarious timeframes, for the artifacts the book analyzes are composed of materials, techniques, meanings, assumptions, and allusions that belong to multiple moments and that age, die, or become obsolete at different paces. Each polychronic object creates different degrees of temporal and historical distance and reveals multitemporal relations of past, present, and future. In inviting us to see how "formal disturbances and collisions … point to competing temporal itineraries that ultimately leave an affective imprint of deep historical significance," O'Quinn makes this temporal multiplicity central to his method.[1] This book *about* mediation, in other words, reflects *on* its modes of mediation, exposing the work done by periodization in constructing our objects of study by determining what belongs to a particular epoch and what is anachronistic or anomalous. In this way, the contribution of *Engaging the Ottoman Empire* is as much methodological as critical and theoretical, and in what follows I address the ways the book's cross-disciplinary approach—indeed, its very structure— generates a reflexive critique of the chronologies that organize our histories.

The book's very title indicates the complexity of its relation to periodization, pitting the present continuous of "engaging" against the neat temporal demarcation of 1690 and 1815. The clean start-and-stop points promised by the precision of these dates is belied by the sedimented layers and temporal striations that run through the media landscape excavated in the book (even the seemingly decisive 1815 points both to the Napoleonic defeat at Waterloo and to Greek independence, a reminder that seemingly neutral chronologies are suffused with political values). While the loss of a battle, the signing of a treaty, the death of a monarch, all generate pivotal dates in the book, the forward march of time is crosscut by structures, allegiances, and practices that generate powerful political, aesthetic, and affective undertows.

These layered landscapes remind us that empires—not only Ottoman but also Roman, Holy Roman, Spanish, Hapsburg, Russian, British, and French—exist in time as well as space. The pivotal dates that punctuate their rise and fall do not, however, neatly correlate with the states of peace and war they are frequently thought to mark. The titles that cleave O'Quinn's book into two sections indicate this imperfect alignment. The first section, "After Peace," names either what follows when peace is declared or the resumption of war when peace is over, while the second, "Beside War," reminds us that peace and war are spatially and temporally proximate. Indeed, peace is a state so beset by the imminence of war that it "seems to happen nowhere in time and in no time, which is not to say it doesn't happen" (28). How is one to capture this elusive state in between?

One answer to this question is to be found in the curious hiatus in the book's chronology, between the first section, covering 1690–1734, and the second, which extends from 1763 (the end of the Seven Years' War) to 1815. Given that this interlude was, O'Quinn tells us, a period during which the Ottoman empire enjoyed peace and economic prosperity, the unnarrated center stages the book's insights about the difficulty of narrating peace. This temporal gap does something more, however, for it also invites us to interrogate the integrity of time cupped between periodizing parentheses and to contemplate the discontinuities and partialities of our own retroactively imposed narratives. The hiatus in the book's chronology, that is, embeds a critique of periodization within its structure, unsettling assumptions about the integrity of the eighteenth century as a historical period, about the continuities imposed by periodization, and the relations of cause and effect these timeframes lock into place. Such discontinuities in chronology also create switch-points that make it possible to alter the trajectory of our histories. For if, as O'Quinn argues, it is necessary for "spatial voids and temporal lacunae [to be] imagined, constituted, and maintained for peace to occur" (28), it is because such lacunae breach formal continuities in order to generate different possible relations between past, present, and future as well as new modes of recognition, sociable connection, and understanding. Even as the treaty negotiations at Karlewitz circle around the "ovoid cypher" (56) of the room where it happened, creating a "void place" (50) that produces a fictive, but necessary neutral zone, an Archimedean point from which peace can be leveraged, so too does the book itself preserve an unfilled center where we can contemplate other relations to the past and register alternative itineraries to the future.

The discontinuity in the book's chronology likewise invites us to read for what is not quite there or does not fit together: for an anomaly in the picture plane, a lacuna in a narrative, an anachronistic figure or term. In the same way that works of art like Jean-Baptiste Vanmour's *View of Istanbul from the Dutch Embassy at Pera* (c. 1720–37) have formal disturbances that indicate something unassimilable to the techniques available to depict their objects, so too does the temporal hiatus generate a ripple or riptide running through the middle of O'Quinn's book that points to what is not fully represented. This temporal hiatus has something to tell us about the ethical reading practice the book seeks to instill. For while the awkward manipulation of perspective in Vanmour's painting indicates his "failure to successfully devise a pictorial solution for intercultural relations" (2), it also reveals his imperfect attempt to grasp the world from another's point of view. The flawed painting that cannot reconcile foreground and background is not failed art, but art that exposes the sites of its own failure to understand. Vanmour's inability to subordinate everything to a coherent aesthetic whole finds a counterpart in the inability of periodization to muster everything into its "proper" time. Even as Vanmour's imperfect painting registers that something can't—shouldn't—be absorbed into a unitary aesthetic system, so too does the temporal hiatus at the heart of O'Quinn's book, by rupturing the smooth chronologies that underwrite periodization, remind us of the partiality of our own perspectives, the violence implicit in the imposition of contemporaneity, and the ways in which the periodizations we invoke stabilize the totality of our own point of view. In tampering with the temporal hinges that delineate the period as an object of study, O'Quinn simultaneously destabilizes the spatial frameworks and historical termini that organize the period around the ascendency of the British empire and make its nineteenth-century global hegemony the only possible consummation of what came before.

The chronological gap in the middle of *Engaging the Ottoman Empire* does something more: it invites us to recognize the exertion of forces adjacent to, but excluded from the field of representation—to translate the spatial mode of metonymic reading modeled in O'Quinn's analysis of antiquarian reproductions of the "Achilles" sarcophagus at Ephesus into a temporal register. In O'Quinn's account, the cropping of images—the inclusion (or exclusion) of a grieving Achilles or the body of Patroclus—indexes shifting social and sexual mores and different degrees of historical distance. By reflecting on the forms and practices that mediate our encounters with others—what frames these encounters and what surrounds (or is occluded by) these frames—we can come to know what we didn't know wasn't there.

It is worth lingering, however, over the way these "unknown unknowns" come to light. To understand the significance of such partial images, O'Quinn notes, it is necessary not "to look for hidden meaning beneath the image, but rather to recognize the meaning generated by adjacent fragments of narrative and by the close encounters between subjects and that which lies beside them. In this image, who and what lies next to whom makes all the difference in the world" (360). The question of "who and what lies next to whom" in different versions of the image is a matter of alliance and action (who stands with whom), erotic affiliation (who lies with whom), and death (who is buried next to whom). We are asked here to read for what is proximate, rather than what is "behind" or "anterior" to the image, as the injunction *not* "to look for hidden meaning beneath the image" sends us sideways, rather than into the depths of the image. This is not, I think, "surface reading" *avant la lettre*, so much as an invitation to recognize and preserve lacunae, rather than filling in what is missing—a mode of reading based on a closeness that doesn't assimilate objects to its protocols, but instead dwells near them without demanding that they be assimilated to a master code or conscripted into a uniform time. This approach does not promise to reinstate a whole, as if the object were fully knowable; instead, we are offered a dawning insight into our own blindness, without the arrogant assumption that what we do not understand is a gap we can necessarily fill, or that all moments can be assimilated to our own histories and chronologies. On these terms, the ongoingness of the "Engaging" in the book's title reminds us of the imperative to intermittently shake up—and even shatter—the neat periodizing vessels into which we seek to decant time.

Notes

1. O'Quinn, *Engaging the Ottoman Empire: Vexed Mediations, 1690–1815* (Philadelphia: University of Pennsylvania Press, 2019), 4. Subsequent citations will be made parenthetically. On the polychronic and multitemporal, see Jonathan Gil Harris, *Untimely Matter in the Time of Shakespeare* (Philadelphia: University of Pennsylvania Press, 2009), 3–5.

Between Geographic and Conceptual Fields: Mapping Microhistories in the Eighteenth-Century Ottoman Empire

KATHERINE CALVIN

When examining the many visual and textual accounts produced at the time of the 1699 Treaty of Karlowitz, Daniel O'Quinn poses a central question using a theatrical metaphor: why is the stage—the simple four-room building constructed "in the middle of nowhere" to house the treaty negotiations—accorded far more attention in these sources than the actors?[1] This question is a characteristic example of how O'Quinn's close examination of a nexus of related images and texts frequently uncovers surprising repetitions, absences, and contradictions at his subject's very center. These are, of course, the "vexed mediations" named in his subtitle that he weaves together to construct a constellatory, rather than a cumulative, history of intercultural communication and representation between Ottomans and Europeans. Such unexpected discoveries of dissonance, instances of something that does not quite fit, exemplify what Carlo Ginzburg and Giovanni Levi, both earlier practitioners of microhistory, might call "clues."[2] The recognition of these clues—in this case, O'Quinn's microscopic observations—is made possible by focusing, singularly, on a particular event, individual, object, or place. This reduction of scale is central to microhistory's methodology.[3] O'Quinn uses microhistorical approaches to identify significant encounters between early modern Ottomans and

Europeans unaccounted for in previous scholarship; however, he innovates with the method by moving beyond a single restricted spatial or temporal scope. Instead, he positions his observations in a vast, interconnected constellatory field, wherein each "clue" operates as a dynamic discursive node, a site with myriad connections to both historical and invented past, present, and future versions of itself. O'Quinn thus guides readers from one microhistorical node to the next—up, down, and around—through the historical and imagined itineraries that linked Europeans and Ottomans in an eighteenth-century imperial field that was, simultaneously, both physical and discursive, both geographical and conceptual.

The origins of microhistory are often traced to a group of Italian historians working in the 1970s who became interested in the possibility that a variation in the scale of one's analysis might lead to radically new interpretations of commonly accepted grand narratives.[4] Indeed, narrative itself became a tool favored in later microhistories by European and American scholars. Robert Darnton, Natalie Zemon Davis, and Emmanuel Le Roy Ladurie turned to microhistory as a way to enliven, rather than merely reconstruct, what cultural anthropologist Clifford Geertz would term "local knowledge," or the experience of reality that originated in people's daily lives.[5] Francesca Trivellato has highlighted how the heterogeneity of findings obtained in such microscopic spheres cannot be automatically transferred to the macroscopic space. This impasse, she argues, is both the greatest difficulty and greatest potential benefit of microhistory.[6] Since its inception, microhistory has contested and complicated "big picture" narratives, such as the emergence of modernity or the operation of empire. Tonio Andrade has similarly argued that, following the turn to globalism in much of the scholarship of the current century, "global microhistory" has provided a necessary counterpart to the proliferation of social science studies focused on modeling large-scale processes, such as trade and migration.[7] Microhistory's biographical, narrative-based approach has continued to highlight instances in which such models break down when considered at the more granular level of individuals, events, or single sites.

O'Quinn's use of microhistorical methods to reduce the scale of analysis and thereby identify "clues," or changes at the level of form or genre in a body of images or texts, is foundational to his examination of intercultural communication because it highlights when and where representational transformations were occurring. A notable example is his investigation of the visual and textual accounts of the site Paul Rycaut termed "the void place" near Karlowitz that was used for treaty discussions in 1699 (50). Two of the formal changes O'Quinn pinpoints as significant "clues" are, first, the large number of depictions focused on the newly constructed conference house in which the negotiations took place and, second, the unprecedented combination of categorically distinct representational forms in these accounts. O'Quinn argues that the Viennese diagram from the *Bericht* (see Figure 1), for example, combines elements of topography and narrative composition as a way to map the negotiation, both geographically and politically, for its European audience. This hybridization of genres is thus a direct result of the need to communicate intercultural information. Indeed, this example evinces a central claim of O'Quinn's book: that microhistorical encounters, and the vexed mediations they provoked, initiated formal, aesthetic transformations in the visual and textual accounts that circulated information regarding the eighteenth-century Ottoman Empire.

Yet microhistory is but one of several equally significant analytical modes that O'Quinn employs in this project. Formal and generic disturbances are not only considered in relation to the specific place and time of their production, but also as dynamic nodes with many connections outward that both affect and are affected by social and cultural tensions in the broader imperial field. To return to the Viennese diagram as an example, O'Quinn posits that the central position of the conference house in this work—and the concurrent erasure of the Ottoman tent that had been used for negotiations while the new conference house was being constructed—functioned to formally

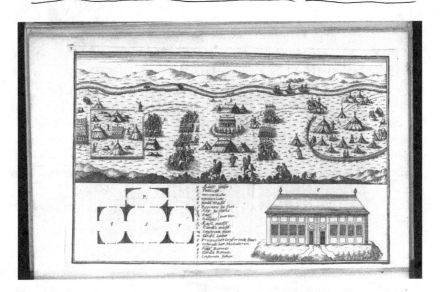

Figure 1. Map of camp, in *Gründ-und Umständlicher Bericht Von Demen Römisch-Kayserlichen Wie auch Ottomannischen Gross-Bothschafften*, engraving, 1702. Getty Research Institute, Los Angeles (2834-604). This appears as figure 8 in O'Quinn, *Engaging the Ottoman Empire.*

displace the Ottomans both from pictorial space and from historical time, thus asserting Habsburg dominance, present and future (59). Considering aesthetic transformation alongside the spatial and temporal itineraries that these images and texts variously depict, reference, and narrate reveals, he explains, "a complex relation to Europe's past that haunts many of my primary observers' present experiences in Ottoman lands" (4). These routes, both real and imagined, are impossible to assess with established microhistorical methods bounded by space and time. Instead, they require a different approach attuned to movement and networks, both geographical and discursive.

It is this positioning of multiple microhistorical studies in a dynamic, constellatory field that makes O'Quinn's approach so innovative. It requires a constant oscillation in both analytical scale (between the singular node and the broader network) and methodological mode, as he switches from microhistorical methods to cultural analysis to assess what he terms "the long view," or the broader imperial field (4). A final example will help further demonstrate how O'Quinn's method of locating multiple microhistorical studies in a constellatory field has particular resonance for cross-cultural studies of travel literature, maps, and other representations of movement through space and time. He points out that *Ionian Antiquities*, an influential account of the travels of Richard Chandler, Nicholas Revett, and William Pars to four ancient sites in the Ottoman Empire, lacks a map. An introductory map had been an essential component of antiquarian travel literature, as it helped European readers locate the narrative (and, by extension, themselves) in relation to sites with biblical, classical, or political significance. Moreover, beyond a single depiction of local residents near the Temple of Bacchus at Teos (see Figure 2), there is no visual or textual evidence in *Ionian Antiquities* of the encompassing Ottoman context in which those sites were encountered. O'Quinn posits that the absence of a map, this moment of microhistorical dissonance, transforms the entire experience of the book: readers are now forced to consider the sites in isolation. And this new mode of reading and viewing, in turn, transforms territory currently in use by the Ottomans into abstracted classical artifacts, detached from the surrounding physical landscape and the people inhabiting it.

The artifact-ization of Ottoman land in *Ionian Antiquities* is one case, then, that can (and should) be mapped, geographically and conceptually, alongside the many contemporaneous instances in which sculptures, architectural fragments, and other antiquities were similarly *made into* artifacts through their integration into European antiquarian frameworks and collections. By attending carefully both to very small units of analysis (a person, an event, a place) and the operation of a vast, unwieldy spatiotemporal field,

Figure 2. Richard Chandler, *Ionian Antiquities* (1769), 1. The headpiece is an engraving after a watercolor by William Pars. Getty Research Institute, Los Angeles (84-B780). The headpiece appears as figure 45 in O'Quinn, *Engaging the Ottoman Empire*.

O'Quinn demonstrates an exciting new way to consider multiple historical scales in a single project. Future eighteenth-century studies of intercultural communication and representation between Europe and the Ottoman Empire will undoubtedly benefit from O'Quinn's identification, analysis, and elevation of the many microhistorical vexed mediations that come with—and have certainly shaped—the field.

Notes

1. O'Quinn, *Engaging the Ottoman Empire: Vexed Mediations, 1690–1815* (Philadelphia: University of Pennsylvania Press, 2019), 49. Subsequent citations will be made parenthetically.

2. See Matti Peltonen, "Clues, Margins, and Monads: The Micro-Macro Link in Historical Research," *History and Theory* 40, no. 3 (2001): 349.

3. Significant theorizations of microhistory by its practitioners include Giovanni Levi, "On Microhistory," in *New Perspectives on Historical Writing*, ed. Peter Burke (Cambridge: Polity Press, 1991), 93–113; Carlo Ginzburg, "Microhistory: Two or Three Things That I Know about It," trans. John and Anne C. Tedeschi, *Critical Inquiry* 20, no. 1 (1993): 10–35; and *Microhistory and the Lost Peoples of Europe*, ed. Edward Muir and Guido Ruggiero (Baltimore: Johns Hopkins University Press, 1991).

4. See Francesca Trivellato, "Microstoria/Microhistoire/Microhistory," *French Politics, Culture & Society* 33, no. 1 (2015): 122. The early *microstoria* practioners in Italy included Simona Cerutti, Edoardo Grendi, Raul Merzario, and Carlo Poni.

5. Darnton, *The Great Cat Massacre and Other Episodes in French Cultural History* (New York: Basic Books, 1984); Davis, *The Return of Martin Guerre* (Cambridge: Harvard University Press, 1983); Ladurie, *Montaillou: The Promised Land of Error*, trans. Barbara Bray (New York: Random House, 1979); Clifford Geertz, *Local Knowledge: Further Essays in Interpretive Anthropology*, 3rd ed. (New York: Basic Books, 2000).

6. Trivellato, "Microstoria/Microhistoire/Microhistory," 123.

7. Andrade, "A Chinese Farmer, Two African Boys, and a Warlord," *Journal of World History* 21, no. 4 (2011): 574.

Rabble, Rubble, Repeat

ZIRWAT CHOWDHURY

A little over two hundred years before anti-racist organizers such as A. Sivanandan retorted "we are here, because you were there" against efforts to delimit British citizenship to an imagined autochthonous whiteness, a group of white British men traveled to one such "there" to find their origins, founding in the process some of the practices and discourses that continue to define cultural heritage preservation today.[1] Britain, they and their elite patrons ruminated, was founded by Brutus, a descendant of Aeneas, the Trojan hero-turned-refugee to whom Virgil traced the origin of Rome.[2] However much their classical learning oriented educated British men to the worlds of ancient Greece and Rome, their proverbial founding father remained an Asian man, who had been displaced following the sack of his homeland in a war made epic by its Homeric narration. The strife of war, and the deferral, rather than resolution, of peace was the unassailable truth of those who inhabited this corner of the ancient world. As Daniel O'Quinn attentively traces in the journeys, pictorial renderings, and commentaries of three men—an artist, William Pars; an architect, Nicholas Revett; and an antiquarian, Richard Chandler—sent by the Society of Dilettanti in 1764 to study, measure, and draw Ionian monuments and ruins in Asia Minor, such truth was also part of the entwined lives of those living in Britain and the Ottoman Empire in the eighteenth century.[3] Indeed, O'Quinn finds in the trio's visual and textual representations of the ancient monuments they encountered and the circumstances of their journeys an aesthetic of entropy, which he not only distinguishes from the narrative of decline that scholars conventionally ascribe to eighteenth-century British portrayals of the contemporary Ottoman Empire but also deploys in order to challenge that narrative. If the idea of *decline* conditions a framework of Orientalist othering that justified British intervention, domination, and ascendance, O'Quinn's discussion of *entropy* lingers instead over the interplay of cooperation, opacity, and hostility—what he calls "intercultural sociability" (34) —that scholars often simplify under the rubric of cross-cultural encounter.

In 1769, British audiences first saw the outcome of the trio's journeys with the exhibition of Pars's watercolors at the Royal Academy of Arts in London, and the publication of the first volume of *Ionian Antiquities*.[4] In prior decades, the likes of Giovanni Battista Piranesi, Revett, and his more renowned counterpart, James "Athenian" Stuart, had already begun to transform the genre of the classical ruin. O'Quinn reminds his readers how imagination and empiricism, the conceptual frameworks often deployed to distinguish the Piranesian oeuvre from that of Revett and Stuart, were often interwoven with one another and that Revett's renderings of the Ionic order of the ruins that he visited during his travels were more conjectural than observational (237). In this vein, he contrasts Revett's act of imaginatively reconstituting classical fragments with the aesthetic of entropy that he observes not only in Pars's watercolors, but also in Chandler's travel narrative of 1775. Before I turn to Pars and Chandler, though, it is worth noting the mutilated quality of the antiquarian print, which assembles, without piecing together on one page, the disconnected limbs, torso, and capital (or head) of a building.[5] This effect is heightened—rather than, as O'Quinn suggests, mitigated—by the prints' diagrammatic organization, especially with the nearly equal division of the page between representation and negative space.

In turning his attention to Pars, O'Quinn invites his readers, especially art historians, to look at artworks that were exhibited alongside history painting, the most prestigious genre of visual art, at the Royal Academy. He draws largely on David Solkin's reading of an imperial aesthetic within the form and content of Benjamin West's *Departure of Regulus from Rome* (1769) (see Figure 1): its compositional distinction of the self-sacrificing, virtuous hero from the mob understood as an allegory of George III's elite Stoicism contrasted with the Wilkite politics of American settler colonists. O'Quinn discerns a similar compositional division in two of the watercolors, both from 1764, that Pars also exhibited in 1769: *Arch at Mylasa* (see Figure 2) and *The Theater at Miletus with the Party Crossing in a Ferry* (see Figure 3). At the Royal Academy, history painting conjoined virtue and virtuosity with quasi-empiricist fiction in its rendering of architectural details. Thus, the

Figure 1. Benjamin West, *Departure of Regulus from Rome*, 1769, oil on canvas. Image courtesy of Royal Collection Trust / © Her Majesty Queen Elizabeth II.

Figure 2. William Pars, *Arch at Mylasa*, 1764–65, watercolor on paper. © The Trustees of the British Museum.

Figure 3. William Pars, *The Theater at Miletus with the Party Crossing in a Ferry*, c. 1764, watercolor on paper. © The Trustees of the British Museum.

colonnade in the background of West's painting is able to signify doubly as both proscenium and Rome. O'Quinn astutely notes Pars's rejection of such theatricality (in both the literal and Friedian senses) in his watercolor of the *Arch at Mylasa*.[6] There the rubble, unlike the rabble in West's painting, on the left gathers not against an immovable hero, but rather a void: arguably, I would add, the affect of a Stoic hero (233). It is this juxtaposition of a withering arch and rubble that for O'Quinn instantiates the cyclicality of history that marks the pages of the first volume of *Ionian Antiquities*. For example, the scattered fragments of the *Temple of Bacchus at Teos* in Pars's headpiece for the first chapter of Volume I are brought together, albeit fragmentarily, in Revett's antiquarian print per the conventions of classical orders. Architecture here, far from attesting to the promise of monumentality, lives in iterations of its continuing entropy, even as it is allegedly preserved on the pages of a book. In this vein, Revett's rebuilding of the Temple of Bacchus at High Wycombe serves more as an act of conjecture, than one of reconstruction (253).

However, O'Quinn's proposition that *The Theater at Miletus with the Party Crossing in a Ferry* is haunted by Roman gladiatorial spectacle, although alluring to consider in the pairing with West's painting, does not wholly work as a visual and historical argument about the slippage implicit in British identification with a site of classical learning transformed by the

Romans into one of deathly entertainment. Rather, unlike West's Regulus who refuses to be moved (emotionally) by the mob, the trio, shown at various stages of boarding the raft in *The Theater at Miletus*, require the full force of Ottoman brokers and interlocutors to move across the landscape left by classical antiquity.[7] O'Quinn attentively extracts from Chandler's narrative how the trio had to rely often upon Ottoman assistance and generosity to navigate equally Ottoman hostility: as, for example, when *ağas* (regional governors) would not recognize the Ottoman Sultan's *firman* (grant) that supported the expedition. Noting Chandler's belated publication of his narrative in 1775, following the conclusion of the Russo-Turkish War (1768–74), he also reads in the *ağas'* recalcitrance against the authority of the Sultan an example of the fragmentation of the Ottoman Empire and its resultant vulnerability to external invasion. Offering close readings of the published narrative, O'Quinn compellingly argues that Chandler's history (especially that of the city of Ephesus) is "one of repeated conquest and almost endless war" (263). Chandler here, in what is arguably one of O'Quinn's most formidable interventions, is neither a melancholy antiquarian, nor an Enlightened imperialist. Rather, he and his Ottoman interlocutors together inhabit a landscape of ruins in which their only continuity with the past is their shared fate of endless war.

O'Quinn's readings of Pars and Chandler, in particular, offer necessary alternatives to more conventional histories of Enlightenment antiquarianism and archaeology, according to which white British men like Pars, Revett, and Chandler step into the arcs of progress that we call modernity by rescuing ancient patrimony from the hands of purportedly declining cultures. Such histories continue to underpin the forms of custodianship that institutions such as the British Museum (controversially) still claim for themselves. Egyptian writer Ahdaf Souief's resignation from the British Museum's Board of Trustees in 2019 in protest of BP's sponsorship reminds us of the continuing paradox at the heart of modernity's preservationist discourse that deems Greece and non-European cultures unsuitable custodians of cultural artifacts, but still profitable purchasers of European and American goods, including weapons and fossil fuels.[8] In lieu of such forms of custodianship, and with O'Quinn's pithy observation that a "desire for the cessation of hostilities incorporates a specific form of historical consciousness" (225), let us look again at *The Theater at Miletus*. Suspended as it is between a genre scene and a topographical view, the watercolor requires the mediation of the actions staged in its foreground in order for British audiences to avail themselves of the history rendered in its background. But the movement from the foreground to the background does not yield a legible monument. It does, however, illuminate a form of historical consciousness wherein one makes sense of one's present in relation to a past that survives in ruins. That is, within the form of the past's continuing presence, one discerns the figure of its (and one's own) destruction.

Despite the centrality of military endeavors to life in eighteenth-century Britain, war itself almost never took place on British soil after 1745. The Wilkite protests and the Gordon Riots were the closest to any form of strife and destruction that those living in Britain experienced immediately and at home, rather than through their own experiences elsewhere, or those of others known to them. The idea that Britain "lost" America, that thirteen of Britain's North American colonies became "foreign soil" in the later eighteenth century as the result of the American Revolution, is among the mythologies to have come out of the distended polity of eighteenth-century Britain, especially in the wake of the Seven Years' War, and it continues to pose important challenges for any scholarship that attends to Britain's American crisis in the 1770s and 1780s. I raise this point as an invitation for scholars to reflect more broadly on the forms of relation that O'Quinn asks us to reimagine within the cross-cultural spaces of the eighteenth century, especially with respect to the mythologies that came out of those spaces and with which we still live. Although scholars of Indigenous Studies (and those in conversation with them) continue to foreground how settlers rebelled against restrictions on their expropriation of Indigenous homelands the American Revolution is still primarily written as a story of the colonists' righteous resistance against the tyranny of a neo-imperialist king's use of his royal prerogative.[9] The archival traces, not to mention the living consequences, of white British settlers' refusal to participate in the society of others, and their translation of Indigenous dispossession for the sake of profit into acts of revolution and liberty are too great for us to continue to ignore. And as O'Quinn poignantly reminds us: when we do not attend to these threads of intercultural sociability, we, too, face the risk of entropy.

Notes

1. Although this aphorism is quoted widely in the literature on Sivanandan, I have yet to locate a source that pinpoints its first use or clarifies whether he borrowed the expression from anti-war and anti-racist organizers, or vice-versa.

2. The founding of Britain by Aeneas's descendant Brutus was first recounted in the twelfth century in Geoffrey of Monmouth's *Historia Regum Britanniae*, which

was translated from Latin to English in 1718 by Aaron Thompson as *The British History*. Note that Troy was located in Asia Minor.

3. Daniel O'Quinn, *Engaging the Ottoman Empire: Vexed Mediations, 1690–1815* (Philadelphia: University of Pennsylvania Press, 2019), 213–66. Subsequent citations will be made parenthetically.

4. The publication for which the trio undertook their travels in 1764–66 came out with staggering delay over the course of the eighteenth, nineteenth, and twentieth centuries, with the five volumes appearing in 1769, 1798, 1840, 1881, and 1915.

5. Analogies between the human body and architecture are commonplace; see, for example, Vitruvius, *Ten Books on Architecture*, trans. Ingrid Rowland (New York: Cambridge University Press, 1999).

6. In Michael Fried's formulation, "theatricality" refers to painting's acknowledgment of the world of its beholder, albeit in order to establish psychic, spatial, and temporal difference from him (the beholder is presumptively male in this framework); see *Absorption and Theatricality: Painting and Beholder in the Age of Diderot* (Berkeley: University of California Press, 1980). My thanks to Hector Reyes for conversation regarding this issue.

7. For an account of Ottoman classicism in these same years, especially its renewed attention to Byzantine architecture, see Ünver Rüstem, *Ottoman Baroque: The Architectural Refashioning of Eighteenth-Century Istanbul* (Princeton: Princeton University Press, 2019), 171–219.

8. Souief also raised, among others, concerns about the Museum's labor practices in "On Resigning from the British Museum's Board of Trustees," *LRB Blog*, 15 July 2019, *https://www.lrb.co.uk/blog/2019/july/on-resigning-from-the-british-museum-s-board-of-trustees*.

9. See, for example, Colin G. Calloway, *The Scratch of a Pen: 1763 and the Transformation of North America* (Oxford: Oxford University Press, 2006), and Jeffers Lennox, "Revolution Expected: The Invasion of Quebec and American Independence," in *Violence, Order, and Unrest: A History of British North America, 1749–1876*, ed. Elizabeth Mancke et al. (Toronto: University of Toronto Press, 2019), 95–116.

On Walls, Bridges, and Temporal Folds: Epic, Empire, and Neoclassicism Revisited

CHARLOTTE SUSSMAN

L ate in his chapter on Lady Mary Wortley Montagu's work in *Engaging the Ottoman Empire*, Daniel O'Quinn calls her letter book, the epistolary account of her travels to Vienna and Constantinople in 1716–18 often known as the *Turkish Embassy Letters*, a "counter epic."[1] It's an arresting claim, comparing a collection of occasional letters to a genre defined by its length, cohesion, and public importance. Lady Mary, according to O'Quinn, "turns the [epic] tradition on itself to reveal what it cannot adequately represent: the recurrent trauma of war" (209). But what does it mean to turn a tradition on itself? And how does that process reveal things previously unseen? Unpacking this argument about Lady Mary's representational practice illuminates important things about O'Quinn's own methodology and the potential that method holds for retooling the way we approach the place of classical genres in eighteenth-century literature and culture.

The epic holds an equivocal place in eighteenth-century literary studies, which is to say that it is little studied and often dismissed. The genre's central role in the period has conventionally been seen as providing the rusty scaffolding upon which the sharp, topical interventions of mock-epic could be hung. If the mock epic has been a perennially fascinating genre, the epic-in-earnest has been viewed as little better than a ruin, with the epistemological battles fought over its rutted ground—between the Ancients and the Moderns, for example—being more interesting than the territory itself. The epic's penumbral place in eighteenth-century studies is perhaps best expressed by the title of an essay by Susan Stewart: "Distressed Genres." Here, Stewart places epic with other literary forms that articulate "an anxiety regarding place, desertion, and the irrevocable silence of the dead." Following M. M. Bakhtin's theory of the epic as a genre that inhabits an "absolute past," "walled off absolutely from all subsequent times," Stewart argues that "in the epic, everything has already *happened*."[2] For the eighteenth century, this strain of criticism goes, the epic was a genre both *about* the past and *of* the past.

In his rethinking of the place of epic in cultural mediation, it is precisely this temporal barrier that O'Quinn proposes that Lady Mary breaches. Epic, he argues, allows her to confront not temporal inaccessibility, but geographical accessibility: she relies on classical epic as a site of translation, a basis for allegory, and a source of allusion to describe and engage the world through which she travels. All three rhetorical practices are "bridging activities" (165) and allow Lady Mary to treat the epic not as standing behind a wall separating one epoch from another, but as a rich terrain of "temporal folds" (181), out of which new articulations of intercultural contact can emerge. By terming Lady Mary's work a "counter-epic," he suggests not only that she turns it back on itself, but also that she disarticulates it into parts in order to stock a toolkit of her own. For Lady Mary, epic is less a ruin than an archive.

The benefits of this practice are perhaps clearest in the case of translation. O'Quinn reminds us that "it is difficult to overstate the importance of classical translation for Augustan literary practice," particularly with regard to the era's "famous willingness to deviate quite forcefully from the original," especially "when the translator is rendering the Latin or Greek with an eye to contemporary politics" (174). Lady Mary, as she moves beyond England's borders, uses translation to map a world of unfamiliar objects.

O'Quinn's argument that classical allusion might be a practice through which to articulate intercultural exchange is more unusual. The word "allusion" derives from the Greek word for play, and it is often associated with mastery of a tradition, the capacity to pepper one's descriptions with references to ancient works that act as a demonstration of one's own authority. O'Quinn shares this understanding of allusion as ludic, terming Lady Mary's practice "subtle play," but hers is not (or not only) an assertion of mastery. In a bravura reading, O'Quinn interrogates Lady Mary's reference to the funeral games for Anchises in Book 6 of the *Aeneid* in her description of a shooting match between women in Vienna, following and unpacking the resonances of the allusion to eventually reveal her sympathy with the women in Virgil who, while these games were going on, burned the Trojans' boats in protest because they valued "security over wars of conflict" (188) and refused to help Aeneas pursue his destiny of conquering Italy and founding Rome. O'Quinn's conclusion, which clearly winds up quite a ways away from the trivial event that prompts the allusion, is the result of an intricate reading that not only compares Lady Mary to John Dryden, but also Virgil to Homer in order to demonstrate her antiwar sentiments. The journey is long and fascinating, not least for its methodology. O'Quinn illuminates the way in which allusion can produce a layering of multiple visions of the world. Drawing on epic for such allusions allows the genre to serve as more than an archive; it approaches the role of a portal, allowing the practitioner to move between cultures.

And it is here that the role of classical genres intersects with O'Quinn's other focus, both in his reading of Lady Mary specifically and throughout the book: namely, the protocols of hospitality. The practice of allusion both offers Lady Mary a way of describing hospitality and is itself an index of hospitality: her allusions signal to the reader that the tradition has welcomed her in. Here too, the discussion recurs to the problem of war. O'Quinn argues that the pattern of Lady Mary's allusions to the *Aeneid* allows her to make visible the trauma incurred by those whose hospitality is violated (most famously, Dido), while also acknowledging her own complicity in the imperialist ambitions that mark both her own travels and Aeneas's: she "makes herself both the prophet and the embodiment of imperial guilt and sadness" (209). O'Quinn argues that "Montagu brings both the necessity and the violence of hospitality into the open" (27). Like allusion, hospitality is a practice that can involve both sharing and taking.

How, then, does this tracing of allusions, this crossing of a rhetorical bridge between one culture and another, generate new methodologies for understanding intercultural contact in the eighteenth century? To begin with, it suggests that the epic was not quite as distressed, or residual, a genre, as we have assumed. For a long time, a time that is perhaps now ending, eighteenth-century studies focused its attention on the "rise" of the novel. But the eighteenth-century novel is a genre that, from Daniel Defoe to Anne Radcliffe, privileges narratives of return: the most interesting part of *Robinson Crusoe* may happen on the island, but it is crucial for the meaning of the narrative that Crusoe, like Moll Flanders, like Tom Jones, like Matthew Bramble, eventually gets to go home. Such homecomings suited a historical era characterized by hegemonic nation-states. Our current moment, however, urges us to be more attentive to mobility, to diaspora, and to the precarity of individual homes as well as empires.

The epic, perhaps surprisingly to those who assume it is a genre of empire and conquest, offers a rubric through which to explore such conditions and experiences. Franco Moretti has argued that in the "modern epic," "the contemporaneity of the non-contemporaneous moves into the foreground: the Before-and-After is transformed into an 'Alongside'—*and history thus becomes a gigantic metaphor for geography*."[3] The epic, in these terms, allows for the juxtaposition of both times and places, something useful for an era like the eighteenth century (or our own moment), in which "empire" was or is "the subject of comparative analysis" (5). But the method of *Engaging the Ottoman Empire* differs from that of Moretti's *Modern Epic*. Where Moretti relies on the "alongside-ness" of metaphor, O'Quinn is more drawn to the far-flung filaments of allusion, the permutations of translation, and what he describes as the "constant deferral" of allegory (165). He terms this the "mediating function of classical literature" (27): not the recapitulation of genre, nor its ruin, but its dispersal, mediation, and reimagining.

Notes

1. Daniel O'Quinn, *Engaging the Ottoman Empire: Vexed Mediations, 1690–1815* (Philadelphia: University of Pennsylvania Press, 2019), 209. Subsequent citations will be made parenthetically.

2. M. M. Bakhtin, "Epic and Novel: Toward a Methodology for the Study of the Novel," in *The Dialogic Imagination: Four Essays,* trans. Caryl Emerson and Michael Holquist (Austin: University of Texas Press, 1981), 15–16; Susan Stewart, *Crimes of Writing: Problems in the Containment of Representation* (New York: Oxford University Press, 1991), 69, 74.

3. Franco Moretti, *Modern Epic: The World System from Goethe to Garcia Marquez* (London: Verso, 1996), 52.

What Eludes Us

DANIEL O'QUINN

Reading these seven essays has been a humbling experience. I am honored that *Studies in Eighteenth-Century Culture* and Ashley Cohen have assembled and curated these multiple viewpoints on *Engaging the Ottoman Empire* from such a wide array of disciplines, and each essay simply confirmed my preexisting admiration for the contributors. Each essayist has crystallized key aspects of the book's argument more powerfully than I had done in the first instance. For a book that was itself already a constellation to have this kind of afterlife among colleagues in quite disparate fields has amplified its argument, but has also activated concerns that had hitherto remained vestigial or were simply overlooked. The strange thing about this book is that I think of it as many books; it had multiple forms, each of which emphasized different problematics. Very little of the book was presented publicly prior to receiving the reports from the Press readers. The multiple acts of reading, the thoughtful suggestions, and the remarkable generosity of groups of scholars who convened at Mansfield College, the British Museum, and Berkeley to workshop various versions produced new writing that has now generated new readings. With each exchange, the project changes. Lynn Festa has perfectly articulated the complex temporal dynamic and the ethical imperative I was trying to code into the book's form: her words complete my thoughts. By brilliantly contextualizing my concern with epic form, Charlotte Sussman brings the book more into dialogue with our field: her concluding distinction between Franco Moretti's approach to epic and my own perfectly captures an aspect of the argument I was struggling to bring to light. In their close attention to how I used performance studies and microhistory not only to understand the mediation of the Treaty of Karlowitz, but also to expand, implicitly, the methodological reach of the analytical tools associated with those practices, Angelina Del Balzo and Katherine Calvin have brought this theoretical concern out into the open. That the estimable art historians Douglas Fordham and Zirwat Chowdhury patiently took my incomplete accounts of Jean-Baptiste Vanmour and William Pars in such productive directions is a sign of both their generosity and their willingness to look with me at visual materials that all too often are ignored or seen as transparent illustrations. Considered in this way, the essays in this cluster demonstrate that *Engaging the Ottoman Empire* achieves a productive level of incompletion.

This, of course, is a charitable way of saying that this long, and at times dense, book leaves a lot of threads hanging. To reframe Ashley Cohen's carpet metaphor slightly, I would suggest that the book weaves together a number of archival strands to establish patterns of analysis, but that the ultimate realization of the design will be the product of a workshop, not a single practitioner. I am using the term "workshop" not in the sense that we speak of Rembrandt's or Peter Paul Rubens's workshop, but rather in the sense of a collective entity working together to modify and transmit a highly refined craft—in this case, cultural analysis. A book whose published form arose in a workshop environment has been taken up with energy and extraordinary rigor by new actors. Looking at the work of this latest iteration of the ongoing workshop, I immediately see new motifs emerging; certain designs are becoming more fully realized, some elements need to be reworked, but what is most intriguing to me is the way in which the collective readings bring me back to the abiding enigma that generated so many different versions of the book and that continues to puzzle me to this day.

That enigma can be expressed as follows: what form does peace take? Or in a slightly different register: how does one describe the time and space of peace? The answers I give to these questions are hardly answers at all, as they turn upon paradox and oxymoron. As Del Balzo and Calvin recognize, the "void place" that I worry over so insistently with regard to the Karlowitz proceedings serves as a figure for the spatial dilemma: peace happens in a vacuum that both can and cannot be described. And yet that void turns out to be an emblematic zone of intercultural exchange. As Festa and Sussman emphasize, the temporality of peace—that which happens in no time, but which happens nonetheless—forces us to reconsider political and literary itineraries in part because it can only be described by negation: either through strategically invoked aporia or through a contemplation of how a seemingly totalizing genre like epic could be activated in other ways, as I believe Lady Mary Wortley Montagu does so eloquently in her letter book. It should come as no surprise that history, the subject of Festa's meditation, and epic, the focus of Sussman's remarks, are so troubled by peace because their classic manifestations are so thoroughly entwined with wartime. Describing such an elusive, transient condition required that I attend to in-between states and intermediary spaces. As someone not trained as an art historian, I am heartened that Fordham found the analysis of the non-committal transitional spaces between the figures in Vanmour's portrait of Lady Mary convincing and that Chowdhury welcomed my entropic comparison of Pars's *Arch at Mylasa* and West's *Departure of Regulus from Rome*. The formal disturbances I found in these works were, to borrow Charlotte Sussman's term, "portals" that enabled me to discern similar deformations or vexed mediations in the archive.

The task of discerning and describing these formal disturbances instantiated an entirely different, unforeseen problematic: one whose dimensions were primarily affective and ultimately ethical. Perhaps because the chapters on the "Achilles" sarcophagus (chapter 7) and Lady Mary's counter-epic (chapter 4)—i.e., those most concerned with love, hospitality, and the negation of attachment during wartime—came first, working on this project inexorably became, to borrow Ashley Cohen's summation, about "the sadness … of seeing the world as it might have been." In affective terms, this meant that I had to devise strategies for dealing with melancholy scenarios that nonetheless exceeded their gravitational pull. The love between Achilles and Patroclus and that between artist and patron encoded into Luigi Mayer's drawing and Lady Mary's affection for Achmet Beg, like so many of the affirming scenes of attachment discussed in the book, become visible at the volatile margin where sociability is ruthlessly destroyed, or, in the case of letter 45 in Lady Mary's letter book, soberly betrayed. It seemed important to me that these affirmations of life and love stay with the reader without clouding the tangible circumstances of their devaluation. A commitment to thought's inherent desire for its own continuation was made especially urgent because so much of the book was dealing with moments of discontinuity and loss. Finding myself in this position, I found that "paying attention to who and what lies next to whom makes all the difference in the world."[1] That sentence came very early on; understanding it, like understanding the temporality of peace, is an ongoing task. Questions such as how narrative units are aggregated, how temporal entities abut against one another, how pictorial spaces are deformed to enable surprising proximities, how persons and peoples are made adjacent or distant, and how eras are made impermeable or flow into one another became vital nodal points of inquiry. All of the essays in this cluster recognize that how we get from *a* to *b*, how we move through time and across space—the very dynamics of translation, allusion, allegory, narrative, composition, mediation, and reception that are the focus of the book's close reading—hold the book together as a viable study of a set of historical and cultural problematics. As Calvin notes, this attention to the connective filaments of textual and pictorial form applies to the book's constellatory structure as well, so watching the critics collected here work with and against that structure is, for me, very thrilling: it suggests that this mode of attention may well live on in a productive form that is necessarily other to itself.

This, of course, is the desire of all practitioners, and to be blessed with such readers is an astonishing privilege. In a way, their generosity, exemplified by what we could refer to as their disciplinary hospitality, is reminiscent of the scenes of affirmative sociability explored throughout *Engaging the Ottoman Empire*. Differences, disciplinary and otherwise, are not here barriers, but rather occasions for what Theodor Adorno described as the inherent happiness of thought: "The happiness that dawns in the eye of the thinking person is the happiness of humanity. The universal tendency of oppression is opposed to thought as such. Thought is happiness, even where it defines unhappiness: by enunciating it. By this alone happiness reaches into the universal unhappiness. Whoever does not let it atrophy has not resigned."[2] But with the invocation of this famous passage, we also have to recognize the precarity of such happiness, because it emerges at the same time that we become aware of its negation. I think that this awareness lies behind Chowdhury's suggestion that my treatment of entropy in chapter 5 speaks to our current predicaments. Started shortly after the second Iraq war and published during the Trump presidency, I would simply add that the urgency generated by oppression inflected every archival encounter and perhaps made the glimpses of happiness, thought, and affection precious indeed.

Let me end with an anecdote. At a certain point in the composition of this book, I knew that its myriad parts would not cohere unless I was able to distill my thoughts on the temporality of peace into some kind of working proposition—the painful work of Introductions. Taking a break from double-checking the Paget papers at SOAS, I decided to go to the British Library, my happy place, in the hopes that I might come up with something. Not surprisingly, I came away with nothing, left the building, and sat down in the courtyard to have a valedictory cup of tea. Sitting there by myself, engrossed by the buzz of conversations all around me, I suddenly saw that this was one of many places where people come to think together and that they were gathered not because they understood what they studied, but precisely because vital questions remained unresolved and potentially unresolvable.

From this point onward, I realized unconsciously that, like the materials I was studying, *Engaging the Ottoman Empire* needed above all to "expose the sites of its own failure to understand ... because such lacunae breach formal continuities in order to generate different possible relations between past, present, and future as well as new modes of recognition, sociable connection, and understanding." These are Lynn Festa's words not mine, and I can't claim to have fully recognized this need. Rather, it expressed itself at the level of affect: by working through the formal disturbances I was finding in the archive, I felt the desire to share the importance of what eludes us, "of com[ing] to know what we didn't know wasn't there."

Notes

1. Daniel O'Quinn, *Engaging the Ottoman Empire: Vexed Mediations, 1690–1815* (Philadelphia: University of Pennsylvania Press, 2019), 360.
2. Theodor Adorno, "Resignation," *Critical Models,* trans. Henry W. Pickford (New York: Columbia University Press, 2005), 293. I am indebted to Helen Deutsch, whose brilliant essay from *The Rambling*, "We Must Keep Moving," sent me back to Adorno's crucial critical statement; *https://the-rambling.com/2020/08/07/issue9-deutsch/*.

Contributors to Volume 51

Nathan D. Brown is Assistant Professor of French at Furman University in Greenville, South Carolina. His primary research interest lies in the transatlantic connections between France and New France in the eighteenth century.

Renee Bryzik holds an M.A. in Eighteenth-Century Studies from King's College, London and a Ph.D. in English from the University of California, Davis. Her writing has appeared in *Eighteenth-Century Studies* and *The Scriblerian*, among other publications. She is an Instructor of English at Saint Clair County Community College in Port Huron, Michigan.

Katherine Calvin is Assistant Professor of Art History at Kenyon College. Her research on early modern travel literature, antiquarianism, and the patronage of European merchants in the Ottoman Empire has been supported by the Williams Andrew Clark Memorial Library and the Lewis Walpole Library. She is currently preparing a book that examines the art and architectural patronage of British Levant Company traders in Aleppo and London.

Noel Chevalier is Associate Professor of English at Luther College, University of Regina. He has a wide range of teaching and research interests, from eighteenth-century drama to biblical intertextuality in literary texts, but his primary research is on pirates and pirate narratives. He has recently published articles on pirate booty and on variants in the various published narratives of the pirate John Gow. The present article is part of a larger study of the social, intellectual, and cultural contexts surrounding Charles Johnson's *General History of the Pyrates*.

Zirwat Chowdhury is Assistant Professor of eighteenth- and nineteenth-century European art at UCLA. Her research explores the interconnected histories of art and visual culture in Britain, France, South Asia, and the Atlantic world. She is currently working on a book that studies the legacy of Lockean extension, understood as a form of imperial relation, in eighteenth-century British art.

285

Ashley L. Cohen is Associate Professor of English at the University of Southern California. She is the author of *The Global Indies: British Imperial Culture and the Reshaping of the World, 1756–1815* (Yale University Press, 2020) and the editor of *Lady Nugent's East India Journal* (Oxford University Press, 2014).

Angelina Del Balzo is Assistant Professor in the Program in Cultures, Civilizations, and Ideas at Bilkent University in Ankara, Turkey. Her work has been published in *Eighteenth-Century Fiction* and *Studies in English Literature, 1500–1900* and has been supported by grants from the Huntington Library, the William Andrews Clark Memorial Library, and McGill University.

Lynn Festa is Professor of English at Rutgers University. She is the author of *Sentimental Figures of Empire in Eighteenth-Century Britain and France* (Johns Hopkins University Press, 2006) and *Fiction without Humanity: Person, Animal, Thing in Early Enlightenment Literature and Culture* (University of Pennsylvania Press, 2019) and the co-editor, with Daniel Carey, of *The Postcolonial Enlightenment: Eighteenth-Century Colonialism and Postcolonial Theory* (Oxford University Press, 2009).

Douglas Fordham is Professor of Art History at the University of Virginia, and the author of two monographs on British Art, most recently *Aquatint Worlds: Travel, Print, and Empire* (Paul Mellon Centre for the Study of British Art and Yale University Press, 2019). He currently holds a Paul Mellon Centre Senior Fellowship in which he is examining the interrelated histories of British imperialism, indigeneity, and the arts.

Dario Galvão is a Ph.D. Candidate in Philosophy at the Université Paris 1 Panthéon-Sorbonne and the Universidade de São Paulo and is a Visiting Ph.D. in History and Philosophy of Science at University College London. He researches the intersections between philosophy and natural history in the eighteenth century. He is a member of the Brazilian Association of Eighteenth-Century Studies and has published articles on David Hume.

Stacey Jocoy is Associate Professor of Musicology at Texas Tech University. She has published essays on a range of topics, including Henry Lawes and Robert Herrick, Caroline court culture, seventeenth-century printed music and censorship, ballads on the Shakespearean stage, and *The Beggar's Opera*. She is the author of "John Playford and the English Musical Market" (in *"Noyses, Sounds, and Sweet Aires": Music in Early Modern England* [Folger Shakespeare Library, 2006]) and editor of a special issue of *Mechademia: Second Arc* on "Soundscapes" (2021). She is currently completing a critical edition of John Playford's *Brief Introduction to the Skill of Musick*.

Aaron Gabriel Montalvo is a doctoral student in English literature at Pennsylvania State University. He is enrolled in the dual-title program in Visual Studies and expects to be among its first graduates. His research primarily focuses on twentieth- and twenty-first century American literature, particularly that of the American West, in conjunction with environmental studies and environmental art. This is his first article.

Maximillian E. Novak is Distinguished Research Professor (Emeritus) at the University of California, Los Angeles. He has written widely on the literature of the Restoration and eighteenth century, especially its drama and fiction. He edited several volumes of *The Works of John Dryden* (University of California Press), is one of the general editors of the Stoke Newington Edition of the writings of Daniel Defoe, and has edited several volumes in that series. In addition to having published five books on Defoe, he has also written books on William Congreve, the latest being *Imaginary Plots and Political Realities in the Plays of William Congreve* (Anthem Press, 2020).

Daniel O'Quinn is Professor in the School of English and Theatre Studies at the University of Guelph. He is the author of *Engaging the Ottoman Empire: Vexed Mediations, 1690–1815* (University of Pennsylvania Press, 2018); *Entertaining Crisis in the Atlantic Imperium, 1770–1790* (Johns Hopkins University Press, 2011); and *Staging Governance: Theatrical Imperialism in London, 1770–1800* (Johns Hopkins University Press, 2005). He has been involved in a range of collaborative projects including, most recently, his work with Jennifer Schacker on *The Routledge Pantomime Reader, 1800–1900* (Routledge, 2021).

Li Qi Peh is a lecturer in the Princeton Writing Program.

David Rosen is Professor of English Literature at Trinity College. He is the author of *Power, Plain English, and the Rise of Modern Poetry* (Yale University Press, 2006); his articles have appeared in *Raritan*, *Modern Language Quarterly*, *The Washington Post*, and elsewhere. He and Aaron Santesso collectively wrote *The Watchman in Pieces: Surveillance, Literature, and Liberal Personhood* (Yale University Press, 2014), which was awarded the MLA's James Russell Lowell Prize. Rosen and Santesso's collaborative work has also been published in *Swift's Travels* (Cambridge University Press, 2008), *The Chronicle of Higher Education,* and the journals *ALH, ELH, Law and Literature*, and the *Birkbeck Law Review.*

Aaron Santesso is Professor of Literature at Georgia Tech. He is the author of *A Careful Longing: The Poetics and Problems of Nostalgia* (University of Delaware Press, 2006); his articles have appeared in *Eighteenth-Century Studies*, *Modern Philology*, *ELH, Modern Fiction Studies*, and elsewhere. He and David Rosen collectively wrote *The Watchman in Pieces: Surveillance, Literature, and Liberal Personhood* (Yale University Press, 2014), which was awarded the MLA's James Russell Lowell Prize. Santesso and Rosen's collaborative work has also been published in *Swift's Travels* (Cambridge University Press, 2008), *The Chronicle of Higher Education,* and the journals *ALH, ELH, Law and Literature*, and the *Birkbeck Law Review.*

Judith Stuchiner is currently Adjunct Professor of English at New Jersey City University. She is interested in the permeability between didactic and fictional texts written in the eighteenth century. In her scholarship, she has traced how religious debates are presented in eighteenth- and nineteenth-century novels. Her publications include "Fielding's Latitudinarian Doubt: Faith 'versus' Works in *Joseph Andrews*" (*Studies in Philology*, 2017) and "*Wuthering Heights*: Brontë's Parable of the Unforgiving Servant" (*Religion and the Arts*, 2020).

Charlotte Sussman is Professor of English at Duke University. She is the author of *Peopling the World: Representing Human Mobility from Milton to Malthus* (University of Pennsylvania Press, 2020), as well as *Eighteenth-Century British Literature, 1660–1789* (Polity, 2012), and *Consuming Anxieties: Consumer Protest, Gender, and British Slavery, 1713–1833* (Stanford University Press, 2000). From 2017 to 2020, she was a convener of Duke's Representing Migration Humanities Lab.

Jesslyn Whittell is a graduate student in the English Department at UCLA, where she works on transhistorical poetics, urban humanities, and the very long eighteenth century.

ASECS Executive Board 2019–20

For information about the
American Society for Eighteenth-Century Studies, please contact:
ASECS
982 Main Street
Suite 4-262
Fishkill, New York 12524
Telephone: (845) 202-0672
E-mail: asecsoffice@gmail.com
Website: http://asecs.org

American Society for Eighteenth-Century Studies

Patron and Lifetime Patron Members, 2019–20

Richard Shane Agin
Stanford Anderson
Paula Backscheider
Joseph F. Bartolomeo
Thomas F. Bonnell
Martha F. Bowden
Leo Braudy
Theodore E. D. Braun
Jane K. Brown
Laura Brown
Marshall Brown
Samara Cahill
Vincent Carretta
Michael J. Conlon
Robert DeMaria, Jr.
Margaret Anne Doody
William F. Edmiston
Daniel Timothy Erwin
Lisa A. Freeman
Jack Fruchtman
Gordon Fulton
Charles E. Gobin

Anita Guerrini
Susan E. Gustafson
Mark Haag
Donald M. Hassler
Nicholas Hudson
J. Paul Hunter
Catherine Ingrassia
Margaret C. Jacob
Alessa Johns
George Justice
Deborah Kennedy
Heather King
Jocelyne Kolb
Susan Lanser
Elizabeth Liebman
Devoney K. Looser
Elizabeth Mansfield
Robert Markley
Jean I. Marsden
Paula McDowell
Heather McPherson
Maureen E. Mulvihill

Felicity Nussbaum
Virginia J. Peacock
Jane Perry-Camp
R. G. Peterson
Clifford Earl Ramsey
Paul Rich
Joseph R. Roach
Harold Schiffman
Volker Schroder
Malinda Snow
Karen Stolley
G. A. Starr
Astrida Orle Tantillo
Downing A. Thomas
Randolph Trumbach
Cynthia S. Wall
Howard D. Weinbrot
Byron R. Wells
Myron D. Yeager
William J. Zachs
Linda Zionkowski

Sponsoring Members, 2019–20

Robert Bernasconi
Jan Fergus
Melvyn New
Douglas Lane Patey

Adam Potkay
Treadwell Ruml II
Peter Sabor
William C. Schrader

John Sitter
Ann T. Straulman
Raymond D. Tumbleson

Institutional Members, 2019–20

American Antiquarian Society
Colonial Williamsburg Foundation, *John D. Rockefeller, Jr. Library*
Newberry Library
Omohundro Institute of Early American History and Culture, *Kellock Library*
Santa Monica College
Smithsonian Institute, *AAPG Library*
Stanford University, *Green Library*
UCLA, *William Andrews Clark Memorial Library*
University of Kentucky, *Young Library*
Yale Center for British Art
Yale University Library

291